D0987141

The Goldwater Coalition

Republican Strategies in 1964

The Bobbs-Merrill Company, Inc.

Indianapolis and New York

The Goldwater Coalition

☆☆☆☆☆☆☆☆☆☆☆☆☆☆☆☆☆☆☆☆☆☆☆☆☆☆☆

Republican Strategies in 1964

JOHN H. KESSEL

Arthur E. Braun Professor of Political Science, Allegheny College

Printed in the United States of America
Library of Congress Catalog Card Number 68-22308

Second Printing

DESIGN: ANITA DUNCAN

For Maggie, Bob, and Tom

Preface

There are a few things I should like to say to the reader about this book. First, I view it as an integrative effort. As a sometime politician, I have been disturbed by the apparent insensitivity of academic political science to many of the crucial strategy choices and organizational problems that confront those seeking major political office. As an academic with theoretical inclinations, I have felt that a political theory which, as V. O. Key, Jr., put it, existed "without influence upon, and without being influenced by, other branches of political science" weakened all political science. And as a student of American politics, I have been troubled by the tendency of many authorities on "political parties" to know little about "voting behavior" and by the tendency of experts on "voting behavior" to give too casual attention to "political parties." In this book I have tried to weave these several strands together.

Second, I had a privileged view of Republican politics in 1964, and I have tried not to abuse this opportunity. I was in a position to observe much of the conduct of the campaign myself, and to get first-hand information about events and decisions which I did not witness. Because of this, I have been able to write more confidently than an outside observer. However, I have not told "inside stories" about the persons involved. My concern is with information that augments our understanding of the American political process, not with gossip or the assignment of praise or blame. As to the authority of what I have said, my feelings are the same as those expressed by De Tocqueville in the introduction to his classic *Democracy in America*. "Here the reader must necessarily rely upon my word. I could frequently have cited names which either are known to him or deserve to be so in support of my assertions; but I have carefully abstained from this practice. . . . I had rather injure the success of my statements than add my name to the list of those . . . who repay generous hospitality . . . by subsequent chagrin and annoyance."

Third, a few words about my own attitudes. I did not favor the nomination of Senator Goldwater. I disagreed with many of the policies he advocated, and thought his candidacy would prove so unattractive to the electorate that many other Republicans would be defeated along with him. Once Senator Goldwater did receive the nomination, however, I felt he was entitled to the full support of the Republican party. Regardless of any other considerations, he was entitled to a *fair* chance to determine the popularity of his positions. After the election was over, I thought it essential to the continued well-being of the Republican party that Goldwater policies be abandoned as quickly as possible. These attitudes did not have any effect on the events discussed in this book. As a member of the Republican National Committee staff, I had to remain neutral during the nomination contest, and my duties during the fall—working for the Republican Governors' Association and acting as a host to foreign visitors—had little bearing on the presidential campaign. To my knowledge, my attitudes did not influence what I have said in this book. I have tried to write as objectively as possible. But I do believe an author has an obligation to let his readers know enough about his attitudes so *they* can judge whether his goal of objectivity has been attained. It is for this reason that I mention these personal views here.

Finally, anyone who writes a book of this kind owes thanks to a great many people. Several friends, Hugh A. Bone, Lewis Bowman, Lewis A. Froman, Jr., Karl A. Lamb, William C. Mitchell, Nelson W. Polsby, Frank J. Sorauf, and Raymond E. Wolfinger, were kind enough to give me critical reactions to portions of this book. If the corresponding segments of the book are better than the drafts they examined, it is because I had their helpful counsel. If errors remain, they are my responsibility alone. I am indebted to the Inter-University Consortium for Political Research for making survey data available, and to Philip E. Converse and Warren E. Miller for guidance in the analysis of these data. I should like to thank the National Center for Education in Politics and the Governmental Affairs Institute for fellowships which enabled me to gather the information reported in this book, the

University of Washington for granting me a leave of absence to accept these fellowships, the Republican National Committee staff for the friendly reception given me during the eighteen months I spent with them, the Pacific Northwest Research Computer Center for providing facilities where some of the early analysis of the survey data was done, and Allegheny College for providing the environment which made it possible to get this book written. Finally, I should like to thank Mrs. Pauline Mooney for turning draft pages into a manuscript, and my editors at Bobbs-Merrill for turning the manuscript into a book.

JOHN H. KESSEL

Meadville, Pennsylvania
November 17, 1967

Contents

1

American Political Parties

Many are the statements that the 1964 presidential campaign was somehow singular, a departure from the rules. "Not in more than forty years," wrote Allan Nevins, "has so sharp a break occurred in the ranks of a major party as that in San Francisco when the Republicans nominated Barry Goldwater."[1] The 1964 election, said Clinton Rossiter, "ranks with the elections of 1800, 1840, 1860, 1896, and 1932 as a very critical one for students of American society. The Democrats, in nominating Lyndon Johnson, made a rather careful decision to adhere to the rules of American politics. The Republicans, in nominating Barry Goldwater, deliberately chose to ignore, to downgrade, perhaps to change these rules."[2] "The presidential election of 1964 was an important event for students of American politics," declared Nelson Polsby, "primarily because it broke some of the rules that politicians had lived by for a generation, and that had been codified in the texts and analytical writings of political scientists."[3] The Democratic strategy, in the view of Stanley Kelley, Jr., "was a carefully constructed response to the

[1] *Washington Star*, August 16, 1964, p. B–3.

[2] "The 1964 Presidential Election in the Perspective of American History," Lecture at the University of Washington, April 22, 1965.

[3] "Strategic Considerations," in Milton Cummings, ed., *The National Election of 1964* (Washington: The Brookings Institution, 1966), p. 82.

Goldwater experiment and was characterized, therefore, by a kind of mirror-image unorthodoxy."[4]

While a much longer list of comments easily could be compiled, there would be little point in doing so. For one thing, this list is sufficient to give the flavor of the observations evoked by the 1964 campaign. But quite beyond this, we are already face-to-face with a central question to which we must address ourselves. Each of these statements claims that one or both of the political parties were engaged in unorthodox behavior. Presumably, then, there exist certain standards of orthodoxy against which the allegedly abnormal behavior can be compared. Consequently, analysis requires that we ask just what the norms of political parties are.

This question cannot be answered in a wholly satisfactory manner. A good deal is known about American political parties, and bench marks abound among these data. Campaign strategies, for example, have been codified in Ivan Hinderaker's *Party Politics*[5] and in *Presidential Elections*[6] by Nelson Polsby and Aaron Wildavsky. But if one is seeking general theories about American political parties, one quickly discovers there is less material available. For almost too long, the student of the subject has wandered through a maze of facts in which adequate theoretical guidelines are missing. While he has been expected to know all about agrarianism, sectionalism, standing committees, county committees, parity, platforms, absentee voting procedures, and countless other topics, there have been formulated few theories to help him distinguish between important facts and extraneous details.

There are perhaps two major reasons for this situation. One has been the concern of our intellectual predecessors with the acquisition of an adequate data base. Such distinguished scholars as Charles E. Merriam and Arthur N. Holcombe were not opposed to theory as such, but they understood that sufficient factual information was a necessary prerequisite to any substantial theory.

> Obviously there can be no real science of politics until we have developed a fact-finding technique, both in finding the facts and in drawing conclusions. Until these problems are more vigorously and successfully attacked, political science cannot make any substantial contribution . . . .[7]

[4] "The Presidential Campaign," in *The National Election of 1964*, p. 58.

[5] New York: Holt, 1956.

[6] New York: Scribner's, 1964.

[7] "Reports of the National Conference on the Science of Politics," *American Political Science Review*, February, 1924, p. 119.

To say that the scholarship of Merriam, Holcombe, and their students (including V. O. Key, Jr., surely the leading authority of his academic generation on political parties) produced enough factual information is understatement indeed. Research of recent decades has produced a rich accumulation of data.

The second consideration has been the emphasis of explicit theory on party responsibility. Many authors have built models around the assertion that a political party ought to offer a coherent program to the electorate, and then be held responsible for implementing that program if the voters elect it to office. Departures from this posited model have then been used to criticize the real world. Those who have sought to understand the real world have produced more complex theories, but their models generally have been implicit. The net result of this theoretical emphasis and the volume of empirically oriented research has been a surfeit of data and a paucity of explicit non-normative theory.

Happily, the present academic generation seems to feel a need to sift through these abundant data and get on with the necessary task of theory-building. Two recent examples of such a trend are Frank Sorauf's *Political Parties in the United States*[8] and Samuel Eldersveld's *Political Parties: A Behavioral Analysis.*[9] Both Sorauf and Eldersveld feel it necessary to spell out a theory of the political party. Neither was willing to continue piling fact on fact without considering which facts had theoretical relevance. It should be noted, however, that the efforts of both show the difficulty of developing an adequate theory. Frank Sorauf suggests that party structure, party functions, party clientele, parties in systems, and the party's environment are all necessary to any sufficient understanding of the political party. Samuel Eldersveld's comprehensive report of the Detroit Area Study views the political party as an almost porous clientele-oriented structure, as an alliance of subcoalitions, as a stratarchy marked by a diffusion of control and a proliferation of centers of decision-making, and as a career system in which individuals are able to overcome the hazards of insecurity and participate at a level determined by their own motivation and the needs of the party. Both Sorauf and Eldersveld have found the political party so complex that it was necessary to use several theoretical vantage points in order to apprehend its essential characteristics.

This book is another attempt to set forth a theory that will aid

[8] Boston: Little, Brown, 1964, Chs. 1, 9.
[9] Chicago: Rand-McNally, 1964. See particularly Chs. 1, 3–7.

in understanding American political parties. Many considerations, of course, go into any effort to devise a theory, but for purposes of simplicity, we shall focus on two. What are the *explicanda*—what facts does the theory need to explain? And what concepts shall be used to organize these data?

The phenomena we want to focus upon are more easily described than defined, so let us begin with a few examples of the party activities we want to talk about.[10] The first begins with two meetings in 1959, one in Palm Beach, the other at Hyannisport.[11] Attending were the Kennedy brothers, their aides, and a few others. The subject under discussion was how the presidential nomination might be obtained for Senator John F. Kennedy. The conclusion was that if New England (with 114 convention votes) could provide a base on which to build, and if Senator Kennedy could do well in the primaries, then he might be able to overcome handicaps of youth, inexperience, and Catholicism. The need to go into the primaries was undeniable. ". . . You had to examine the nominating process, which is not a free open popular vote, but a process which is dominated and influenced by all the groups in the Democratic coalition—the farmers, labor, the South, the big-city people, et cetera. These groups are more influential in a convention than they are in the country as a whole. Therefore he had to prove to them that he could win. And to prove that to them, he'd have to fight hard to make them give it to him. . . . So it evolved from the top down that you had to go into the primaries."[12]

As a matter of fact, Kennedy's first big victory came without his having to enter a primary. Ohio's Governor Michael V. DiSalle, hoping to act to

[10] This is not an attempt to define the substantive content of "political parties," "politics," or "political science," an enterprise I regard as among the less rewarding scholarly tasks. Although there have been proposed some ingenious and useful definitions, definition-makers usually draw their boundaries so as to include the things they are interested in and to exclude subjects they find dull. Since almost all researchers go where they think the action is, anyhow, there seems little point in dancing through this particular ballet. Accordingly, the examples which follow should be regarded as nothing more than some of the subjects which I regard as important.

[11] The description which follows is drawn from Theodore H. White, *The Making of the President 1960* (New York: Atheneum, 1961), Chs. 2, 4, 5, 6; Theodore C. Sorenson, *Kennedy* (New York: Harper & Row, 1965), Chs. 5, 6; Harry W. Ernst, *The Primary That Made a President: West Virginia 1960* (New York: McGraw-Hill, 1962); and Paul Tillett, ed., *Inside Politics: The National Conventions 1960* (Dobbs Ferry, N.Y.: Oceana, 1962), Chs. 2, 4, 10, 17, 21, 22.

[12] This quote from Theodore Sorenson is from *The Making of the President 1960*, p. 54.

maximize Buckeye influence (and his own stature) within the Democratic party, spoke about running as a favorite son to hold the state's sixty-four votes as a bloc. But in a series of conferences, the Governor was told bluntly that if he did run as a favorite son, John Kennedy would run against him and beat him. Furthermore, he was shown survey results which indicated this was more than a hollow threat. Governor DiSalle did not like being given orders, but he knew that his bargaining position was weak. So he made an announcement (drafted by Kennedy's office) that he would run as a favorite son with delegates pledged to Kennedy as long as the Massachusetts senator had a chance for the nomination.

The next important move was a decision to challenge Hubert Humphrey in the Wisconsin primary. Humphrey, from neighboring Minnesota, had many important supporters in Wisconsin, but a Harris survey indicated Kennedy had a good chance. Both candidates worked very hard, but the vote proved that the intensiveness of the Kennedy campaign and the effectiveness with which Wisconsin Kennedy volunteers were organized was enough to crystallize the support the Harris poll had detected. Nevertheless, the results were disappointing to Kennedy. There was too high a correlation between Catholicism and the Kennedy vote to convince *neutral* Democrats of Kennedy's attractiveness as a vote-getter. Wisconsin did not provide any bargaining power.

West Virginia did. The important differences between Wisconsin and West Virginia were that Hubert Humphrey had lacked the money to put on an effective campaign, and that John Kennedy decided to bring the religious question into the open. No one had questioned his fitness to fight for his country, Kennedy reminded his mountaineer audiences, and as president he would be sworn to defend the separation between church and state. The vote in West Virginia turned out to be a pleasant surprise for the Massachusetts senator. He won 60 per cent of the vote in a state which was 95 per cent Protestant. And, in case this was not sufficient to convince those watching from the sidelines, John Kennedy went on to win 73 per cent of the primary vote in Oregon against favorite son Wayne Morse, and swept through uncontested primaries in Indiana, Nebraska, and Maryland.

While the Senator had been engaging in the primary election contests, as-yet-uncommitted Democrats were being assiduously wooed. With the increased influence resulting from impressive primary showings, this effort now began to pay dividends. In early June, 1960, Senator Kennedy journeyed to Mackinac Island, where Michigan's Governor Williams announced that he was endorsing the Kennedy candidacy. Three weeks later, a poll at the New York State convention revealed 87 Empire State votes would be cast for him. Smaller states did not swell the Kennedy vote total as dramatically, but neither were they neglected. The result was that by late June the Massachusetts senator could claim 710 first ballot votes.

Seven hundred and sixty-one votes were needed to nominate, but with 710 votes in hand John Kennedy went to Los Angeles with far more bargaining power than any other candidate. Four big states were uncommitted: Pennsylvania, Illinois, California, and New Jersey. Governor David Lawrence and Mayor Richard Daley led Pennsylvania and Illinois into the Kennedy camp; Governor Edmund (Pat) Brown brought in part of the California delegation; Governor Robert Meyner kept New Jersey outside. These additions, together with some contributions from smaller delegations, swelled the Kennedy total—and the Senator's brother Edward persuaded Wyoming to take advantage of its position at the end of the alphabetic roll call, cast all fifteen votes as a bloc, and give John Kennedy the few more votes he needed for a first ballot victory.

The next example of party politics begins with an announcement. The Doorkeeper of the House of Representatives, William M. Miller, known to attentive televiewers as "Fishbait," cries out: "Mr. Speaker, the President of the United States!" And the president walks into the chamber to deliver his State of the Union message. The beginning of this ceremony is the same whether the president's name is Eisenhower, Kennedy, or Johnson. He receives a standing ovation from the assembled senators and representatives as he walks down the center aisle, he shakes hands with the speaker and the vice president as he reaches the rostrum, and he is introduced by the Speaker of the House. But from the time the president begins to read his address, significant variations occur—and whether his name is Eisenhower, Kennedy, or Johnson makes a good deal of difference. To see this, let us examine certain items which were recommended by these presidents as part of the legislative programs they submitted in 1954, 1962, and 1965.[13]

[13] There is a problem in the selection of which presidential programs to compare because there is no such thing as a "typical year." The examples we are using here are the programs submitted after the administrations had been in office for a year. The administrations are still close enough to the beginning of their responsibilities to have some initial momentum left, and have been in office long enough to have made a reasonably thorough canvass of what needs to be done. Presidential programs usually have not been treated as part of "party politics," but there are a couple of quotes which point up the true relationship. In Decem-

Dwight Eisenhower's domestic welfare requests included a program of limited government reinsurance of high-risk medical problems to encourage an expansion of private and nonprofit health insurance, a national conference to study "the nation's educational problems and recommend solutions," an increase in social security benefits and an expansion of the program to cover ten million additional persons, a program of loans and grants to communities for slum clearance and renovation, and construction of 140,000 units of low-cost housing over a four-year period. In 1962, John F. Kennedy asked for Medicare under the social security program, an increase of funds for the National Institutes of Health and creation of two new institutes, a bill to "improve the quality" of education, a program of aid to higher education, enactment of previously submitted aid-to-education bills (though these were not pushed), a Department of Urban Affairs and Housing, and expenditure of $500 million over a three-year period on urban transit problems. In 1965, Lyndon Johnson asked for Medicare under social security, regional medical centers, a program of federal aid to education with a first-year appropriation of $1.5 billion, Operation Head Start, a Department of Housing and Urban Development, a $100 million appropriation for urban facilities, extension of urban renewal programs, rent supplements for low-income families, air and water pollution control measures, elimination of the national origins quota system from immigration legislation, assistance to Appalachia, doubling the money spent on the "War on Poverty," and an increase in social security benefits.

All three presidents had to deal with agricultural problems. When President Eisenhower came to office, he found a farm program of fixed 90 per cent parity payments which was of greater benefit to large commercial

---

ber, 1953, President Eisenhower told the Republican legislative leaders: "In 1954 the party should deliver on commitments made in the platform of 1952. There are minimum limits of achievement below which we must not fall" (*Mandate for Change* [New York: Signet Books, 1965], p. 349). And in the fall of 1965, the Democratic National Committee issued a brochure called *President Johnson and the 89th Congress: A Study in Party Responsibility*: "It has been said that the platforms of American political parties are electioneering documents and not blueprints for action. The Democratic Party platform of 1964 clearly refutes this. *One Nation, One People* was a precise, forthright espousal of programs designed to build a better America. It has been charged that the promises of political parties are forgotten the day after the election. The Johnson Administration and the Democratic 89th Congress have obviously contradicted this." And the pamphlet went on to document this point by quoting passages from the platform and the corresponding legislative actions.

farmers than to small producers. He asked for a farm program with flexible parity payments, whereby the Secretary of Agriculture could adjust the parity payment from 90 per cent down to 75 per cent in case of overproduction, and authority to spend $1 billion over a three-year period to distribute (or sell for "soft" currencies) existing surpluses in foreign countries. President Kennedy responded to essentially the same situation by asking for continuation of the parity payments together with stringent production and marketing controls on feed grains, dairy products, and wheat (but not on cotton, tobacco, or peanuts). President Johnson did not call for alterations in the support programs, but did ask for a long-term cropland retirement program, a home mortgage program to increase rural credit, and creation of a Rural Community Development Service to funnel federal money into agricultural areas.

There are other matters on which quite similar action has been requested by all three presidents. Dwight Eisenhower asked for a Mutual Security appropriation of $3,500,000,000 in 1954; John Kennedy asked for foreign aid funds in the amount of $4,878,500,000 (and an additional $600,000,000 to launch the Alliance for Progress) in 1962; Lyndon Johnson asked for a foreign aid appropriation of $3,380,370,000 in 1965. President Eisenhower's State of the Union message said: "It is apparent that the substantial savings already made, and to be made, by the Post Office Department cannot eliminate the postal deficit. I recommend, therefore, that Congress approve (an increase in postal rates), and that Congress create a permanent commission to establish fair and reasonable postal rates from time to time in the future." In 1962, President Kennedy renewed a request for legislation submitted in 1961 for a postal rate increase in the amount of $741 million to offset the postal deficit. And in his 1965 Budget Message, President Johnson announced that he was creating a panel to look into the problem of the postal deficit, and that it was to report to him by April 1. The panel, headed by Postmaster General Gronouski, duly recommended a further increase in postal rates.

So inspection of these portions of presidential programs tells us that in some areas, like domestic welfare and farm legislation, presidential requests have been quite different, while on other topics, foreign aid appropriations and postal rate increases, presidents have tended to make rather similar requests. The nature of presidential programs is surely a topic that a theory of political parties ought to help us understand.

Another important question is the treatment given to presidential requests when they reach Capitol Hill. In 1961, for example, the Kennedy administration asked for an authorization of $95 million to add electric generating facilities to a dual-purpose reactor whose construction at Hanford, Washington, had been authorized in 1958.[14] The 1958 authorization for the plutonium reactor had not encountered serious opposition, but, in 1961, Republican members of the Atomic Energy Committee joined with coal and private power interests to fight against the generating facilities. The burden of the July 13 debate in favor of the conversion facilities was carried by Democratic members of the Atomic Energy Committee, joined at times by a few liberals and members from the Pacific Northwest. They argued that heat was being produced in any case and the alternative to converting it to usable electricity was to dump it into the Columbia River, that experience could be gained in the operation of a nuclear power plant in conjunction with a power system, and that since the 800,000 kilowatts would be the greatest quantity of electricity generated by a reactor anywhere in the world, construction of the conversion facilities would be a significant boost to U.S. prestige.

The opposition was led by Republican members of the Atomic Energy Committee with assistance from coal state congressmen and a number of "middle-western non-spenders." They argued that it would not produce power economically because the available steam would be at too low a pressure, and that the electricity was not needed in the Northwest. But, in addition to these technical points used to counter the arguments of proponents, the Hanford steamplant was depicted as a threat to the coal industry, to private power interests, and to depressed areas. These arguments touched sensitive political nerves, and the proposal was defeated by a teller vote of 176 to 140. This verdict was confirmed in three August and September roll call votes involving instructions to conferees and the conference report. The Republicans voted almost solidly against the Hanford proposal, and they were joined by Democrats from New England, the Coal States, (Pennsylvania, West Virginia, and Kentucky), and most of the South.

In 1962, a rather different proposal was submitted to Congress. The basic difference was that the construction of the power conversion facilities was now to be financed by a group of local utilities, the Washington Public Power Supply System. This, too, reached the floor of the House in mid-

[14] For additional information about this, see my "Washington Congressional Delegation" in *Mid-West Journal of Political Science*, February, 1964, pp. 1–21.

July, where it was defeated by a vote along the same lines as those of the previous year. The Washington delegation, the principal proponents of the new measure, were discouraged by this, but decided to see what could be done. The new bill was being supported by all but one member of the Atomic Energy Committee (Pennsylvania's James Van Zandt), and the Senate could be expected to approve the Hanford proposal when it considered the bill. The Washingtonians felt they had no chance of gaining Coal State support, so selected 52 Republicans and 21 Southern Democrats whose views might be shifted before the next vote on the measure.

In the month before the conference report came back to the House, the Washington delegation tried to reach as many of the potential converts as possible to stress the differences between the 1961 and 1962 versions. They had help in this from Craig Hosmer, a Republican member of the Atomic Energy Committee who had switched his vote. Hosmer mailed a brochure to House members entitled "Only the Name's the Same." A matter of timing also proved important. The next time the subject was called up on the House floor, it came immediately after the House had voted by a narrow margin for accelerated public works. Nine Pennsylvania Republicans, including James Van Zandt, voted with the Democratic majority on this, and this angered other Republicans. And, during the floor debate, Rules Chairman Howard W. Smith, a most influential Southern Democrat, asked some questions enabling the proponents to repeat once again that this was a local project which did not obligate the federal government. In short, several things occurred which were likely to convert some Republicans and Southern Democrats.

This is exactly what happened. Thirty-five Republicans and forty-eight Democrats switched their votes. New Republican support came from California, the Dakotas, Minnesota, New York, New Jersey, and Maine. Some Republican opponents were to be found in New England, but most were from Pennsylvania or the Middle West. There was now almost solid Democratic support for the measure. The remaining Democratic opposition was concentrated in the Pennsylvania, West Virginia, and North Carolina delegations. The congressmen who had led the anti-Hanford majority on previous votes remained as the determined minority in this occasion.

Finally, a theory of parties ought to enable us to comprehend the behavior of voters. The examples of *explicanda* given thus far all deal with the activities of candidates, presidents, and congressmen. How do the voters react to this? Much of this activity, of course, escapes their attention. Citizens are involved in a host of private activities, and their threshold of awareness is high. But politicians are continually making news. Some of this is bound to get through to at least some of the voters, and that which is communicated acts to reinforce or to modify their attitudes about political affairs.

There is evidence of such impact in the detailed studies of voting executed in recent decades. V. O. Key, Jr., estimated that between one-eighth and one-fifth of the voters switch their votes from election to election.[15] And it is probable that the behavior of officeholders is quite as important in producing these shifts as the statements made during campaigns. The early Erie County study found that 21 per cent of the 1936 Democratic voters intended to vote Republican by May, 1940, as compared with 8 per cent of these voters who changed their minds during the campaign.[16] The authors of the more recent *American Voter* were likewise struck by the impact of the activities of the Eisenhower administration on voters' perceptions. ". . . The Republican party was unable for twenty years to dispel the notion that its return to office would jeopardize our economic well being. Despite the earnest campaign declarations of Landon, Willkie, Dewey, and Eisenhower, this theme remained strongly in perceptions of the party in the campaign of 1952. Not until economic prosperity had been experienced with a Republican in the White House did the party make any substantial headway against this theme. The point is not that economic prosperity during Eisenhower's first term was any better evidence for the Republican case than what had been cited by Messrs. Landon, Willkie, and Dewey. . . . The point is rather that the evidence was visible enough that it could enter the awareness of the mass electorate and have a broad impact on perceptions of parties."[17]

Now what kind of concepts do we want to use to organize these data? This choice depends on our approach to theory-building. There are two general approaches which can be used. The basic distinction between them corresponds to that between a valid argument (one which is logically correct) and a true argument (a valid argument proceeding from true premises). The first approach, favored by many economists, makes very simple assumptions, then constructs a deductive argument on the basis of

[15] *The Responsible Electorate* (Cambridge: The Belknap Press, 1966), pp. 16–22.

[16] Paul F. Lazarsfeld, *et al., The People's Choice* (2nd ed.; New York: Columbia University Press, 1948), p. 102.

[17] Angus Campbell, *et al., The American Voter* (New York: Wiley, 1960), p. 61.

these assumptions. This method is employed by Anthony Downs in *An Economic Theory of Democracy*.[18] In defining his concept of a political party, Downs writes: "In the broadest sense, a political party is a coalition of men seeking to control the governing apparatus by legal means. . . . [But,] such a coalition does not possess a unique, consistent preference-ordering. Its members agree on some goals, but they disagree on many others. Hence the actions taken by the party as a whole are likely to form a hodgepodge of compromises—the result of an internal power struggle rather than any rational decision-making. . . . To avoid this result, we redefine party as follows: a political party is a team of men seeking to control the governing apparatus by gaining office in a duly constituted election. By *team*, we mean a coalition whose members agree on all their goals instead of just part of them."[19] Having deliberately adopted simplified concepts of this kind, Downs is able to show how political parties would behave in a completely certain, rational model world. This permits him to compare his conclusions with behavior in the uncertain real world. "Theoretical models," he tells us, "should be tested primarily by the accuracy of their predictions rather than by the reality of their assumptions."[20]

This is an honorable genre, one which has raised theoretical points of real importance.[21] However, there is another approach to theory construction, one which stresses concern for rules of correspondence with the real world when defining basic concepts. I believe there are compelling reasons for proceeding thus. First, there is no longer any need to begin with such artificial constructs as man in a state of nature or a hedonistic calculus because of lack of information. The behavioral sciences have learned a great deal about human beings, and it is foolish not to take advantage of these intellectual riches. Second, if one begins an argument with realistic assumptions, the chances of arriving at accurate conclusions are greatly increased. Third, although using concepts with real world counterparts is more cumbersome,

[18] New York: Harper, 1957.

[19] Downs, *Economic Theory*, pp. 24–25.

[20] *Ibid.*, p. 21.

[21] In addition to Downs, leading works include Duncan Black, *The Theory of Committees and Elections* (Cambridge: Cambridge University Press, 1958) and James Buchanan and Gordon Tullock, *The Calculus of Consent* (Ann Arbor: University of Michigan Press, 1962). For a splendid account of the importance of this work to political science, see William C. Mitchell, "The Shape of the Political Theory to Come," a paper prepared for delivery to the 1967 Annual Meeting of the American Political Science Association, Chicago, Illinois, September 5–9, 1967.

the analysis can be simpler. Over-simplified premises often force a theorist to engage in logical acrobatics to save his argument. Fourth, whether expressed in Donald Matthews' frank reference to "those of us who prefer to muddle along rather close to the data"[22] or in Donald Stokes's stylish prose, "Bringing (real world cognitive) variables into the (Downs) model would lessen its elegance and parsimony in some respects but would vastly increase the scientific interest of the model as a theory of party systems,"[23] a healthy respect for a data base is part of the professional outlook I find congenial.

Four concepts will be used to organize our data: *electorate*, *group*, *coalition*, and *institution*. None of these concepts is new. Each has been used by political scientists for years. But it is worth taking time to define them for two reasons. Formal definitions do remove some ambiguity from discussion. And these concepts can be defined so as to facilitate speculation about their relationship to each other. We will define each in terms of three sets: a set of persons (or a collectivity of persons), a set of attitudes, and a set of behaviors.

The definition of *electorate* will be quite familiar to anyone who has read the spate of voting studies published in recent years. The electorate is the set of all potential voters. It is further defined by a set of attitudes, valenced cognitions about political objects. The most central of these attitudes concerns the political party. Other important attitudes relate to such objects as personalities, issues, civic duty, political efficacy, and the like.[24] The set of behaviors refers to the range of citizen activity which varies from belonging to political organizations, working for candidates, giving money, attending rallies, and persuading friends in the highly politicized stratum to simply talking politics and voting for the average person to non-participation for the politically inert.[25]

A *group* is a much smaller set of persons. The individuals constituting

[22] Donald R. Matthews, "Patterns of Influence in the U.S. Senate: Five Approaches," a paper prepared for delivery at the 1960 Annual Meeting of the American Political Science Association, New York City, September 8–10, 1960, p. 2.

[23] Donald E. Stokes, "Spatial Models of Party Competition," in Angus Campbell, *et al., Elections and the Political Order* (New York: Wiley, 1966), p. 176.

[24] Angus Campbell, *et al., The American Voter.*

[25] There is a considerable literature on this, much of it based on the work of the University of Michigan Survey Research Center. See, for example, Lester Milbrath, *Political Participation* (Chicago: Rand-McNally, 1965); V. O. Key, Jr., *Public Opinion and American Democracy* (New York: Knopf, 1961), Ch. 8; and Donald R. Matthews and James W. Prothro, *Negroes and the New Southern Politics* (New York: Harcourt Brace, 1967), Chs. 3–11.

the group must share a set of attitudes with one another. Typically, these attitudes concern role expectations within the group, the nature of the group's goals, and the environment within which the group functions. The set of behaviors must include a reasonably stabilized pattern of interaction between the members.[26]

This is not an elaborate definition of a group, but it has certain advantages which make it useful in this context. First, it raises a question about the characteristics of the persons who are drawn from the electorate into the more intense activity of group participation. Second, the definition permits flexibility. Since it focuses on individuals, we are able to handle groups in which one individual is dominant (such as the president among his own aides). Some alternative definitions would have made this more difficult. Third, since this definition simply encapsulates the observations of social psychologists, it does not require us to carry around any extraneous philosophical baggage.[27] So, for our purposes, this is a serviceable definition.

Still, we do not want to stretch this concept too far. Herbert Simon has argued persuasively that there is a level of activity not easily understood either through the micro-theory of primary groups or the macro-theory of institutions.[28] For us, the concept which stands between the group and the institutional level is the coalition. A *coalition* is a set of groups. Its set of attitudes lies within the intersection of the sets of attitudes of the member groups, and its set of behaviors is comprised of those activities which form an interdependent system. The difference between the characteristic behavior of the group and the coalition is important. A group requires interaction; a coalition only interdependent activity. This looser requirement admits the possibility of a coalition without overt coordination between the member groups.

[26] There is a voluminous literature on groups. This definition is essentially that used by David Truman. See *The Governmental Process* (New York: Knopf, 1951). See also George C. Homans, *The Human Group* (New York: Harcourt Brace, 1950); Sidney Verba, *Small Groups and Political Behavior* (Princeton: Princeton University Press, 1961); A. Paul Hare, *Handbook of Small Group Research* (New York: The Free Press of Glencoe, 1962); Robert T. Golembiewski, *The Small Group* (Chicago: University of Chicago Press, 1962); and Theodore M. Newcomb, Ralph H. Turner, and Philip E. Converse, *Social Psychology: The Study of Human Interaction* (New York: Holt, Rinehart & Winston, 1965).

[27] While on the subject of what this definition does *not* imply, it should be noted that it does not imply any necessary concern with interest groups.

[28] Comments on the Theory of Organization," *American Political Science Review*, December, 1952, pp. 1130–39.

The attitudes of the member groups lead to certain conclusions about the likelihood of coalition formation, and the problems of coalition leadership. A group which views the environment as hostile may choose not to participate in any coalition, preferring instead the isolated splendor of advocating its own pure goals. Non-ideological coalitions may sometimes be formed. For example, groups may combine in a coalition because they have similar attitudes about the environment in which they are situated, or because they share role expectations such as a desire that leadership should be polyarchal rather than hierarchical. If a group has too specific expectations about its own leadership role, the person playing this role may find the requirements of intragroup and intergroup leadership so different that he cannot become the leader of a coalition. Many coalitions may be ideologically based and easily led, but these other possibilities ought to be kept in mind.

The concept of coalition, of course, has long occupied a central place in the study of American political parties. "To understand a political party," Arthur Holcombe wrote in 1924, it "is necessary to become acquainted with its members and ascertain what its interests are and what their responses may be expected to be under the various circumstances with which they may be called upon to deal."[29] "All national leaders," concluded Wilfred E. Binkley after examining the history of American political parties, "had to discover the points of agreement, the centripetal ideas, that would give cohesive force to a multi-group combination."[30] Working from the mathematics of n-person games, William Riker has developed an elegant theory emphasizing the size principle: "In n-person, zero-sum games, where side payments are permitted, where players are rational, and where they have perfect information, only minimal winning coalitions occur."[31]

The concept used here is closer to the traditional definition than to Riker's. In particular, the emphasis on overlap between attitudes provides a different key to the processes of coalition formation than a concern with the number of players involved. Without even entering into the difficult questions of rationality and perfect information, the applicability of side payments to many political situations may be questioned. In an economic game where coalition members can share, say, the profits of a corporation, this assumption is quite plausible. In political matters, however, the

[29] *Political Parties of Today* (New York: Harper, 1924), pp. 348–49.
[30] *American Political Parties* (3rd ed.; New York: Knopf, 1958), pp. xi–xii.
[31] *Theory of Political Coalitions* (New Haven: Yale University Press, 1962), p. 32.

"reward" of simply being a member of the majority is an insufficient motivation unless that majority stands for policies acceptable to the member groups. Fortunately, we do not need to decide between these two concepts solely by questioning the plausibility of assumptions. Both make some predictions. Riker's concept states that coalitions will be of a minimum size. Our concept says that coalition formation will be governed by the attitudes of the member groups, and that the coalition attitudes will fall into the overlap between the attitudes of the member groups. To be sure, Riker's requires some quite restrictive conditions (a zero-sum game with side payments, perfect information, and rationality) to be met, and a test of our concept requires that the attitudes of the member groups be known. But since Riker himself presents an illustration from American politics of the 1820's where all four restrictive conditions clearly were not met, these difficulties should not be interpreted as eliminating all possibility of real world comparison.

Institutions, too, have long concerned political scientists. It is notable, however, that many seem to write *about* institutions without ever specifying what an institution is. For our purposes, an *institution* is a set of coalitions.[32] Its set of attitudes consists of the attitudes of coalition leaders toward functions stipulated by the society (culture, polity) of which the institution is a part. These functions may be formally stated, as in a constitution, or simply be matters of tradition. The institution's set of behaviors contains those which form a regularized pattern of activity concerned with nominations, elections, administration, or legislation.[33]

By conceiving institutional attitudes and behaviors as being distinct from those of the member coalitions, we recognize what David Truman has called the "influence of office."

> When a man enters a legislative position he takes on a new role that is prescribed for him by society. His success as a legislator depends in large part on how well he performs that role. . . . (Legislative norms) require some behaviors and forbid others; still others are a matter of the officeholder's

[32] Here it becomes important to remember that a set may have a single member. Hence an institution, such as the Presidency, may be made up of a single coalition.

[33] This is close to the definition suggested by S. F. Nadel. His phrase is "a standardized mode of coactivity." See *The Foundations of Social Anthropology* (New York: Holt, 1947), pp. 287–92. Ralph Linton's discussion is also germane: "It is one of the primary aims of culture to transform (an aggregate of individuals) into a society by organizing the *attitudes and behaviors* of the aggregate's members" (emphasis added); *The Study of Man* (New York: Appleton-Century-Crofts, 1936), p. 412.

discretion. . . . The occupant of an executive position in the government is no less exposed to such expectations than is the legislative politician. He too has learned, before he entered upon his position, some expectations concerning the role, including such matters as "loyalty" to the chief executive; he too has entered his position through certain semi-ritualistic procedures. . . .[34]

Distinguishing between coalition goals and institutional requirements is helpful in reminding us of the difficulty of political leadership. The behavior pattern of coalitions is dictated by both the composition of the coalition *and* the necessities of office. If these demands happen to coincide, it is easy to meet the requirements of coalition leadership and institutional leadership simultaneously. When coalition goals and institutional requirements do not mesh, however, political leaders are subject to considerable strain.

Institutional behavior, of course, is not completely prescribed. Since many functions are assigned to an institution, there is no one way of fulfilling them. Variations in the leaders' attitudes about any single function can also lead to varying behavior patterns within one and the same institution.[35] By calling our attention to the leaders' attitudes toward the functions of their particular institution, our concept accounts for some of the flexibility in institutional life.

Another advantage of this definition is that progress in the study of political parties has been inhibited by our tendency to confine our attention to those institutions which happened to be called "political parties." This focused study on only part of the relevant activities, specifically on those concerned with nominations and elections. If we wanted to discuss voters or United States senators, we felt it necessary to extend the word party by such phrases as "party-in-the-electorate" or "party-in-the-government." There was a time when such restricted usage made some sense. Some decades ago, the activities of county chairmen and precinct workers had more impact on party fortunes than today, when national leaders can communicate directly with the voters. But whatever the past justification for narrow conceptualization may have been, we now need concepts which call our attention to all the relevant actors.

[34] *The Governmental Process*, pp. 347, 447.

[35] Robert Peabody has pointed out that Republican legislative leaders have sometimes regarded the function of the minority party as cooperation with the majority, sometimes as partisan opposition, and sometimes as proposing constructure alternatives ("House Republican Leadership: Change and Consolidation in a Minority Party," a paper prepared for delivery at the 1966 Annual Meeting of the American Political Science Association, New York City, September 6–10, 1966).

Mentioning these four institutions also reminds us that party leaders operate from a specific institutional base. There is at least an implication in writing about "the Republicans" or "Democratic leaders" that there is some kind of inclusive aggregate encompassing all those who participate in party affairs. Such an encompassing collectivity exists only as an ideal. Because of this ideal construct, it is possible to speak meaningfully about the goals of the party, the needs of the party, or the pledges of the party. However, there is no Grand Council in charge of party affairs. There are occasions when the various institutional leaders sit down around the same table. This occurs at the President's Tuesday morning meeting with congressional leaders, when a governor sits down with his legislative leadership and the state chairman is in attendance, and at meetings of the new Republican Coordinating Committee.[36] But even when such meetings do take place, the actors behave in a manner described by Robert A. Dahl: "If hierarchy appears, it is weak and may rest exclusively on a central position in the network of communications occupied by a particular leader or set of leaders. Thus, although a few chiefs may be somewhat more influential than others, they are all highly dependent on one another for the successful attainment of their policies."[37] Each of the participants, in other words, has some particular institutional base of power, and each is treated with the deference due a man of independent influence. Our definition of institution calls attention to the leaders' differing bases of power. It also implies that their goals may sometimes conflict because we have specified that power within an institution rests on a particular coalition made up of particular groups.

Electorate, group, coalition, institution. To restate the definitions assigned to these terms, we can write:[38]

$$(1) \qquad E = \{P_1, P_2, P_3 \cdots P_n; A_E; B_E\}$$

where

$$A_E = \{a \mid a \text{ is an attitude toward some political object}\}$$

$$B_E = \{b \mid b \text{ is a behavior which falls within the range of citizen activity}\}$$

[36] The significance of the name should not be missed. Its very existence testifies to the problems resulting from the absence of the centripetal influence of the president in the out-party.

[37] This is the leadership pattern which Dahl calls "a coalition of chieftains" (*Who Governs?* [New Haven: Yale University Press, 1961], p. 187).

[38] If you have not encountered set theory before, be not alarmed! There are two methods of writing the elements of a set, the *roster method* and the *defining*

(2)
$$G=\{P_1, P_2, P_3 \cdots P_n; A_G; B_G\}$$
where
$$P_{n_G} << P_{n_E}$$

$A_G = \{a \mid$ a is a shared attitude re group goals, role behavior within the group, or the group's environment$\}$

$B_G = \{b \mid$ b is a reasonably stabilized pattern of interaction$\}$

(3)
$$C=\{G_1, G_2, G_3 \cdots G_n; A_C; B_C\}$$
where
$$A_C=\{A_{G_1} \cap A_{G_2} \cap A_{G_3} \cdots \cap A_{G_n}\}$$

$B_C = \{b \mid$ b is a behavior which is part of an interdependent system$\}$

(4)
$$I=\{C_1, C_2, C_3 \cdots C_n; A_I; B_I\}$$
where

$A_I = \{a \mid$ is a coalition leader's attitude toward functions assigned to the institution by society$\}$

$B_I = \{b \mid$ b is a behavior which is part of a regularized pattern re nominations, elections, administration, or legislation$\}$

So, now we have four concepts which can serve as the beginning of a theory about American political parties. Only the beginning, because, while we have defined the concepts, we have said little about the relationships between them. We have said that an institution is a set of coalitions, a coalition is a set of groups, and that the attitudes of the coalition will fall within the intersection of the sets of attitudes of the member groups. These have

property method. The roster method lists the members of the set. "$E=\{P_1, P_2, P_3, \ldots P_n\}$" would be read "E (the electorate) is a finite set whose members are P_1 (person number one) through P_n (person number n)." The defining property method states a property and indicates that the objects having this property, and only those objects, are members of the set. "$A_E = \{a \mid$ a is an attitude toward some political object$\}$" should be read "A_E (the attitudes of the electorate) is the set of those elements a such that a is an attitude toward some political object." These equations, in other words, are simply formal statements of the concepts defined in the preceding pages.

been the only relationships which have been specified, and, until the concepts are tied together more neatly than this, we cannot say that we have much of a theory.

But if we do not have a complete theory, we do have a basic vocabulary. This vocabulary can be used to talk about the activities we said a theory of political parties ought to be able to explain, and to discuss them in a way which facilitates an understanding of them. The nomination example began with meetings of a group whose shared goal was to obtain the nomination for John F. Kennedy. This core group had to devise a strategy of coalition formation which could be implemented in the institutional setting of Democratic nomination politics. The first step of this strategy was to have groups of New England delegates with many common attitudes toward public policy and a common desire to enhance the prestige of New England join to form the base for a Kennedy coalition. Once this was accomplished, primary elections had to be won to demonstrate Kennedy's popularity with the voters. This was not accomplished in Wisconsin, but it was in West Virginia and succeeding primaries. Now bargaining could be conducted with groups from Michigan and New York by stressing that Kennedy was an attractive candidate who was taking policy positions acceptable in these states. And when the Senator went to Los Angeles with a near-winning coalition, final bargaining could be carried on with groups from Pennsylvania, Illinois, and California on the ground that the Kennedy coalition was very likely to win, and there would be greater rewards for groups who were members of the coalition than for those who were not.

Presidential programs are fast becoming, if they are not already, what Bagehot called the nineteenth-century British Cabinet, "a hyphen which joins, a buckle which fastens, the legislative part of the state to the executive part of the state." Viewed from the perspective of our concepts, the items included reflect the attitudes of the groups in the presidential coalition, the coalition leaders' attitudes toward their continuing institutional responsibilities, and their expectations about the nature of the legislative coalitions which will support or oppose their proposals. The Eisenhower domestic welfare requests showed the "administration's determination to provide for the needs of all Americans, particularly the little fellow,"[39] but they also reflected a Republican emphasis on measures which would stimulate private or local initiative. The Kennedy domestic welfare requests, on the

[39] Dwight D. Eisenhower, *Mandate for Change*, p. 360.

other hand, mirrored the attitude of Democrats that programs should be carried out on the federal level. The Johnson administration asked for still more federal activity in 1965 because its legislative requests were going to be acted upon by sympathetic legislative coalitions.

The Eisenhower support for flexible farm supports not only stemmed from a Republican attitude of opposition to continuing federal activity, but also reflected the personal views of two key members of that presidential coalition, Agriculture Secretary Ezra Taft Benson and Milton Eisenhower, the President's brother who had spent fourteen years in the Department of Agriculture. The Kennedy agricultural requests suggested a Democratic willingness to use federal controls, the views of University of Minnesota Professor Willard Cochran who was advising Agricultural Secretary Orville Freeman, and perhaps a decision to begin the use of controls on crops grown in Western states (which had voted for Nixon) rather than in Southern states (which had voted for Kennedy). The Johnson requests did not attempt to disturb the agricultural status quo while some eighty-eight other "must" measures were being submitted, but did seek to use federal money to alleviate some of the rural poverty Lyndon Johnson could so easily remember. And the requests for foreign aid appropriations and postal rate increases by all three Presidents did not reflect any desire to use up presidential bargaining counters in supporting politically unpopular causes, but rather institutional responsibilities to conduct foreign policy and to try to curb the postal deficit at a time when the federal budget was subject to so many other pressures.

The handling of the Hanford requests in the House illustrates a legislative struggle between two coalitions. A group of Democrats on the Atomic Energy Committee and a group of congressmen from the Pacific Northwest were joined by most Northern and Western Democrats to form a pro-Hanford coalition. An anti-Hanford coalition was led by coal state Republicans. They were joined by almost all other Republicans, by Southern Democrats, and by Coal State Democrats. The strategic problem facing the congressmen from the Pacific Northwest in 1962 was how to detach enough groups from the anti-Hanford coalition to change their losing coalition into a winning one. They were able to do this with coastal Republicans and Southern Democrats by stressing the local financing feature of the new Hanford proposal, and by having the luck to have the Hanford measure acted on at a time when some Coal State congressmen had just angered some of the other groups in their coalition. So when the vote was taken, the Coal State congressmen found there were only two major groups remaining in the anti-Hanford coalition, themselves and their staunchest allies, the middle-western Republicans.

The examples of voter reaction begin to hint at another relationship between the concepts. The attitudes of the voters are subject to modification by the behavior of the coalitions in their several institutional settings. The evidence we have noted indicates that the voters' attitudes are not forever fixed, but that some of these attitudes are subject to modification as the voters receive a continual flow of new information. Normally the voters cognize new information in accordance with their previous attitudes, and under ordinary circumstances the number of voters who shift their attitudes in a pro-Republican direction is offset by the number of voters who shift their attitudes in a pro-Democratic direction. But on occasion highly visible behavior by a particular coalition provides information on an important subject about which there was heretofore inadequate knowledge. This was what happened in the early fifties. Not only was the behavior of the Eisenhower coalition in relation to the recession of 1954 visible to many people, but really credible information on this subject had been missing for more than two decades. The conditions were right for behavior of the Eisenhower coalition to have a visible impact, and it did. It produced a *net* change in the attitudes of the electorate.

Since we have been able to restate our examples in terms of our concepts, we can now argue that there is a "fit" between our *explicanda*, the phenomena we seek to understand, and the concepts as we have defined them. We have been able to talk about nomination contests, presidential programs, legislative fights, and voting in terms of the attitudes and behavior of the electorate, groups, coalitions, and institutions. But these brief examples are an insufficient challenge to our attempt-at-a-theory. So, let us go about our main business and see if we can handle a much more detailed set of data, the nomination and electoral politics of 1964, by using these concepts.

ONE

☆☆☆☆☆☆☆☆☆☆☆☆☆☆☆☆☆☆☆☆☆☆☆☆☆☆☆☆

Coalition Formation

2

Available Candidates and Contending Groups

The nomination process of the party out of power provides an ideal setting in which to study coalition formation.[1] Consider the characteristics of this brand of politics. First, achieving the nomination is the most important function. There are, of course, other functions for coalitions in nomination politics. These include giving voice to a particular ideology, maximizing the influence of a particular state through the device of a favorite son, and helping the chances of another candidate whose views are acceptable. But it happens that, as a coalition increases in size, it becomes easier to achieve all of these ends. Whether the aspirant is a genuine candidate, a spokesman for a point of view, a symbol of his state's pride, or a stalking-horse for a stronger candidate, his influence is maximized when he has the largest

[1]One of the major findings of the David, Moos, and Goldman study was that out-party nominations are quite different from those of the party in power. The party in power tends to continue with its existing leadership. See Paul T. David, Ralph M. Goldman, and Richard C. Bain, *The Politics of National Party Conventions* (Washington: The Brookings Institution, 1960). Other recent studies of nomination politics include Gerald Pomper, *Nominating the President* (Evanston: Northwestern University Press, 1963); James W. Davis, *Presidential Primaries: Road to the White House* (New York: Crowell, 1967); and Polsby and Wildavsky, *Presidential Elections*, Ch. 2.

possible number of votes committed to him. Consequently, coalition leaders spend a good deal of time trying to increase the size of their coalitions.

Second, none of the member groups is large enough to act decisively without considerable help from other groups. If a state delegation is split into groups preferring Candidates A, B, and C, each of these groups is dependent on out-state assistance to give it stature vis-à-vis its home state rivals. Even if there is a united state delegation (which can be considered as a single group because of a reasonably stable pattern of interaction and shared attitudes), its own power is quite limited. New York, the state with the largest delegation, had only 15 per cent of the votes necessary for a nomination at the 1964 Democratic convention and 14 per cent of the votes needed to nominate at the 1964 Republican conclave.

Third, there are many incentives for groups to join coalitions. In addition to the obvious political payoffs, there are many personal motivations. For those whose careers have been devoted to state politics, this is a chance to participate in an important national decision. A governor who cannot succeed himself may want to continue his career in a federal post. The intensive television coverage provides an opportunity for reputations to be made. Washington's Don Eastvold won his state's nomination for Attorney General after a speech at the 1952 Republican convention, and Wyoming delegates are remembered for putting John Kennedy over the top at the Democratic Convention in 1960.

Fourth, there are no party leaders in a position to control the nomination process. Even national party leadership comes from the support of a specific coalition in a specific institution. Consequently, the influence of any leader is sharply curtailed outside his own institution. Floor leaders can speak for the dominant coalitions in the United States Senate or in the House of Representatives, but presidential nominations are not made on Capitol Hill. A governor can be influential with his own delegation, but his influence stops at the state line. The chairman of the national committee has responsibility without power[2] and is forced toward neutrality because of his role in making the arrangements for the convention. Former presidents evoke nostalgic memories of the party's days of glory, but their wishes do not carry the authority they did when expressed on White House stationery. A "titular leader's" mandate to command his party is effective only until the

[2] The phrase "responsibility without power" comes from Cornelius Cotter and Bernard Hennessy. See *Politics Without Power* (New York: Atherton Press, 1964), Chs. 4–5.

first Tuesday after the first Monday in November in the year of his nomination. In short, when editorial writers declare "party leaders must realize they need to choose an attractive candidate this year," they miss the point. National party leaders already know it would be desirable to have an attractive nominee, but they are not in a position to control the process of coalition formation which will ultimately determine the nominee's identity.

State leaders are likely to lack experience. A high rate of turnover in volunteer posts is one of the basic facts of life in American politics. Only four of the Republican state chairmen in 1964 had held their posts during the immediately preceding presidential campaign, and only nine of the 1964 state chairmen remained in office as long as September, 1967. New state leaders are more likely to be learning the rules of the game themselves than they are to be devising brilliant new tactical moves.

A high rate of turnover is also a characteristic of convention delegates and alternates. Of the slightly more than ten thousand delegates and alternates attending the last four Republican National Conventions, nearly four-fifths had *not* been elected to the convention meeting four years earlier.[3] The proportion of returning delegates and alternates is reasonably constant. The highest rate of delegate continuity (23.6%) was between 1956 and 1960; the lowest rate of delegate continuity (19.6%) was between 1952 and 1956. States with stable party organizations, such as New York, usually return a somewhat larger proportion of their delegates. In part for this reason, the highest rate of Republican delegate continuity is found in the East (27.3%) and the lowest in the West (15.4%).[4] But the general rule remains that many delegates and alternates are newcomers. Therefore, it is not unusual to find many of the groups involved in nomination politics

[3] This is a fact which should be recognized in interpreting the Munger-Blackhurst argument about consistency in voting from convention to convention. They point out that certain state delegations have regularly voted for liberal or conservative candidates at Republican and Democratic conventions. This probably comes about because the shared attitudes of the groups selected in each state are likely to reflect the ideological tone of the party in that state even though different delegates are selected from convention to convention. See "Factionalism in the National Conventions, 1940–1964: An Analysis of Ideological Consistency in State Delegation Voting," *Journal of Politics*, May, 1965, pp. 375–94.

[4] These studies of delegate continuity were done by Paul Friedman and Steven Wolinetz. At the time, both were students of Theodore Lowi at Cornell University. I should like to thank Professor Lowi for calling these unpublished data to my attention.

behaving in a very tentative and hesitant fashion.[5] This is because they are seeking their footing on unfamiliar terrain.

To recapitulate, the most important institutional function requires that a winning coalition be formed, other functions are facilitated by increasing the size of proto-coalitions, the member groups are too small to act by themselves, there are incentives for group leaders to bring their groups into a coalition, and there are neither national nor state leaders in a position to force the coalition formation to follow any predetermined course. Taken together, these conditions form an almost classic *coalition situation.*[6] "A *full-fledged coalition situation,*" according to William A. Gamson, "is one in which the following conditions are present:

1. There is a decision to be made and there are more than two social units attempting to maximize their share of the payoffs.

2. No single alternative will maximize the payoff to all participants.

3. No participant has dictatorial powers, i.e., no one has initial resources sufficient to control the decision by himself.

4. No participant has veto power, i.e., no member *must* be included in every winning coalition."[7]

Since there is such a close correspondence between the situation envisaged by coalition theory and the real world, out-party nomination politics appears to be an ideal arena for the study of coalition formation.

The details vary from nomination to nomination, but the coalition formation process passes through some generally recognizable stages. The business of campaigning for a nomination these days is a long term proposition. An aspirant may begin preparing the groundwork almost as soon as the preceding presidential election is over. At this stage, publicity and con-

[5] See the studies of state delegations in Paul Tillett, ed., *Inside Politics: The National Conventions,* 1960 for a discussion of ways in which the delegates adapted themselves to an unfamiliar situation. The chapters by Aaron Wildavsky on the Ohio Democrats and by David Derge on the Indiana Republicans are particularly good on this point.

[6] A situation, in Riker's usage, is "the abstract and instantaneous-eternal boundary of events" (*Theory of Political Coalitions,* p. 105). The "nature of the coalition situation" is also a major variable in the model developed by Michael A. Leiserson. See "Coalitions in Politics: A Theoretical and Empirical Study," unpublished doctoral dissertation, Yale University, 1966, Ch. 6.

[7] "A Theory of Coalition Formation," *American Sociological Review,* June, 1961, p. 374. Gamson has operationalized his theory and applied it to presidential nominations himself. See "Coalition Formation at Presidential Nominating Conventions," *American Journal of Sociology,* September, 1962, pp. 157–71.

tacts are necessary. This often means fairly extensive travel, both foreign and domestic. The aspirant visits distant lands and hobnobs with world leaders. This generates publicity, gives the candidate some background information about international affairs, and furnishes pictures which can be included in campaign brochures one day as evidence that the candidate "understands the world situation." The time spent in domestic travel is even more important. Here the candidate is interested in showing that he is a willing party worker, giving local party leaders evidence of his appeal, and making contact with potential delegates. Very few bargains are made at this early stage. Until the mid-term elections have taken place, guessing about the identity of the participants in the next convention is a very risky business. Groups of delegates usually do not want to cast their fortunes with a particular candidate until they are sure that no more attractive candidate is going to appear on the scene. Aspirants might like to have delegate pledges, but don't want to solicit the aid of, say, a governor until they are sure he is going to be re-elected and therefore leading his state's delegation at the coming convention. So, at first, campaigning is a very gentlemanly business. Few pledges of support are offered and few are sought. The aspirant must first create the resources which his managers can use one day to build a coalition around him.

Sometime after the mid-term elections, the candidate sits down with his closest friends and advisers to decide whether he ought to seek the nomination. It would appear that the answer to this question is usually in the affirmative. This impression might be illusory. After all, we don't often hear of meetings when the consensus is: "Forget it, Bob! You wouldn't have a prayer of getting the nomination." But neither should it be forgotten that if a candidate has spoken at fund-raising dinners and party rallies across the country, many are urging him to enter the presidential lists. It is sometimes easier to agree to let one's friend's "do what they can" than to say no to a host of potential supporters.

If the decision is that a coalition should be assembled in support of the candidate, those present usually form the core group around which the coalition is constructed, and many of them become coalition leaders. Of all the participants in the nomination process, the coalition leaders probably have the greatest freedom to do as they see fit. There are constraints which stem from such factors as the characteristics of the particular candidate, and expectations of others that he will enter certain primaries or will not seek delegates in a state where the governor is a favorite son. But the candidate and his immediate advisers have the option of selecting the basic tactics. If an open candidacy with an announcement to the press, which primaries should the contender enter and which should he try to avoid? If a covert candidacy, should the candidate's friends assure state leaders the candidate will accept a draft or would it be better to remain a true dark horse who makes no move unless there is a convention deadlock? The coalition leaders lose some flexibility once they have committed themselves to a course of action, and they lose maneuverability as the coalition grows in size. But, given the absence of national party leaders in a position to control the process, the inexperience of many state leaders and delegates, and the likelihood that the coalition leaders have superior information about the attitudes of groups of delegates, the coalition leaders are in a better position to take the initiative than anyone else. When the coalition leaders understand the rules of the game (as Dewey's experienced managers did in 1948), their possession of the initiative may be the most significant feature of the whole process.[8]

The first group to join the coalition (after the core group of confidants and leaders) is normally the candidate's home state delegation.[9] If the candidate is from an unusually small state, then he may be put forward as a regional candidate. In this case, votes are sought in the immediately surrounding states so as to broaden his initial support. The next groups to be recruited are the candidate's most natural allies: the groups whose defining attitudes have the greatest extent of overlap with the candidate's own attitudes. Since there are only so many groups in sufficiently complete accord with the candidate on goals, an ideological argument to join a coalition can be used only so long. Then emphasis has to shift to some other element in the group's set of attitudes, such as desire to be part of a winning coalition or hope for some specific political reward. Consequently, the argument presented to potential recruits shifts as the coalition grows. It begins with an appeal to support "our very own Governor." Then the managers can approach natural allies and say: "Our Governor has 50 votes and has exactly the attitudes you want in a presidential candidate." When the Governor reaches 250 votes, the delegate hunters can say, "He's almost the ideal can-

[8] Coalition leaders may, of course, be new to nomination politics. When there are uninitiated participants in the state delegations *and* in the camps of presidential hopefuls, the behavior of everyone tends to become rather cautious. Even so, inexperience often leads to tactical errors.

[9] If the aspirant has held national office, he may have supporters in many parts of the country rather than a single base in his home state. The number of candidates with national rather than local bases will probably increase with time, but this is still an unusual situation.

didate for you." With 400 convention votes the argument can be softened to "he's your kind of guy," and with 600 delegate pledges in hand, the coalition leaders can assert "the Governor's going to win anyway." This is not to argue that there are certain "magic numbers" which govern shifts in strategy, but simply to point out that the recruitment of groups to a coalition proceeds from most natural to least natural allies, and that the less natural allies can be wooed because of the increased leverage which stems from already committed delegates.

There is another implication to this growth process. This is that the increase in coalition size should be a continuous process. As long as the coalition is adding groups, the coalition leaders can point to this growth as a portent of eventual success. But the converse is also true. If a candidate acquires, say, 225 votes and holds at that level, his rivals will say that he is never going to reach the total needed to nominate. Not only does this make it difficult for the candidate to attract more recruits, but his managers soon find they are spending much of their time reassuring supporters who are being approached about switching "as soon as your man releases you." Consequently, it is helpful if announcements about new groups joining the coalition can be made one at a time to create the impression of continuous growth.

A final key to understanding this process is that blocking coalitions rarely form. As one coalition nears the size needed to nominate its man, it might seem to be in the interests of the other coalitions to join in an effort to stop the front runner. Yet, this has not happened very often lately. In 1948, Judah and Smith tell us,

> . . . it was impossible to form an anti-Dewey coalition. Taft had previously refused to combine with Vandenberg in a pre-convention stop-Dewey move and Warren's views were closer to Dewey's than Taft's. Stassen and Taft were separated by personal ill-feeling as well as policy differences. Nevertheless they did meet. The conference was held in a freight elevator to insure secrecy. Nothing came of it. . . .[10]

In the 1960 Democratic convention, it is said, Stevenson managers approached others about a rules change to prevent voting switches at the end of the first ballot. (The assumption was that Kennedy might not have quite enough votes on the first ballot, and might lose some support on a second ballot.) Symington managers were agreeable, but Johnson's were not. So again a blocking coalition did not form. In part, this is because the simple

[10] Charles Judah and George Winston Smith, *The Unchosen* (New York: Coward-McCann, 1962), p. 241.

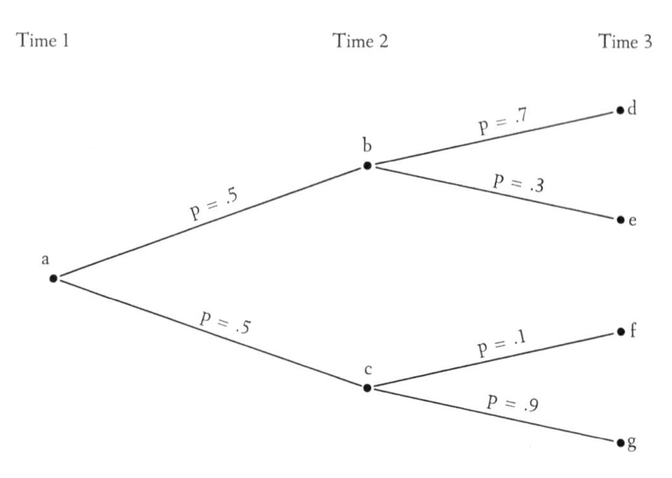

Figure 1 *A Simple Stochastic Process*

desire to stop a front-runner is too slender a reed to bind a coalition together. In part, it is because of the power of the argument that a candidate is about to win.

William A. Gamson calculates 41 per cent as the approximate point when the process "goes critical" and a stampede to the winner begins.[11] Once the identity of the winning coalition becomes obvious, only those groups whose characteristic attitudes are hostile to the attitudes of the winning coalition have sufficient reason to stay outside. So the general process of group combination proceeds from most natural to least natural allies. Because of the difficulty of recruiting less natural allies, the process may slow down a bit at this point. But, once the coalition reaches a size where a bandwagon begins to roll, the process speeds up again. A larger-than-necessary coalition often results.

The bare bones of coalition formation may be thought of as a stochastic process, a simple version of which is shown in tree-form in Figure 1. Here one is concerned with "state probabilities," the likelihood that

[11] "Coalition Formation at Presidential Nominating Conventions," *American Journal of Sociology*, September, 1962, p. 166. Gamson's model for coalition formation stresses factors similar to those being used here: "A candidate will prefer that coalition *within* a class which maximizes the similarity to his own ideology where the ideology of the coalition members is a weighted average of the ideology score of the prospective members—weighted by their percentage of resources in the coalition."

a phenomenon will be in a given state at a given time, and "transition probabilities," the chances that the phenomenon will change from one state to another between successive intervals. In the illustration, we are certain that if we begin in State *a* at Time 1, there is an even chance of going to State *b* or State *c* as we move from Time 1 to Time 2, a somewhat better chance of going from State *b* to State *d* than State *b* to State *e*, and a much better chance of going from State *c* to State *g* than of going from State *c* to State *f* as we move from Time 2 to Time 3. We have an initial state probability of 1 (certainty) since the process can be only in State *a* at Time 1. Therefore the state probabilities at Time 2 will be the transition probabilities from Time 1, and the state probabilities at Time 3 will be the products of the two transition probabilities involved. The state probability for State *e*, for example, reflects the chances that the process will follow path *a-b-e*. Since the transition probability for *a-b* is .5, and the transition probability for *b-e* is .3, the state probability for *e* is .15.

A similar figure (Figure 2) can be used to visualize the essentials of the

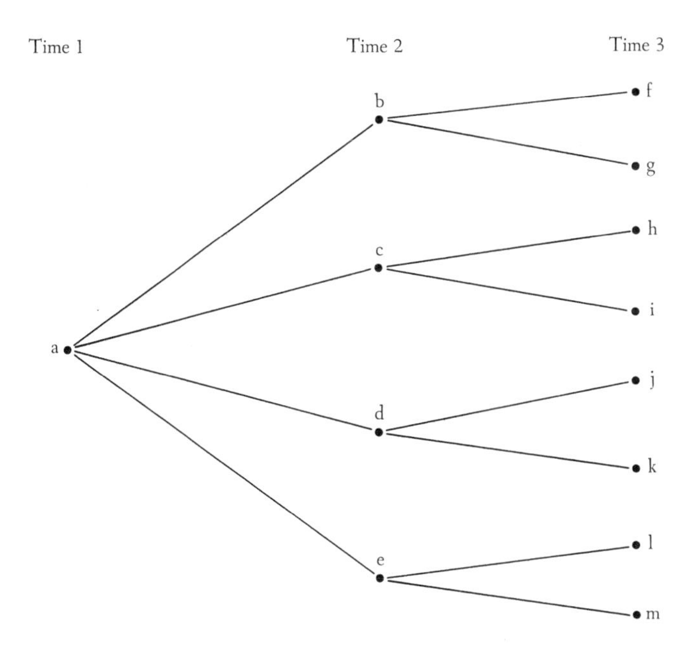

Figure 2 *Nomination Politics as a Stochastic Process*

nomination process. There are three basic questions: What is the likelihood that a group of delegates will be selected to participate in the nomination process (State *a*)? What is the likelihood that the group of delegates will decide to join one of, say, four coalitions (State *b*, State *c*, State *d*, or State *e*)? After a group joins a coalition—once, for example, the process goes from State *a* to State *c*—what is the likelihood that this particular coalition will win (State *h*) or lose (State *i*)?

The initial state probability governing the emergence of a group of delegates depends on the characteristics of the population from which the group is to be selected. The transition probabilities depend on the overlap in attitudes and a step function which reflects selected characteristics of the coalition. When considering the possibility that a group will join a coalition, the relevant attitudes are those of the group and the coalition it might join. When estimating the chances that a given coalition might win, one focuses on the intersection between that coalition's attitudes and the attitudes of as yet unrecruited groups.

The step function takes on different values according to the size of the coalition. When the coalition is attracting its first recruits, it has a value of 1 if the group resides in the coalition candidate's home state, but otherwise falls off as a function of distance from the home state approaching a limit of 0. Once the coalition has attracted $1/n$th of the votes needed to nominate (where n is the number of serious candidates), the step function takes on the value of the proportion of the votes needed to nominate that are already in the coalition. In other words, if the coalition has 300 votes when 600 are needed to nominate, the step function has a value of .5. When it finally becomes evident the coalition is going to win, the step function assumes a value of 1, and the extent of overlap in attitudes drops out of the calculation of the transition probabilities. There is one exception to this. If there is no substantial overlap in attitudes, the transition probability governing whether the group will join the winning coalition remains a joint function. The logical meaning of this is that it is certain the coalition will win, it is certain those groups who share a substantial number of attitudes will join the coalition, and the likelihood the groups that are in minimal agreement will join depends solely on the extent of overlap in attitudes between each such group and the winning coalition.

The total process, of course, is much more complex. Dozens of groups are involved. The transition probabilities change almost every time any group joins an existing coalition. But the extent of the overlap in attitudes and the size of the coalition are the crucial questions. Therefore it is useful to conceptualize the nomination process in this way.

Prior to 1964, the most recent Republican experience with out-party coalition formation had been in 1952. At that point in time, there were experienced coalition leaders and many veteran state leaders. The Eisenhower and Taft coalitions[12] included participants who had been active in the Dewey and Taft coalitions, and these coalitions had figured prominently in every Republican presidential contest since 1940. In part because of this, Republican groups formed into "classic" coalitions in 1952.

The base for the Eisenhower coalition was provided by New York. The Empire State had 96 votes, 92 of which were ultimately cast for Dwight Eisenhower. The attitudes stressed included a commitment to an internationalist foreign policy, the importance of military and foreign affairs in the postwar world, and the party's need, after a generation without a national victory, for a candidate who could not only win, but win with a large enough margin to carry in other Republicans. The action prescription implied by these attitudes, of course, was the nomination of Dwight Eisenhower.[13]

In each of three succeeding conventions, Ohio had contributed her 56 votes as the base for a nomination drive by a native son. In 1940, the candidate had been Senator Robert A. Taft; in 1944, Governor John W. Bricker; in 1948, Taft again. Following the senior Senator's re-election by 437,000 votes in 1950, a fourth campaign was launched from the Buckeye State. The attitudes stressed by the leaders of the Taft coalition included a quite negative view of the New Deal-Fair Deal ideology, a conviction that Republicans could win by making a frontal attack on "creeping socialism," a belief that a liberal phase had ended in the late 1940's and it was time for conservatives to return to power, and the importance of rewarding faithful service to the party. The conclusion to be drawn from these attitudes was that the party should nominate a "real Republican"—as it had not done during the 1940's—and have it out with the New Dealers once and for all.

[12] The terms "Eisenhower coalition" and "Taft coalition" imply that these nomination coalitions were made up of specific groups supporting specific candidates rather than representing any contest between a mythical "eastern establishment" and "the midwestern conservatives." This is *not* a trivial point.

[13] Paul T. David, Malcolm Moos, and Ralph M. Goldman, *Presidential Nominating Politics in 1952* (Baltimore: Johns Hopkins Press, 1954), Vol. I, p. 48. Much of the description which follows has been abstracted from this comprehensive study.

The most natural allies for an Eisenhower coalition were to be found in neighboring New Jersey and New England. New Jersey, following the lead of Governor Alfred E. Driscoll, contributed 33 votes. Eighty-six more were garnered from New England states where Eisenhower groups, following the pattern set in New Hampshire, won out over Taft groups. (These struggles sometimes left scars. In Massachusetts, for example, New Bedford publisher Basil Brewer, a Taft supporter, became very active in behalf of John Kennedy's successful attempt to take a Senate seat away from Eisenhower leader Henry Cabot Lodge.) New York, New Jersey, and New England votes together came to a total of 218, a respectable number with which to begin a serious campaign. Similarly, groups most easily coopted into the Taft coalition came from states close to Ohio. Indiana, Illinois, and Wisconsin sent almost solid Taft delegations: 113 votes in all. Fifty-four more came from Kentucky, Tennessee, and West Virginia on the southern side of the Ohio River. These easily allied groups gave the Taft coalition a pool of 223 votes with which to begin bargaining.

Throughout the spring, delegate hunters from both the Eisenhower and Taft coalitions roamed the country. Taft did better in the more conservative South. There was support for both candidates, but there were 80 clear Taft votes to 43 for Eisenhower. The two coalitions did almost equally well west of the Mississippi. Taft groups were in control in certain Plains States (Nebraska and the Dakotas) and along the western ridges of the Rockies (Idaho, Utah, Arizona). Eisenhower groups did better in the General's home state of Kansas, in Iowa, Missouri, and Colorado, and in the Pacific Northwest. All told, the Taft coalition gleaned 130 votes from this area while the Eisenhower coalition got 144 votes. There was a scattering of Taft support (ultimately 31 votes) in the East, and a hint of Eisenhower support (a dozen votes) in Indiana, Illinois, and Minnesota. When these groups from other parts of the country were added to the 200-plus votes each candidate had from his natural allies, the Eisenhower coalition had something like 425 votes and the Taft coalition about 450.

As the convention neared, the leaders of both coalitions turned their attention to the search for the necessary additional votes. There were three possible sources. One hundred and forty votes were to be cast by three states—Maryland, Michigan, and Pennsylvania—which had not yet declared openly for either candidate. Second, there were 68 contested seats in three Southern states, Georgia, Louisiana, and Texas, where Taft groups and Eisenhower groups had both sent "duly elected" delegations. Third, there were a little more than a hundred votes, principally from California and Minnesota, committed to Warren, Stassen, or MacArthur.

The Eisenhower coalition was more successful at this stage of the nomination contest. Governor McKeldin was asked to nominate Eisenhower and was able to produce 16 Maryland votes for the General. The Michigan delegation, astutely led by Arthur Summerfield, split 35 to 11 for Eisenhower after it became apparent that General Motors and Ford favored Eisenhower and that the World War II commander would be the more popular candidate in most of the delegates' home districts. The Pennsylvania delegation was split into three groups, an Eisenhower group led by Senator James Duff, a Taft group led by National Committeeman G. Mason Owlett, and a "neutral" group responsive to Governor John S. Fine. After conferences with Michigan chairman Summerfield, as well as extensive consultation with Pennsylvania delegates, county chairmen, and state legislators, Fine announced he thought Eisenhower would be more likely to win and thus help the Republican ticket in Pennsylvania. Consequently, the Keystone State had two groups (53 votes) for Eisenhower and one (15 votes) for Taft.

While these 104 votes were being added to the Eisenhower coalition, the coalition leaders were also giving attention to the disputed Southern delegates. They made a moral issue out of the seating of these delegates by offering a "fair-play" amendment which prevented any disputed delegate from voting on any credentials contest. This kept a bloc of potential Taft votes out of the balloting, and the Eisenhower coalition picked up the Warren and Stassen votes on this issue. The result was a demonstration of Eisenhower strength and 60 more Eisenhower votes. Therefore, Eisenhower had 595 votes at the end of the first ballot—only nine less than were needed to nominate. Minnesota then switched from its solitary role in support of former Governor Stassen and it was all over.

The point which historians remember is that Dwight Eisenhower was nominated at Chicago. The point of importance to our analysis, however, is that when almost all of the groups in the Republican party had joined either the Eisenhower or Taft coalition, the two coalitions were of approximately equal strength. Before the vote switches at the end of the first ballot, the Eisenhower coalition had 595 votes while the Taft coalition had 500 votes. Both the Eisenhower and Taft coalitions were past the 41 per cent figure Gamson regards as critical. If the Taft forces had won the contest on the disputed Southern delegates, Taft would have led 560 to 535. It happened that the leaders of the Eisenhower coalition were more skillful and more fortunate in the final stages of coalition formation in 1952, but it is not difficult to imagine slightly different circumstances which would have led to a Taft victory.[14] This was not a case of liberal Republicans winning an automatic victory, nor was it a case of the will of the conservative majority being thwarted by a few Eastern kingmakers—although quite a few people accepted one or the other of these simplified versions later on. The 1952 contest was a very close thing. So, in estimating the probabilities in the next Republican exercise in coalition formation, it is well to ask what happened to the groups who composed the Eisenhower and Taft coalitions in the ensuing dozen years.

By and large, members of the Eisenhower core group had retired from politics. General Eisenhower himself was determined to remain neutral in order to serve as a unifying influence after the nomination contest was over. Thomas E. Dewey and Herbert Brownell were both engaged in profitable law practices in New York City. Sherman Adams had retired to a quiet life in New Hampshire. Henry Cabot Lodge was still in active public life, but halfway around the world in Saigon. Lucius Clay and Walter Williams were both investment bankers. James Duff had been retired from the Senate by Joseph Clark, and was now 81 years old. There were some experienced moderate leaders around in 1964—Thomas Stevens and Hugh Scott, for example—but their ranks were a good deal thinner than they had been in 1952.

In 1952, Republican governors played an important role. On at least one vital occasion, they acted as a group themselves. A manifesto, signed by 23 of the 25 governors, urging the "fair-play" procedure in resolving the delegate contests from Texas, Louisiana, and Georgia was released to the press just before the convention opened. The governors also played key roles in leading state groups into the Eisenhower coalition. In our brief review, we already have noted the activity of Governors Dewey, Adams, Driscoll, Fine, and McKeldin. The most cursory examination of activity elsewhere reveals key roles being played by Governors John Davis Lodge, Dan Thornton, Arthur Langlie, Douglas McKay, and many others. But, during the 1950's, there was a general attrition in Republican strength at the state level. By the end of the decade, there were only fifteen Republican gover-

[14] The logical possibilities here would include a deadlock with both coalitions falling just short of the required majority, but, as a matter of empirical fact, it should be noted that a convention deadlock has not occurred since the 1920's.

nors in office. Some attractive new faces appeared on the scene in the 1962 elections—John Chafee, William Scranton, George Romney, and John Love, for example—but these men were not experienced in nomination politics. Nelson Rockefeller, Robert Smylie, and Mark Hatfield had national experience, but Rockefeller was involved for many months with his own candidacy, and Smylie and Hatfield came from such sparsely populated states that they lacked the easy visibility associated with being governor of California or Ohio. A fairly high rate of turnover is normal in nomination politics, but, even so, there was an unusually small number of experienced chief executives on hand as 1964 approached.

The Southern groups were quite weak in 1952. In some parts of the South—the mountain areas and a few metropolitan areas—Republican groups were led by those interested in winning elections. But generally, Southern Republican leaders of that vintage

> might be called palace or bureaucratic politicians, since their chief preoccupation is not with voters but with maneuvers to gain and keep control of the state party machinery, an endeavor that requires convention manipulation at home and intrigue with national party leaders up North. So complex is Republican factional politics in some states that only those with a high order of skill in palace politics can stay on top for long. . . . Presidential aspirants, invariably nonsouthern, are interested in control of state organizations only because of the votes they can deliver in national conventions.[15]

By 1964, however, it was no longer possible to "buy" Southern delegations. A number of factors lay behind this development, but one of the more important was "Operation Dixie."

Republican strength had been developing in the South for some time. Population mobility—Northerners moving to the South and Southerners gaining more experience outside their native region—and the integration of the South into the national economy had been eroding sectional isolation. In 1957, National Chairman H. Meade Alcorn decided to act to try to accelerate the growth of Southern Republicanism. He created a Southern Division in the National Committee staff, and placed an affable Virginian, I. Lee Potter, in charge. During the next seven years, Lee Potter concentrated on publicity and recruitment. He made hundreds of speeches on the growth of Southern Republicanism, and these received widespread

[15] V. O. Key, Jr., *Southern Politics in State and Nation* (New York: Knopf, 1950), p. 272.

coverage in the regional press. "Every time I'd make a speech in which I discussed the South," he recalled, "almost every paper from Florida to Arkansas picked it up." The weakness of the existing party structure also gave him a chance to do some active recruiting. Usually national leaders can only hope able party leaders will emerge in the states, but by telling them their chances of promotion were better, Potter was able to entice some ambitious young men into Republican ranks. By 1964, the average age of the Southern state chairmen was just over thirty-six.

The pace was hastened by the election of John Tower to the Senate from Texas in 1961 and the near election of James Martin from Alabama in 1962. A good many Republicans had been elected in the Southwest and in the Border States. Howard Pyle, Barry Goldwater, and Paul Fannin in Arizona, Edwin Meecham in New Mexico, Henry Bellmon in Oklahoma, James Kem in Missouri, John Sherman Cooper and Thruston Morton in Kentucky, Cecil Underwood in West Virginia, and Theodore McKeldin, John Marshall Butler, and J. Glenn Beall in Maryland had all won post-war elections. But John Tower's election as the first Republican United States Senator from the Old Confederacy and James Martin's 49 per cent of the vote in a Black Belt state lent credence to the belief that victory was possible in the Deep South. Southern groups, led by such men as John Grenier of Alabama, Peter O'Donnell of Texas, Drake Edens of South Carolina, and Wirt Yerger of Mississippi, now scented victory. Though relatively inexperienced on the national scene, they were prepared to play politics for keeps. They wanted a candidate who would be attractive in their home states—and they knew if they held together, the Southern states could provide such a candidate with an impressive base of 279 votes.[16]

In the years between 1960 and 1964, conservative groups were also being mobilized outside the South. There were quite a few Republicans whose belief in some of the central attitudes of the Taft coalition—that the New Dealers could be defeated in an ideological confrontation, that there were conservative voters who were staying at home when faced with a

[16] George L. Grassmuck, "Emergent Republicanism in the South," a paper prepared for presentation at the 1964 Annual Meeting of the American Political Science Association, Chicago, Illinois, September 9–12, 1964. See also Allan P. Sindler, ed., *Change in the Contemporary South* (Durham, N.C.: Duke University Press, 1963), and Bernard Cosman, *Five States for Goldwater* (University, Alabama: University of Alabama Press, 1967).

choice between two liberals, and so on—had never really been shaken. Political scientists may have viewed the 1960 election as one in which Richard Nixon received a larger proportion than the "normal" Republican vote of 46 per cent,[17] but to these conservatives, 1960 was just another election opportunity kicked away by the me-too approach. One key person holding these views was F. Clifton White. White was a one-time national chairman of the Young Republicans who had been active in the cooptation of several more conservatives for that post, and who operated an agency in New York to advise industrial concerns on political problems. As a New Yorker, he had been active in the Dewey and Eisenhower coalitions, and he had been national organization director of the Nixon-Lodge Volunteers in 1960. Clif White, in other words, was an experienced political technician with extensive contacts in Republican and industrial circles. Shortly after Nixon's defeat, White began talking with friends such as Charles Barr of Standard Oil of Indiana about the desirability of nominating a conservative in 1964.

On October 8, 1961, some twenty of White's associates met in a Chicago motel for a serious discussion of the necessary steps to bring about the nomination of a conservative (who had not yet been chosen). White was commissioned to act as the group's agent. He increased his travel schedule in order to encourage conservatives to run for precinct, county, and state party positions of little visibility which would enable them to select conservative delegates in 1964. In 1964, one state chairman recalled an earlier meeting:

> There were seven of us sitting around the living room. We were talking about who was going to do what and they said to me: "You're going to run for state chairman." And you know, thinking back on that meeting later I realized that everyone there was a pretty strong Goldwater man.[18]

Such living-room conversations were precisely what Clif White wanted to encourage.

Following the 1962 elections, the White group—now grown to around fifty—met again in Chicago. This time they decided that the 1962 election

[17] Donald E. Stokes, "1960 and the Problem of Deviating Elections," a paper prepared for delivery at the 1961 Annual Meeting of the American Political Science Association, St. Louis, Missouri, Sept. 6–9, 1961.

[18] This sort of activity provides a good illustration of the processes by which "potential groups" (to use David Truman's concept) in the electorate become actual groups participating in politics.

results were encouraging enough for them to proceed, talked in considerable detail about budget, and picked certain states for intensive efforts. In February, 1963, they resolved that, in view of Barry Goldwater's own reluctance to become a candidate, they would emerge as a National Draft Goldwater Committee. The surfacing of this organization took place in April, 1963, when a press conference was held at which Texas State Chairman Peter O'Donnell was introduced as chairman. Goldwater was cool to the idea and the committee, but took no position on the ground that it was "their time and their money." Considerable time and some money was spent throughout 1963, and by the time the Senator finally announced his candidacy for the presidency, the Draft Goldwater Committee had state chairmen and an organization down to the congressional district or county level in forty states.[19]

Needless to add, moderate Republicans were not inactive during this period. A good deal of activity was taking place on behalf of Nelson Rockefeller. But if one begins with the fact that the Eisenhower and Taft coalitions were of approximately equal size in 1952, and then asks what had happened to the groups making up these coalitions during the ensuing period, a reasonably clear pattern emerges. The moderate groups were weaker—particularly in leadership. The leaders of the old Dewey coalition had retired from politics, and too few skillful younger men had stepped into their shoes. Conservative groups, on the other hand, were in a good deal stronger position. The Republican party in the South was no longer in the hands of "post office politicians," and conservatives throughout the country were being mobilized by some quiet technicians anxious for a chance to demonstrate their skill at coalition formation.

Groups do not come together at random to form coalitions in nomination politics. Rather, specific groups are attracted to specific candidates, and while one can envision an ideal candidate around which a coalition might form, in real life the choice is restricted to a finite list of flesh-and-blood hopefuls who are on the scene at the time. In January, 1964, interviewers from the University of Michigan Survey Research Center asked a national sample: "If you had a choice, which Republican leader do you think would be the

[19] F. Clifton White, "Selection of Delegates to the 1964 Republican Nominating Convention," a paper prepared for the 1965 Annual Meeting of the Western Political Science Association, Victoria, British Columbia, March 19, 1965. The story has been told in much more detail in White's *Suite 3505: The Story of the Draft Goldwater Movement* (New Rochelle, New York: Arlington House, 1967).

best for our country in 1964?" Some 36.4 per cent of those interviewed did not have a choice. Of those who did, the preferences were as follows:[20]

Nelson Rockefeller	29.5%
Richard Nixon	28.1
Barry Goldwater	21.1
Henry Cabot Lodge	8.6
George Romney	5.5
William Scranton	4.1

This was the list from which the 1964 Republican nominee was to be chosen, and—with the exception of Henry Cabot Lodge who was off in Saigon—these were the speakers introduced to the Republican faithful over closed-circuit television at a series of fund-raising dinners held on the evening of January 29, 1964. Their words are worth our attention because they suggest the attitudes that would be stressed in any coalition built around any of these candidates.

New York's Governor Nelson A. Rockefeller spoke from Los Angeles. He attacked Lyndon Johnson for promising everything in his State of the Union Message, but failing to deal with the causes of unemployment, failing to indicate things were going badly in Vietnam, Cuba, and Panama, and failing to call attention to the deterioration of our alliances. "The American people," he continued, "need, deserve, and want better leadership than this. The American people want leadership that will unshackle the free enterprise system so it can play its rightful role in providing jobs; that will re-establish the strength and vitality of our relationships with other free nations; that will face the realities of the Communist threat; that believes in the federal system of shared sovereignty; and that deeply believes in the worth and dignity of every individual human being."

This was the language spoken by all recent Republican presidential candidates, and Nelson Rockefeller certainly had the credentials to run for president. Virtually his whole adult life had been devoted to public affairs. He had been Assistant Secretary of State for Latin American Affairs under Franklin Roosevelt, Chairman of the International Development Advisory

[20] These data are from an SRC code book made available through the Inter-University Consortium for Political Research. Three per cent of the respondents picked some other candidate.

Board under Harry Truman, Under Secretary of Health, Education and Welfare at the outset of the Eisenhower administration, and Dwight Eisenhower's personal assistant for international security matters. After deciding he would be better able to advance the causes in which he believed if elected to office himself, he left the federal government to seek the New York governorship in 1958. Elected twice by margins of more than half a million votes, he had impressed observers as an able administrator in the Empire State.

The Executive Mansion in Albany has been a traditional starting point for presidential aspirants. Alfred E. Smith, Franklin D. Roosevelt, and Thomas E. Dewey were all in office at the time of their nominations, and there was no doubt that Nelson Rockefeller wanted to follow in their footsteps. Once he discovered that Richard Nixon had the nomination all locked up in 1960, the Governor began building for 1964. He surrounded himself with an exceptionally able core group. New York's National Comitteeman George Hinman talked with his many friends among Republican leaders about the virtues of a Rockefeller candidacy. John A. Wells and William L. Pfiffer, whose experience in the formation of nomination coalitions extended over two decades, accepted key organizational assignments. Roswell Perkins, a wunderkind of the Eisenhower administration, developed positions on issues. Regional directors, such as Washington's talented Mort Frayn, began to organize Rockefeller groups in various states. These political veterans were given ample resources, too. Nelson Rockefeller had access to the money necessary to finance a major political campaign.

In the spring of 1963, Republican leaders had been "certain" that Nelson Rockefeller was going to be nominated. He was the leading spokesman of moderate Republicans; he had the experience, ambition, and organization necessary to capture the nomination. He had been in political difficulty because of a tax increase and his divorce, but had been re-elected in 1962 with almost as large a margin as four years earlier. Besides, they asked, who else was there? Richard Nixon seemed to have renounced politics after his California defeat, and Barry Goldwater, popular as he was in the eyes of his devoted followers, did not have enough strength with the general public.

All this changed on May 4. This was the day Governor Rockefeller married Mrs. Margaretta "Happy" Murphy, a recently divorced mother of four young children. It soon became apparent that the Governor's remarriage was a serious political liability. The Gallup Poll had shown Rockefeller leading Goldwater by 43 per cent to 26 per cent among Republicans. The first Gallup Poll after the remarriage—available in late May—showed the Arizonan leading the New Yorker among Republicans by a margin of 35 per cent to 30 per cent. Republican leaders uninvolved in the presidential contest agreed the Governor had lost much of his appeal. Said one: "I've just heard too much about this remarriage from women. If there hadn't been any children involved, it might have been another story. But as of now, I think Rocky's out of the box." Echoed another: "Rocky's got the best delegate hunters in the country. But with this remarriage, all they can do is sit up there on the 56th floor in Rockefeller Center. No one wants to talk to them."

For a Rockefeller coalition to win, primary victories were a must. He could count on a New York group and a few more groups of natural allies. But the only way a Rockefeller coalition could grow beyond minimal size was on the strength of primary victories which would demonstrate his popularity and occasionally (as in California) add a large group of delegates. Successfully contested primaries would give Rockefeller workers in convention states leverage to persuade some state parties to send groups of Rockefeller delegates to San Francisco. If Rockefeller came to the convention with a string of primary victories and a respectable number of delegates, then he would be in a position for the hard bargaining necessary to increase his coalition to winning size. So, in early November, Nelson Rockefeller faced a battery of television cameras and said: "I am here this morning—and I shall go to New Hampshire immediately following this meeting—formally to announce my candidacy for the Republican Presidential nomination. . . . I have reached this decision because I believe that vital principles are at stake in the next Presidential election . . . ." By the time of the January fund-raising dinner, he was fully engaged in the Granite State primary campaign.

The familiar voice of Richard Nixon came over the video circuit from New York City. "Tonight let us . . . [instill] in each one of us that essential ingredient for political success—the spirit of victory. That spirit money cannot buy. It comes from belief in our cause, willingness to fight for it and the conviction that we shall win . . . . We shall not win by resort to image-making, by being everything to everybody, by trying to appear liberal to the liberals, and conservative to the conservatives. The present occupant of the White House is a past master of that kind of political shell game. We shall win by standing for principle on a great issue. I believe there is such an issue—the need for America to regain the initiative in the fight against world communism . . . . There is no major area of the world where the cause of freedom is not worse off today than it was four years ago . . . . Now is the time for a new team to go to Washington, D.C., to reverse the tide of defeat and launch an offensive for victory without war for the forces of freedom."

This speech showed the political skill which had carried Richard Nixon to party leadership so quickly. There was hardly a phrase which would not serve to unite various groups in the Republican coalition. His major attack was directed at Lyndon Johnson, an unlikely recruit to any Republican coalition. He stressed the importance of dedicated work (a salient attitude for party stalwarts), the possibility of winning (a happy thought to any member of a minority party), and then went on to develop his major appeal on foreign policy, an issue which had generally attracted votes to the Republican party. In developing his appeal, there was just enough of a hint of "Why Not Victory?" to be acceptable to hard-liners, and just enough emphasis on the ineptitude with which the Democratic administration was pursuing foreign policy goals to appeal to the party's internationalists.

Had Richard Nixon been speaking as one whose post-1960 political participation had been limited to working for the national party and acting as its public spokesman, the former Vice-President very possibly would have been the prime contender for the 1964 nomination. His experience in office, his near victory in 1960, and his central position in the party would have made him an aspirant around which a coalition could have been formed fairly easily. But such was not the case. He had returned to California in 1961 and generally had been unavailable for fund-raising appearances. He had sought to hold the Republican party in the Golden State together by running for governor in 1962, but his bitter statement on the morrow of defeat had raised questions about his ability to withstand pressure and the defeat itself had left the party badly disorganized. Then, in 1963, he had left his native state to join a New York City law firm. So 1964 found him without a political base and with a number of political scars he had not borne four years earlier.

All this made it a little difficult to imagine how a Nixon coalition might be put together. It could not be done in the classic fashion by beginning with one's home state and building out from there. Some natural support could perhaps be found in the Midwest where there were Republican groups whose attitudes were more moderate than in the South and less liberal than in the East. If a respected party figure, ideally someone of the stature of Ohio's Ray Bliss, came forward and said, "Dick, we need you to keep this party from splitting," something might begin to jell. In the absence of this, Nixon's friends could portray him as a national leader and try to pick up the beginnings of a Nixon coalition here and there by recruiting delegates friendly to Nixon since his vice-presidential days. These delegates would have to be Nixon loyalists who were positively attracted to him if they were to stick by him long enough to keep Nixon's candidacy credible. If there were 50 to 100 votes committed to Nixon, other groups might eventually join a Nixon coalition. But since these additional groups would most likely come from some other candidate's coalition, Nixon ought not to attack other candidates. This would only cause then pro-Rockefeller or pro-Goldwater groups to form anti-Nixon attitudes and reduce Nixon's chances of eventual success.[21] Consequently, Nixon's gambit had to be very quiet campaigning while he kept himself visible as best he could and hoped none of the others put together a winning coalition.

Another voice came from the dinner being held in Pittsburgh. "This election year is not one just for the record books," declared Senator Barry Goldwater. "It is one for the history books. . . . There are *two* paths that face us and a great choice between them. One path is toward growing control, coercion, regulation, and regimentation by the executive branch of the federal government; toward the growing power of an entrenched bureaucracy responsive to no constituency but the White House; toward the million miles of red tape that bind our lives, our hopes, our futures, our initiative, and even our prayers; toward the default of international responsibility in trying to sugar-coat problems rather than solve them, to avoid them rather than confront them; toward the befriending of enemies and the offending of allies; and toward the isolation of this, the mightiest nation on earth, behind walls of indecision while the world cries for the leadership that could restore liberty and greatness. The other path is toward increased freedom by an increase of reliance on individual responsibility, initiative, creativity, and integrity; toward increased welfare by increased freedom to work without hindrance, to work wisely, to work hard, to enjoy the rewards of that work; toward increased strength of the great alliance of free nations to face the challenge of Communism and force its withdrawal from conquest, subversion, and threats to the peace; toward the restoration of checks and

[21] Similar calculations seem to offer front-runners immunity from attack by candidates who hope to inherit some of their support. The resulting lack of criticism may be a reason why front-runners have so frequently gone on to win the nomination in recent years.

balances in our government, particularly in regard to the role and responsibility of Congress; and toward restoration of the fiscal and moral integrity that can assure a prosperous nation and a peaceful and *free* world. These are not differences in detail. . . . These are differences in principle. These should be the differences in parties. They can be the basis for the great choice Americans can and must make in the next election."

Like other political leaders who use uncompromising language, Senator Barry Goldwater had many detractors and many admirers. The result of expressing himself in frank and colorful language was a polarization of opinion. There were many to whom Goldwaterism was a synonym for not being quite with it; there were others who felt that the Arizonan was the most virtuous candidate to appear on the political scene for decades. His long public record—and he had expressed himself on almost every conceivable topic—included many statements that invited public attack, but there were many true believers who were willing to rush to his defense when he was attacked. Fortunately for one who aspired to the Republican nomination, Barry Goldwater's devoted following was concentrated within the Republican party.

This following in the Republican party rested on more than his uncompromising assertion of conservative principles. He had also shown himself willing to work for the party. His speech withdrawing his name from nomination at the 1960 Republican convention showed both these characteristics. From the rostrum at Chicago, there had been a declaration that Republican moderates were following unwise strategies. "We must remember that Republicans have not been losing elections because of more Democratic voters. Now, get this. We have been losing elections because conservatives too often fail to vote." There was an invitation to make the Republican party more conservative. "Let's grow up, conservatives. If we want to take this Party back, and I think we can someday, let's get to work." But there was also a ringing declaration of support for Republican candidates. "I am a conservative and I am going to devote all my time from now until November to electing Republicans from the top of the ticket to the bottom of the ticket, and I call upon my fellow conservatives to do the same." The Senator illustrated his point by making 126 speeches for the Nixon-Lodge ticket that fall, and emerged as something of a hero—a man willing to work loyally for his party even though he disagreed with many of the programs then being advocated. After John Kennedy's election, Barry Goldwater kept right on working for the Republican party. While many other Republican leaders were looking the other way, the Arizonan was willing to come in for fund-raising dinners to help reduce the debt incurred in 1960. He made 225 appearances during 1961, and his schedule was even more crowded during the first part of 1962. A warm and attractive human being, Barry Goldwater left friends wherever he spoke.

Many of the people he contacted were one day to lead groups into the Goldwater coalition, but his speaking junkets were not undertaken with the presidential nomination consciously in mind. In fact, as presidential talk grew in 1962, the Arizonan sharply curtailed his speaking schedule. He was of two minds about the grand prize. On the one hand, he felt an obligation as the leader of the conservative cause. On the other, he was reluctant to seek the presidency, and felt that if he were unsuccessful in seeking the nomination or in the general election campaign, the cause of conservatism would be set back. He therefore took steps compatible with a presidential race *or* a contest for re-election to the Senate from Arizona. He brought his old friend, lawyer Denison Kitchel, to Washington to make preparations for whichever campaign the Senator should ultimately find himself involved in. Mr. Kitchel began an analysis of the positions Goldwater had taken in his public life. He also kept himself informed about the activities of the Draft Goldwater organization—but was most careful not to express any opinion lest the Draft Goldwater leaders take it as interest on the part of the Senator.

Barry Goldwater had just about made up his mind to run for the presidency in the fall of 1963. Then the assassination of President Kennedy forced a painful reassessment. Not only was there the shock of the death of a man of whom Goldwater was personally fond, but the political situation was different with Johnson in the White House. Goldwater supporters had been counting on Southern electoral votes because this was a region of Goldwater strength and Kennedy weakness; now the White House was occupied by the first Southerner since the Civil War. There was also a question whether the conservative support building behind Goldwater had been a manifestation of opposition to John F. Kennedy rather than real backing for Goldwater himself. In the end, Goldwater gave in to the pleading of his many backers who wanted him to enter the lists. Standing in the sunshine outside his Arizona home on January 3, 1964, the Senator made his announcement: "I have decided to [seek the Republican presidential nomination] because of the principles in which I believe and because I am convinced that millions of Americans share my belief in those principles. . . . I will offer a choice, not an echo. This will not be an engagement of personalities. It will be an engagement of principles."

If Barry Goldwater's decision to seek the presidency had been reluctant, he was firm about another point. This was that the campaign was going to be run *his* way. He was not going to become the captive of groups who had been urging him to run because they wanted a conservative champion in the race. Consequently, his core group was made up of personal friends from the Arizona political world. Denison Kitchel would be "head honcho," the man in charge. Dean Burch of Tucson, who had been the Senator's administrative assistant, would be Kitchel's immediate assistant. Richard Kleindienst, former Arizona Republican state chairman, would be director of field operations, and Ann-Eve Johnson, who had been national committeewoman from Arizona, would be in charge of women's activities. Without exception, these Arizonans lacked national political experience. The only ranking Goldwaterite who had been through a presidential campaign, Clif White of the now expired Draft Goldwater Committee, was placed in a subordinate position.

A strategy which could be used to put together a Goldwater coalition had been obvious since at least the time of John Tower's election in 1961. Arizona was too small to provide much of a nucleus, but Texas had 56 votes in the Republican National Convention. Texas also provided a base from which a "Southwestern" candidate could appeal to Southern groups and to Western groups. Actually, a Goldwater coalition of respectable size was already in existence by the time of the Senator's announcement. The talk at the Republican Southern Leadership Conference in November, 1963, was that Southern groups were unwilling to accept any other candidate, and conservative groups in the West had also been busy. A fair estimate of the size of the Goldwater coalition in January, 1964, would have been in excess of 300 votes. His problem was to move from there to the 655 votes needed to nominate. But it was possible that more groups could be added as the citizen activity stimulated by Clif White produced delegate votes at the end of the precinct-caucus, county-caucus, district-caucus, and state-caucus process, and as party workers throughout the country remembered the number of times Barry Goldwater had flown through bad weather to address fund-raising dinners. And if Barry Goldwater could demonstrate his popularity in one or two primaries to overcome the reluctance of groups who felt he might not be an attractive candidate in the general election, a large enough coalition might be put together to produce a massive convention victory.

Henry Cabot Lodge was not among those who addressed the Republican fund-raising dinner. He was absent because of his responsibilities in

Saigon, but those who remembered words spoken on other occasions knew his attitudes on both domestic and foreign policy were progressive. He had once written: "We Republicans should say to the voter: We offer you a welfare society without a welfare state . . . . We think the desire for security is normal and human and good, in war and in peace, and that we can have it without red tape, without bureaucracy . . . without sacrifice of opportunity, and without loss of personal liberty." On civil rights, he had said: "If we are to win the struggle for the minds of men—particularly in Africa and Asia—we must show at home that we practice what we preach about equal rights for all, and that what we do is animated by spiritual values." Lodge had supported foreign aid for somewhat similar reasons. "My years at the U.N. convince me that many of the peoples on the sidelines—in Asia, Africa, and the Middle East—do not by any means take it for granted that the western style of freedom is better than communism. They don't listen much to what we *say* about communism, but they care a great deal about what we *do* for the national independence and better material life which they desire." The former Ambassador to the United Nations was perhaps best known for his highly publicized arguments with various Soviet representatives. For example, he had responded to Soviet charges about the U-2 overflight by arguing: "Here is a government, well known for its expansionist proclivities and armed to the teeth, which . . . has repeatedly used force. . . . When such a government insists on secrecy it is in effect also insisting on preserving its ability to make a surprise attack on humanity . . . . If it ever should be accepted that the Soviet Union can maintain a double standard whereby they have thousands of spies and subversive agents everywhere while protesting one harmless observation flight, the free world would surely be in great and peculiar danger."[22]

Henry Cabot Lodge's name had not figured in much public or private speculation about the Republican nomination until Lyndon Johnson became president. Mr. Gallup's interviewers had failed to find any public support while John Kennedy was in the White House, but in the first survey after the assassination, one out of six Republican voters named Lodge as their preferred candidate. And some party leaders, who had not thought of running Massachusetts' Lodge against Massachusetts' Kennedy, now gave serious consideration to him. In essence, the case for the Ambassador was

[22] These quotations appeared in "The Public Record of Henry Cabot Lodge," *Congressional Quarterly*, March 13, 1964, pp. 508–9.

that he was strong where the President was weak. He was popular in the populous industrial states of the Northeast which might hesitate in voting for a Texan. He had long experience with foreign policy, whereas Lyndon Johnson was a newcomer to these problems. And Lodge's demeanor suggested high standards of public morality which contrasted sharply with Lyndon Johnson's contacts with Bobby Baker. Balanced against this was the risk inherent in his position as Ambassador to South Vietnam. He was closely tied to what might well become the administration's major foreign policy failure. And Lodge had been more of a "loner" than "one of the boys" throughout his career. He was unpopular with the leaders of many important Republican groups.

It could be argued that his greatest strength and his greatest weakness came from the same source: the 1960 campaign. Surveys conducted during the 1960 campaign found that he was widely known and very popular among the voters. Nearly half (48%) of the respondents queried by interviewers from the University of Michigan Survey Research Center reported they had strong opinions about Henry Cabot Lodge. A fantastic 96 per cent of those having strong opinions about the Ambassador stated their opinions were favorable.[23] Ironically, the same campaign gave rise to a story accepted by many Republican professionals that Lodge was not a good campaigner. Lodge believed that he could do a better job of campaigning if he was not overscheduled. He often took time for an afternoon nap to break the eighteen-hour days which were necessary. From the standpoint of the campaign managers, the Ambassador's habits "created scheduling difficulties." When a congressional candidate with important constituents in tow was told the vice-presidential nominee was taking a nap, the reaction was likely to be unprintable.

The core group for a Lodge coalition was made up of persons from two generations. The elder generation was made up of Lodge's former political associates. At the outset, the most important persons here were Robert R. Mullen, a Washington public relations man who had been in charge of the 1952 Draft Eisenhower headquarters, and Irving Salomon, a retired business-

[23] These figures are from SRC code books made available through the Inter-University Consortium for Political Research. The comparable figures for other vice-presidential candidates are: Sparkman, 14% having strong opinions, 50% of these opinions favorable; Nixon (1952), 31% strong opinions, 78% favorable; Kefauver, 39% strong opinions, 68% favorable; Nixon (1956), 48% strong opinions, 48% favorable; Johnson, 34% strong opinions, 61% favorable.

man who had worked with Lodge at the United Nations. The younger generation consisted of persons who had held key positions in the 1962 Senate campaign of George Lodge, the Ambassador's son. Notable among these were Paul Grindle, a Boston importer of scientific instruments, and David Goldberg, a Boston lawyer in his mid-thirties. In the table of organization of the Draft Lodge Committee, Salomon appeared as National Finance Chairman and Mullen was listed as National Coordinator.

The classic coalition-building strategy for a candidate from Massachusets who is popular with the general public but viewed with skepticism by political leaders is that followed by John Kennedy in 1960. You first put together a solid block of New England votes to make your candidacy credible, then enter primaries to give a convincing demonstration of your personal popularity with the voters. This worked with Kennedy, but there were some differences in the situation facing the Lodge core group. Not the least of these were differences in financing and the amount of time available for delegate contact. With Lodge's popularity with the general public as the only card they had to play, the best they could do was to concentrate on relatively inexpensive primary campaigns in small states. Their hope was that a chain reaction would develop. Popularity would lead to a primary victory which would lead to a jump in Lodge's standing in the polls which would lead to another primary victory and so on. If Lodge's popularity got high enough, leaders of various groups might decide they had to join the Lodge coalition. This strategy was consistent with the resources available to the Lodge leaders, but it was relatively inflexible. If the process was stopped at any point, there was no alternate strategy available.

In Washington, D.C., Michigan's Governor George Romney was telling party contributors that what "America desperately needs is a program based on a modern application to our present-day problems of proven American principles. What is wrong with America today? Well, for one thing as spending goes up, morality goes down. One of the strongest forces at work to undermine our morality is the relentless growth of centralism with its corresponding decline in individual morality." After pointing to Northern Democrats who felt that all things must be accomplished at the federal level and to Southern Democrats who used states' rights as a cloak for inaction, Romney declared: "The Republican position must be that each state not only has *responsibilities,* but each state must move to meet these responsibilities. . . . Only the Republican party is in a position to prevent the substitution of centralism for the limited and balanced government established by the Constitution. By doing so, we will make a modern application of proven American principles to one of today's pressing problems."

The evangelistic emphasis on morality and principles was typical of the Michigan Governor. A former President of the Detroit Stake of the (Mormon) Church of Jesus Christ of Latter-Day Saints, George Romney brought missionary zeal to all of life's enterprises. During his years as President of the Nash-Kelvinator Corporation (later American Motors), he had revitalized the firm and sold the nation on the virtues of the compact Rambler. An advocate of citizen participation in government, his own entry into politics was as Vice-President of the 1961-62 Michigan Constitutional Convention. In the fall of 1962, he had ended fourteen years of Democratic rule by defeating John Swainson for the Michigan governorship. After a year as that state's chief executive, George Romney could document his thesis that "we Republicans are demonstrating the positive role that state government plays." He could point to the passage of a new state constitution, the elimination (with the help of some financial good fortune) of a chronic state deficit, leadership in civil rights, and an increase in funds available for education and mental health.

Michigan was a large enough state to provide a respectable base for a Romney coalition. Its delegates were to cast forty-eight votes at the Republican National Convention. Moreover, geography provided a chance that many of the early recruits to the old Taft coalition might be attracted to a Romney coalition. There was no other serious Midwestern contender, so a regional appeal could be directed to the other industrialized states in the Great Lakes region. Delegates from the old Northwest Territory (including Michigan) would cast 252 votes in San Francisco. It would be overly optimistic to assume that all these votes would be cast for Romney, but some additional groups could probably be recruited from the Mountain West because of the Governor's Mormon ties. Moreover, if George Romney were to enter, say, the Wisconsin primary on April 7, the Illinois primary on April 14, and the Indiana primary on May 5 in the process of bringing natural allies into a Romney coalition, he might very well emerge with a string of primary triumphs which would make him a most attractive candidate to groups elsewhere in the nation. It was perfectly conceivable that a powerful Romney coalition could be put together.

All this was not to be. In 1964, George Romney was not in a position to play a leading role in presidential politics. He had promised Michigan voters in 1962 that he would not run for president in 1964, and had repeated that pledge publicly and privately a number of times since. Another important consideration was that the job of rebuilding the Republican party in Michigan was barely under way. Romney's own term as governor expired in 1964, and Michigan Republicans had no other candidate of stature ready to run if Romney entered the presidential lists. Consequently, favorite-son status was George Romney's closest venture to active candidacy in 1964. He filed an affidavit with the Oregon Secretary of State declaring that he was not a presidential candidate, and soon announced his candidacy for re-election as Governor of Michigan.

Another new Republican governor was addressing Republican diners in Indianapolis that January evening. "Through the great part of its history, through the greatest of its successes," asserted Pennsylvania's William W. Scranton, "the Republican party served America not by standing as the negative party, but by serving as the party of positive accomplishment . . . . In that spirit Republicans rally tonight. . . . We seek hands, and hearts, and votes—not because politics is the science of scratching backs, but because politics is the art of serving a nation. We must unfetter Americans from excesses and needless taxes, but we must also demand the integrity of a great nation's tax dollar. We must keep America in the leadership of the Free World, and to do so we must strengthen our moral foundations at home. We must defend the equal rights of all Americans under the law, but we must also courageously say that the real battlefields of human rights are not in the law books, but in human hearts. We must lead America towards solutions for the human problems created by the age of automation, but we must also provide a framework of free enterprise under which American business—not American government—creates prosperity. Through the whole gamut of the great issues, the Republican Party today ought to be for progress, not for procrastination; for prosperity, not for poverty; for performance, not promises. It's time we begin to stress the great positive accomplishments of modern Republicanism . . . . On such a platform we are prepared to seek a mandate from the people and, on such principles, we can and shall lead America into the finest hour of her history."

The completely self-confident man who uttered these phrases was the scion of a family closely connected with Republican politics since the origin of the party. One of the first Scrantons to settle in Pennsylvania, George Scranton, was elected to the U.S. House of Representatives in 1859. The

Governor's great-grandfather, Joseph A. Scranton, founder of the *Scranton Daily Republican*, served five terms in the House between 1881 and 1897. His mother, Mrs. Worthington Scranton (popularly known as the Duchess) was Republican National Committeewoman from Pennsylvania for twenty-three years.

Governor Scranton had a fierce loyalty to the party to which his family had devoted so much effort, but he also maintained a perspective which restrained him from overestimating his impact on the national scene. His personal participation in public life extended only over five years. After a period as a private assistant to John Foster Dulles and Christian Herter, he had served a single term in Congress. Picked to run for Governor of Pennsylvania in 1962, he had shown real vote-getting power in amassing a plurality of nearly half a million votes. But as a new governor he was pre-occupied with the problems of his own state—and he had another reason to reject the urgings of those who wanted him to seek the presidency. It was uncomplicated. He simply did not want to do so.

If the Governor was reluctant, there were many others who were anxious to start to put together a Scranton coalition. Pennsylvania alone could give its governor a bloc of 64 votes to begin with. Another 98 votes could be found in Ohio and New Jersey on Pennsylvania's western and eastern borders. New York would doubtless stay with its own governor, Nelson Rockefeller, but three other middle states, Connecticut, Delaware, and Maryland, had another 48 votes. If most of the groups from these nearby states could be enticed into a Scranton coalition, it would have a size of between 150 and 200 votes. And at that point, other groups would be likely to join the coalition of a candidate who was an attractive new face without apparent political handicaps.

When these six strategies are compared, it at once becomes obvious that all could not be executed at the same time. The success of more than one coalition depended on its ability to attract the same group of delegates. The natural allies in a Rockefeller coalition based on New York included New England and Pennsylvania, but at least part of New England would be pre-empted if there were an active attempt to put together a Lodge coalition and Pennsylvania would be the natural base of a Scranton coalition. There might likewise be a collision if the two new governors, Scranton and Romney, both became active candidates. Ohio bordered on both Pennsylvania and Michigan. And in the event Scranton and Romney sought the support of Ohio groups, they might also encounter opposition from the veteran Ohio state chairman. Ray C. Bliss might want to keep Ohio neutral so an Ohio group could join a potentially winning coalition at a propitious time.

It is also significant that the potential conflicts in strategy were concentrated among the moderate candidates. A Goldwater coalition would face opposition from the Rockefeller coalition in California, and if Rockefeller picked up momentum from primary victories, Goldwater leaders would face competition from Rockefeller leaders in some of the Western states where delegates were picked by convention. There was also potential Scranton support among Western moderates, and potential Romney support in Utah and Idaho if coalitions were constructed on behalf of either of these governors. But no other coalition was following the Goldwater strategy of recruiting conservative groups from the South and West. This meant that the leaders of the Goldwater coalition were free to execute their strategy while the leaders of moderate coalitions had to be careful about each other. As we shall see, this was to be an important Goldwater advantage as the nomination contest developed.

3

The Primaries

The strategies of the three active candidates—Goldwater, Rockefeller, and Lodge—all depended to some degree on the primaries. The extent to which the potential strategies of the then inactive candidates might be pursued also depended on how well these three fared. So the eyes of political observers turned toward New Hampshire where the first major primary was to take place.

Senator Goldwater's strategy did not require primary victories to give it momentum. Still, it was thought to be desirable to show that the Arizonan had appeal for the voters as well as a devoted following among party workers. New Hampshire seemed to be well suited for Goldwater's purposes. "For some time now," wrote Duane Lockard in the late 1950's, "the leadership elements of both factions (of the New Hampshire Republican party) have been of decidedly conservative hue—the distinction has been that of more-conservative versus the less-conservative."[1] The structure of the New Hampshire Republican party had become a good deal more chaotic since the death of the long-time leader of the more-conservative faction, Senator Styles Bridges, but it was still accurate to characterize the majority of the state's Republicans as conservative. Surveys of this population in the fall of 1963 showed Goldwater with a 3-to-1 edge over Rockefeller. In addition, most

[1] *New England State Politics* (Princeton: Princeton University Press, 1959), p. 50.

New Hampshire Republican leaders favored the Arizona senator. The Goldwater group in the Granite State included such men as Senator Norris Cotton, former Governor Lane Dwinell, and the state legislative leaders, House Speaker Stewart Lamprey and Senate President Philip Dunlap.

The New Hampshire leaders designed a campaign which stressed handshaking and meeting with small groups of people. This was to take advantage of Senator Goldwater's normally engaging personality and was the usual method of campaigning in the state. This plan was accepted by the national Goldwater leaders, but it did not pay off. The Senator, in some pain from recent surgery for a calcium deposit on his heel, was tired out by poor scheduling. He seemed aloof, sometimes even surly, in his personal campaigning. Quarrels developed between New Hampshire Goldwater leaders over tactics, and more basic strain showed up between such responsible figures as Senator Norris Cotton and such volatile far-right types as Delores Bridges and *Manchester Union-Leader* publisher William Loeb. Still other disputes took place between the national and state levels as each group discovered the other was not ready to conduct an efficiently organized campaign. In short, the campaign was ineffective, and the stress generated by campaign difficulties catalyzed a good deal of intergroup rivalry within the fledgling Goldwater coalition.

These internal difficulties, however, were as nothing compared to the troubles caused by many of Barry Goldwater's public statements. Senator Goldwater did not, at this time, have access to competent public relations advice, and he made a series of utterances which were to haunt him until November. In Portsmouth, New Hampshire, he voiced his opinion that America's long-range missiles were not dependable. Before the Economic Club in New York City, he stated a belief that "most people who have no skills have no education for the same reason—low intelligence or low ambition." In Washington, D.C., he told Young Republicans that "at best, political platforms are a packet of misinformation and lies." And before he had learned the full story of Fidel Castro's action in cutting off the water supply to the naval base at Guantánamo, he declared in Kingston, New Hampshire, that Castro should be told to turn the water on "or the Marines are going to turn it on for you and keep it on." All these statements stressed the same viewpoints: militarism abroad and a rejection of long accepted social and political tenets at home. These declarations caused many who had intended to vote for Goldwater when their information about him was limited to the single fact that he was a conservative to have real doubts about whether they agreed with *these* attitudes.

As we have already noted, the early polls gave Barry Goldwater a substantial edge among New Hampshire Republicans, but Nelson Rockefeller had been moving to exploit any opportunity that came his way. If winning primaries would be helpful to the Goldwater strategy, such victories were absolutely essential to the chances of the New York Governor. Characteristically, his staff had made a thorough study of the features of the state, of past primary campaigns there, and of issues which might be particularly salient in the New Hampshire political environment. It was disappointing to Nelson Rockefeller, a Dartmouth graduate, to find so many New Hampshire Republicans backing Barry Goldwater, but he put together the best slate of delegates he could. His New Hampshire group was led by former Governor Hugh Gregg and Perkins Bass, the Congressman who had lost a 1962 bid to move to the United States Senate.

Rockefeller's personal campaigning was better organized than that of his opponent. Between his announcement on November 7 and the election on March 10, he spent a total of twenty days in New Hampshire. During that time, he visited eighty-two communities. Friendly observers credited him with shaking an estimated fifty thousand hands. But far more important than numbers was the fact that the New York Governor enjoyed this kind of personal contact. Although the schedule tired his staff, Rockefeller seemed to thrive on it. As the campaign progressed, Nelson Rockefeller's great empathy with people began to pay off.

A significant measure of the Governor's improving chances was the number of questions he was asked about issues. It was, of course, in Rockefeller's interest to shift as much public attention as possible from his personal life to the positions he was taking. He had carefully selected issues which would accent the contrast between himself and Senator Goldwater. Generally, this approach took advantage of controversial statements made by the Arizonan. In appearance after appearance, Governor Rockefeller stated his belief that hemispheric cooperation rather than sending in the Marines was the right way to deal with Cuba, and that imperfect operation of the free enterprise system was to blame for unemployment rather than was the laziness or stupidity of those who were out of work. In town after town, the New Yorker attacked Senator Goldwater for his statements about social security and the graduated income tax, and for his votes against federal aid to education. And, gradually, the Rockefeller coalition began to show signs of optimism.

The combined effect of Goldwater difficulties and Rockefeller efforts began to appear in the polls. In January, the Gallup Poll had found Rockefeller running slightly behind Goldwater among all voters in the United States, 44 per cent to 42 per cent. Figures published in mid-February showed the Governor ahead, 49 per cent to 36 per cent. More to the point in nomination politics, Nelson Rockefeller had almost closed the gap in the estimate of Republican voters. The January standings gave Senator Goldwater a lead with Republican voters of 57 per cent to 35 per cent. A month later, the Arizonan led by only 44 per cent to 41 per cent. Similar shifts of opinion were detected in polls of New Hampshire voters. Not all of the survey information was cheering to Nelson Rockefeller, though. He needed a straight fight between himself and Barry Goldwater in order to attract the less conservative New Hampshire Republicans to his banner. But the conclusion Rockefeller staffers were reaching as they studied polls from the Granite State was: "We think we've made it so far as Goldwater is concerned, but what worries us now is the increasing support for Lodge."

The New Hampshire Lodge campaign had a casual air to it. All that was visible was the arrival in Concord of four Lodge volunteers who opened a headquarters. These were Paul Grindle and David Goldberg of the 1962 George Lodge for Senator campaign, and two attractive recent college graduates, Sally Saltonstall and Caroline Williams. When a Rumford businessman by the name of J. Richard Jackman, who was quite unknown to the Lodge leaders, filed papers as a Lodge delegate, he was promptly designated chairman of the New Hampshire Draft Lodge Committee. But if the New Hampshire Lodge campaign was limited, the activities it undertook were basic. Some senior members of the Lodge core group remembered the 1952 Eisenhower campaign in the Granite State. The Lodge forces had access to an old mailing list of 95,000 New Hampshire Republicans. Possession of such a list, even if not up-to-date, was a not inconsiderable advantage in a primary contest in which only 94,870 votes were to be cast. A basic mailing was sent to this list, and some 10,000 pledge cards came back stating the signers would write in Lodge's name. A second mailing went out to known Lodge supporters just before the election. This contained precise instructions on how to write in Lodge's name. The Lodge group also made use of a 1960 television spot in which Dwight Eisenhower told voters how highly he regarded Cabot Lodge.

This Lodge activity went almost unnoticed by the small army of newsmen who had gone to New Hampshire. Their concentration on the Rockefeller and Goldwater candidacies was such that Lodge workers found the best way to distribute their press releases was to leave them on the press bus following one of the major candidates. But opinion polls, as has been noted, began to detect significant support for Ambassador Lodge. A Louis Harris poll, published a week before the election, showed Goldwater and Rockefeller tied for the lead when choice was restricted to names printed on the ballot. When New Hampshire respondents were given their choice of all possible Republican candidates, though, Henry Cabot Lodge was the preference of 31 per cent while Goldwater won 18 per cent and Rockefeller 12 per cent. The conclusion generally reached was that Lodge would have been a strong candidate if he had filed, but that voters would not go to the trouble of writing in a candidate's name.

When it became apparent that Lodge possessed the ability to attract a considerable vote, and that much of that vote would come from potential Rockefeller supporters, pleas were directed to Lodge leaders to abandon their efforts. It was argued that Lodge would only be a "spoiler" who would prevent a clear repudiation of the Goldwater candidacy. But the poll findings which were seen as ominous by Rockefeller leaders were seen as encouraging by the Lodge leaders. And, if primary victories were vital to the Rockefeller strategy, they were even more important in the Lodge strategy. The Ambassador's popularity with the voters was virtually the only asset the Lodge coalition had. Consequently, they were unlikely to abandon their efforts just when it looked as though they might receive some tangible evidence of that popularity.

The results of the New Hampshire primary suggested there had been a great deal of last minute decision-making, and that the primary beneficiary of this had been Henry Cabot Lodge. The Ambassador received 35.5 per cent of the vote, while Goldwater got 23.2 per cent and Rockefeller 21.0 per cent. Richard M. Nixon, in whose behalf former Governor Wesley Powell had been campaigning, also received a substantial write-in-vote, 16.8 per cent. Senator Margaret Chase Smith and Harold Stassen, who were also listed on the ballot, received very small votes. By giving more than half their votes to absent candidates, New Hampshire voters rejected the candidacies of the two major contenders who had gone to such effort to win their support. By casting such a large write-in vote for Henry Cabot Lodge, they showed they regarded him as a very attractive candidate, indeed.

The effects of New Hampshire on the process of coalition formation can best be understood by recalling the strategies being followed by each aspirant. Richard M. Nixon's chances were enhanced. His strategy called for very quiet campaigning and was dependent on none of the declared candidates being able to execute his strategy. When the New Hampshire results were in, this continued to look like a feasible approach. Nixon advocates could argue that the former Vice President's vote was quite respectable in view of the small-scale campaign conducted in his behalf and that the vote had not advanced the strategies of either the Rockefeller or Goldwater coalitions.

Nixon himself moved to emphasize his position as a unifying figure in the Republican party. On March 11, the day after the New Hampshire primary, he told newsmen that as titular leader of the party, he would work to press the case against President Johnson. "There is no man in the country who can make a case against Mr. Johnson more effectively than I can," he stated in Newark. And, on March 20, two Springfield attorneys revealed that Mr. Nixon had asked them not to sponsor a write-in campaign for him because it "might prove detrimental to party harmony in Illinois."

So saying, Richard Nixon departed on a business trip to Asia which had the effect of reminding people of his competence in foreign affairs. He held press conferences in Beirut, Hong Kong, and Tokyo. He stopped in Saigon to be photographed with Henry Cabot Lodge, and to learn firsthand about events in South Vietnam. In Taipei, he said the United States must do "whatever is necessary to win" the war against the Vietcong.

On returning from his twenty-four-day junket, the former Vice President appeared before two prestige audiences to spell out his views on foreign policy. On April 16, Mr. Nixon addressed the New York Chamber of Commerce, and two days later spoke to the American Society of Newspaper Editors in Washington, D.C. He said Asian leaders had told him American foreign policy was inconsistent, that they couldn't "depend on the United States when the chips are down." He said the war in South Vietnam had to be won because the outcome there would determine the future of other countries in the area, and a Communist takeover in the region would be "a signal to the rest of the world that the United States does not have an answer." Nixon suggested South Vietnam ought to have the same goal in the war as the Vietcong, and ought to be allowed to invoke the doctrine of hot pursuit to cross over into North Vietnam.

An omen that Richard Nixon was being regarded as a strong contender was made public the following day. An Associated Press poll released April 19 showed more Republican county chairmen expected Nixon to emerge as the eventual nominee than any other aspirant.[2] But the former Vice President was still a candidate without a coalition, and groups of delegates were needed if this condition was to change. At the end of the month, he went to Ohio. He had carried Ohio in 1960, and had maintained close ties with the state's Republican leaders. In Dayton, Ohio, where he was going to speak to a well-attended party rally, Nixon told reporters he thought the California primary would be crucial. Trying to keep the possibility of his own nomination in the forefront of attention, and at the same time avoid giving any offense to the dedicated followers of Barry Goldwater, he refused to predict that Goldwater would win the nomination, but forecast it would not go to anyone Goldwater didn't like. There was much interest in a Nixon candidacy when he left Dayton, but still no Nixon delegates.

Another effort to give wings to a Nixon candidacy and perhaps produce a group of delegates was going forward in Nebraska.[3] The Cornhusker State had a non-binding presidential primary scheduled for May 12. Barry Goldwater was the only candidate formally entered, but Richard Nixon had friends in Nebraska, particularly former Secretary of the Interior Fred Seaton. On May 7, Nixon came to Omaha for a speech before another prestige audience, the National Conference of Christians and Jews. The next morning, a mass mailing was sent out to Nebraska Republicans urging them to write in Nixon's name and explaining how this might be accomplished. When the votes were counted, Nixon had 35 per cent. Together with the 16 per cent that went to Henry Cabot Lodge, this was sufficient to keep Barry Goldwater's total under a majority. The Nixon vote was too low, however, to dramatize his candidacy—or to cause Nebraska's group of Goldwater delegates to think about shifting to a Nixon coalition.

Still another Nixon effort to conduct a low visibility campaign to call attention to his candidacy came in Oregon. His name had been placed on the Oregon ballot by the secretary of state under the Oregon statute which

[2] 1,489 county chairmen stated their expectations about the eventual victor: 35.3% chose Nixon, 28.7% Goldwater, 12.7% Lodge, 10.8% Scranton, and 3.4% Rockefeller. 1,606 county chairmen gave their own preferences: 45.0% wanted Goldwater, 18.1% Nixon, 12.0% Lodge, 11.9% Scranton, and 5.2% Rockefeller.

[3] This Nebraska campaign is described in Robert D. Novak, *The Agony of the G.O.P. 1964* (New York: Macmillan, 1965), pp. 367–68.

said that all should be listed who were "generally advocated or recognized in national news media," and the Oregon results were binding. Only eighteen delegates were involved, but this could be the beginning of a real Nixon coalition. A campaign for Nixon was organized by Donald F. Myrick and former state chairman Wendell Wyatt. When Nixon headquarters were opened in mid-April, Wyatt announced there would be a "serious and determined" effort in Mr. Nixon's behalf. Some radio and television time was purchased, and one mailing was sent out. At the heart of the Nixon campaign, however, was a telephone "blitz," a technique which had proven successful in Nixon's 1960 campaign. Some fifty telephones were used by trained operators from 9:00 a.m. to 9:00 p.m. for two-and-a-half weeks before the May 15 Oregon election. In that time, 125,000 registered Republicans in the Portland area were called and urged to cast ballots for the former Vice President.

There was not much discussion among party leaders about how the New Hampshire results affected the strategy which might have been followed to form a Romney coalition. The Michigan Governor had clearly taken himself out of competition for 1964. There was, however, considerable speculation about Pennsylvania's William W. Scranton. He had given a widely reported speech before the Economic Club of New York a week before the New Hampshire primary. "The forces which have combined to become the Democratic party," declared the Pennsylvanian, "are forces which by their very nature collide in deadlock. It is the party of dreams, on the one hand, and of reaction on the other. . . . The party when it governs is hamstrung by its reactionaries, who smash the dreams and leave the political landscape strewn with the broken promises of a deadlocked party." Turning to the possibility of Republican action, the Governor continued: "The whole point of Republican insistence on strong state governments is the Republican belief that state governments can in many areas accomplish more and do the job better than the central government can. . . . We can devise a hundred bold new attacks on the problems of America and we can do it without going outside the framework of the Constitution and the federal principle. But none of these things, our recent history makes clear, can be achieved by the deadlocked Democratic party. Progress, today, can be achieved only through the Republican party." Barely below the surface of this analysis lay a strategy for a general election campaign. Hit the Democratic coalition hard in the middle; split it; leave the middle ground to the Republicans.

The task of putting together a coalition which would make William Scranton the Republican nominee appeared to be easier to carry out after the New Hampshire primary. The immediate problem of building a coalition around a Pennsylvania base was the candidacy of New York's Nelson Rockefeller. As the prospects for a New York based coalition contracted, it became more likely that groups from New Jersey, Connecticut, and other neighboring states would be receptive to invitations to join a Scranton coalition. Moderates in other sections of the country also reverberated when a possible Scranton candidacy was mentioned.[4] Replying to a conversational point that the party needed to arrive in San Francisco with an electable candidate whose reputation had not been too seriously damaged in the primaries, a leading Kansas Republican exclaimed: "That's why it's *got* to be Scranton." "Well", mused a veteran of Colorado politics, "all of the people I respect out here think it's going to turn out to be Scranton." So the potential for a Scranton coalition was certainly present in the early spring.

If others were concerned about promoting this candidacy, William Scranton was not. He was being flooded with out-of-state speaking requests, but was turning down almost every one, lest acceptance suggest an interest in the nomination. His attention, in fact, was being devoted primarily to getting through his legislature a controversial plan to reform Pennsylvania's unemployment compensation. After this was accomplished by a bare constitutional majority, Governor Scranton departed for Florida to rest and meditate under the sun. On his return in early April, he called a news conference to clarify his position. The Governor almost announced flatly that he would not accept the nomination even if drafted. "Only the fact that I believe no American has the right to take that position," Scranton explained, "prevents me from so doing. But I want those who have been supporting my possible candidacy to clearly understand how close I came to making that decision. From this day forward I cannot be held accountable for encouraging their efforts in the slightest degree. My efforts will be devoted to my duties as Governor of Pennsylvania."

Given this determination to avoid presidential politics, not even private coalition-building was possible. Party leaders in Harrisburg felt Republicans elsewhere should manifest their interest in Governor Scranton, but party pro-

[4] This view was limited to party leaders. Scranton was almost unknown to the general public.

fessionals were not going to lead groups into a Scranton coalition without some sign that Scranton was interested. Those who believed in that mythical group, "the Eastern Establishment," behaved as if they expected someone in an Eastern skyscraper to pick up a phone and say: "It's going to be Scranton." This, however, is the way nominations are obtained in late-late movies, not the way coalitions are formed in the real world.[5] Draft Scranton headquarters were opened in several major cities, and buttons reading "Draft Bill, Sure We Will" continued to be available in Harrisburg. But the genuine optimism of Scranton backers turned into strained hope as the weeks passed by. Governor Scranton remained a potentially strong candidate, but nothing was happening to mobilize groups into a Scranton coalition.

The Goldwater coalition was less dependent on primary success than was any other. As long as groups already committed to, or leaning toward, a Goldwater coalition were not scared off by the adverse primary results, the Goldwater coalition would continue to grow. Still, the New Hampshire defeat had important consequences for the Goldwater forces. The most important was the realization that something was wrong with what they had been doing. Barry Goldwater expressed this view with the characteristically blunt admission: "I goofed up somewhere!" For the loyal, but naïve, core group of Arizonans, the New Hampshire primary was a trial-and-error learning experience, and when their efforts were not rewarded they assumed that there was some fault in their approach. In the period of re-examination after the New Hampshire primary, everything was open to question.

Some important changes resulted. One was the addition of professional campaign talent to the inexperienced group of Arizonans who had been conducting operations to that point. F. Clifton White, the New Yorker who had been directing the mobilization of conservative groups throughout the country for the past two-and-a-half years, was promoted to co-director of field operations, whence he assumed effective command of the hunt for Goldwater delegates at the convention. Karl Hess, a veteran conservative speech writer who already had been making contributions, moved into the

[5] It is of no little interest that so much had been written about "the Eastern Establishment" that a good many politicians behaved as if such a group was a reality. After the nomination, many moderate Republicans were chagrined that they had waited for "the Eastern Establishment" to "take action." Conservatives, on the other hand, were jubilant that they had finally "triumphed over the Eastern Establishment."

Senator's headquarters to devote all his efforts to the Goldwater candidacy. Charles Lichenstein, who had worked on the 1960 and 1962 Nixon campaigns, joined the staff to give his expert attention to other Goldwater propaganda operations.

There occurred certain changes in campaign technique as well. From this point on, set speeches were the order of the day. There were to be fewer press conferences. This increased reliance on the written word was, of course, an effort to avoid the off-the-cuff remarks that had caused so much trouble in New Hampshire. Senator Goldwater's own campaign schedule was cut back. The candidate was to be given enough rest so he would be in good spirits for his campaign appearances. In short, campaign techniques were adopted which fit the special needs of a unique human being named Barry Goldwater rather than being designed to have Barry Goldwater imitate the campaign methods used successfully by others.

These new techniques were in evidence when Senator Goldwater visited Oregon in early April. Shortly after this visit, another change of plans came to light. It was announced that Senator Goldwater would be unable to make further appearances in Oregon, as his presence was required in the United States Senate for the civil rights debate. A strategic decision had been made to write off the Oregon primary. The Senator's prospects had never been bright in Oregon, a state with a strong progressive tradition.[6] Now published polls showed he had dropped to fourth place behind Lodge, Rockefeller, and Nixon. Since he had little hope for winning, he would at least avoid adverse consequences by conducting a minimal campaign. Billboards bearing the Senator's handsome likeness and the slogan "You Know Where He Stands" lined Oregon's highways. Some money was spent on television, radio, and newspaper advertising. The Goldwater campaign did cost more than those conducted for Lodge and Nixon, but it did not begin to rival the Rockefeller effort. This was important. With limited time and limited cash, the Goldwater coalition had decided to concentrate these scarce resources on the crucial California primary.

Taken as a whole, the Goldwater campaign was proceeding rather well. It is true that the Senator was having some trouble in primary elections, but some 715 of the 1,308 national delegates are not elected. They are

[6] Styles Bridges was a typical conservative Republican from New Hampshire, but Charles McNary and Mark Hatfield are typical progressive Republicans from Oregon. Thomas E. Dewey won Oregon's primary in 1948; Dwight Eisenhower did so in 1952.

chosen by state conventions or state committees. From January through April, Pennsylvania, North Carolina, Oklahoma, South Carolina, North Dakota, Kentucky, the Virgin Islands, Arizona, Kansas, Louisiana, Iowa, and Nevada had selected 205 national convention delegates in conventions. Senator Goldwater was certainly getting his share of these delegates.

Exact details of the process of delegate selection differ from state to state, but it commonly involves a long series of indirect elections. First, precinct caucuses are held to select delegates to county conventions. The county conventions select delegates to go to congressional district conventions. The district conventions pick two national convention delegates themselves as well as other delegates to the state convention where the state's at-large delegates are chosen. This elaborate process fitted into the Goldwater strategy nicely. The Senator had spent the better part of a decade befriending the party activists who were making these decisions,[7] and the Goldwater field organization was set up to translate this friendship into votes.

Working under Clif White and Dick Kleindienst were regional directors such as Alabama state chairman John Grenier in the South, Arizona campaign strategist Stephen Shadegg in the Far West, and Nebraska businessman Dick Herman in the Plains States. These men saw to it that Goldwater supporters were alerted at the time of the precinct meetings to insure the selection of Goldwater delegates to the county conventions. By starting this way and following the selection of delegates through the several stages of selection, they were sure that Goldwater groups would send some delegates to the state conventions. At each state convention, the state director, regional director, and one of the national field directors were present. They assigned supporters to important committees, such as resolutions and credentials, and prepared a slate of firmly committed Goldwater delegates to the national convention.

In every state, the Goldwater leaders maintained pressure for the selection of groups of Goldwater delegates. In North Carolina, John Grenier moved across the state in the company of state Republican leaders as the Tarheel state chose its delegates. In Oklahoma, a southwestern state naturally attracted to an Arizona-Texas based coalition, state party leaders prepared to pick, in accordance with state custom, an uninstructed delegation. Goldwaterites from Oklahoma City demanded an instructed Gold-

[7] The poll of Republican county chairmen which showed that 35 per cent thought Nixon was going to be the nominee also revealed that 45 per cent *wanted* Goldwater.

water delegation, and they got it. In Kansas, where the Goldwater group was a little weaker, it used traditional arguments for its own purposes. Here the Republican national committeewoman traditionally had been a member of the national convention delegation while the Republican governor traditionally had not. So the Goldwater leaders ran retiring national committeewoman Mrs. Effie Semple, a Goldwater supporter, against moderate governor John Anderson. They won, and gained an 11 to 9 majority in the Kansas delegation. In Nevada, no substantial opposition developed to the Goldwater for President group. And so it went. The district and state conventions mentioned above sent 130 Goldwater delegates to San Francisco. Other aspirants were represented at *some* of the state conventions, but none was able to show the solid results of the Goldwater coalition.

If one looked at the national polls or read much political commentary during this period, one would be inclined to discount the possibility of a Goldwater nomination. An April Harris Poll, for example, showed that Goldwater was the preferred candidate of only 10 per cent of the *Republican* voters. The same survey revealed Goldwater running behind Johnson in a trial heat by a 66 per cent to 26 per cent margin. And in reporting the results of the Illinois primary and an exchange between Senator Goldwater and the Defense Department, *Newsweek* said in a fairly typical comment: "Barry Goldwater took on two challengers last week and came up a bit short."[8] Only three weeks later, *Newsweek* had a lead article entitled, "Can Barry Goldwater Be Stopped?"[9] The situation had not changed, of course. The interpretation depended on which set of facts caught the observer's attention. If you paid attention to Barry Goldwater's popularity with the general public, the Arizona Senator seemed to be an unlikely nominee. If you looked at the size of the Goldwater coalition, it was clear that Goldwater had established a sizeable lead. If the group of eighty-six California delegates could be added to the Goldwater coalition, Barry Goldwater would stand a

[8] *Newsweek*, April 27, 1964, p. 29.

[9] *Newsweek*, May 18, 1964, pp. 27–31. This is not meant as a criticism of *Newsweek*'s coverage. In fact, many of the participants were failing to perceive cues about the growing size of the Goldwater coalition. Those who focused on the popularity of the candidates were paying close attention to information from primary elections and polls. Hence they simply were missing cues from other sources about the size of Goldwater's following in the party. This was not the only case in which selective perception was important in the contest for the nomination. As we shall see, party leaders' generally adverse perception of Henry Cabot Lodge posed a real problem to leaders of the Lodge coalition.

very good chance of becoming the Republican nominee. And the polls showed that Goldwater was running ahead in California.

For some time, it looked as if the one man who could stop Goldwater was the winner of the New Hampshire primary: Henry Cabot Lodge. The results of the Granite State contest were, of course, exactly those required by the strategy of the Lodge coalition, whose hope was to translate Lodge's popularity into a primary victory, and then parlay this success into greater Lodge popularity. The New Hampshire results gave the Lodge coalition its first group of fourteen delegates, and the national surveys showed that the Ambassador clearly had become the first choice of Republican voters throughout the country. The last pre-New Hampshire Gallup Poll of Republican voters' presidential choices showed: Nixon, 34%; Goldwater, 17%; Lodge, 16%; and Rockefeller, 13%. The next trial revealed a dramatic improvement in the Ambassador's position: Lodge, 42%; Nixon, 26%; Goldwater, 14%; and Rockefeller, 6%. A Harris Poll showed substantially the same thing so far as the preferences of Republican voters were concerned. When Harris trial heats compared the attractiveness of possible G.O.P. nominees with Lyndon B. Johnson among all voters, only 52 per cent of the respondents said they would vote for the President rather than Henry Cabot Lodge. This was by far the best showing of any Republican possibility.

The New Hampshire victory also altered the leadership of the Lodge coalition. More experienced men were brought into the Lodge core group. Max Rabb, a long-time Lodge aide from Massachusetts who had become secretary of the Eisenhower cabinet, was brought in to take general charge of the campaign. Milton Katz, Director of International Legal Studies at the Harvard Law School, began to work with Cambridge colleagues to prepare research material on campaign issues. In Washington, D.C., retired Major General C. T. "Buck" Lanham, a skillful wordsmith who had been a key Eisenhower aide at NATO headquarters and was presently a vice-president of Xerox, began to fashion speeches for use if Lodge returned from Vietnam.

Groups of Lodge volunteers also began to emerge around the country. For a short period after the New Hampshire primary, so many Lodge enthusiasts were turning up that the Lodge core group was having real trouble staying in control of the situation. Eventually, lines of communications were established, and local supporters were organized into Draft Lodge Committees in forty-five states. Relatively few of these volunteers, however, were persons who had been active in Republican politics. The New Hampshire results also produced a reaction from leaders of Republican groups throughout the country, but their commitment to a Lodge coalition was less complete. Prior to New Hampshire, they had been quite cool to Lodge national coordinator Bob Mullen. Now they told him: "Let's stay in touch. Let me give you my home phone number." State leaders were not yet ready to join a Lodge coalition, but they wanted to be in a position to do so if the Lodge candidacy continued to prosper.

A series of hasty decisions had to be made about possible alterations in strategy. Volunteers were anxious to mount campaigns in a number of state primaries. If Lodge could win in California, or Illinois, or Texas, it would demonstrate that he was more than a regional candidate and, at least in California, add a large enough group of delegates to the Lodge coalition so that the Ambassador would become a very serious contender. California was excluded because Lodge would have had to have filed an endorsement of the slate of Lodge delegates with the California secretary of state on March 9, the day before the New Hampshire primary. It was decided to exclude Texas and Illinois because the state organizations, particularly that in Texas, were sympathetic to Goldwater. Moreover, limitations of cash and experienced personnel made the Lodge core group generally wary of expensive primaries in large states.[10] If these resources had been available to the Lodge coalition, its chances of ultimate success would have been a good deal better. For many weeks, the Field Poll (the California Poll) showed Lodge as the most popular candidate in California, and national polls suggested that he might have done very well in other states. Given the necessary resources, Henry Cabot Lodge probably could have won in California and Illinois. With his popularity, Lodge might even have been able to win some other primaries without much of a campaign being waged in his behalf. It would have been a risky business to enter the California primary without money or manpower, but the over-all risk to the Lodge coalition might not have been greater than that resulting from the inflexibility of the strategy it was following.

For some weeks, good fortune attended the Lodge coalition. Each succeeding primary election gave new evidence of the Ambassador's popularity. In Illinois, where Barry Goldwater and Margaret Chase Smith were on

[10] Herbert E. Alexander estimates that about $4,000,000 was spent on the Rockefeller and Goldwater campaigns in the California primary alone. The *entire* Lodge campaign cost about $100,000 (*Financing the* 1964 *Election* [Princeton, N.J.: Citizens Research Foundation, 1966], pp. 35, 27).

the ballot, 8 per cent of the voters wrote in Lodge's name. In New Jersey, with no names printed on the ballot, the Ambassador received a clear plurality with 40 per cent of the write-in votes. In Pennsylvania, where the Republican state organization was working hard to produce a write-in vote for Governor Scranton, Lodge drew 21 per cent of the vote. In Texas, the base of the Goldwater coalition, where the state leaders planned to demonstrate Goldwater's popularity by staging a primary in which the declared candidates (Goldwater, Rockefeller, Mrs. Smith, and Stassen) would be on the ballot and undeclared candidates would not, 8 per cent of the Republicans wrote in the name of the gentleman from Massachusetts. In Nebraska, where a very modest campaign had been conducted for Lodge, he drew 16 per cent of the vote. Even more important, the Lodge coalition was gaining groups of delegates. Some nineteen delegates selected at the Iowa state convention indicated at least an interest in joining the Lodge coalition, and in his home state of Massachusetts, Henry Cabot Lodge formally gained the allegiance of a group of thirty delegates the same day he was garnering 79 per cent of the write-in vote in the Bay State primary.

Demonstrated popularity with the general public and sixty delegates around which to build a real coalition were tangible assets in nomination politics, but these did not alter the antipathy of many Republican leaders toward Henry Cabot Lodge. A number of reasons can be cited for this coolness toward Lodge. An aristocrat who went through Harvard College in three years, he had a tendency to ride roughshod over opposition. A "loner" throughout his political career, he did not seem to fit into a political organization. He had made a number of enemies because of his opposition to Robert A. Taft in the United States Senate,[11] and because of his activities as a leader of the 1952 Eisenhower coalition. Finally, a good deal of the animosity resulting from the close defeat of the Nixon-Lodge ticket in 1960 found expression in anger directed at the Ambassador's mode of campaigning.

Any real comprehension of Lodge's potential as a vote-getter would have been incongruent with the prevalent anti-Lodge attitudes. To avoid cognitive imbalance, party leaders used a number of dissonance reduction mechanisms to handle information about Lodge's popularity. Some simply failed to perceive Lodge's reputation with the voter. Of all the statements of

[11] Lodge, as the candidate of the liberal Republicans in the Senate, had run against Taft for the chairmanship of the Senate Republican Policy Committee in 1949. Taft won by a vote of 28 to 14.

Republican leaders carried by the wire services following the New Hampshire primary, only one (by Washington's national committeeman Robert Timm) stated flatly that things were now changed and that Lodge was now a strong candidate. Most wrote the victory off as an expression of support for a favorite son. Some New Englanders (who presumably had special competence in interpreting New Hampshire results) were quoted as saying: "Don't mistake this for real pro-Lodge sentiment." Less favorable information about Lodge was stressed. A frequently heard characterization was that he was an "ambulatory disaster," a phrase often accompanied by reference to some event of the 1960 campaign. Finally, when Oregon polls showed him running ahead in that state, it was "explained" that Governor Mark Hatfield wanted to be vice president; that he thought his best chance was on a Lodge ticket; and that Lodge's standing in Oregon was "really" just a reflection of Hatfield's popularity. Thus the Lodge coalition was encountering significant opposition from party leaders at the same time that the Goldwater coalition was growing rapidly.

A turning point in the Lodge candidacy came in late April. It was then that National Draft Lodge coordinator Bob Mullen was told by one friendly Republican leader who had assessed the situation that the Goldwater coalition already had a delegate strength of about five hundred votes. He was authorized to transmit this information to Saigon together with the strong suggestion that if Lodge was interested in the nomination, he ought to come home and campaign actively. At this point, an argument could have been made for such a move. The Ambassador could have given the popular demand evidenced by his primary victories as the reason for his resignation. He would have left Vietnam with honor and thereby freed his own candidacy from the risk of being associated with a possible foreign policy disaster. His return from the battlefield would have been an "event" comparable to Eisenhower's return from the NATO command in 1952 that would have generated wide publicity. But Cabot Lodge's reply was that he felt he must remain in Saigon. He was the living symbol of American determination to remain in a dangerous situation. As one whose family had served commonwealth and country for many generations, he did not feel he could leave his post while Americans were dying in battle.

Without the candidate, the only alternative open to the Lodge forces was to continue with their chosen strategy. The campaign in Oregon was being managed by the same group who had run the successful campaign in New Hampshire, and the tactics were almost identical. A headquarters was opened in Portland. Television time was purchased to run the 1960 spot in which Eisenhower endorsed Lodge. And the centerpiece of the campaign was a direct mail effort to locate and activate Lodge support throughout the state. More important in-state backing was available than had been the case in New Hampshire. The chairman of the Draft Lodge Committee was George "Bun" Stadleman, well known to the public as a former all-American football player at the University of Oregon, but the Lodge group in the Beaver State also included Phil Roth, a very able former Republican state chairman. The influential *Portland Oregonian* endorsed Lodge's candidacy nearly a month before the election. The *Oregonian* Poll found Lodge the choice of 40 per cent of Oregon Republicans throughout April. This survey, published April 26, showed the other contenders trailing far behind: Rockefeller, 21%; Nixon, 15%; Goldwater, 12%; Scranton, 4%; Mrs. Smith, 1%.

The position of being the front-runner, however, exposed the Ambassador to certain dangers he had not faced in the Granite State. Opponents paid more attention to him. In particular, Goldwater leaders asked General Eisenhower if the use of the 1960 film clip endorsing Lodge meant that Eisenhower had departed from his position of neutrality. Eisenhower replied with a statement that while he had a high regard for Henry Cabot Lodge, his 1960 endorsement should not be taken to mean that he necessarily preferred Lodge as the 1964 nominee. This probably dulled the impact of the film clip. Whether or no, the polls began to show some slippage in the Lodge standings as election day neared. The *Oregonian* Poll a week before the election showed Lodge had slipped from 40 per cent to 36 per cent. The Harris Poll announced that Lodge had fallen from a high of 46 per cent to only 32 per cent two days before the voters went to the polls. And Samuel Lubell wrote shortly before the election that a surprise might be in the making in Oregon.

One reason for the attenuation of Lodge's popular appeal in Oregon was the careful planning and determined campaigning of Nelson A. Rockefeller. The New Hampshire results, of course, had been disastrous to the Rockefeller strategy. He needed evidence of his popular appeal in order to build his coalition beyond minimal size. In New Hampshire, he had not only failed to win, but had run third behind Goldwater. Never mind that he had done almost as well as Goldwater with 21.0 per cent of the vote to Goldwater's 22.3 per cent; this was a horse race with "win," "place," and "show" results. With these results, a less resolute candidate might have given up. But Nelson Rockefeller had put in months of effort and was not of a mind to abandon his candidacy.

Not the least of the advantages stemming from Rockefeller's early effort in Oregon was the leadership which had been recruited to head the Rockefeller group in Oregon. George Hinman and Mort Frayn had persuaded William Walsh, a veteran of several presidential contests who was serving as president of the State Board of Higher Education, to act as Rockefeller's Oregon chairman. In turn, Walsh tapped able younger leaders. Portland attorney William Moshofsky was to be the top strategist for the Portland metropolitan area; F. F. "Monty" Montgomery, Republican leader in the state house of representatives, was to manage affairs in the other thirty-three counties; Clay Meyers, who had been quite active in Young Republican affairs, was to head the speakers' bureau. Each of the other candidates was able to recruit at least one Oregon leader of some standing, but none of the others was able to assemble an equally able pool of talent.

When this group first began its Saturday meetings, its assumption—reflecting the thinking of the national Rockefeller leaders—was that its principal opponent would be Senator Goldwater. Its plan was to meet Goldwater on a number of major issues, and at the same time present an affirmative program for Rockefeller. The major decisions on policy were to be made in New York, with the Oregon group planning the Governor's tours through the state and advising on the adaptation of the general strategy to Oregon conditions. This plan was in effect as Governor and Mrs. Rockefeller made their first tour through western Oregon on February 7, 8, and 9.

By the time Rockefeller returned for a tour though central and eastern Oregon at the end of March, the situation had changed markedly. Now—after the New Hampshire primary—support for both Rockefeller and Goldwater was disappearing. The New Yorker continued to stress the attitude that "the Republican party must not let itself be captured by militant extremism," but the only opponent who had significant support among Republican voters at this point was Henry Cabot Lodge. Rockefeller's problem was to persuade Oregon voters who had little intention of voting for Goldwater to pick him as the alternative rather than the Ambassador to South Vietnam. Rockefeller and his advisers felt he had a chance to do this because Oregon had a history of responding to vigorous personal campaigning.

The tide began to turn on April 17, when Nelson Rockefeller arrived back in the state for his third campaign swing. He had finished dealing with problems in the New York legislature at 9:00 p.m. the evening before, but arrived in Corvallis to speak to Oregon State students early the following morning. Some five thousand students heard the Governor call for a new program of federal scholarships. This was followed by a major policy address before the Portland City Club in which he urged the states be given greater authority on tax matters and a larger sector of the available tax revenues. He completed his day with appearances before a suburban chamber of commerce and at a high school mock convention. The crowd response was so good that Walsh began urging increased personal contact, and a few days later editorials began appearing in Oregon papers stating that Governor Rockefeller had earned their endorsement.

Next came a telethon. Questions were put to the Governor, at his insistence, "cold off the deck" to give him a chance to display his very considerable knowledge of public affairs. The reaction to this was sufficiently favorable that another major television production was scheduled two weeks before the election. This was patterned on "This Is Your Life," and, of course, emphasized Nelson Rockefeller's extensive background in governmental affairs. Nor were other campaign techniques neglected. A direct mail campaign was carried on in his behalf. Three separate mailings were sent to each of Oregon's 350,000 registered Republicans. A reply card in one of these mailings brought in names of many volunteers who were put to work on a telephone campaign for the Governor.[12]

Compared with the other candidates, Governor Rockefeller had a most comprehensive campaign in Oregon. Goldwater, after making some early appearances in the state, concentrated on television and billboards. The core of the Lodge campaign was a direct mail effort. The Nixon group relied primarily on the telephone. These efforts cost $109,000, $54,000, and $49,000, respectively. Rockefeller's campaign employed all these techniques, and cost some $460,000.[13] But more important than effort or expenditure was the fact that Rockefeller was on hand. Late in the campaign, Rockefeller had decided on a whirlwind personal tour of Oregon. During the final two weeks of the campaign, he was exposed to an estimated 25,000 people. He reveled in his role as the Lone Ranger. "Who would make the speeches," he would ask, "if I were to drop out of the campaign?"

The net effect of all this was to convince many Oregonians of his

[12] Much of the foregoing description of the Rockefeller Oregon campaign is based on statements by Mr. Walsh published in a newspaper article by Doug McConnell, "Rocky's Oregon Campaign Chairman Explains Winning Political Moves," *Portland Oregonian*, May 18, 1964, pp. 1, 14.

[13] Herbert E. Alexander, *Financing the 1964 Election*, p. 34.

sincere interest in public affairs. "I'm in politics," the Governor had explained, "because I'm concerned with the future of our country." As he campaigned throughout the state, he managed to communicate this concern. The result was to shift the focus of voters' attention from his personal life to his position on issues—that is, from his weakness to his strength.

As in New Hampshire, there was a good deal of last-minute decision-making, but this time the beneficiary was Governor Rockefeller. The tide toward Rockefeller ran most strongly in the cities—Portland, Eugene, and Salem—and the suburbs. The CBS News-I.B.M. Vote Profile Analysis showed Rockefeller ran better than Lodge in the cities and suburbs, about the same as Lodge in the towns, and behind Lodge in the rural areas. In Oregon, as in most of the country, the bulk of the electorate now resides in urbanized areas. Hence, Rockefeller, who was able to mobilize an urban vote, led with 33 per cent. Lodge ran a very creditable second with about 28 per cent of the vote. Goldwater and Nixon ran third and fourth, with slightly more and slightly less than 17 per cent, respectively.

The results of the Oregon primary were decisive for only one of the contenders, Henry Cabot Lodge. Oregon proved the end of any realistic hope that he might be nominated. At 7:55 p.m. on May 15, Lodge supporters could still dream of the popular Ambassador returning from battle-torn Vietnam to lead the Republican party. When the polls closed five minutes later, this dream was dead. This might seem ironic in view of his relatively strong showing, but an Oregon victory was an essential ingredient in the strategy of building a Lodge coalition. Many Republican leaders were reluctant to lead groups into a Lodge coalition, and the only hope of Lodge leaders was to obtain such compelling evidence of public support that the politicos would have to give heed to it. A strong second place just wasn't good enough.

The Oregon results left Nixon and Goldwater right where they had been before. Nixon was still a candidate without a coalition. Oregon failed to provide any dramatic evidence of potential strength in the former Vice President's candidacy, so Mr. Nixon had to continue to wait and hope none of the other coalitions would grow to winning size. It is true Goldwater's third-place showing suggested the Arizonan was not very popular with the voters, but this was hardly new intelligence. Moreover, the Goldwater core group had already provided an excuse for a poor showing by putting out the word it wasn't really trying in Oregon. Consequently, the results had minimal impact on the candidate's delegate strength.

The Oregon results did improve the chances of the Rockefeller coalition.

It proved the New York Governor could win an election, remarriage or no, when a number of attractive competitors were on the ballot. It gave him a group of eighteen delegates. It revived interest in what had appeared to many to be a hopeless exercise in coalition formation.[14] Leaders of uncommitted Republican groups suddenly found time to talk with the Governor's emissaries. And, potentially most important of all, it gave a lift to the Rockefeller campaign in the crucial California primary. If Rockefeller could win this, two huge groups of delegates would be added to his coalition the same day.[15] And this would at least give Nelson Rockefeller important bargaining power at the convention.

California was a hard testing ground for the Rockefeller candidacy. If one considered only the state's progressive tradition, exemplified by such political leaders as Hiram Johnson, Earl Warren, and Thomas Kuchel, it would seem that the moderate ought to do well in a straight fight between a moderate and a conservative. But at this point in time, California Republicans were out of office and conservative groups were growing in power. In 1962, conservatives had taken 36 per cent of the vote away from Richard Nixon in the Republican primary,[16] and in the leadership vacuum that resulted from Nixon's defeat in the general election (and subsequent move to New York), conservatives had captured control of several party organs. In 1963, conservative groups won leadership of the California Young Republicans and of the California Federation of Republican Women, and formed their own volunteer group, the United Republicans of California. By the time moderate Republicans became aware of the seriousness of the challenge, conservatives were already in a very powerful position. They were certainly entrenched in Southern California, and since three southern counties (Los Angeles, San Diego, and Orange) contain half the state's population, conservative candidates had a more than adequate springboard for statewide contests.

In an important sense, Barry Goldwater and the California conservatives were made for each other. His candidacy furnished them with a rallying point. They were able to step up their recruiting and keep their troops

[14] It also revived interest in a possible Scranton candidacy on the assumption that Rockefeller would be strong enough to stop Goldwater, but not strong enough to win the nomination himself.

[15] The New York state convention was also scheduled for June 2.

[16] One major reason for the Nixon gubernatorial candidacy was the need for a Republican leader of sufficient standing to hold the contending groups together.

marching in approximately the same direction. In turn, the militant conservatives provided the precinct workers who were able to accomplish heroic tasks for the Senator. When petitions began to circulate on March 4, Goldwater volunteers collected eighteen thousand signatures by two o'clock in the afternoon. And they were able to bring some four thousand people to a hundred-dollar-a-plate fund-raising dinner shortly after the New Hampshire primary. With this kind of backing, Senator Goldwater was not going to be easy to beat in California.

Moderate Republicans, by this time thoroughly alarmed, rallied around Nelson Rockefeller as the one man with the financial and organizational resources to have a chance of defeating Goldwater in California. Senator Kuchel, who had held somewhat aloof from organization politics, was ready and anxious to aid the New Yorker in this fight. National committeeman Joseph Martin, Jr. resigned to work for Rockefeller "to prevent the Republican Party in California from becoming a branch of the John Birch Society." Former Governor Goodwin Knight and San Francisco Mayor George Christopher entered the contest as Rockefeller delegates. Also, some conservative Republicans were supporting the New York Governor because they were anxious about the number of zealots gaining positions of influence in the party. Southern California Rockefeller chairman Leonard K. Firestone was such an individual.

The advice these Californians gave Rockefeller was that if he wanted to come from behind, he had to "get busy, roll up his sleeves, and go to work." Nelson Rockefeller, never one to duck a challenge, was willing to do just that. He hired Spencer-Roberts, one of the best of the campaign management firms which flourish in the chaotic California political setting, as his campaign managers and gave them the money they needed to work with.

For some time, the Rockefeller campaign had trouble getting off the ground. One problem was the Governor's inability to catch the attention of primary voters with a positive discussion of issues. In a poll of those likely to vote in the Republican primary, respondents were asked to select issues about which they were especially concerned. Fifty-three per cent picked government spending and the national debt; 49% selected Cuba; 42% noted juvenile delinquency; 42% pointed to the threat of subversion and espionage in the United States; and 41% chose Negro racial problems. The problems of most concern to California Republicans in 1964 simply were not Nelson Rockefeller's issues.

In April, the Rockefeller forces decided upon a strong attack on Barry

Goldwater. An analysis of the Goldwater voting record on twenty-five issues on which the Republican platform had taken a stand was released to California newspapers. This showed that while Senator Kuchel had voted in favor of the platform position on all twenty-five occasions, and a majority of Senate Republicans had so voted on twenty-three occasions, Senator Goldwater had voted against the Republican platform position on every one of these twenty-five issues. Governor Rockefeller began making speeches containing phrases such as "Americans should not respond to a political creed that cherishes the past solely because it offers an excuse for shutting out the hard facts and the difficult tasks of the present." And Californians began to hear a good deal more about two issues on which Senator Goldwater had taken vulnerable positions: nuclear warfare and social security.

Even with this shift in emphasis, the Rockefeller managers still faced another basic problem. Barry Goldwater was not the most popular candidate, but Nelson Rockefeller was so much less popular that it was difficult for groups who preferred someone other than Goldwater to rally around him. The California Poll results (which were almost constant during April and early May) illustrate this dilemma. When asked to name their first choice for President, the preferences of California Republicans were: Lodge, 33%; Goldwater, 26%; Nixon, 18%; Rockefeller, 10%; Romney, 3%; Scranton, 2%, Smith, 1%; and Don't Know, 7%. If a moderate candidate who could have commanded the support distributed between the several moderate possibilities had been running, he ought to have been able to beat Barry Goldwater fairly easily. But the flesh-and-blood candidate who was on the ballot was Nelson Rockefeller, and when the poll choices were restricted to Goldwater and Rockefeller, the Arizonan held a 46 per cent to 27 per cent lead over the New Yorker.

This was more than a threat to Nelson Rockefeller. It was a threat to every coalition except Barry Goldwater's. In view of the size and growth rate of the Goldwater coalition, a California victory would be very likely to increase it to winning size. This was a point where, in theory, a blocking coalition might have formed in California behind Nelson Rockefeller. To consider this possibility, we must ask what joining a blocking coalition would have meant to the strategy being followed by each of the other contenders. Richard Nixon still had a large following in California, but his strategy excluded any move which would have given offense to the supporters of another candidate. Romney and Scranton groups might join, but Governor Romney was concerned with his re-election in Michigan and

Governor Scranton had been almost Sherman-like in his statements of lack of interest in the nomination. Lodge groups perhaps had the clearest reason to join a coalition. Lodge was not on the ballot, but if Rockefeller won the primary after being endorsed by Lodge while Lodge continued to lead the polls, Lodge leaders could claim that Californians were really demonstrating their preference for the Ambassador. Rockefeller leaders would, of course, dispute any such interpretation, but divergent interests *after* the California primary should not prevent recognition of parallel interests *during* the primary.[17] So there was some basis for the formation of a blocking coalition behind Rockefeller, but surely not enough to make the formation of such a coalition a certain event.

One stop-Goldwater group emerged in early May, apparently without action by any candidate. This was a "Committee of Responsible Republicans," led by Douglas Myles, vice chairman of the Los Angeles County Republican Assembly. Their position was that they were not enchanted with either Goldwater or Rockefeller, and were therefore making their choice on the basis of the quality of the delegates supporting the two candidates. They felt the Rockefeller delegates were more likely to switch their votes to an acceptable candidate than were the Goldwater delegates, and therefore urged support of the New Yorker.

A more substantial announcement came right after the Rockefeller victory in the Oregon primary. On May 18, the Lodge leaders assembled in Los Angeles and announced that they were urging all Lodge supporters to vote for Nelson Rockefeller in the California primary. (A week later, George Lodge flew to Los Angeles to say: "The surest way to endorse Ambassador Lodge in California is to elect Rockefeller delegates on Tuesday.") The Lodge core group was aware of the need for Rockefeller to win in California, and even though its own chances of winning were almost nil after the Oregon primary, it was trying to lead its followers into a blocking coalition.[18] Queried by newsmen in New York, Governor Scranton made it

[17] The possibility of a later clash did not make it any easier to form a coalition. Even though there were many overlapping attitudes between the Lodge and Rockefeller groups, there were reasons why the candidates would be reluctant to cooperate. Why, for example, should Rockefeller step aside for any other candidate after months of work for the nomination? And why should Lodge endorse Rockefeller if it would not aid his own chances?

[18] Remember that the definition of coalition we are using does not require any overt coordination—only that there be some jointly held attitudes and that the behavior of the groups in the coalition be in some way interdependent.

clear that he was not a part of a stop-Goldwater coalition. "This is an arrangement made by the Lodge and Rockefeller proponents in California," he declared. But at the same time, Scranton referred to it as a "moral and logical move" for those engaged in nomination politics. "If I were a candidate, like Lodge," the Governor continued, "I might do the same thing."

With Rockefeller now openly backed by at least part of a moderate coalition, endorsed by the influential *Los Angeles Times*, and, even more important than these two considerations, possessing fresh glamour as the winner of the Oregon primary, pollsters found a shift in the candidate standings. A California Poll conducted between May 20 and May 23 determined that with the choice restricted to Rockefeller and Goldwater, the New Yorker now led among Republican voters by a margin of 46 per cent to 33 per cent. This was a dramatic change, perhaps too dramatic for Rockefeller's own good. It called attention to the significant improvement in Rockefeller's chances, and tended to divert attention from the fragile nature of the Governor's new lead. Those who read beyond the headlines found that on the basis of voters' being asked to give their first choice among all candidates, Rockefeller led Goldwater by only 26 per cent to 22 per cent, that Rockefeller's big gain had been among previously undecided voters, that Rockefeller had only a 1 per cent lead in Southern California where 62 per cent of the state's Republican voters lived, and that Goldwater supporters were more intense in their devotion to their candidate. "One interpretation of these figures," the report concluded, "might be that Rockefeller's supporters will be somewhat more prone to slip away from him in the heat of the campaign to come and that fewer of them are also likely to go to the polls on June 2. If Goldwater's campaign regains its momentum, therefore, and if there is any fall-off in turnout, Rockefeller's present lead could fall away as rapidly as it has grown."[19]

In keeping with the pattern of all Rockefeller campaigns, Rockefeller money, Rockefeller energy, and Rockefeller organizational skill was poured into California. The Governor himself flew around the state shaking as many hands as possible. Everything Bill Roberts and Stu Spencer could think of in the way of campaigning was done. This included a saturation radio-television campaign depicting the Governor as the "responsible Republican," a telephone campaign, and a mailing to 1,800,000 Republican households.

[19] The California Poll, Release #438, May 28, 1964.

The telephone drive, centered in Los Angeles County, concentrated on locating the voters favorable to Rockefeller and getting additional campaign material to undecided voters. Every registered Republican household in the county was called. Those who reported indecision were mailed a special letter, and were then phoned once again on the weekend before the election. The final call included the message: "Please keep in mind that the Rockefeller delegation is composed of moderate Republicans who like Mr. Lodge, Mr. Nixon, and Mr. Scranton and would be more inclined to support a moderate candidate during the convention."

The flyer mailed throughout California was likewise anti-Goldwater and designed to encourage voters to think of the Governor as the candidate of a moderate coalition. The major question posed attacked Senator Goldwater on the nuclear issue. "Whom do you want," the pamphlet asked, "in the room with the H-Bomb Button?" When opened, the pamphlet showed pictures of Governor Rockefeller and Senator Goldwater. "This Man?," the query continued, or "This Man?" The brochure also contained pictures of Richard Nixon, William Scranton, George Romney, and Henry Cabot Lodge. "These men stand together on the party's principles," the pamphlet proclaimed. The implication was clear. If the voter favored any other candidate besides Barry Goldwater, he should cast his vote for Nelson A. Rockefeller.

This flyer proved to be hotly controversial. The nuclear reference was very strong medicine even for a bitterly contested primary. And, even more important so far as the shaky moderate coalition was concerned, the pamphlet had not been cleared with those who were represented as being in fundamental agreement with Governor Rockefeller. Therefore, when Senator Goldwater inquired whether the other candidates were part of a stop-Goldwater movement as the pamphlet implied, Richard Nixon released a statement to the press declaring: "I'm not supporting or opposing either of the two candidates running in the California primary." George Romney wired: "I am part of no such movement." And William Scranton, who had appeared to endorse the moderate coalition by calling it a moral and logical move, wrote: "I have refused to join 'stop-Goldwater,' 'stop-Rockefeller,' or 'stop-anybody' movements." This left only the Lodge and Rockefeller groups in the moderate coalition. The Lodge leaders were loyal, but, as one of them was to recall later: "We did everything we could, but only about a third of our people would work for Rockefeller." What had happened was that at a point where a real blocking coalition was needed, only a pale reflection of one could be assembled behind Governor Rockefeller.[20] This weak moderate coalition fell apart when it met its first test. Nelson Rockefeller was on his own.

In Oregon, the New York Governor had been able to win by communicating his concern with public issues and thus shifting attention away from his private life. But now, on the weekend just before the California primary, Nelson Rockefeller raced back to New York because of the birth of Nelson A. Rockefeller, Jr. This was a delightful event for a man devoted to his wife and children, a happy private event for a man who had been engaging in a grueling public effort for a considerable period of time. But it was an inauspicious event for candidate Rockefeller. The resulting headlines would inevitably increase the salience of his remarriage on the eve of the crucial election.

This was also a period of intense Goldwater activity. In Washington, Denison Kitchel understood that the situation in California was *in extremis*. The polls showed the Senator running behind. The California Goldwater groups had been able to raise huge amounts of money and had great plans for winning the election. But more money was needed, and there was little evidence that the plans on paper were in fact being executed. So Kitchel summoned to Washington men who could raise money and dispatched a task group led by Dean Burch to California to make sure that necessary jobs were being done.

The money-raisers, George Humphrey, Arthur Summerfield, Dan Gainey, Robert Herberger, and others, were given telephones and lists of wealthy businessmen to be contacted. In two telephone blitzes, they managed to raise nearly half a million dollars. Most of this went into extensive newspaper and television campaigns just before the California election.

The pamphlets and newspaper publicity were designed to communicate the message that Senator Goldwater was a spokesman for true Republican views rather than an extremist. A Goldwater flyer raised the question: "Where is the Republican Mainstream?" It contained statements on a variety of issues by Republican leaders who represented almost the whole spectrum of thought in the party together with similar statements by Barry Goldwater. Without the names, it would have been almost impossible to

[20] This is not unusual. As was pointed out in the last chapter, blocking coalitions have been much discussed in theory, but rarely occur in modern American nomination politics.

tell which statements had been made by Goldwater and which by moderate leaders. In an effort to spread the word that Barry Goldwater was the true Republican, full-page ads were taken in California papers. Five appeared in the *Los Angeles Times* on the day before the election. Perhaps the most effective of these was a reproduction of a letter Nelson Rockefeller had written Barry Goldwater praising the Arizonan for his efforts to build the Republican party.

Television programs were designed to show the Senator doing things which he naturally did well. One showed him addressing devoted followers at what amounted to a patriotic rally at Knotts' Berry Farm. In another telecast, Goldwater answered questions put to him by individuals whose pictures appeared on a large back screen in the studio. He had been told the nature of the questions before he went on, but was photographed the first time he saw the individuals ask the questions. This lent some spontaneity to the show, as when a little old man shook his finger and said: "I hear you're going to take away my social security." A look of astonishment spread over the Arizonan's face as he replied: "Why, I don't know where you ever got that idea."

The crucial operation, though, was the precinct drive managed by Dean Burch and Dick Kleindienst, and carried out by the Goldwater volunteers. Goldwater was running behind in the polls, but that need not make any difference if the Goldwater supporters turned out in greater numbers than the Rockefeller voters. The Goldwater precinct organization had been busy for months registering Goldwater supporters and locating additional volunteers. On Saturday, May 23, they were ready for "Operation Determination" in Los Angeles County. Eight thousand volunteers took the streets to canvass nearly 600,000 homes. Only about half the Republicans could be contacted that day, but by election day the volunteers had compiled a list of 300,000 pro-Goldwater voters. These names were listed on "walking sheets," and distributed to fifty-five area headquarters for the use of individual precinct workers. Each volunteer was asked to stay in his precinct, and contact only those pro-Goldwater voters listed on his walking sheet. Special squads of workers were sent into precincts where large numbers of pro-Goldwater voters had not voted by four o'clock in the afternoon. Ten thousand volunteers took part in this effort which almost blanketed Los Angeles County. By contrast, the Rockefeller forces had only about 2,000 volunteers. They were able to do comparable work in less than a fifth of the precincts.

"All those little old ladies in tennis shoes that you called right wing nuts and kooks," a delighted Dick Kleindienst remarked as the election returns came in, "they're the best volunteer political organization that's ever been put together, and they proved it today." Kleindienst had every right to be happy. In California, there had once again been a lot of last-minute decision-making.[21] The polls taken after the birth of the Rockefeller baby and the last-minute Goldwater advertising barrage showed Goldwater almost catching up with Rockefeller. Whether he actually had done so is a moot question. Goldwater won the election because he was at least close enough to be in striking distance, because many potential Goldwater supporters were more intense in their attitudes and so more likely to vote, and because Goldwater groups in Los Angeles and Orange counties had enough volunteers to reach the pro-Goldwater voters who needed to be reminded.

Nelson Rockefeller did very well in many parts of the state. He ran very well in the San Francisco Bay area, in farm and mountain regions, received backing from minority groups throughout the state, and even did better than expected in normally conservative San Diego. Fifty-four of California's fifty-eight counties went for the New Yorker. But the margin Nelson Rockefeller built up there was for naught; Orange County went for Goldwater by almost two to one, and Los Angeles County gave the Arizonan a staggering 207,000 vote majority. Los Angeles County has the largest single bloc of suburbanites in the country. Since the vote here gave Senator Goldwater a narrow statewide victory, and since his California win was the most important single event in his drive for the nomination, one could conclude that the activity of Goldwater groups in contacting their fellow suburbanites was the most crucial episode in the process of coalition formation in 1964.

As with New Hampshire and Oregon, the California primary was important because of its bearing on the strategies being followed by the various coalitions. Both Goldwater and Rockefeller had to win California in order to be able to carry out their strategies, and the strategies of the undeclared candidates depended on a California winner who could not go

[21] The absence of the relatively stable attitude of party identification from the cluster of relevant attitudes means that voters' tentative decisions in primary elections are less well anchored. If a Republican voter has real doubts about voting for a Republican or a Democrat, he is likely to resolve these doubts by casting his ballot for his fellow partisan. When he is choosing between Republican aspirants in a primary, he does not have this familiar guide available to him.

on to build his own coalition to winning size. But another key to the importance of the Golden State contest lies in its timing with respect to the selection of groups of delegates in other states. Three hundred and thirty-five delegates were to be chosen in state conventions scheduled after the California primary.[22] Some of these states—Texas and Alabama, for example—were certain to send groups of Goldwater delegates. Other states, such as Connecticut, were unlikely to do so. But many conventions were scheduled in states such as Washington, Colorado, Minnesota, and Virginia where Goldwater groups and moderate groups had been contending for power. The effect of the California primary was to decisively strengthen the bargaining power of the Goldwater group in almost every one of these contested states.

Colorado, for example, was a state where a number of important Republicans either favored a moderate candidate or at least wanted to keep the group of Colorado delegates out of anybody's coalition for the time being. Senator Allott had announced that he would be willing to serve as a favorite son; Governor Love had long been a personal friend of Governor Scranton; former Republican state chairman Jean Tool was a regional director for Rockefeller. Luis D. Rovira, a Denver attorney and Colorado Rockefeller leader; John Elliott, a Denver water engineer and Colorado head of the Draft Lodge Committee; and William Griffith, a state representative who headed the Draft Scranton Committee in the state, drew up plans to submit a slate of moderate delegates to the state convention meeting in Pueblo on June 6.[23] But the Goldwater enthusiasts had been working their way up through the delegate selection process, and, when the state convention met after the California primary, they chose an eighteen-member delegation which included seven diehard Goldwater supporters and seven more delegates who would be very likely to vote for the Arizona Senator.[24]

So it was in almost all the "contested" states. Some months earlier, a Rockefeller leader familiar with Washington politics estimated the Rockefeller coalition might pick up a group of eleven delegates from that state. When the state convention met, twenty-two Goldwater delegates out of

[22] Some of these state conventions had been scheduled for June by leaders who assumed the identity of the probable nominee would be unknown until after the California primary.

[23] *Denver Post*, May 17, 1964, p. 5AA.

[24] F. Clifton White, "Selection of Delegates to the 1964 Republican Nominating Convention," p. 6.

twenty-four were selected and voted for a Republican national committee-woman whose appeal was that she was "a thousand per cent for Goldwater." The process had gone critical. Groups of delegates were hastening to join what looked to be the winning coalition. The Texas state convention met on June 16, and when the Lone Star State's fifty-six votes were formally committed to Barry Goldwater, the number of delegate pledges in hand passed the 50 per cent mark. A winning coalition had been formed. All the Goldwater leaders had to do was hold it together until the balloting took place in San Francisco.

4

☆☆☆☆☆☆☆☆☆☆☆☆☆☆☆☆☆☆☆☆☆☆☆☆☆☆☆☆☆

Victory Is Confirmed

The Fifty-sixth Annual Governors' Conference was scheduled to meet in Cleveland the weekend following the California primary. For some time this meeting had been important in nomination politics. It provided an opportunity for coordinated action by the states' chief executives—as in 1952, when many Republican governors had appealed for the "Fair Play" rules change which aided the chances of the Eisenhower coalition. In 1964, the Republican governors faced a difficult problem. In their own states, many were carrying out programs they regarded as positive. A Goldwater nomination would place them in an embarrassing position. If they endorsed Goldwater, they would be called upon to explain why they were supporting a nominee whose programs were different from their own. If they did not endorse the Senator, they were likely to be asked why they were not supporting their party's nominee. And, far more serious than the prospect of being caught in an awkward public posture, there was the possibility of an electoral disaster in the fall. But with a winning coalition already in being,[1] what could be done?

There were several logical possibilities. One was to acquiesce in the Goldwater victory and attempt to diminish the distance between the gov-

[1] Not all Republican governors understood that Goldwater already had an effective majority among the delegates. One root of this misperception was the number of Republican governors who were new to nomination politics.

ernors' attitudes[2] and those of the Goldwater coalition in order to make the situation less embarrassing in the fall. A second was to form a coalition behind some other candidate in the hope that enough groups could be wooed away from the Goldwater coalition before mid-July to block a Goldwater victory and nominate a candidate whose attitudes were closer to those of the governors. A third possibility was to form a coalition behind a candidate who had no hope of victory, but who would accent progressive attitudes in his speeches. The moderate governors could publicly identify with this champion before accepting the inevitable in San Francisco.

If either the second or the third strategy was to be followed, who would the candidate be?[3] Richard Nixon was anxious to run, but mention of a Nixon candidacy did not generate much enthusiasm among the governors. Nelson Rockefeller could have been urged back into an active candidacy if the governors decided on the third strategy and drafted him to carry the moderate banner, but a Rockefeller coalition was almost certain to lose. This left the two new governors who had not been very active in nomination politics thus far: Michigan's George Romney and Pennsylvania's William Scranton. Neither of these men bore any scars from primary fights. Both had progressive programs their fellow governors could gladly endorse. And even though it would be very difficult, it was conceivable that enough groups could be gathered around either of them to form a winning coalition. But, it was very late in the day, and the strength of the Goldwater coalition left little room for error at this point. If *any* strategy was to be followed by the governors in Cleveland—reaching an accommodation with the Goldwater coalition, trying to form a winning coalition behind another candidate, or joining ranks in a losing coalition to dramatize their differences with the Goldwater coalition—the principal actors could not afford to be at cross-purposes. But, in fact, there were few prior arrangements. The telephone lines between Albany, Harrisburg, and Lansing were silent.

The three potential contenders were developing similar attitudes about the undesirability of a Goldwater nomination before the meeting convened.

[2] I am referring here to the attitudes of the majority of governors. There were some Goldwater supporters among the governors (Fannin of Arizona, for example) who shared the attitudes of the Goldwater coalition.

[3] By asking this question, I mean to imply only that there had to be *a* candidate to execute either the second or the third strategy, not that these were somehow preferable to the first alternative of trying to reach an accommodation with the existing Goldwater coalition.

Dwight Eisenhower was telling William Scranton that he should not be so rigid in his insistence that he would accept the nomination only if there was a draft. George Romney had decided that the situation was so grave that he was ready to relax his normal religious ban against Sunday political activity. Nelson Rockefeller, though weary, continued to believe that a Goldwater nomination would be disastrous for the Republican party. That these three men were unable to translate their attitudes into an effective course of action was due to three things: the lack of prior communication; the existence of a group of moderate Western governors, including Mark Hatfield and Robert Smylie, whose experience told them it was too late to launch a non-Goldwater candidacy; and a timetable which kept Scranton, Romney, and Rockefeller from having any private conversation in Cleveland before they had made some conflicting public statements.

Governor Romney was in Cleveland for a Sunday breakfast of Republican governors, but both Governors Scranton and Rockefeller were arriving by air and had to drive through metropolitan traffic before they could reach the meeting. Discussion had begun before either man got there. Governor Scranton was even later than Governor Rockefeller because he paused in his room for an urgent call from General Eisenhower. Eisenhower was trying to maintain two conflicting attitudes, admiration for the Governor of Pennsylvania and determination to keep himself neutral in nomination politics. In Pennsylvania on Saturday he had indicated that if Scranton announced his availability, he, Eisenhower, would indicate publicly how much he admired Scranton when he arrived in Cleveland. In the phone call Sunday morning, he stressed the attitude of neutrality by saying that he did not care to be part of an anti-Goldwater cabal. This conversation was very much on William Scranton's mind when he went downstairs to join his gubernatorial colleagues.

The Republican governors were still attending to the normal business of their association when Scranton arrived: announcements about plans for the Republican National Convention from various party officials and discussion of plans for a gubernatorial campaign conference which was scheduled for August. About eleven o'clock, George Romney said that he thought there should be some frank talk about the political situation and the governors' association went into executive session. The Michigan governor told his colleagues that he felt the time had come to speak out about the dangers of a Goldwater nomination. This statement brought criticism from two directions. Paul Fannin replied with a defense of his fellow Arizonan as might have been expected. But moderate Mark Hatfield responded by telling Romney that the war was over and that to oppose Goldwater now would be an exercise in futility. The discussion had been underway for only half an hour when Governor Scranton had to leave to drive across town to a "Face the Nation" telecast. Not too much later, Governor Romney departed for a scheduled noon news conference.

Ordinarily, such minutiae as comings and goings are of little consequence, but, in this case, Governor Romney left for his twelve o'clock news conference without having an opportunity to learn what Governor Scranton intended to say on his twelve-thirty television interview. The Pennsylvanian was similarly without opportunity to know whether his Michigan colleague was going to speak out. As it happened, George Romney arrived at his news conference still believing that this was the time to speak up:

> It is my conviction that the Republican party in its 1964 convention will either take actions that will enable the party to provide the leadership the nation needs, or commence the suicidal destruction of the Republican party as an effective instrument in meeting the nation's needs.
>
> . . . If [Goldwater's] views are in fact as clearly in variance with the nation's needs and the Republican party's needs, and if his views deviate as indicated from the heritage of our party, I will do everything within my power to keep him from becoming the party's presidential candidate.
>
> I'm not so naïve that I don't know what the odds are. I realize it is late. I am fully aware of the delegate strength. But plenty of uphill battles have been won.

While Romney was on the attack, William Scranton was en route to his telecast. Mindful of the Eisenhower phone call and interpreting the gubernatorial conversation as meaning that a coalition would be very difficult to put together, he decided not to announce his availability. He did not read the statement that referred to a Goldwater nomination as a blueprint for "political disaster." Among other things, Scranton said that Senator Goldwater "more than likely had the nomination in his pocket" and "I don't plan to go out and try to defeat Goldwater." There were a good many other news conferences and statements that Sunday, but by the time Romney and Scranton finished with their public statements, the chances of forming a coalition behind any non-Goldwater candidate were dimmer than ever. The following morning the *New York Times* headlined : "G.O.P. GOVERNORS FORESEE VICTORY FOR GOLDWATER."

There occurred one further effort at coalition formation. Governor Scranton got together with Governors Rockefeller and Rhodes Sunday night and discussed the possibility of a Romney coalition. They phoned Romney, who had flown back to Michigan to act as host when Richard Nixon appeared in Detroit the next day, and he agreed to explore the matter when he returned on Tuesday. Tuesday morning saw another confusing series of breakfast meetings.[4] Suffice it to say there was some support for a Romney coalition, particularly from the large industrial states, but in the end Romney's pledges to remain as Governor of Michigan determined his course of action. By mid-afternoon, George Romney released a flat statement to counter widespread speculation: "I am not considering becoming a candidate."

Actually, the strategy which came closest to fruition was one which generated relatively few headlines. There was a determined effort to reach some kind of accommodation with the Goldwater coalition which would suit the purposes of both the governors and the Goldwaterites. The idea of a meeting with Senator Goldwater was one that appealed to the governors from industrial states who faced political disaster, to the Western moderates who thought it was too late to launch a non-Goldwater candidacy, and to the pro-Goldwater governors who were conscious of their minority position among Republican chief executives. If substantial agreement could be reached at such a meeting, then everyone would be off the hook. A tentative statement of principles was drafted calling for a strong civil rights plank in the platform, compulsory social security, and continued American membership in the United Nations. Near unanimity was reached on this, and Arizona's Paul Fannin conceded that the statement offered terms for a reasonable agreement between Senator Goldwater and his critics.

[4] Not the least confusing aspect of these meetings was the role of Richard Nixon, who had come to Cleveland at the invitation of Governor Rhodes. In his public statements, Nixon said (a) "it would be a tragedy for the Republican party if Goldwater's views, as previously stated, are not repudiated by the party platform," (b) "the [developing] Governor Romney effort is not a stop-Goldwater movement, but an attempt to write a good platform in keeping with the progressive traditions of the Republican party," and (c) he would not become an active candidate himself, but "would be available for the nomination at the convention if called upon." Anti-Nixon accounts of the Tuesday morning breakfasts say many governors believed Nixon hoped an anti-Goldwater candidate would produce a deadlock which would benefit Nixon's own strategy. Pro-Nixon accounts stress that the former vice president was appalled by the political blunders being committed by the relatively inexperienced governors. There is doubtless some basis in fact for each of these interpretations, but the perceptions of "what really happened" vary too widely to be reconciled.

This idea may have been attractive to the Republican governors, but it had little appeal to Barry Goldwater. From his point of view, there was little reason why he should be summoned to Cleveland to be interrogated by a group of men who had all but failed in their efforts to keep him from the nomination. The Senator did fly out to Cleveland to attend a public session addressed by Dwight Eisenhower. He spoke to his rivals in friendly terms at the open banquet session, and was photographed shaking hands with the former President. But he did not meet with any group of governors, and flew right back to the nation's capital to be present for Senate voting on the civil rights bill. Aides distributed campaign leaflets to the governors so they could learn what Senator Goldwater's stands were.[5] This was not to be the last time that moderate Republicans would try—and fail—to reach an accord with the Goldwater coalition.

Cleveland did not produce a decision about a non-Goldwater strategy, but, within two days of the adjournment of the governors' conference, William Scranton had made his own decision to run. The Governor was moved to the point of decision by a number of factors which impinged on his central values. Family-man Scranton was impressed when his wife changed her mind and encouraged him to run. Pennsylvanian Scranton gave credence to a report from a delegation of state legislators (including many from conservative areas) that support for Senator Goldwater in Pennsylvania was almost nil and to a telephone canvass of county chairmen which confirmed this. The long-time believer in civil rights was terribly irritated by Goldwater's vote against cloture on Tuesday in the Senate. And the scion of the family which had supported the Republican party for over a century was dejected by the lack of positive action in Cleveland and appalled by the prospect that his party might be torn to shreds in the ensuing election. So after discussing the situation at a meeting with his family, members of his staff, and Pennsylvania Republican leaders, William Scranton at last made up his mind to enter upon an active candidacy.

The first hours of the Scranton campaign were busy and exciting. The staff of the Republican State Committee was called back to work. Phone calls were placed and telegrams were dispatched to leaders of Republican groups throughout the country notifying them of the gubernatorial decision. Craig

[5] Distribution of these campaign pamphlets was not as deliberately discourteous as it might seem on the surface. It was in line with the policy of reliance on the written word which had been followed since the New Hampshire primary.

Truax and his assistant, Joseph Bye, flew off to Baltimore to make arrangements for the Governor to address the Maryland Republican state convention the following day while William Keisling, Malcolm Moos, and James Reichley went to work on a speech. The following morning the Governor flew to Baltimore with his wife and two of his children to make his public announcement:

> We have waited dangerously long to call upon our party's conscience, upon its wisdom, upon its will. For too many months we have been too slow to act, but fast to say that it could not happen to us, not to our party. I share responsibility with others of our leaders who until now have failed to act. I frankly express my admiration for those who earlier entered the lists, with energy, and dedication. . . .
>
> The Republican party is in danger. And some say our country may be, too. We could send down to defeat good men and good women who stand ready to carry our banner in the several states. We could take the responsibility, the reason, the Lincoln, the heart and the soul—all of these things we could take out of our party. We will do so if we let an exclusion-minded minority dominate our platform and choose our candidate.
>
> But we have a choice. And that is why I have come here today. I have come here to offer our party a choice. I reject the echo we have thus far been handed, the echo of fear, of reaction, the echo from the never-never land that puts our Nation on the road backward to a lesser place in the world of free men. I come here to announce I am a candidate for the Presidency of the United States.

The initial news following the announcement was cheering to the Scranton forces. New Jersey state chairman Webster Todd announced that the Scranton declaration would make his forty-member delegation "stop, look, and listen." Lodge spokesman Max Rabb went to Gettysburg for a conference with Dwight Eisenhower and afterward told newsmen that the two-party system was at stake. This meant groups of delegates from Massachusetts and New Hampshire. The Connecticut state convention heard a speech by Scranton on Saturday, and then selected twelve more Scranton delegates. The following Monday, Nelson Rockefeller announced he would give his "full support to Governor Scranton for the nomination." This meant not only a large group of delegates from New York, but also the support of the veterans of nomination politics from the Rockefeller core group.

This rush of support was heartening, but the real situation facing the Scranton coalition was far from promising. The announcements of support had all come from natural allies, from Eastern states which either bordered on Pennsylvania or were very close to it. All the votes of Pennsylvania, Maryland, New Jersey, Massachusetts, New Hampshire, Connecticut, and New York taken together added up to only 264, and since small Goldwater groups were on most of these delegations, the real strength of the Scranton coalition was closer to 200 votes. Moreover, the Texas state convention selected its delegates the day following Governor Rockefeller's announcement of support for Scranton, and in so doing formally confirmed the existence of a winning Goldwater coalition.

The strategy the Scranton coalition had to follow was inherent in the regional composition of the two coalitions now contending. The majority coalition was essentially a southern and western coalition built around a Texas axis. The minority coalition had an eastern base. The essential task facing the Scranton coalition was to woo some groups away from the Goldwater coalition. This could be done most easily around the periphery of Goldwater country: the Pacific Northwest, Florida, and a long arc of states cutting through Minnesota, Iowa, Wisconsin, Illinois, Indiana, Ohio, Kentucky, West Virginia, and Virginia. These middle-western and border states represented the balance between the coalitions fighting for the 1964 Republican nomination. If these states joined with those lying to the east and north to cast a solid vote, they would form a majority with 689 votes. If the states lying along this arc cast a solid vote with those lying to the south and west, they would form a majority with 959 votes. It is oversimplifying things to speak of solid regional votes, but it is accurate to say that it was here that the contest between the Scranton and Goldwater coalitions was focused. The Scranton coalition had to persuade groups committed or leaning to the Goldwater coalition that a Goldwater nomination would lead to an electoral disaster in their home states in the fall.[6] The Goldwater coalition had to keep their groups loyal to the conservative standard bearer.

A more precise understanding of the task facing the Scranton coalition can be gained by asking what groups of delegates had been chosen in some of these states and what issues the Scranton coalition might use to appeal to them.

[6] A somewhat weaker argument that Scranton was a more desirable candidate than Goldwater might have been sufficient before the groups had joined the Goldwater coalition. A stronger argument was necessary in light of the need to persuade groups to leave an existing winning coalition.

☆ *Florida.* There was some hope here. The Florida Republican party had put together a slate which included a group of Goldwater delegates and a group of uncommitted delegates. This interfered with the Goldwater strategy which called for solid southern support, and the organization slate had been opposed by a group of diehard Goldwaterites. The organization slate had won, and with fresh memories of an unpleasant primary contest the winners were less disposed to Goldwater than might have otherwise been the case. Another argument available to the Scranton coalition was that many Florida voters were retired persons sensitive to Goldwater's stand on social security.

☆ *Virginia.* There were some groups of moderate Republicans in Virginia, but they had only a single representative on the delegation. A resolution passed at the state convention had instructed the delegation to vote for Goldwater until released.

☆ *Kentucky.* Senator Goldwater would be a weak candidate here because of his statement about selling TVA and because most Republican victories in Kentucky had depended on getting a good vote in the urbanized area around Louisville. Senator Cooper was staunchly anti-Goldwater, and Senator Morton and state leaders had attempted to maintain a posture of neutrality. A majority of the delegation, however, favored Goldwater.

☆ *Ohio.* The large Ohio delegation was formally committed to the favorite son candidacy of Governor James A. Rhodes, but was split into three groups. There was a group of fifteen Goldwaterites, a group of about a dozen moderates, and a large uncommitted group responsive to the wishes of state leaders. The Scranton coalition could gain the support of the moderates and might be able to recruit the "swing" group if it could convince them that a Goldwater nomination was not inevitable and that a Goldwater candidacy would spell trouble for the Taft Senate race in the fall.

☆ *Indiana.* The Indiana delegation was bound by primary law to vote for Goldwater on the first ballot. Given the conservative attitudes of Indiana Republicans, most delegates were likely to continue to do so for as many ballots as necessary.

☆ *Illinois.* Here the Scranton coalition could point out that a Goldwater candidacy could be disastrous because of the unattractiveness of Goldwater's positions in and around Chicago, and because all members of the Illinois legislature had to run at large in 1964. However, the strongest Illinois moderate, gubernatorial candidate Charles Percy, had promised to vote for the winner of the Illinois primary (Goldwater), and the Arizona Senator had the dedicated support of many who had been active in Illinois politics for years and years.

☆ *Wisconsin.* The Wisconsin delegation was formally committed to the favorite son candidacy of Representative John Byrnes, but at least twenty of the thirty delegates favored Goldwater and would be likely to vote for him when released.

☆ *Minnesota.* Goldwater and moderate groups had fought hard for places on the Minnesota delegation. The result was a group of eight Goldwaterites and another group of eighteen moderates banded together behind the favorite son candidacy of Walter Judd. If Goldwater could be held past the first ballot, the Scranton coalition might recruit most of the moderates rather easily but the Goldwater group was cemented into its coalition.

☆ *Pacific Northwest.* The Oregon delegation was legally bound to vote for the winner of that state's primary—Rockefeller—on the first two ballots unless he received less than 35 per cent of the vote on the first ballot. If and when released, a group of three would join the Goldwater coalition and a group of fifteen would join the Scranton coalition. In Washington, however, the Goldwater group had twenty-two of the twenty-four seats on the delegation tied down.

Given this situation in mid-June, one would have to conclude the prognosis for the Scranton coalition was not good. To be sure, there were at least some moderates on most of these delegations. There were also attitudes which could have been used to persuade *neutral* groups they ought to support Scranton. But, given Scranton's need *to recruit almost all* these groups to win, and the relatively easy task of the Goldwater leaders to *hold some* of these groups to keep a winning coalition in being, the odds were very much on the latter possibility.

Governor Scranton devoted most of June to a twelve-state tour concentrating on those groups whose support he hoped to win. Though some time was spent in the East—a speech at the Massachusetts state convention and a meeting with New Jersey delegates—more attention was devoted to states lying on the periphery of Goldwater country. His speeches were keyed to salient attitudes in the areas where they were delivered. In Iowa on

June 16, he declared: "This is not the hour for us to join those extreme reactionaries, who are anything but conservative, those radicals of the right who would launch a system of dime-store feudalism that is foreign to the American way of thinking." In Louisville, Kentucky, close to the hard-core poverty of Appalachia, Scranton attacked Goldwater on June 19, saying: "I believe it is most unfortunate that the present front-running candidate for our presidential nomination has embarrassed our party by announcing that people who are poor have only their stupidity or their laziness to blame." Questioned about Senator Goldwater's civil rights position on CBS's *Face the Nation* on June 21, he answered: "Anybody who has voted as (Goldwater) has consistently over the last few days on this subject . . . would have great difficulty going along with a platform that was in favor of this (civil rights) bill." In Cleveland, Ohio, on June 25, Scranton met with members of the Ohio delegation, and contrasted the views of the late Senator Taft, "the greatest conservative of our time," with Senator Goldwater's ideas, "a technicolor fantasy behind which the problems of the present . . . are to be concealed." In an address before the Detroit Press Club on June 26, the Governor declared that automation should be harnessed "to translate its benefit into a happier, more productive future for all our people" by launching a massive program of job retraining and establishing "a coordinated labor market to match available workers with available jobs." And in Knoxville, Tennessee, on June 29, the Governor said nothing would be more unwise than to sell the Tennessee Valley Authority as Senator Goldwater had suggested.

An appeal to anti-Goldwater attitudes was not the only technique used by the Scranton coalition in its attempt to win groups away from the Goldwater coalition. Another was publicity given to survey evidence that Senator Goldwater would run a weak race in the fall. At the time the Governor made his decision to run, he told his staff: "My best guess is that the analysis of a very poor showing by Barry is true. But by convention time, I want no guesswork. I want the most accurate scientific information possible." The first results of the surveys Scranton had ordered were released by him in Miami, Florida on June 24. Studies by John Bucci,[7] Central Surveys of Iowa, and the Minnesota Poll gave estimates of Goldwater support in the fall election by *Republican* voters as 45 per cent in North

[7] Bucci is a Swarthmore, Pennsylvania, pollster who was regularly employed by Scranton.

Dakota, 44 per cent in Minnesota, 34 per cent in Iowa, 27 per cent in Maryland, 20 per cent in New Jersey, and 17 per cent in Ohio. A nationwide poll by Bucci gave an estimate of the total Johnson vote of 78 per cent as compared with 14 per cent for Goldwater. These data were substantially confirmed by a Gallup Poll released a week later which showed Johnson with a 77 per cent to 18 per cent margin over the Arizona Senator.

The same Gallup Poll revealed that Scranton had greater appeal to the electorate than Goldwater. A majority (55 per cent) of the Republican voters desired Scranton as the nominee as opposed to 34 per cent who wanted Goldwater. With Independent voters, Scranton was viewed as the preferred nominee by 62 per cent as opposed to 24 per cent who wanted to see Goldwater at the head of the Republican ticket.[8] Continuing his appeal for public support, Governor Scranton went on nationwide television (CBS) on the evening of June 28. He said that the Arizona Senator had "given every evidence of being a man who is seeking not to lead the Republican party, but to start a new political party of his own." He asked that members of the party write or wire him immediately if they agreed this was "an hour of crisis for the Republican party and for our nation." This appeal, and a similar one over NBC a week later, brought nearly a quarter of a million answers by the time the convention was called to order. Needless to add, this mail was heavily pro-Scranton. The televised plea for support also brought in some $40,000 in small contributions.[9]

It proved difficult to use this evidence of public support as a tactic to sway Goldwater groups. One problem was that the same polls that indicated that Goldwater was an almost certain loser led to the same conclusion about Governor Scranton. The Pennsylvanian, to be sure, would run a stronger race. The Gallup figures suggested that he would do about 8 per cent better than Goldwater. But the gap between Johnson and Goldwater was due as much to the popularity the President was enjoying in his first months in office as it was to Goldwater's weakness. The electorate's attitudes at this point in time were such that surveys indicated Lyndon Johnson would pull about 70 per cent of the vote against Scranton. As long as they were going to lose the election anyway, Goldwater supporters could ask, why not lose with the nominee they really wanted?

[8] None of these sample estimates add up to 100 per cent as I have been excluding those who were undecided or had no preference.

[9] Alexander, *Financing the 1964 Election*, p. 26.

Whatever the reason, no change had been produced in the roster of groups comprising the Scranton and Goldwater coalitions. The clearest signal of the problems facing Scranton came at the end of June in Chicago. Illinois had been a key state in the Scranton strategy—not because it was an easy target but because if Scranton could win a substantial group in the large Illinois delegation, it might cause other Goldwater groups to re-examine their loyalties. And if the Scranton coalition could not extend its influence from Pennsylvania to Illinois, it was unlikely to win anyhow, so why not try? The Illinois delegation was scheduled to meet at the O'Hare Inn in Chicago on June 30, and both Scranton and Goldwater were scheduled to speak. The delegates listened to the two contenders, but already they were aware of the arguments and their views were unchanged. A poll of the delegation registered the strong Goldwater sentiment: forty-eight votes for Goldwater, ten undecided, none for Scranton.

Scranton's difficulty was symbolized by the reaction of the Illinois delegation leader, Senator Everett Dirksen. Scranton forces had hoped that he would oppose Goldwater because the Arizonan had voted against the civil rights bill which Dirksen had supported. Scranton had said that Dirksen would be a fine favorite son for Illinois, and might well become a vice presidential nominee. But the Scranton core group misunderstood the Goldwater position on civil rights, and failed to calculate Dirksen's reaction. Goldwater had voted against the civil rights bill because he had been convinced it was bad constitutional law, not because he hoped for political gain.[10] The key passage in Goldwater's speech explaining his vote was:

> I wish to make myself perfectly clear. The two portions of this bill to which I have constantly and consistently voiced objections, and which are of such overriding importance that they are determinative of my vote on the entire measure are those which would embark the Federal Government on a regulatory course of action with regard to private enterprise in the area of so-called public accommodations and in the area of employment. . . . I find no constitutional basis for the exercise of Federal regulatory authority in either of these areas. . . . If it is the wish of the American people that the Federal Government should be granted the power to regulate in either of these areas and in the manner contemplated by this bill, then I say that the Constitution should be so amended. . . . If my vote be misconstrued, let it be, and let

[10] Lawyer Denison Kitchel was probably the most influential person Goldwater consulted in making this decision, and Kitchel's advice reflected his interpretation of constitutional law.

me suffer the consequences. Just let me be judged in this by the real concern I have voiced here and not by words others may speak or by what others may say about what I think.

Senator Dirksen was satisfied this was perfectly consistent with stands Senator Goldwater had taken as a member of the Senate Labor Committee, and consequently did not regard his vote against the civil rights bill as a reason for opposing him. Dirksen was quite uninterested in the vice presidency, explaining: "There are four years of my [Senate] term left to serve. I want to leave a little mark on the pages of history." In fact, given the support for Goldwater in the Illinois delegation and the existence of a winning Goldwater coalition, the Illinois Senator was persuaded to nominate Barry Goldwater.[11] "Barry earned his spurs as a Republican," Senator Dirksen told friends. "He traveled the length and breadth of this land year after year for Republican candidates."[12]

Governor Scranton gamely continued his efforts after the Illinois debacle. At a press conference in Seattle the next day, he declared there were "literally hundreds of delegates who are still movable." For all practical purposes, though, the chances of recruiting more groups to the Scranton coalition before the convention were nil. The scene of the contest between the Scranton and Goldwater coalitions now shifted to San Francisco, where the platform hearings were scheduled to begin on July 6.

The strategies of the two coalitions were summed up in a comment by a Scranton leader the evening before the platform hearings began. "We need a battleground," he said, "but they've got the screws turned down real tight." The Scranton coalition needed an issue that would produce a test vote minimizing the strength of the Goldwater coalition. The latter, on the other hand, was intent on avoiding any unnecessary fight. It adopted a strategy of supporting anything proposed by the party officials who were running the convention. Some Goldwaterites chafed at this restriction, but the Goldwater core group was far more interested in the presidential nomination than in getting involved in some ancillary contest with unpredictable consequences. It was able to hold to this strategy because the Goldwater groups were well enough disciplined to follow their leaders' instructions. So

[11] This had some historic meaning. Dirksen had presented the name of "Mr. Republican," Robert Taft, to the 1952 Republican Convention.

[12] Rowland Evans and Robert Novak, "Barry Captures Dirksen," *Washington Post*, July 1, 1964.

to interpret events in San Francisco, one must remember that the Scranton coalition was trying to upset the normal course of events with a fight on an issue or issues advantageous to it while the Goldwater coalition was supporting the decisions of previously selected convention officials. And the convention officials, while obviously not disposed to embarrass the party's probable nominee, were working within an established institutional pattern rather than out of any desire to help or hinder the chances of any particular candidate.

Each national convention sets into motion the machinery for convening the succeeding convention. The rules adopted at the convention consist of three parts. The first concerns the conduct of business at that convention. The second stipulates that there shall be a national committee to conduct the business of the party until the next national convention. The third section sets forth the procedure to be followed by the national committee in making the arrangements for the next national convention four years later. Everything done by the national committee in making preparations for the 1964 convention in San Francisco, in other words, was in accordance with an institutional pattern set forth by the 1960 convention in Chicago.[13]

A convention organizes itself through an elaborate ballet of committee actions. The prescribed sequence reflects an underlying dispersion of power which reduces the probability that any one coalition will dominate all the official machinery of a convention. The national committee appoints a site committee which picks the city, a committee on call which issues the official call for a convention to be held, an arrangements committee which works through subcommittees on housing, tickets, badges, and so on, and a committee on contests which gathers information in case the election of any delegate is disputed. These committees report to the national committee, and, if there arises any business requiring convention action, the national committee makes recommendations to the convention.

When the convention meets, it appoints four more committees to take certain actions and then report back to it. The credentials committee passes on the qualifications of the delegates and presents a permanent roll to the convention for confirmation. The rules committee moves the adoption of its proposals for procedures to govern the remaining business, to establish

[13] In theory, a national committee would cease to exist if a national convention failed to adopt rules authorizing it. In practice, each national convention simply confirms most, if not all, the rules adopted by its predecessor.

a national committee for the next four years, and to elect delegates to the next convention. The committee on permanent organization presents the slate of officers who will preside over the convention. Finally, the resolutions committee presents a draft platform for adoption by the convention.

Two things should be borne in mind about these convention committees. The first is that, while they are theoretically chosen by the convention, some preparation is necessary for them to submit their reports on time. Therefore, the chairmen of these committees are informally designated in advance. If the amount of preparation is substantial, the pre-convention activities of the chairman and those with whom he consults may be quite as important as the activities of the formal committee. This is particularly true of the platform committee. The other important institutional consideration is that these committees are made up of one man and one woman from each state and territory. Therefore, Nevada and New York have equal voting strength in these committees even though New York has much greater strength on the floor. Since there is over-representation of small state conservative influence on the committees, it is not unusual for amendments to be offered on the floor, where the large industrial states have greater power. The reports of each of the four committees has occasioned a floor fight at one time or another in the past, but contests have come most frequently over the report of the credentials committee or the platform committee. This "classic" script was followed in 1964, with the important exception that the moderate forces were outnumbered and simply lacked the votes to overturn the committee recommendations.

The resolutions (platform) committee has long been of special interest to congressional Republicans. Legislative proposals implementing its planks are normally introduced by senior Republicans in the Congress; it is consulted regularly at meetings of the House-Senate Republican leadership; the platform chairman has usually been an important congressional Republican. In 1952, the platform committee was chaired by Senator Eugene Millikin, in 1948 by Senator Henry Cabot Lodge, and in 1944 by Senator Robert A. Taft.[14] National chairman William E. Miller, himself a congressman, followed this precedent in designating Representative Melvin R. Laird of Wisconsin as 1964 platform chairman.

In formulating his plans, Laird had two principal concerns. One was

[14] The designation of Charles Percy as platform chairman in 1960 was an exception to the general rule.

to prevent a repetition of 1960 difficulties when a "runaway" civil rights subcommittee presented a plank inconsistent with the wishes of national party leaders.[15] In 1964, Laird wanted to keep the drafting process in responsible hands. During the months preceding the convention, he and his immediate assistants sounded out a number of subject-matter experts (e.g., Allan Dulles, Lucius Clay, Robert Murphy) on ideas which might be included. The ideas obtained were combined into a "working paper" which went through some fifteen drafts before San Francisco. When the platform committee met, subcommittees were organized, but responsibility for preparation of the draft to be presented to the full committee was kept in the hands of an executive committee chaired by Laird himself. (The words "draft," "working paper," and so forth lose literal meaning here because of the need to do the necessary preparatory work while maintaining the fiction that no "platform" is written before the resolutions committee meets. Regardless of its name, some kind of tentative document provides the agenda for the series of committees who work on the platform at the time of the convention. Detailed discussion is focused on those segments of the tentative document which cause disagreement among the committee members.)

Representative Laird's second concern was to maintain a balance between moderate and conservative groups in the party. In part, this was because much of the preliminary work had to be done in the spring when the identity of the probable nominee was not yet clear. But beyond this, Laird was determined to write a platform which any Republican could run on and which congressional Republicans could live with for the next four years regardless of the outcome of the election. So he chose as his assistant for national security affairs, Representative Glenard P. Lipscomb, a conservative, and as his assistant for domestic affairs, Representative Charles E. Goodell, a moderate. Responsibility for the "working paper" was assigned to three veteran speechwriters: Malcolm Moos, a political scientist of moderate views; Bryce Harlow, an Eisenhower aide who frequently drafts speeches for the former President; and Karl Hess, a contributor to conservative journals. (By convention time, Moos was so busy with the Scranton campaign and Hess so involved in the Goldwater effort that Harlow did most of the writing.) Laird assigned conservative and moderate co-chairmen to head each of

[15] On the 1960 platform, see Karl A. Lamb, "Civil Rights and the 1960 Republican Platform," in Paul Tillett, ed., *Inside Politics: The National Conventions, 1960*, Ch. 6.

the four subcommittees who were hearing testimony. And the executive committee which had responsibility for presenting a draft to the full platform committee consisted of Laird, Lipscomb, Goodell, the eight subcommittee co-chairmen, Senator Hugh Scott of Pennsylvania, a Scranton spokesman, and Congressman John Rhodes of Arizona, a close associate of Senator Goldwater.[16]

These arrangements were designed to keep control of the drafting process, and to insure that the platform would reflect the views of all important groups in the Republican party, but they also had the effect of making it difficult for any dissatisfied coalition to challenge the work of the platform committee. So when the Scranton coalition found itself "in need of a battleground," it was in fact challenging a committee chairman who had placed himself in a very strong position. To add to their difficulties, the moderates' points of possible contention were limited because Laird had seen to it that many Scranton positions were included in the platform. Governor Scranton had written the platform chairman outlining "thoughts which are uppermost in my mind" on federal-state relationships, civil rights, extremist groups, medical care for the aged, urban problems, poverty, automation, agriculture, conservation, education, reapportionment, foreign policy, military preparedness, and fiscal responsibility. With the exception of positions on civil rights and extremism, the platform reflected these views. Therefore, the contest between the Scranton coalition and the platform committee[17] focused on these two issues (civil rights and extremism) and the additional question of the delegation of presidential authority to use nuclear arms.

The attitudes of the majority of the platform committee members can be illustrated in their reaction to the public testimony of the two candidates. Governor Scranton appeared before the committee on Thursday, July 9.

[16] To say that this executive committee was balanced between moderates and conservatives requires an assumption that Laird's views placed him in the center of the party. If one claims—and there is evidence to support this—that Laird's views were more conservative than centrist, then it follows that the executive committee was balanced to the right. The fact remains, however, that from Laird's point of view, this committee was balanced.

[17] The platform committee had the tacit backing of the winning Goldwater coalition, but the Scranton coalition and the platform committee were the protagonists. Laird's behavior would probably have been the same if a moderate had been about to win the nomination and the platform committee had been under attack by a losing Goldwater coalition.

His testimony stressed the contrast between his views and those of Senator Goldwater. He began by arguing:

> In our own party there exists a small minority who claim that platforms "at best" are "a packet of lies and misinformation."
>
> I reject that view. To the contrary I believe that the 100 distinguished Republicans who make up this committee are guardians of the soul of the Republican party. . . .
>
> I am not unaware of the political implications of the decision which lies before you.
>
> It is not possible to separate the Republican platform from the Republican Presidential candidate.
>
> . . . In effect, your task is to decide what is the true conscience of a conservative.

The Governor continued by calling attention to differences between his views and Goldwater's in several substantive areas.

> First, there is the matter of extremist groups and their relationship to the Republican Party.
>
> You have two points of view from which to choose.
>
> One says that "A lot of people in my home town have been attracted to it—that is, the John Birch Society—and I am impressed by the type of people in it. They are the kind we need in politics. They are generally impressive, intelligent people."
>
> The other point of view, with which I agree, says that the radical extremist groups are alien to our shores. I can find in them no saving grace whatsoever.
>
> Our platform should say so. Frankly, I cannot for one second conceive why you would hesitate to specifically name the John Birch Society as a prime example of this weird presence in America.

Whenever Scranton attacked Goldwater in this manner—and he did so throughout his testimony—there would be a low buzz of conversation among platform committee members. They were not sufficiently familiar with Goldwater's positions to recognize the direct quotes to which Scranton was taking exception, but they knew their hero was being attacked and they didn't like it at all.

When Senator Barry Goldwater appeared the following day, he did not challenge the committee in this way. Rather, he identified with them. Referring to the testimony of other witnesses, Goldwater said:

> Some who have appeared have cajoled, sweetly reasoned with you, frankly lobbied, or sincerely espoused programs and principles. A few threat-

ened you, in effect, by pointing only to the destructive results of *not* heeding their demands. . . .

I have sufficient confidence in your good judgment that I know you step forward on principle and with the courage of your convictions, and that you will reject all suggestions to step back on expedient, narrow, or personal grounds.

I will speak to you only of how this Republican views the world in which we must live and in which hopefully we will be given the mandate to lead. . . .

His testimony after he had made the point was rather brief. It was a simple restatement of some of the Senator's central attitudes.

The standard we raise at home is one to which men can repair around the world. In our reluctance to impose our own ways on others we must not be blind to the fact that the world, whether we like it or not, *is* in a time of choosing. . . .

Our party can responsibly remind all free men that Communism *is* the enemy, *not* a friend and *certainly not* a fiction. Our party will reject unfounded assumptions of Communist change and base its policies upon the observable facts of Communism's continued, unchanged, and unabated intentions to destroy Western Society and replace it with Communist society.

The platform committee responded to this testimony by giving the Senator a standing ovation. And the contrast between the applause for Goldwater and the murmured suspicion about Scranton was an accurate precursor of the further actions the committee would take. Every motion offered by spokesmen of the Scranton coalition, whether procedural or substantive, was rejected by a lopsided margin.

This is not to say that the actions of the platform committee were meaningless. There was, for example, substantial and informed debate about the civil rights plank in which the leading role was played by William McCulloch, the veteran congressman who had played a crucial role in obtaining House approval of the 1964 civil rights bill. Southern attempts to obtain a weaker plank than that of 1960 (most of the provisions of which had been incorporated in the 1964 civil rights bill) were rejected. In general, the domestic portions of the platform approved by the committee were not very different than they had been in 1960. "If the platform is no mandate for the kind of economic policy that the progressive wing of the Republican party would like to see," wrote Yale economist Henry C. Wallich, an adviser to the platform committee, "neither is it inconsistent with such a policy."[18]

[18] Henry C. Wallich, "An Economic Analysis of the Republican Platform," *Journal of Commerce,* August 3, 1964.

Some shift of emphasis from four years earlier was evident in the foreign policy planks. The last Eisenhower platform had declared:

> The pre-eminence of this Republic requires of us a vigorous, resolute foreign policy—inflexible against every tyrannical encroachment, and mighty in its advance toward our own affirmative goals.

On the same point, the 1964 platform averred:

> The supreme challenge to [American] policy is atheistic imperialism-Communism. Our nation's leadership must be judged by—indeed, American independence and even survival are dependent upon—the stand it takes toward Communism.

Many observers pointed to this militant anti-Communism as proof of Goldwater domination of the platform. It is true that this passage is consistent with the testimony of Senator Goldwater quoted above, but it is also true that the foreign policy portions of the Republican platform were consistent with the views expressed in *A House Divided: America's Strategy Gap*, a book published by Representative Laird in 1962. Laird was correct in his claim that the platform presented to the convention was "not a Goldwater platform, not a Rockefeller platform, not a Scranton platform, but a Republican platform." What he did not add, but which would have been equally correct, was that it was also very much a Laird platform.

The final opportunity for the Scranton coalition to capture the initiative came when the resolutions committee made its report to the convention on Tuesday evening, July 14. Senator Scott had made an agreement with Representative Laird and Senator Thruston Morton, the permanent chairman of the convention, that the Scranton forces would offer only three amendments: extremism, civil rights, and nuclear responsibility. Governor Romney decided to offer separate amendments on extremism and civil rights to give the convention an opportunity to express itself on the principles involved without regard to their relationship to the nomination, so there were actually five amendments offered from the floor. The convention officers agreed to permit one roll call, and the leaders of the Scranton coalition decided to take it on the civil rights amendment.

The arguments had been heard before. Nelson Rockefeller spoke first in behalf of an anti-extremism amendment:

> The Republican Party fully respects the contribution of responsible criticism and defends the right of dissent in the democratic process, but we repudiate the efforts of irresponsible extremist groups, such as the Communists, the Ku Klux Klan, the John Birch Society, and others to discredit our Party

by their efforts to infiltrate positions of responsibility in the Party or to attach themselves to its candidates.

The Governor declared that a minority wholly alien to honest conservatism was trying to take over the party, and that he had personally experienced anonymous phone calls, hate literature, and bomb threats. The platform was defended by Representative John Byrnes of Wisconsin. "It is the essence of liberty," he said, "that there be no bar to the unhampered clash of ideas. . . . This amendment puts this Party in the posture of seeking to destroy ideas, not by condemning the ideas but by ostracizing their source." The amendment was rejected by a standing vote. Governor Romney then mounted the rostrum to plead for an amendment worded identically, except that it did not name any specific groups. He pointed out that Lincoln had not hesitated to denounce the extremist Know-Nothings of his day, and that, if the Republican party lacked the wisdom to take a similar stand in 1964, "Our opponents will use this with great effectiveness against us." This Michigan amendment was opposed by Senator Peter Dominick of Colorado, who quoted from an alleged May 30, 1765, *New York Times* editorial attacking Patrick Henry as "a lawyer whose credentials are dubious" and one who "has long been a spokesman of that small but vocal minority who seek to undermine confidence in the Crown. . ." .[19] The Romney amendment was also defeated by a standing vote.

The next amendment to be called up was the Scranton coalition's proposed addition to the relatively brief civil rights plank. It would have added a number of specific pledges. Among other things, it would have committed the Republican party to increased staffing for the Justice Department's Civil Rights Division, to legislation requiring all school boards to adopt plans for compliance with the Supreme Court's desegregation decision, to apply the voting guarantees of the 1964 civil rights act to state as well as federal elections, and to action against discrimination in employment. Speaker Joseph Carlino of the New York State Assembly gave the lead-off speech for this amendment. He was supported by Edward Brooke of Massachusetts, John Lindsay of New York, and Senator Clifford Case of New Jersey. The rebuttal came from five members of the platform committee, of whom the most important was Representative McCulloch. In a short,

[19] When it was later pointed out that the *New York Times* was not published in 1765, Dominick replied that he had simply been using the supposed quotation as an illustration.

unimpassioned speech, he pointed to his own work in behalf of civil rights, and advanced his sincere belief that the plank as drafted contained "language noble in security, clear in aim, and based on the Constitution." On the roll call there were 897 votes against the civil rights amendment; only 409 for it.

The next figure to appear before the convention was former Secretary of State Christian A. Herter who had been chosen to present the Scranton coalition's plank reaffirming that the authority to use nuclear weapons belonged only to the President of the United States. "These three short sentences," Herter explained, "do nothing but reiterate the policy that existed during the Eisenhower administration. . . . The Republican Party in its statements on foreign policy has been a responsible party . . . one that has carried out the pledges that kept peace during very difficult times and has handled its nuclear capability with great skill. I am really asking . . . that there be a continuation of that policy that has been so clearly enunciated in days gone by." Actually though, President Eisenhower had advised Laird against putting a statement on this topic in the platform on the ground that presidential freedom to take emergency action should not be circumscribed. But, whatever the arguments, the delegates were getting tired. It was after midnight now, and they had sat through an Eisenhower speech and a reading of the entire platform before the debate on amendments had begun. The convention majority was opposed to the amendment, and it was defeated by a standing vote.

The final action of the evening came on a milder civil rights amendment offered by Michigan's George Romney. This pledged

> action at the state, local and private levels to eliminate discrimination on the basis of race, religion, color, or national origin in education, housing, employment opportunities, and access to public accommodations.

Romney was joined in his plea for his amendment by Governor John Chafee of Rhode Island and Representative Clark McGregor of Minnesota. Platform committee spokesmen Laird and McCulloch answered by saying that the amendment was unnecessary, and this, too, was defeated by a voice vote.[20]

[20] I have not named all the speakers or mentioned all the arguments. For the full debate, see Republican National Committee, *Proceedings of the Twenty-Eighth Republican National Convention* (Washington, D.C.: Republican National Committee, 1967), pp. 216–63.

The convention actions on this long Tuesday evening must be described from four different points of view to be understood. From the perspective of the platform committee, they represented vindication for the long and very hard work of Representative Laird and his colleagues. Mel Laird's behavior was exactly that to be expected of a strong committee chairman in the House of Representatives. One works very hard in committee to achieve at least consensus, and unanimity if possible, among committee members, and then defends the actions of the committee when the bill is called up on the floor of the House. Every effort is made to win House approval for the bill as written by the committee, and the Appropriations Committee (of which Laird is a member) is successful 90 per cent of the time.[21] This is just how Laird behaved in San Francisco.

To the person watching his television set at home, unfamiliar with the details of convention procedure or the norms of the House of Representatives, the dominant themes were probably discourtesy and negativism. Governor Rockefeller was repeatedly interrupted in his presentation by booing and chants of "We Want Barry." Most of this was coming from the balcony, specifically from the seats controlled by the California and Texas delegations. But the viewer at home had no way of distinguishing between meaningful floor activity and meaningless shouts from the gallery. All he could tell was that a distinguished Republican leader was being interrupted, presumably by Goldwaterites. Similarly, it is doubtful that the platform debate presented an affirmative case for the platform. The thrust of the amendments, after all, was to oppose conspiratorial politics, to advance civil rights, and to reduce the danger of nuclear warfare—all reasonably popular positions. And five times the convention voted no. Except for those viewers whose own attitudes on these subjects were decidedly pro-Goldwater, and those viewers who took the trouble to follow the platform debate rather carefully, the message communicated probably was "NO, NO, NO, NO, NO."

From the standpoint of the Goldwater coalition, the platform debate represented another step toward the nomination. By standing behind the previously chosen platform committee—casting its votes in favor of its proposals, but not attempting to dictate terms to it, the Goldwater coalition maximized its strength. A number of delegates who were opposed to

[21] For a brilliant description of the attitudes of the Appropriations Committee, see Richard F. Fenno, *Power of the Purse* (Boston: Little, Brown, 1966).

Goldwater's nomination nevertheless cast votes to uphold the platform committee.[22] The refusal to accept any amendment also foreshadowed a determination on the part of the Goldwater coalition to run the party its way rather than a concern to make it easy for groups then in the Scranton coalition to join in support of Goldwater in the general election. Given the strength of his position in the convention, it would have been a simple matter for Goldwater to pass the word to "give them something" if he had been interested in reaching a *modus vivendi* with his opponents. Both of the amendments proposed by Governor Romney were consistent with positions Senator Goldwater had taken, and acceptance of either one of them would have held out an olive branch to about-to-be-defeated opponents.

From the standpoint of the Scranton coalition, fighting against the platform committee as well as against the Goldwater coalition minimized the size of the vote it could muster on the floor of the convention. The basic need of the Scranton coalition was to acquire the support of groups around the periphery of the Goldwater coalition, but members of the platform committee from these states were defending the platform. To take but a single example, Ohio is an industrialized state whose Republican leaders have almost always taken strong stands in favor of civil rights. Its interests ought to be about the same as neighboring Pennsylvania's on this issue. But the platform spokesman on civil rights was William McCulloch, who had a reputation as one of the most capable Speakers ever to preside over the Ohio House of Representatives long before he became the senior Republican on the U. S. House Judiciary Committee. So it was hardly a surprise that Ohio's fifty-eight votes were cast in favor of the plank McCulloch had drafted. The moderate banners were held high during the debate by distinguished leaders from Pennsylvania, New York, New Jersey, Connecticut, Massachusetts, and Rhode Island. But the circumstances of the contest were such that the Scranton coalition was able to get only a hundred votes outside the East, and most of those came from Michigan, Minnesota, and Oregon, states who have been members of moderate coalitions in all modern Republican conventions.

The platform battle, however, was only the latest in a series of frustrations encountered by the Scranton coalition in what it now knew to be a

[22] 897 delegates voted to uphold the platform committee; 883 voted for Goldwater's nomination the following night. The difference is not large, but the near certainty that Goldwater would be nominated also operated to maximize the size of the Goldwater coalition on the first ballot.

losing battle. On Thursday, July 9, Governor James Rhodes of Ohio had released Ohio delegates from their favorite son commitment to him. Some went eagerly, others reluctantly, but all save one in the direction of the Goldwater coalition. On Sunday, July 12, a Scranton aide sent a letter to Goldwater over the Governor's signature which was so strongly worded (i.e., "with open contempt for the dignity, integrity, and common sense of the convention, your managers say in effect that *the delegates are little more than a flock of chickens whose necks will be wrung at will*") that it was perceived as an attack on the delegates. On Monday, July 13, the Scranton coalition had sought a temporary rules change which would have forced the seating of a Negro delegate from Tennessee. The Goldwater forces followed their general strategy of supporting the convention officers, and this proposal was defeated on a voice vote. On Wednesday, July 15, Wisconsin favorite son John Byrnes released his delegates, and all of them joined the Goldwater coalition. The only thing left was the counting of the votes, and when the resonant Southern voice of Drake Edens was heard to say: "Humbly grateful that we can do this for America, South Carolina casts sixteen votes for Senator Barry Goldwater," the Arizonan formally became the Republican nominee for President of the United States.

While the balloting was going on, William Scranton was waiting backstage at the Cow Palace to make a speech of concession. When the roll of the states was completed, the Pennsylvania Governor was recognized:

> . . . To those who have been so steadfast in their loyalty to me and to the principles for which we fought in common, I now say that the time has come for us to shift the scene of the battle. To the victor I extend my very warm congratulations. He has made the long, hard campaign and every man can applaud the labor that has brought about the victory that now is his, just as I do now.
>
> The Republican party . . . must now emphasize its unity, not its differences. We must now be about the business of defeating the Democrats. As I have always pledged to do, I shall work for and fully support the ticket chosen by this convention. . . .
>
> Some of us did not prevail at this convention but let it be clearly understood that this great Republican party is our historic house. . . . Let the Democratic party find no comfort in the spirited campaign we have waged within our own party. Let me remind our Democratic friends that we have hardly begun to give them the full attention that is coming to them. We have every intention of speaking bluntly to the American people this fall. We shall demonstrate to all Americans that the Johnson Administration is pursuing no policy abroad and a bad policy at home. . . .

Governor Scranton was playing the classic role of a defeated contender. He was acting to unify all the groups in the party behind the nominee. And in so doing, he was giving the leaders of the Goldwater coalition yet another opportunity to broaden their base of support for the electoral battle to come.

Barry Goldwater, watching the proceedings from his suite in the Mark Hopkins Hotel, was paying little attention to what William Scranton was saying. When the Governor came to the point in his remarks when he said, "This great Republican party is our historic house," Barry Goldwater muttered, "That's what he should have been saying all along . . . ," and began discussing another matter with his advisers.[23] The nominee already knew what he was going to tell the delegates the following night. He had finished working with his speechwriters on his acceptance speech, and they were pleased with the address they had prepared:

> . . . We Republicans see [recent history] as more, much more, than the result of mere political differences or mere political mistakes. We see this as the result of a fundamentally and absolutely wrong view of man, his nature and his destiny. . . .
>
> It is the cause of Republicanism to ensure that power remains in the hands of the people. . . . It is further the cause of Republicanism to restore a clear understanding of the tyranny of man over man in the world at large. It is our cause to dispel the foggy thinking, which avoids hard decisions in the illusion that a world of conflict will somehow mysteriously resolve itself into a world of harmony, if we don't rock the boat or irritate the forces of aggression—and this is hogwash. . . .
>
> The Republican cause demands that we brand communism as a principal disturber of the peace in the world today. Indeed, we should brand it as the only significant disturber of the peace, and we should make it clear that until its goals of conquest are absolutely renounced and its relations with all nations tempered, communism and the governments it now controls are enemies of every man on earth who is or wants to be free. . . .
>
> I seek an America proud of its past, proud of its ways, proud of its dreams, and determined actively to proclaim them. . . . This Nation, whose creative people have enhanced this entire span of history, should again thrive upon the greatness of all the things which we, as individual citizens, can and should do. During Republican years, this again will be a Nation of men and women, of families proud of their roles, jealous of their responsibilities, unlimited in their aspirations—a Nation where all who can will be self-reliant.
>
> We Republicans see in our constitutional form of government the great

[23] There is a film of this, portions of which were shown on the nationally televised program, "The Making of the President 1964."

framework which assures the orderly but dynamic fulfillment of the whole man, and we see the whole man as the great reason for instituting orderly government in the first place. We see in private property and in an economy based upon and fostering private property, the one way to make government a durable ally of the whole man. . . .

Anyone who cares to join us in all sincerity, we welcome. Those who do not care for our cause, we don't expect to enter our ranks in any case. And let our Republicanism, so focused and so dedicated, not be made fuzzy by unthinking and stupid labels.

I would remind you that extremism in the defense of liberty is no vice. And let me remind you that moderation in the pursuit of justice is no virtue. . . .

As it turned out, the meaning conveyed by the speech depended largely on the context in which the last two sentences were understood. If coupled with the immediately preceding sentence, they were a plea to judge issues on their merits rather than prejudging them by applying "unthinking labels" such as "moderation" and "extremism."[24] In this context, the reference was nothing more than a request that voters decide whether they were for or against a militant anti-communism, greater reliance on the individual, respect for constitutional precedent, and so forth, rather than making a categorical judgment on the basis that they did not regard themselves as "extremists."

When read in the context of the entire address, however, the sentences took on a different meaning. The speech as a whole equated dedicated Republicanism with the central attitudes of the Goldwater coalition. When this was followed by the sentences, "Anyone who cares to join us in all sincerity, we welcome. Those who do not care for our cause, we don't expect to enter our ranks in any case," the implication was that only Goldwater Republicanism would be acceptable to the new leaders of the party. In this context, the controversial reference seemed to be a declaration that when the new leaders thought strong measures were called for, they would be employed whether other groups approved of them or not.

Finally, if Governor Scranton's concession speech of the previous evening is joined with Senator Goldwater's acceptance speech and the two are

[24] The academician who first suggested these sentences had in mind Aristotle's point in the *Nicomachean Ethics* that there are circumstances where the golden mean is inappropriate as a standard of conduct. He had made his suggestion when material was being drafted for possible use during debate on the platform. Material was not needed for this purpose, but Goldwater leaders liked the sentences, saved them, and gave them a prominent place in the acceptance speech.

viewed as a dialogue between the leaders of the losing and winning coalitions, the moderate groups appear to have offered their aid and to have been told that they were welcome to join the Goldwater coalition if and only if they abandoned their ideas in favor of Goldwater's. In the weeks after the California primary, moderate leaders had made three serious attempts to come to terms with the Goldwater coalition: the request for a meeting between Goldwater and the Republican governors at Cleveland, the relatively mild civil rights and anti-extremism platform amendments proposed by Governor Romney, and Governor Scranton's offer of full support in the fall campaign. Each time, the moderate leaders had been rebuffed or ignored. The Goldwater coalition was determined to act as it saw fit.

TWO

☆☆☆☆☆☆☆☆☆☆☆☆☆☆☆☆☆☆☆☆☆☆☆☆☆☆☆☆

Coalition Leadership

5

☆☆☆☆☆☆☆☆☆☆☆☆☆☆☆☆☆☆☆☆☆☆☆☆☆☆☆☆

The Goldwater Coalition Takes Charge

A nomination coalition ceases to exist at the moment of its victory. A successful coalition is immediately confronted with the problem of electing the candidate it has just nominated. Because of these new responsibilities, a new set of institutional attitudes becomes salient which in turn modifies patterns of behavior. And, unless the nomination coalition includes all of the groups in a majority party, it is necessary to add more groups (usually from coalitions who have lost their party's nomination) in order to broaden the base of support in the election to come. So a nomination coalition is forced to transform itself into an electoral coalition which has a different behavior pattern and normally is larger than the antecedent nomination coalition.

The organization which exists for the purposes of national electoral politics is the national committee staff.[1] A candidate may choose to use this

[1] For detailed discussions of the national committee staffs see Cornelius P. Cotter and Bernard C. Hennessy, *Politics Without Power* (New York: Atherton, 1964); Daniel L. Ogden, Jr. and Arthur L. Peterson, *Electing the President: 1964* (San Francisco: Chandler, 1964); Hugh A. Bone, *Party Committees and National Politics* (Seattle: University of Washington Press, 1958).

organization to run his campaign (as Kennedy did in 1960) or set up a parallel "Jones for President Committee" which duplicates many of the functions of the national committee staff (as Nixon did in 1960). In either case, a knowledge of the basic activities carried on by the national committee staff tells much about the institutional responsibilities facing the new electoral coalition.

The lines drawn on an organization chart (when one can be found) for a national committee staff vary over time. A high rate of personnel turnover, periodic reorganizations, and frequent decisions to undertake "vital new programs" all contribute to an unstable institutional pattern. But there are certain responsibilities which are standard, and campaign committees frequently have divisions with directors whose assignments bear a rough correspondence to these functions. First of all,[2] there is public relations. The public relations personnel usually have had some media experience, and at least understand the special needs of each medium. They know, for example, that a news conference should be held no later than mid-afternoon if the television networks are to be expected to develop their film in time for use on an early evening newscast. They are frequently billed as "image makers," but, in fact, their chief task is to see to it that the words spoken by the candidate or national chairman are made available to media which are likely to use them. A public relations man does write speeches and frequently makes suggestions, but spends much of his time processing the thoughts of others rather than creating new ideas of his own.

A second basic task is that called research. One assignment which falls to this division is speech writing, which usually means pulling ideas together into a speech draft.[3] Researchers also spend a good deal of time getting information into a form which makes for easy retrieval. This is so the exact words of the opposing candidate or the exact sequence of events in an international crisis may be produced quickly if the presidential candidate wants to respond to an opposition charge or if, say, a congressional candidate in Iowa wants to give a speech on a particular topic. The demand for instant information during campaigns is great enough that "answer desks" are often set up to handle phoned requests for particular facts. The research division

[2] I do not mean to imply any ordering of importance among these jobs. All must be done.

[3] Candidates vary a great deal in the way they work with speechwriters, but they frequently take a draft and put their own gloss on it.

also issues summaries of election laws, analyses of election results,[4] and "fact books" which speakers can draw upon when debating opponents.

The third principal task is fund raising, a function which is becoming more and more bureaucratic. There was perhaps a time when a few large contributors could supply most of the cash needed for a campaign. This set of circumstances disappeared with the graduated income tax and the use of such costly items as jet aircraft and television. Today, long lists of contributors are maintained and finance campaigns are managed by efficient young men whose skills are the same as those of the efficient young men who raise money for the Red Cross, the United Fund, or a university alumni appeal. An even more recent development has been the intensive cultivation of the small contributor. Solicitation of $10 "sustaining memberships" by the Republican party in the early 1960's was in fact the program which permitted the party to keep its headquarters in operation.

Next there is the campaign division, a composite which includes persons with expertise on groups the party is interested in reaching. The groups may be chosen on a geographical, ethnic, or vocational basis. In early 1964, for example, the campaign division of the Republican National Committee was carrying on programs to improve the standing of the party with Southerners, Negroes, nationality groups (i.e., non-Negro minority groups), farmers, professors, workers, and senior citizens. Essentially, the persons in charge of these programs attempt to explain the attitudes of their clientele to party leaders and to explain what the party is doing in terms their clientele can understand. The campaign division also directs such political activities as registration campaigns, canvassing, and election day procedures, and trains party workers to carry on these activities on the state or local level. A responsibility which consumes a great deal of energy while a campaign is in progress is scheduling speeches for candidates and other party notables, sending "advance men" around the country to make sure the arrangements for public appearances are in order, and planning the necessary transportation.

Finally, there is a series of miscellaneous functions which cannot be easily included in any of these normal categories. There are the "auxiliary organizations"—women's organizations, youth groups, and the like—whose officers have desks at national headquarters in the hope that their programs

[4] There are very good analyses produced by the Research Division of the Republican National Committee which usually appear in the spring following each major election. These avoid esoteric techniques in view of the lack of sophistication on the part of the intended audience, but are quite thorough and accurate.

will be coordinated with those of other party leaders. The party in power normally has persons who devote full attention to the problems of patronage. The two parties employ the few people in the United States who know how to stage a national political convention. And, as with any organization of comparable size, some energy must be devoted to questions of personnel, budget, and communication in order to achieve a modicum of administrative control.

There is one striking omission from this list of functions. The national committee staff is not a programmatic agency. It is not concerned with the development of party policy on economic questions, civil rights, foreign policy, or other substantive questions. Positions in these topics are developed by those who have been elected to office, by candidates for elective office, and by members of the platform committee at the national convention. The tasks of a national committee staff are concerned with the logistics of a campaign. They place resources at a candidate's disposal which enable him to pursue the strategy he selects, but they do not dictate the nature of that strategy. Both conservative and liberal candidates need to have press releases distributed, speeches written, essential facts turned up, money raised, and so forth. At least in theory, a campaign organization which possesses these skills ought to be able to serve any presidential candidate the party selects.[5]

The period immediately following the selection of a new presidential nominee is a crucial one to this organization. There is a rapid expansion of the staff *and* a high rate of turnover among the key personnel. The organization must have enough manpower to accomplish the tasks just discussed during the campaign. The Democratic National Committee staff grew from 70 in 1963 to 302 in 1964; the Republican National Committee staff grew from 124 in 1963 to 618 in 1964.[6] The new presidential nominee usually designates a new national chairman and the new chairman frequently appoints men of his own choosing to top staff positions at the national committee.

The members of the existing national committee staff approach this transition with some apprehension. They are uncertain as to who their new bosses are going to be, whether they will continue to be employed them-

[5] This lack of concern with policy often surprises visitors—especially from Europe—who come to party headquarters full of questions about the party's stands on a host of issues.

[6] Hugh A. Bone, *American Politics and the Party System* (New York: McGraw Hill, 1965), p. 193.

selves, and what is going to happen to their own institutional goals under the new regime. In order to reduce this uncertainty, as well as to smooth the transition, recent out-party chairmen, Paul Butler in 1960 and William E. Miller in 1964, made careful plans in the pre-convention period. Advertising agencies were hired, gradual staff build-ups took place, and some thought was given to a strategy which "the candidate" could easily follow.[7] In 1964, Chairman Miller obtained promises of cooperation from all serious Republican contenders, and offered each office space so a liaison man could be aware of what the national committee staff was doing. The problem with this was that while assurances of cooperation were readily given, the top level personnel in each aspirant's core group were so busy with the priority task of winning the nomination that they lacked time to concern themselves with less pressing matters. The attention of the winning coalition tends to focus on the tasks of conducting an election campaign only after it has nominated its candidate. And when these tasks do arrest its attention, its strategy is determined by the attitudes of the groups who make up the new electoral coalition. Similarly, the key personnel for the campaign organization normally reflect the membership of this coalition.

The question of who is selected for key campaign assignments is closely related to the other major question facing a winning nomination coalition as it transforms itself into an electoral coalition: How much must it expand in order to broaden its base of support for the election campaign? How many groups who were members of losing coalitions will be invited to join the electoral coalition to insure united party support for the nominee in the November election? Almost every coalition which has won an out-party nomination has expanded by adding groups who supported an unsuccessful contender. Frequently, the unsuccessful aspirant has become the party's candidate for vice president. This was the case with Governor John Bricker of Ohio in 1944, Governor Earl Warren of California in 1948, Senator Estes Kefauver of Tennessee in 1956, and Senator Lyndon Johnson of Texas in 1960. Senator Robert Taft did not become the vice presidential nominee in 1952, but the Eisenhower-Taft meeting in Morningside Heights served as a symbol of the inclusion of Taft groups in the Eisenhower electoral coalition.

The problem facing the Goldwater coalition in 1964 was particularly acute because of lack of support for Senator Goldwater within the Re-

[7] For a description of the 1960 Democratic efforts see Ogden and Peterson, *Electing the President: 1964*, pp. 237–39.

publican party. Good data on this point are available from the 1964 election study of the University of Michigan Survey Research Center. All respondents were asked whom they preferred as the Republican nominee, and how strongly they felt about this.[8] One-third of the Republicans reported no preference at all, but analysis of the desires of those who did favor a particular candidate makes it clear that Senator Goldwater was a "minority candidate of a minority party."[9] Nearly all the Goldwater supporters reported they were particularly happy he was nominated, but only 23.4% of the Republicans fell into this category. A slightly larger proportion, 29.8%, said that, while preferred some other aspirant, Goldwater was nearly as good. But almost half the Republican respondents, 46.8%, stated they favored the nomination of someone other than Goldwater *and* they were particularly unhappy when Goldwater got the nomination. It would be a reasonable assumption that those Republicans who agreed that Goldwater was nearly as good as their own choice would join the original Goldwater supporters in backing the Republican nominee, but whether those who were particularly unhappy about Goldwater's nomination would do so was another question.

The distribution of Goldwater support within the Republican party was also very uneven. Twice as many party activists (those who had made a financial contribution, or attended a political meeting, or belonged to a political organization, or did some work for a candidate) had wanted Goldwater to be the nominee as those who had not been involved in party affairs.[10] Conversely, as Table I indicates, a good many more persons un-

[8] The exact questions were: "You will remember that there was some doubt as to who would win the Republican presidential nomination at the San Francisco convention. Was there anyone in particular you hoped that the Republicans would nominate there?" IF SO, "Who was that?" IF GOLDWATER, "Were you particularly happy that Goldwater got the nomination or would some other candidate have been just about as good?" IF OTHER THAN GOLDWATER, "Were you particularly unhappy that Goldwater got the nomination or did you think he was nearly as good as your man?"

[9] Philip E. Converse, Aage R. Clausen, and Warren E. Miller, "Electoral Myth and Reality: The 1964 Election," in *American Political Science Review*, June, 1965, pp. 321–36.

[10] The importance of the activist/nonactivist distinction was called to my attention by Leon Epstein. See Leon D. Epstein and Austin Ranney, "Who Voted for Goldwater: The Wisconsin Case," in *Political Science Quarterly*, March, 1966, pp. 82–94. Their activist category included only those who had made a contribution, or were members of a party organization, or had done some work for a candidate.

happy about Goldwater's nomination were to be found among the "grass-roots" Republicans. The concentration of Goldwater support among the activists was an important factor in winning the nomination, but the concentration of opposition among "grass-roots" Republicans meant that the Goldwater activists faced real problems in persuading their less involved friends. The distribution of support by region, also shown in Table I, illustrates this same problem from a slightly different perspective. Only in the South did the proportion of Goldwater supporters in the party outnumber the proportion of those who were unhappy about his nomination. Among Western Republicans there were four Goldwater opponents (i.e., those unhappy about his nomination) for every three Goldwater supporters; among Midwestern Republicans two Goldwater opponents for every Goldwater supporter; among Eastern Republicans twelve Goldwater opponents for every Goldwater supporter. Given the weakness of Goldwater support among the less involved Republicans, and given the lack of support among Republicans in areas of the country where votes were needed in November,[11] the question of how much the Goldwater coalition should be expanded as it was transformed into an electoral coalition was urgent, indeed.

"Senator Goldwater has won the nomination, but it is quite clear that

Table I *Goldwater Support Among Republicans**

		Prefer Someone Else		
	Prefer Goldwater as Nominee	Goldwater as Good	Unhappy about Goldwater	N
Party Activity				
Activists	32.4%	31.0%	36.0%	111
Nonactivists	16.3	28.4	55.3	141
Region				
East	5.4%	34.6%	60.0%	75
Midwest	24.1	29.9	46.0	87
West	32.7	24.5	42.8	49
South	37.8	33.3	28.9	45

*Excluding the one-third of the Republicans who had no choice.

[11] So far as electoral strategy was concerned, the opposition to Goldwater among Midwestern and Western Republicans was more important than the concentrated opposition among Eastern Republicans. This will be discussed in the section on coalition strategy.

he does not yet have the leadership of the party. Acquiring the reins of the leadership is going to be a very delicate operation." So spoke one Goldwater supporter shortly after San Francisco. His perception of the situation confronting the Goldwater coalition, however, was not typical. Most members of the Goldwater core group had no previous experience with presidential campaigns, most were not nearly so sensitive as this person, and most behaved as if party headquarters was a military command post from which orders were to be issued to obedient troops. They expanded their coalition only to the extent of including a group of organizational loyalists, men such as former National Chairman Leonard Hall, Ohio State Chairman Ray C. Bliss, and Fred C. Scribner, general counsel to the Republican National Committee, men whose identification with the Republican party was so complete that they were accepted even though they had not supported Barry Goldwater in his fight for the nomination. And none of these men was ever accepted into the core group making the most crucial decisions about campaign strategy. The Goldwater nomination coalition was transformed into an electoral coalition with only a minimal expansion.

There are several ways of describing the groups who formed around the core group of Arizonans to make up the Goldwater nomination coalition. For a detailed roster, one could list the groups in each state which joined the coalition as it was being formed. In terms of sections, one could say the coalition was made up of Southerners, Westerners, some from the Middle West, and a very few Easterners. From the perspective of origins, one could point to erstwhile Taft conservatives, some Young Republicans and members of the Young Americans for Freedom, writers for such conservative publications as the *National Review*, and businessmen who were determined supporters of free enterprise. On the basis of ideas, there were three groups: conservative ideologues, foreign policy hard-liners, and Southerners. Any of these descriptions would be reasonably accurate, and all of the groups named would fit our definition of a group as a set of persons with shared attitudes and a reasonably stabilized pattern of interaction. To any of them, therefore, one can add the group of organizational loyalists, long-time Republicans who were prepared to support the Senator on the ground that he was now the Republican nominee, and obtain the composition of the Goldwater electoral coalition.

Now how did this coalition organize its campaign? Here the key fact is that no thought had been given to this matter until Goldwater had won the nomination. The calendars at Goldwater for President headquarters showed the number of days left until July 15, the date for the presidential balloting at the Republican National Convention. After that there was nothing. What followed was much more in the nature of improvisation, making decisions as questions became visible to the decision-makers, than it was implementing any master plan. No master plan existed.

Nor was there any concentration of experience in the Goldwater core group. The Senator himself had been chairman of the Senate Republican Campaign Committee during 1960. Clif White had been organization director for Nixon-Lodge Volunteers; Charles Lichenstein had written speeches for Mr. Nixon. Wayne Hood had been active in the 1952 campaign, but had been out of politics until the Goldwater campaign. Beyond this, no major figure had been active on the national level in a presidential campaign.

There were, however, a few ideas about campaigning which governed the underlying organizational pattern. First, Senator Goldwater was determined not to repeat mistakes from the 1960 campaign.[12] Vice President Nixon had set up an organization parallel to the national committee that year, and the campaign staff was housed in several different buildings. "I wanted to contact Bob Finch [Nixon's 1960 campaign director, now Lieutenant Governor of California]," Senator Goldwater once recalled; "I called five different headquarters. There wasn't one where the telephone operator knew who Bob Finch was!"[13] To the Senator's mind, this was a symptom of the problems of a split organization. He wanted to have a unified campaign organization.[14] And, as a party loyalist, he wanted to re-establish an

[12] It could be argued that this is a general characteristic of political parties. The rate of personnel turnover is so high that organizational memory is short. There are some who remember the mistakes of the last campaign; few whose experience stretches over several campaigns. This sometimes leads to the dysfunction of overcompensation for the mistakes of the last campaign without awareness of other organizational problems.

[13] It should be pointed out here that the regular telephone operators at the Republican National Committee are most capable. They know the working habits of personnel well enough to locate an individual for important calls wherever he may be. The campaign problem is that the regular operators don't have the budget to hire *and train* campaign operators before the national convention. When new girls come to work during August and September, they are untrained and swamped with incoming calls.

[14] This was the pattern employed by James A. Farley in the Roosevelt campaign in 1932 and by Robert F. Kennedy in his brother's campaign in 1960 (Ogden and Peterson, *Electing the President: 1964*, pp. 72–80).

important role for the Republican National Committee. So there was to be a single campaign organization, and that was to be the national committee staff.

A second key to the organizational thinking of ranking members of the Goldwater coalition was a 1963 memorandum prepared by that veteran adviser of presidential candidates, Raymond Moley. Moley suggested the substantive policy aspects and the political aspects of a campaign should be handled by different people. One team should concentrate on questions of campaign strategy, policy statements, speeches, and the like. Another should handle contacts with party members around the country, travel arrangements, and the rest of the logistical side of the campaign. A single person should coordinate the activities of these two components. The reason for limiting the contact in this way was to insulate the policy staff from political messages that the candidate "must say" such-and-such or that the candidate "has to respond" to a particular opposition attack. The absence of such "distractions," it was thought, would permit the policy staff to concentrate on what the candidate *ought* to say.

A third basic factor was a skepticism of the judgment of almost all other persons. This grew out of the experience of the core group in the early months of 1964. It believed that many mistakes had been made in the New Hampshire primary as a result of listening to New Hampshire politicos. It knew it had won in California when it had run the campaign as it saw fit. Moreover, it knew it had won the nomination after a campaign in which many pollsters, political writers, and not a few Republican politicians had said, "Goldwater lost whatever chance he had in New Hampshire," or "The party wouldn't dare nominate anyone with Goldwater's views." It might be stating matters too strongly to say that the coalition leaders' experience led to confidence in their own competence and distrust of advice from outside sources, but at least they formed the habit of making their own decisions and then telling others what they intended to do.[15]

Barry Goldwater made the key personnel decisions at San Francisco, and he chose to surround himself with men he was sure would be responsive to his wishes. Essentially, he placed members of his own core group

[15] This should remind us once again that the non-ideological attitudes of a coalition may be quite as important in determining its behavior as the policy goals of concern to it.

in the crucial positions at the top of his campaign organization. Denison Kitchel, his "Head Honcho," was to be general campaign manager and serve as liaison man between the policy group and the rest of the campaign staff. Dean Burch was to serve as chairman of the Republican National Committee, to be in charge of the campaign staff, and to implement the decisions of the policy group wherever necessary. John Grenier, Southern regional director during the nomination campaign, was to be Burch's immediate assistant as executive director of the National Committee. Edward McCabe was to work with the policy group and continued to bear the title of director of research. Karl Hess was to be with the policy group as chief speechwriter, and Charles Lichenstein was placed in charge of the day-to-day operations of the policy group as deputy director of research.

Having made these decisions, the presidential nominee went off for a cruise on the yacht *Sundance* and left his aides with the task of making plans for campaign strategy[16] and organizing the campaign staff. Denison Kitchel turned the latter task over to the two men, thirty-six-year-old Dean Burch and thirty-three-year-old John Grenier, who would have to supervise this staff after it had been assembled. This, incidentally, was the first of a series of important delegations of power on Kitchel's part. During the campaign, Kitchel would simply tell Burch of decisions which had been made and trust him to carry them out.

As Burch and Grenier saw their task, they had to do four things. First, they had to structure their organization. Next, they had to recruit leadership for this organization. Third, they had to staff the committee, to fill the five hundred or so positions to provide the leadership with necessary staff backing. Finally, they had to make budgetary plans. While some of these steps overlapped rather than followed each other in a precise chronology, there is some analytical convenience in discussing these actions in this order.

Burch and Grenier began their thinking about structuring the organization with the basic assumption that there were going to be two ultimate decision makers in the campaign: Barry Goldwater and Denison Kitchel. They would receive their orders from the candidate and general campaign manager. Their conception of their own positions, in other words, was that they were administrators rather than basic policy-makers. They stood as middlemen in a hierarchy running from the candidate to the voters. And,

[16] See Chapter 7.

in order to reach the voters, they wanted the organization they were to create to be primarily concerned with two tasks—motivation and mobilization. Motivation was to be supplied by the candidates with the assistance of the policy group, public relations personnel, and the tour committee which would arrange the candidates' travel. The campaign division, citizens' committee, women's divisions, and Young Republicans were to mobilize the electorate to make sure every possible Goldwater vote was cast on November 3.

Responsibility for organizing the policy group was given to Charles Lichenstein, the deputy research director. For all practical purposes, the name of one of his units, the candidate support unit, stated the purpose of his research division. The tasks assigned to this unit were those necessary to prepare major statements of policy for the candidate: analysis of issue, political analysis, recruitment of task forces of experts in various fields, quality control (screening proposed statements to make sure they fit into the general campaign strategy), liaison with other political leaders, and manning the Recordak (an information retrieval device which gave quick access to earlier statements made by Goldwater and Johnson). A separate speechwriting unit was also included in Lichenstein's original plan, but, except for Karl Hess, the chief speechwriter who traveled with Goldwater during the campaign, the distinction between speechwriters and those working in candidate support simply disappeared during the campaign. These people were far too busy to care about organization charts.

Most of the pre-San Francisco research division was designated as an "information center." These staff members, and those in the arts and sciences unit, a group concerned with liaison with the academic community, were permitted to continue with the chores they were already handling. Occasionally, they were called upon for "back-up" tasks, but were not drawn into the vortex of the policy group.

The organization of the public relations division was not unusual. This division was assigned three main areas of responsibility: radio and television, campaign materials, and press relations. Preparation of television material of course implied liaison with an advertising agency which could advise on making the most effective use of this expensive medium while simpler tasks (distribution of spot announcements) could be handled by national committee staff members. Campaign pamphlets and other materials for use in direct mail were to be prepared by staff writers and artists. Catalogs had to be compiled advising state and local party units of the availability of these items, as well as commercial sources from which campaign buttons and other novelty items could be obtained. Press releases were to be prepared for distribution to the various printed media, a press lounge set up for the convenience of members of the Washington press corps, and daily press advisories prepared for internal circulation giving the gist of important news to busy personnel.

The third activity on the motivational side of the campaign was making arrangements to move the candidates and other leading party figures around the country. This was the principal responsibility of the tour committee, another standard item in national campaign organization. The tour committee screens the requests which come from all parts of the country for appearances by the candidates, decides (or receives word from ranking campaign strategists) where the candidate ought to be spending his time, recruits and dispatches "advance men" who arrive in a locality five to ten days ahead of the candidate, check out all of the arrangements, and coordinate travel arrangements for the candidate and his party. A Speakers' Bureau coordinates requests for appearances by less notable party leaders, and a "Truth Squad" travels around the country in the wake of opposition candidates giving the Republican side of the story.

Most of the rest of the organizational arrangements made by Burch and Grenier[17] were concerned with mobilizing the Goldwater vote. The campaign division, now charged with liaison with party members throughout the country, came in for a major structural change. While it still embraced certain standard activities (the tour committee, training of party workers, etc.), the major portion of the campaign division was reorganized on a geographical rather than a group basis. The pre-San Francisco campaign division had sought to maintain contact with various groups of voters: farmers, union members, Negroes, senior citizens, and so on. In their reorganization, Burch and Grenier divided responsibility along regional lines. Region I contained five states casting large electoral votes: New York, Pennsylvania, Ohio, Texas, and California. Regions II through VII were composed of

[17] Sometimes their structuring involved new campaign units such as the policy group concerned with candidate support; often it involved only approval of fairly standard organizational arrangements such as the public relations division and the tour committee.

states in well-recognized geographical areas such as the Plains States, the South, and so forth.[18] Each of these units was headed by a regional director who had full authority to speak for the national chairman in his area. Each had two assistants who divided their time between travel in his region and working in national headquarters to make sure there would always be someone at the national committee with a fresh feel for the situation as it was developing. The regional directors and their assistants were backed up by coordinators who worked in still smaller areas. The arrangement was designed to make it possible to work more closely with the state organizations, to let them know what services the national committee could provide, and to give each state chairman a point of contact with the national committee staff. If all fifty state chairmen were to try to contact the national chairman, communications bottlenecks would develop. The state chairman could, however, report to regional directors, who could see to it that the ranking officials were kept informed.

The existing program for political education and training was to be much expanded. Since 1962, a single organizer had been traveling around the country arousing the enthusiasm of party workers and giving advice to party leaders on basic campaign techniques. His activities were deemed to be important. He was placed at the head of a staff of half a dozen campaign organizers, and this staff was assigned key responsibilities in the mobilization side of the campaign.

The third structure with some responsibility for the mobilization of Goldwater voters was the Citizens for Goldwater-Miller. It is perhaps the most difficult organizational component to describe because it was composed of "leftovers," activities which didn't quite fit into the national committee staff as Dean Burch and John Grenier were structuring it. Whenever confronted with a pre-existing unit which didn't seem to fit anywhere, there was a tendency to assign it to the Citizens. On paper, the Citizens had a complete campaign staff duplicating almost all of the responsibilities of the

[18] Region II included four Middle Atlantic states, Maryland, West Virginia, New Jersey, and Delaware. Region III was New England. Region IV was composed of five Great Lakes states, Illinois, Indiana, Michigan, Wisconsin, and Minnesota. Region V was made up of Plains States, Oklahoma, Missouri, Kansas, Colorado, Nebraska, and the Dakotas. Region VI included Virginia, North Carolina, South Carolina, Georgia, Florida, Alabama, Mississippi, Louisiana, Arkansas, Tennessee, and Kentucky. Region VII was made up of Montana, Wyoming, New Mexico, Arizona, Utah, Nevada, Idaho, Washington, Oregon, Alaska. and Hawaii.

national committee. But some elements of this staff were very active while others were almost inert.

A major group transferred to the Citizens was the bulk of the pre-existing campaign division. The pre-San Francisco campaign division had included programs to develop Republican support among farmers, organized labor, veterans, senior citizens, and so forth. John Grenier's conception was that the national committee ought to speak, as the presidential candidate ought to speak, to a national audience. The national committee ought not have the responsibility for reaching specialized segments of society. Consequently, virtually all these programs were transferred to the Citizens for Goldwater-Miller.[19]

Another problem "solved" by the creation of the Citizens organization was what to do with the many Goldwater clubs which had been organized during the nomination drive. Relations between the Goldwater followers and the state party organizations were quite uneven. In some states, the Goldwater organization was coterminous with the regular party organization; in others, relations between the two separate organizations were friendly enough for them to work together easily; in still other states, members of both groups bristled when the name of the other was as much as mentioned in conversation. Creation of a National Citizens organization established some lines of influence to the state Goldwater organizations, and policy regarding the role of each in the campaign could be set according to the situation existing in that particular state.

The last important element on the mobilization side of the campaign was composed of the auxiliary units: the women's division, the National Federation of Republican Women's Clubs, and the Young Republicans. None of these units presented any important organizational question. They had been in existence for a long enough time, and their programs were sufficiently well developed that they presented little opportunity for change. These units were simply moved to a distant part of the building, and permitted to continue with their established programs.

[19] There were two exceptions to this generalization. The nationalities division (which dealt with non-Negro ethnic groups) remained at the national committee with a large suite because it was headed during the campaign by Congressman Edward Derwinski of Illinois. Derwinski had been a strong Goldwater supporter during the nomination campaign. The other exception was the arts and sciences division which maintained liaison with the academic community. This was transferred to the research division during the campaign.

The next task facing Burch and Grenier was recruitment of leadership. This, of course, posed the crucial question of how the Goldwater coalition would be adapted for its new responsibilities. There were now two fixed points around which the decision-makers had to work. One was the composition of the electoral coalition; the other was the division of labor they had decided upon to permit the national committee staff to accomplish its goals. In theory, they could appoint anyone they chose to the positions they had created. In practice, virtually all the key posts went to leaders of groups making up their coalition. The selection of personnel is not only a crucial phase in organizational development, but it also determines much of the pay-off a group receives for its participation in the earlier coalition victory. If a group is represented in a position where key decisions are being made, its influence on the behavior of the coalition will be much enhanced. Without such representation, its influence will be diminished.

While the theoretical implications of the importance of this task in coalition leadership are quite clear, it is also important that this not be confused with the conscious motivation of the decision-makers.[20] From their point of view, they want the best qualified men who have the specific skills needed for each assignment. It is also desirable that the appointees be fully committed to the candidate. Where are such men to be found? In order to increase their chances of obtaining this combination of skill and commitment, the decision-makers are likely to select from those with whom they are personally acquainted. If they do not know such men themselves, then they rely on the recommendations of men they do know and trust. So even though the decision-makers may not conceive of their task in coalition terms, the probability that the key posts will go to leaders of groups in the coalition (or at least to persons recommended by them) is very high, indeed.

In the top personnel decisions made by the Senator at San Francisco, each of the major groups in the Goldwater coalition had been given some key post. The core group of Arizonans was represented by Denison Kitchel and Dean Burch, the Southerners by John Grenier, the foreign policy hardliners by Karl Hess, the conservative ideologues by Charles Lichenstein, and

[20] That we should not confuse our theoretical perspective with the motivation of the actors is a familiar point. In this instance, the decision-makers may think of their task in terms of coalition leadership, especially if they reflect on the nature of their job or have long political experience. In 1964, the decision-makers did not do so.

the organizational loyalists by Edward McCabe. Now who else would these people select to fill other key posts?

Those asked to join the policy group were conservatives with experience in universities or foundations. Professor G. Warren Nutter of the University of Virginia was an economist who had done a good deal of work on the Soviet Union. W. Glenn Campbell, another economist, took leave from his position as director of the Hoover Institute on War, Revolution and Peace at Stanford University. Richard A. Ware, a political scientist, came from his post as secretary of the Relm Foundation in Detroit. Miss Ann Brunsdale had been a friend of Lichenstein's from the time both had been graduate students in political science at Yale.

The name of the most important man in the policy group never appeared on any list of committee employees. This was William Baroody, the president of the American Enterprise Institute for Public Policy Research. Baroody, a close personal friend of Goldwater's with many contacts among conservative academics, had been serving for some time without any formal designation as a ranking policy adviser. He took leave from his position to continue this work during the campaign, and came to fill a portion of the role originally envisioned for Denison Kitchel. Since Kitchel was traveling with the candidate most of the time, he was not present when many decisions had to be made. Baroody acted informally in his behalf.

Immediately after the convention, thirty-one-year-old W. Lee Edwards, press secretary to Senator Goldwater during the primary campaign, was designated as director of public relations. Edwards had once served as press secretary to former U.S. Senator John Marshall Butler and had been quite active in the affairs of the Young Republicans and the Young Americans for Freedom. Edwards' first order of business as public relations director was to put a large number of his Young Republican and YAF friends on the national committee payroll. His second was to issue an order that *nothing* could be mimeographed without his express consent. It rapidly became apparent that there was a critical shortage of talent in the public relations division. Edwards' experience as editor of such publications as the *Young Republican National Federation News* might have been a start toward a journalistic career, but it was hardly adequate background for the demands of a presidential campaign—and his young friends had a good deal less experience than Edwards himself.

Whether Edwards' appointment was ever intended to be permanent is open to question. Denison Kitchel had been aware of Senator Goldwater's urgent need for topflight public relations support for some time, but unable to recruit any. When this question came up in the post-convention period, organizational loyalists such as Leonard Hall argued that the public relations post was one where skills were indispensable, and urged the appointment of L. Richard Guylay. Guylay had two decades of experience in handling major political campaigns. He was involved in national campaigns in 1944 and 1948, had been public relations director in Robert Taft's successful senatorial campaign in 1950 (when he began a practice of routinely distributing material to small-town weekly newspapers), and had been public relations director for the Republican National Committee during the 1956 and 1960 presidential campaigns. So Lou Guylay was put in at the head of a public relations division composed of a few permanent employees and a large number of young conservatives.

The appointment of Guylay also involved a change of advertising agencies. The Leo Burnett Agency of Chicago had been hired by the Republican National Committee in 1962 as part of the preparation for the coming campaign. In August, 1964, however, the contract with Burnett was severed, and Erwin Wasey, Ruthrauff & Ryan, a unit in the nationwide Interpublic Group of agencies, was hired. Their task, in Guylay's words, was "to use the power of mass communications to present a persuasive image of the candidate selectively, strategically, tactically, economically, and successively." Al Tilt, an agency vice president who was account executive for the national committee, came to Washington to handle liaison with the agency and worked in an office next to Lou Guylay's.

The most important personnel choice made by Dean Burch and John Grenier alone was the selection of Wayne J. Hood to head the campaign division. Hood was a fifty-one-year-old Wisconsin businessman who had some political experience. He had been Wisconsin Republican chairman from 1950 to 1953, and had been named executive director of the Republican National Committee during the 1952 Eisenhower campaign. (Though Hood held the title of executive director, he had functioned as office manager. There is considerable difference in these positions. The executive director is the second-ranking person at the committee with authority to act on his own in the chairman's absence. The office manager supervises administrative services within the office itself.) Mr. Hood had dropped out of politics after the 1952 campaign to devote full time to his business affairs, and had not become active again until the Goldwater campaign. Then he had served as Great Lakes regional director during the nomination drive.

The man selected to head the tour committee was one Mr. Hood remembered from the 1952 campaign, Douglas Whitlock. Whitlock's chief contribution to American politics had been the founding of the first Young Republican Club in the United States in 1928. He had worked with the tour committee in 1952, and had been secretary of the Eisenhower inaugural committee in 1957, but, like Hood, had been in private business (a Washington, D.C. law practice) and out of touch with politics for a number of years.

Aside from the tour committee, the most important posts to be filled in the campaign division were the regional directorships, the men who would speak for the national chairman and provide liaison with the state organizations. Wayne Hood took the responsibility for Region I, the five large states, himself. Stephen Shadegg, regional director for eleven Western states during the primary campaign, was asked to continue in that position, as was Richard L. Herman, regional director for the Plains States. Shadegg had held many positions in Arizona politics: state chairman, national committeeman, chairman of the Arizona Citizens for Eisenhower. He had managed Goldwater's Senate campaigns in 1952 and 1958, had written a biography of Goldwater and a book on campaign tactics, and had been one of the ranking Goldwater advisers until he had shown signs of desiring a Senate seat himself. Herman was in the petroleum transport business in Omaha, and had been a past president of the Nebraska Motor Carriers Association. He had been quite active in the 1960 Senate campaign of conservative stalwart Carl Curtis, and had thereby come to Goldwater's attention. Hood, Shaddegg, and Herman thus filled three of the posts, but since two of the regional directors from the primary campaign (Grenier and Hood) had been promoted to more responsible posts, there were four new appointments to be made.

The regional directorship which was filled immediately was the Southern post. This went to Sam V. Claiborne, a Tennessee state legislator. Claiborne had traveled through every county in Tennessee with John Grenier in his capacity as Tennessee chairman in the Goldwater for President committee. Given the Senator's statement about the desirability of disposing of the TVA, Tennessee was not an easy place to look for Goldwater delegates. Nonetheless, the Tennessee convention endorsed Goldwater, passed a unit rule, and twenty-two of the twenty-eight places on the delegation were filled by loyal Goldwaterites. Consequently, Claiborne became Southern regional director.

In early September, another Wisconsin industrialist-politician,[21] Sam M. Hay, was appointed as Great Lakes regional director. Hay was assistant personnel manager of the Allen-Bradley Company, had been both vice chairman and chairman of the Republican party in Milwaukee county, and had served as vice chairman of the Wisconsin Goldwater for President committee. It was not until late September that the appointment of David Nichols was announced as New England regional director. Nichols had been active in Maine politics, and had just completed a term as Republican state chairman. No one could be persuaded to serve as regional director in the Middle Atlantic states, so Maine's faithful Fred C. Scribner, Jr., general counsel to the national committee, took on the assignment. Management of the campaign in the East, in other words, was being left in the hands of organizational loyalists, but the lack of speed in making these appointments clearly implied that these were not regarded as vital posts.

Raymond V. Humphreys, a veteran political organizer, was left in his position as director of the division of political education and training. Humphreys, a native of West Virginia, combined two important talents, a working knowledge of the techniques of precinct politics and an ability to give rousing speeches to party workers on the importance of this precinct work. He had been employed by the Republican Congressional Campaign Committee for some years prior to 1962 when he began travelling in behalf of the national committee. In the course of his travels about the country, he had impressed members of the Goldwater coalition with his technical skills, with the result that his job was upgraded when they came to power.

Humphreys heretofore had been working alone. Now he was given a staff of half a dozen experienced aides. His immediate assistants were Hugh F. Bell, an Iowa lawyer, and Sumner Gerard, whose income came from cattle in Montana. Important specific responsibilities were given to Mrs. Rita Bass of Dallas, Texas, and Harlington Wood, Jr., an Illinois attorney. Mrs. Bass was a *cum laude* graduate of the University of Texas who had become active in civic affairs as a member of the board of the University of Dallas and a member of the Dallas Public Affairs Luncheon Club. Politically, she had

[21] There are several businessmen-politicians to be found among Wisconsin Republicans. It is a reasonably common practice for industries to permit younger executives to spend a large portion of their time on party affairs. These men tend to be more efficient than their volunteer counterparts in other states, but are often more closely attuned to the conservative thoughts of their industrial colleagues than to public opinion.

organized a very successful canvassing program in her home city. Now she was charged with directing a similar program on the national level. Mr. Wood had been U.S. Attorney for the Southern District of Illinois during the Eisenhower administration, and was currently a member of the Illinois Crime Investigating Commission. He had detailed personal knowledge of various forms of vote fraud encountered in Chicago. Wood was placed in charge of a program of ballot security designed to make sure that the votes would be counted as they were cast.

The Citizens for Goldwater-Miller were nominally headed by James H. Doolittle and Clare Booth Luce. Retired Lieutenant General Doolittle agreed to lend his name in support of Major General Goldwater, and the need for Mrs. Luce to serve as co-chairman of the Citizens was one factor in her decision to give up a projected race as the Conservative Party's Senate candidate in New York. (Incumbent Republican Senator Kenneth Keating faced enough trouble running against Democrat Robert Kennedy in 1964.) The post of national director of the Citizens went to F. Clifton White, who had done so much in organizing conservatives around the country to produce Goldwater votes at San Francisco. White had wanted very much to become chairman of the Republican National Committee. Since the Senator had selected his trusted personal aide, Dean Burch, for the national chairmanship rather than the accomplished political technician, White was given the directorship of the Citizens, perhaps as something of a consolation prize.

As we have already noted, on paper the Citizens duplicated most of the functions of the national committee. In practice, however, there were a few posts which were particularly important. James M. Day, a lawyer who had served as office manager at the national committee during the crucial organizing period in early August,[22] became director of special activities. He guided the units which were appealing to various groups: veterans, farmers, senior citizens, movie stars, pilots, sportsmen, doctors, veterinarians, homebuilders, and Notre Dame graduates. Some of these units, such as the farm division headed by veteran agricultural specialist Rollis Nelson, carried on the same range of activities in which they would have engaged had they been left in the campaign division at the national committee. Others, such as the Pilots for Goldwater, were principally fund-raising units.

The field organization, keeping in contact with the Goldwater clubs

[22] This was a most responsible position during this time. Day had authority to make *all* personnel decisions below the level of division head.

White had stimulated across the nation, was headed by a White protegé from Kansas, Tom R. Van Sickle.[23] As with the field organization at the national committee, this organization was filled out unevenly. David Nichols, New England regional director for the national committee was given another title as New England regional director for the Citizens, and no appointment was ever made for the Middle Atlantic region. There were working appointments made, however, in the Midwest, West and South, where the campaign was in high gear.

The Citizens' public relations director was Rus Walton. Walton was the organizer of the United Republicans of California, a volunteer organization with a pronounced conservative orientation formed in 1963. It had unanimously endorsed Senator Goldwater in the California primary. Walton's contributions to the national campaign were the film "Choice" (later disavowed by Senator Goldwater) and the organization, "Mothers for a Moral America," which was billed as the sponsoring group for the film. Also working in the public relations shop was Travis Cross, Governor Mark Hatfield's very talented assistant who was "lent" to the Goldwater forces for the duration of the campaign. Cross was responsible for some of the most tasteful and effective pamphlets to come out of the 1964 campaign.[24]

Only one of the auxiliary posts presented any personnel question. The president of the National Federation of Republican Women's Clubs, Mrs. Dorothy Elston, and the chairman of the National Federation of Young Republicans, Donald "Buzz" Lukens, had been elected by their own memberships. Moreover, both happened to be strong Goldwater supporters. But it was necessary to pick an assistant chairman for the Republican National Committee. Mrs. Elly Peterson, who had been in charge of the women's division[25] for the preceding year, had become the Republican Senate candidate from Michigan. The preferred candidate for this post was said to be Mrs. Laddie F. "Pat" Hutar of Illinois. Mrs. Hutar, a very good-looking

[23] In 1965, Van Sickle, following the path of a number of other White protegés, was to be elected national chairman of the Young Republicans.

[24] The difference between the film "Choice" and the expert public relations job done by Travis Cross, incidentally, illustrates the difficulty of making valid general statements about the Citizens.

[25] The origin of the distinction between the National Federation of Republican Women's Clubs and the women's division is obscure. At present, however, the National Federation tends to be more independent in its actions and the more conservative of the two.

free-lance writer (e.g., co-author of *The Investment Club Way to Stock Market Success*) and clubwoman from Chicago, had been active in Young Republican politics, serving as co-chairman of the National Federation from 1961 to 1963. She had been one of the key links in the Illinois Goldwater organization during the nomination contest, but it was difficult for her to accept the assistant chairmanship as she was the mother of a two-and-a-half-year-old daughter. Finally, however, satisfactory arrangements were made, and her appointment was announced at the end of August.

The finance posts were filled, not unexpectedly, by businessmen and bankers. Ralph J. Cordiner, who had retired in December, 1963, as chairman and chief executive officer of General Electric, was prevailed upon to accept the national chairmanship of the finance committee. J. William Middendorf II, a partner in a New York City brokerage firm who had been one of the important fund raisers during the nomination campaign, was appointed treasurer of the national committee. And Frank J. Kovac, whose prior experience included thirteen years with the Standard Oil Company of Ohio, three with the Republican national finance committee, and a year with the Goldwater for President committee, returned to the national committee staff in the executive post of finance director.

The appointment of Ralph Cordiner had an important bearing on the handling of campaign finances. Mr. Cordiner had insisted, and Senator Goldwater had agreed, that deficit financing should be avoided. No expenditures were to be made unless the funds were in hand at the time. This placed a unique constraint on the campaign. Presidential campaigns normally cost more than the money the party is able to raise during the same time period. In part, this is because of the constantly rising costs of such items as television and jet transport. In part, it is because money tends to come in shortly before the election when contributors get excited, whereas plans and commitments have to be made much earlier. In part, it is because the prize of the presidency is so desirable that there is an inclination to run up the bills as necessary and worry about payments later. Consequently, the conventional pattern is for both parties to end the campaign with a deficit. The winning party has the help of the president in wiping out its deficit. The losing party struggles with its obligations as best it can until the next campaign.

For planning purposes, Burch and Cordiner asked all the division heads who had been appointed to turn in budget requests. These were examined, approved, and combined into a general campaign budget by mid-August.

Table II *Allocations in 1964 Republican Campaign Budget*

Television	34.2%
Campaign material, literature, etc.	12.1
Citizens for Goldwater-Miller	12.1
Candidates' tours	8.2
Congressional and senatorial campaigns	7.3
Administration	6.3
Speakers' tours	6.2
Regional coordination and training	3.7
Fund raising	4.3
Polls, etc.	2.2
All other expenses	3.4

They found the budget they had inherited[26] was inadequate in three respects. It did not allow for internal control procedures called for by the new organization structure. It did not include any money for a citizens' organization. And it did not reflect the 40 per cent increase in television production costs since 1960 or the 25 per cent increase in television time costs in the same time period. Since television was projected as the largest single cost in the campaign, these deficiencies meant a need to increase the campaign budget to a total of twelve million dollars. Table II gives the allocations by purpose.

The plans called for spending three-quarters of the 1964 budget in the two months immediately prior to the election, and it was hoped that the money could be raised at a rate of a million dollars a week so some of the cash would be in hand before the expenditures had to be made. As it developed, this budget was adhered to fairly closely throughout the campaign. Television costs were about half a million dollars higher than had been planned originally, but this was the only substantial departure.[27] Consequently, the budget was reasonably effective as a device for administrative control. Moreover, the campaign did end up with a surplus estimated at half

[26] The Republican National Finance Committee reviews the requests of the Republican National Committee, the Congressional Campaign Committee, and the Senatorial Campaign Committee and sets a general budget each December. The budget in effect in the summer of 1964 reflected decisions made in December, 1963.

[27] Alexander, *Financing the 1964 Election*, p. 47. For a much more detailed discussion of campaign finance, see this study, Chs. 4, 5, and 7.

a million dollars in the Republican treasury. But the funds were not raised in advance as had been planned. Money came in very slowly during September. The surplus resulted from contributions of nearly three million dollars which came in during the last week before the election.

In fact, two men deserve principal credit for the Republican financial success in 1964 and neither one was on the finance committee. One was William S. Warner, who had served as executive director of the national committee under the chairmanship of William E. Miller. Warner had inaugurated the first really successful drive for small ($10) contributions in the history of American politics. Launched in 1962, this program was so well established that it brought in more than two million dollars in 1964.[28] The other person responsible for the surplus was public relations director L. Richard Guylay. Guylay urged Dean Burch to make a televised appeal for funds in mid-October;[29] it raised more than a million dollars. When such television appeals were repeated, they helped bring in the flood of "late money" which arrived just before the election. Warner's sustaining program and Guylay's televised appeals for donations were responsible for raising many times the surplus available at the end of the campaign.

As the campaign organization was now structured, there were supposed to be two levels of general decision-making. One was a strategy committee which was to meet every Sunday afternoon. This relatively large group included top leaders of all the groups in the Goldwater coalition. The membership of this strategy committee included Arizonans Denison Kitchel and Dean Burch, Southerner John Grenier, businessmen Ralph Cordiner and Wayne Hood, organizational loyalists Leonard Hall, Ray Bliss, Lou Guylay, Edward McCabe, and William S. Warner,[30] and conservatives William Baroody, Clif White, and William Knowland. (All these persons did not attend all the meetings as some had to come from out of town.) Meetings of the core group of ranking advisers such as Kitchel, Baroody, Burch, and Grenier were also scheduled for Mondays. Perceptions of the importance of the Sunday strategy committee consequently varied according to whether one was also a member of the inner circle of advisers. An organi-

[28] During the first quarter of 1964, the sustaining program brought in $559,000 while the Republican National Finance Committee was raising $34,000.

[29] For the details of this, see Ch. 7.

[30] Warner had become director of the vice-presidential campaign and had assembled a small staff including many of the ablest members of the pre-San Francisco national committee staff.

zational loyalist who was a member of the strategy committee only said, "That's where tours, radio and television schedules, issues, images, polls—where all that is decided." A member of the core group, however, commented, "This is an advisory committee only. It does not make decisions." From the perspective of the total coalition, the Sunday strategy committee was *the* group of decision-makers. From the point of view of the core group, it was a useful sounding board, a group of persons whose reactions offered valuable advice to those who were making the decisions.

As things worked out, many of the discussions of the Sunday strategy committee dealt with problems of scheduling. The responsibility for planning when and where the candidate should make his appearances had been assigned formally to the tour committee headed by Douglas Whitlock. Within the tour committee, one person was supposed to be responsible for scheduling Barry Goldwater, another for scheduling William E. Miller, still another for scheduling Dwight Eisenhower and Richard Nixon. They were to receive all requests for appearances by these party leaders, keep track of commitments made for appearances by them, and coordinate their schedules so as to make the most effective use of their time. But certain personality difficulties stood in the way of putting these plans into effect. According to one observer:

> The trouble is that Doug Whitlock wants to take all of the phone calls himself and make all of the decisions. He won't tell the people working for him anything. He just wants them to push a pencil, and they won't put up with it.

By mid-September, three persons "in charge of" the Goldwater desk had resigned rather than work under these conditions. Comments about the clandestine way in which the tour committee was conducting its operation were heard from others who needed information.[31] In view of these difficulties and in view of the importance of getting scheduling decisions made at least long enough in advance to permit necessary arrangements to be made, Whitlock's organizational superiors had to intervene. A good share of campaign director Wayne Hood's time had to be devoted to problems of scheduling, and this subject became the major subject for the Sunday strategy

[31] One story making the rounds was that Denison Kitchel had been heard to make the comment: "Say, if anybody is able to get a copy of the complete schedule, do you think I could have one?"

committee. The strategy committee tried to get a firm schedule two weeks in advance, and to discuss possibilities for the third week.[32]

Meetings of the core group had originally been intended for Mondays. Few of them took place, however, because other high priority tasks required the attention of the coalition's ranking members. Consequently, decisions were made informally as questions presented themselves. During October, for example, Senator Goldwater gave two very important speeches, one on morality in the Mormon Tabernacle in Salt Lake City, the other on civil rights in Chicago. Members of the core group had to decide whether to show one or both on nationwide television. William Baroody, Dean Burch, and John Grenier discussed the matter and concluded that both should be shown. At this point, the finance people said that they could not advance enough money to put both of them on the air. That evening Baroody, Burch, and Grenier flew to Dallas to present the matter to Senator Goldwater for decision. The Senator resolved the matter by declaring that both speeches should be aired.

Questions of campaign scheduling and finance are, of course, important in any campaign. Because of the assignment of institutional responsibilities to particular individuals in the Goldwater coalition, they consumed an unusual amount of the coalition leaders' time and attention in 1964. This tells us something about the nature of the organization created by Burch and

[32] Stanley Kelley, Jr., has studied the Goldwater campaign schedule with great care. "A presidential candidate's time is a scarce resource. Given a modicum of rationality on the part of the strategists of a presidential campaign, the way the candidate's time is distributed among the states should reflect, at least roughly, the allocation of the other scarce campaign resources. . . . The strategies of the Republican presidential campaigns of 1964 and 1960 . . . differed only marginally in the states selected as the foci of the most intensive campaigning. . . . Goldwater gave less time to the Northeast and more time to the South than Nixon had. The list of ten states where Nixon was scheduled to campaign longest, however, includes seven of the ten states that appear in a similar Goldwater list" ("The Presidential Campaign," in Milton Cummings, ed., *The National Election of 1964*, pp. 50–51, 75). There are two problems with this analysis. One has to do with a lack of correspondence between the rationality of Professor Kelley's model and the way the schedule decisions were actually being made. A more serious question has to do with interpretation. According to the data presented, Senator Goldwater spent 40 per cent more of his available time in the South and West than did Vice President Nixon. How much change in emphasis is necessary before it is considered as more than "marginal?"

Grenier, and it is for this purpose that these examples are included here.[33] But these instances cast only incidental light on how this organization went about the business of mobilizing and motivating the electorate. Since these were the institutional goals toward which the coalition leaders were directing their efforts, they deserve much fuller discussion. So we shall concern ourselves with these topics in the following chapters.

[33]For a more extended discussion of decision-making *per se*, see Karl A. Lamb and Paul A. Smith, *Strategies for Political Decision* (Belmont, California: Wadsworth, In Press).

6

Mobilizing the Coalition

Selection of the personnel who will have the key jobs is only the beginning of the job of managing a presidential campaign, but it is a crucial step. A political campaign does not allow much time to replace key men who fail to live up to expectation. But the jobs done with whatever skill by the national committee staff members represent only a small fraction of the effort necessary in a national campaign. A staff of seven hundred cannot make contact directly with an electorate of seventy million. Consequently, a great deal of attention must be given to communications with groups who can provide external support[1] (such as political writers) and with other party units who can help mobilize loyal voters.

The maintenance of effective communications is a particularly important problem in American political parties because of their characteristic dispersion of power. Samuel J. Eldersveld has suggested Lasswell and Kaplan's term *stratarchy* should be used to imply the diffusion of authority among the several layers of party organization.

> The very heterogeneity of membership, and the subcoalitional system, make centralized control not only difficult but unwise. In the process of adap-

[1] The need for external support is a familiar theme in administrative theory. See Herbert Simon, Donald Smithburg, and Victor Thompson, *Public Administration* (New York: Knopf, 1950), Chs. 18–19; Norton E. Long, *The Polity* (Chicago: Rand McNally, 1962), Ch. 4. Cf. Philip Selznick, "A Theory of Organizational Commitments," in Robert K. Merton *et al.*, *Reader in Bureaucracy* (Glencoe, Ill.: The Free Press, 1952), pp. 194–202.

tation, the party develops its own hierarchical pattern of stratified devolution of responsibility for the settlement of conflicts, rather than jeopardize the viability of the total organization by carrying such conflicts to the top command levels of the party. Further, the party must cope with widely varying milieus of opinion, tradition, and social structure, and this encourages the recognition and acceptance of local leadership, local strategy, local power. In addition, the desperate need in all parties for votes, which are scarcely mobilized at the apex of the hierarchy, results in at least some, if not pronounced deference to local structural strata where votes are won or lost. Thus a kind of "balkanization" of power relations occurs, with variations in the extent of autonomy in middle and lower strata from one habitat to the next.[2]

Eldersveld's model is at variance with the views of elite theorists who see all party activity run from the top. The best known elite model is, of course, Roberto Michels' "Iron Law of Oligarchy," which holds that power gravitates to the leadership strata of a party organization. Additional research is needed to learn whether Eldersveld's or Michels' model has more general applicability, but Eldersveld's certainly provides a better fit with American data. Political parties in the United States, as David B. Truman has pointed out, are "composed of a tremendous variety of elements imperfectly and rather unpredictably articulated, capable of showing a remarkable degree of separatism and autonomy."[3]

Consider the number of separate units involved in the Republican campaign in 1964. We have already mentioned four formally autonomous units, the National Federation of Republican Women, the Young Republican National Federation, the National Republican Finance Committee, and the Citizens for Goldwater-Miller. Add to this the Republican Congressional Campaign Committee (which has a large staff of its own), the Republican Senatorial Campaign Committee, the Republican Governors' Association, and the Republican State Chairmen's Advisory Committee, a national group which includes the Northeastern State Chairmen's Association, the Southern State Chairmen's Association, the Western State Chairmen's Association, and the Midwest State Chairmen's Association. Each of

[2] *Political Parties: A Behaviorial Analysis* (Chicago: Rand McNally, 1964), p. 9; see also Ch. 5 and the earlier literature cited on pp. 98 and 99.

[3] "Federalism and the Party System," in Arthur W. Macmahon, ed., *Federalism Mature and Emergent* (Garden City, N.Y.: Doubleday, 1955). The distinction between oligarchy and stratarchy is analogous to the distinction drawn by Robert A. Dahl and Charles E. Lindbloom between hierarchy and bargaining; see *Politics, Economics and Welfare* (New York: Harper, 1953), Chs. 8, 9, 12, 13.

the state chairmen, of course, heads a committee of his own, usually called a state central committee. Then there are the county committees in most of the three-thousand-odd counties across the country—and so on down to the precinct level. And this description of formal organizational units only hints at the group and coalition activity within each one of these elements. Complexity, indeed, and whatever plans Senator Goldwater and his advisers might have about mobilizing the electorate would have to be communicated down through this elaborate organizational network if they were to be put into effect.

The need to maintain liaison with this multiplicity of organizational units was reflected in the previously discussed structuring of the campaign division on a regional basis. This followed a pattern Ohio Republican chairman Ray C. Bliss had been using for some time. Bliss, who had been chairman of Summit County (Akron) before his promotion to the state post, had to deal with eighty-eight county organizations in the Buckeye State. He did not try to design a campaign which would take all the variation from county to county into account, but planned a general state campaign and relied on the county chairmen to adapt this as necessary to meet local conditions. To make sure that he was in touch with what was happening in each of the counties (and that the county chairmen were fully informed about his wishes), he employed a number of field men. Each of these young men spent most of his time in the area of the state to which he had been assigned, but also reported periodically to Bliss in Columbus. Thus the state chairman structured things in a way which permitted flexibility to meet varying local circumstances and promoted adequate liaison to tie the county organizations into the overall state campaign. The organization of the campaign division on the basis of regions in 1964 carried this idea to the national level.[4]

The latest technical equipment was also installed to permit high speed communication between various parts of the country.[5] DATA speed transmitting machines enabled the national committee staff to send copy to nine

[4] While organization of a campaign staff on a regional basis facilitates liaison, there is an argument against it which has particular force if divisions within the party happen to correspond with regional interests. If, for example, most Easterners and most Southerners take opposing positions on a series of issues, a form of organization which carries these views to the top of the party may accent conflict within the party rather than reducing it.

[5] This was partly due to Senator Goldwater's personal fascination with electronic gadgetry.

regional headquarters at a rate of 1,050 words per minute. There was at least one regional headquarters in each of the seven political regions. From these regional headquarters, two-way traffic was possible with both national headquarters and the state headquarters via TWX equipment at a rate of 100 words per minute. The regional headquarters could re-transmit messages for general distribution to all state headquarters, or relay specific inquiries to the designated addressee. State headquarters could also initiate requests for information it needed in a hurry. In addition to this teletype equipment, WATS lines (Wide Area Telephone Service, long distance lines leased at a flat rate) permitted national committee staff members oral conversations whenever this was more desirable. To supervise this equipment the 1964 national committee staff had a communications director, Nicholas J. Volcheff, a Bell System employee who worked full time with the committee during the campaign.

High-speed communications equipment was also placed aboard Senator Goldwater's campaign jet, Yia Bi Ken.[6] There was a "Radio Communications Airborne Command Center" which permitted the aircraft to transmit and receive messages with various points on the ground. News aides could release statements while the plane was airborne, and radio them to the Washington, D. C., communications center for simultaneous release from the Republican National Committee. Elaborate telephone equipment on board the plane could be connected with a plug-in device whenever the plane was on the ground. Similar equipment aboard the Niagaran, the jet-prop aircraft being used by William E. Miller, permitted the Senator to exchange messages with his vice presidential running mate.

This high-speed communications network was invaluable for maintaining positive contact between headquarters and the traveling party.[7] It was also very helpful when speed was required to respond to some unexpected development in the campaign, such as Khrushchev's fall from power in mid-October. But the channel capacity of the teletype network was greater than the amount of information it had to handle. It was anticipated that the DATA and TWX equipment would carry a great deal of high priority

[6] This was Navajo for "House in the Sky." Senator Goldwater selected the name because of its similarity to Be Nun I Kin, "House on the Hill," his home in Phoenix.

[7] This was true even though there was some radio trouble with the Niagaran at the outset of the campaign which made it necessary to wait to use the telephone when the plane was on the ground. This is considerably easier than trying to establish contact with a traveling party late at night when it finally checks in at a hotel to sleep.

traffic such as press releases, detailed scheduling information, research requests and information, and administrative traffic. In practice, there was a tendency to use the telephone WATS lines for high priority inquiries while the teletype equipment handled routine messages. The national communication network resembled the intra-office network in the sense that telephones were employed when one would engage in personal conversation in the office while the teletype network carried the same kind of routine announcement which came from the office mimeograph machine.

The most important traffic carried on the DATA-TWX network was probably the "Victory Bulletin" transmitted each evening so as to be available at the beginning of the following work day. This served as a kind of internal house organ, carrying a summary of political developments and announcements of coming events. The "Victory Bulletin" of September 15, for example, began with an announcement about Senator Goldwater's schedule for appearances in the South that week, and a Goldwater charge that the Democrats were timing their handling of foreign policy crises to suit domestic political needs. The next item was Congressman Miller's schedule for a swing through the Midwest. Then came a summary of opposition activities. President Johnson had a speech scheduled for Sacramento; there had been a meeting of Rural Americans for Johnson-Humphrey; Senator Humphrey was in the Midwest and due to speak at the National Plowing Contest; and Senator Fulbright (who had generally voted against civil rights) had attacked Senator Goldwater for his civil rights stand. Next came a brief announcement that Senator Goldwater would take a whistle-stop tour through Ohio, Indiana, and Illinois; then protests from Senator Dirksen and Chairman Burch about the Democrats' "daisy girl" commercial. Assistant Chairman Pat Hutar was speaking in New Jersey, and Congressman Chamberlain of Michigan was demanding that Secretary McNamara tell why a deputy project director had been fired. The names of members of a new Republican National Committee executive committee, to be released to the press later in the day, were given, as was the announcement that Barry Goldwater, Jr. was campaigning in Pennsylvania and Ohio. The "Bulletin" closed with an announcement about some television shows, and the appointment of Ronald Reagan and M. Philip Davis as co-chairmen of California Citizens for Goldwater-Miller.

The "Victory Bulletin" for October 1 opened with highlights about Senator Goldwater's speeches in Ohio and Congressman Miller's attack on the Americans for Democratic Action in Nebraska. Next came a reference to a speech of Senator Humphrey's in Detroit, an announcement that Goldwater's third television speech would be on October 6, notice that Congressman Miller's daughters would be honored at Notre Dame, and an item on the efforts of the Republican Truth Squad. The next had to do with the election of officers by the National Federation of Republican Women, including the re-election of Mrs. Dorothy Elston as president, and the election of Mrs. Phyllis Schlafly (of *A Choice Not an Echo*) as first vice president. The next intelligence was that *TV Prevue*, a local guide circulating in northwest Oregon, had endorsed Senator Goldwater (the "Victory Bulletin" didn't let much favorable information go unnoticed), and there was a joke about a mistake in a Democratic fund-raising letter. Texas Chairman Peter O'Donnell sent word that in June, 1960, Lyndon Johnson had said, "The worst Democrat is better than the best Republican," and Governor Mark Hatfield was reported to be busy helping his party on the campaign trail. The final items concerned a contribution from a member of the Brotherhood of Railway Clerks who objected to his union supporting the Democratic ticket, and the formation of a campaign unit known as "Hams for Barry." These "editions" of the "Bulletin" were typical. The bulk of the information was either available in public sources or trivial, but the "Bulletin" did get it to state leaders quickly and in a form which could be easily digested. And, quite aside from its content, the existence of the "Bulletin" gave state leaders a sense of being tied into a national campaign.

Memos circulated to members of the national committee staff also testify to the amount of effort devoted to establishing an adequate communications network. Almost all these memoranda can be placed in one of three categories: office procedure (care of rented furniture or wearing identification tags), events the staff was invited to attend (Goldwater departure on a whistle-stop tour or breakfast with the candidate), and communications. The memos which somehow concerned handling messages or routing correspondence were as numerous as those about office procedure and campaign events taken together.

The tone of some of these memoranda suggests the urgency of the communications problem.

TO: ALL DIVISION HEADS
FROM: Dean Burch

I wish to remind all division heads that information for the daily "Victory Bulletin" *must* be submitted to Carol Bauman in the News Room *daily*. This is a *most important* communications link with Republican State

Chairmen, and can be essential to us in transmitting vital information to them instantly.

Will *each* division head submit a report to Carol *today?* Even if you have nothing to report, please report in so she can proceed with the bulletin. As I stated in a memo dated Aug. 29, this material is sent via our TWX system each evening.

Let me emphasize that we need to get your information out into the field. . . .

TO: STAFF
FROM: John Grenier

It is requested that all personnel refrain from using the WATS lines between 10:00 a.m. and 1:00 p.m. and 4:00 p.m. and 7:00 p.m., unless the call is of the utmost importance. These hours should be reserved as much as possible for the Regional Directors. It is further requested that you make one initial request for a WATS line. Please do not call up five minutes later and ask a WATS line again for the same call. This only tends to confuse the operator and causes inefficiency in our communications operation.

TO: ENTIRE STAFF
FROM: Ray Hurley

It has come to my attention, that there is entirely too much confusion and disorganization here at the Committee with respect to requests and calls from Senators and Congressmen and their assistants.

When you receive calls and requests from Senators and Congressmen, and are not able *immediately* to offer them assistance, please transfer this call to me or my secretary . . .

These memoranda, it should be noted, were all dated in early September. There was some improvement in the situation as the committee "shook down," and staff members learned how to get necessary messages through in a relatively efficient manner. However, another memo dated October 8 suggests that the problem of internal communication was of a magnitude which did not admit of any really satisfactory solution.

TO: STAFF
FROM: John Grenier

When placing calls through the switchboard, please be sure to have the extension number of your party well in mind before placing your call.

Our switchboard is overloaded and this is partly the result of calls being placed by name instead of by extension numbers. The new staff directory was distributed this week and contains a list of all employees with their extension numbers.

There was not enough time to establish and test a communications network before it had to be subjected to the very heavy demands of a national campaign. Those who had to use the network developed a clear preference for oral communication over written with the result that the telephone network was overloaded while the teletype system was sitting idle much of the time.

The preference for oral communication is easy to understand. Given the hectic pace of a campaign, it is often preferable to get an answer to a question "right now" over the phone than it is to wait four or five days for an exchange of correspondence or even the hour or so required for a TWX inquiry and answer. As Harold Guetzkow reminds us:

> Telephones have the advantage of a technologically based demand for the complete momentary attention of the receiver, as well as the caller. . . . Although written messages, such as letters and memoranda, are in relatively permanent form, they suffer not only in competition with the demanding oral forms of communication, but also by competing among themselves for reading time. In fact, if the circulation of written memos is not severely restricted, irrelevant messages may prevent the reading of relevant ones.[8]

When eight different letters arrive from national headquarters the same morning, they all go into the "in" basket to be attended to as soon as possible. The fact that they may be stamped IMMEDIATE ACTION in red ink makes no difference, especially if several of them bear the same high priority designation. Telephone calls evoke a more immediate response. Sooner or later participants discover this, with the result that telephone busy signals multiply while written forms of communication are used for lower priority matters.

As a matter of fact, the communications network we have been discussing was used for amplification of campaign details rather than for setting forth the basic plans. These had been disseminated in a series of conferences beginning in early August. First came a meeting with the joint Senate-House Republican leadership which Goldwater, as a Senator, was accustomed to

[8] Harold Guetzkow, "Communications in Organizations," in James G. March, ed., *Handbook of Organizations* (Chicago: Rand McNally, 1965), pp. 538–39.

regard as *the* Republican leadership group. Next came a meeting with those Republican members of the House of Representatives who had supported the Arizona Senator before San Francisco. Then came a series of more general legislative meetings. The candidates appeared at a pair of breakfast conferences on August 5 and August 6. The first meeting was for all Republican congressmen and was hosted by Congressman Robert Dole of Kansas. The second was for Republican senators with Senator John Tower of Texas acting as master of ceremonies. On August 6, Senator Goldwater appeared before Republican congressional candidates at a campaign school being conducted by the Republican Congressional Campaign Committee. (Dean Burch, John Grenier, and Wayne Hood also appeared the following day.)

Discussions at these early meetings was very general. It almost had to be, because at that point few detailed plans had been worked out. Dean Burch and John Grenier had just finished structuring their organization, and were just getting into personnel questions. But the candidates did give speeches, and responded to questions that followed. The items covered were the broad outlines of strategy—Goldwater said he could defeat Johnson by carrying California, Texas, Illinois, Indiana, and Ohio in addition to states where he was already leading—and such topics as the importance of party unity and the need for the congressmen and candidates to maintain good communications.

More important meetings came the following week. On August 12, Goldwater, Miller, and the top leadership at the national committee journeyed to Hershey, Pennsylvania, for a unity meeting with Dwight Eisenhower, Richard Nixon, the incumbent Republican governors, and the Republican gubernatorial candidates.[9] And on Saturday, August 15, an all-day meeting was held with the Republican State Chairmen's Advisory Committee. This was a meeting which the Republican state chairmen had voted to hold some time before the convention. They felt it important that they meet with the new leaders of the national committee (whoever they might turn out to be) to learn the detailed plans for the campaign to come.

By the time of the August 15 meeting with the state chairmen, Dean Burch and his associates were ready for serious business. By this time, the major personnel decisions had been made, the budget had been reviewed and approved, the calculations had been completed for the vote quota

[9] This meeting was the beginning (and the end) of the first phase of Goldwater's campaign strategy. It will be discussed in some detail in the next chapter.

program (about which more shortly), and a forty-two page mimeographed organizational handbook was ready for distribution. John Grenier discussed the general structure of the Republican National Committee staff, Ray Humphreys went over the vote quota program, and Wayne Hood explained how the speaking schedules were being worked out. Senator Goldwater and Congressman Miller spoke at a closed luncheon meeting, and then the state chairmen returned to hear Lou Guylay give a detailed presentation on plans for a public relations campaign. Wayne Hood followed with an explanation of the regional structuring of the campaign division, and introduced Clif White, who promised complete cooperation, and said that no state chairmen for the Citizens for Goldwater-Miller would be appointed until they had been cleared with the Republican state chairmen. John Grenier then went over the budget, and Dean Burch closed the meeting by saying that the national leadership hoped to stay in constant touch with the state chairmen by means of the field force (working for the regional directors) and the TWX system. After the close of the formal sessions, three regional directors, Steve Shadegg of the West, Dick Herman of the Plains States, and Sam Claiborne of the South,[10] hosted parties for the state chairmen from their areas.

Most of the communication at this meeting was one-way. The national committee division heads lectured and the state chairmen listened. This was significant in two respects. First, it was indicative of the institutional attitudes of the leaders of the Goldwater coalition, specifically their tendency to think of party structure more in terms of hierarchy than stratarchy. Second, it suggested that if the state chairmen had any reservations about the plans presented to them,[11] they did not choose to express them openly. Such doubts as they might have were expressed in private conversation with each other. They did not regard this as a proper time to challenge the Goldwater leadership.

Still more detailed presentations of campaign plans were made at a series of nine regional meetings in late August and early September. A team headed by Executive Director John Grenier and Director of Political Edu-

[10] These were the only three regional directors who had been appointed at the time.

[11] This does not imply that the state chairmen were necessarily skeptical. In view of the turnover rate—only four had been state chairmen during the 1960 presidential campaign—many were too inexperienced to do anything more than try to absorb what was being presented to them.

cation and Training Raymond V. Humphreys appeared at nine regional workshops. Local leaders from California, Hawaii, and Alaska came to Sacramento on August 26; those from the Pacific Northwest assembled in Boise on August 27; a workshop for the Rocky Mountain states was held in Denver on August 28; a meeting with Republican leaders in the Plains States was held in Omaha on August 29. The touring team rested on Sunday, then resumed with a meeting with the South Central states in Dallas on August 31, a workshop for the South Atlantic states in Columbia, South Carolina on September 1, a session with Great Lakes political leaders in Indianapolis on September 2, a meeting for the Mid-Atlantic states in Harrisburg on September 3, and concluded its trip with a New England workshop in Hartford on September 4.[12]

John Grenier did most of the talking at these workshops. His presentation informed the state and local leaders about campaign plans in general and organizational plans in particular. Most of the organizational discussion summarized decisions made by coalition leaders up to that point, material which has been reviewed in the last chapter. The action item communicated at these workshops, though, was the plan for the mobilization side of the national campaign. Mobilizing loyal voters has been a basic task of party organizations as long as they have existed. Republican campaign manuals carry in admonition about its importance from Abraham Lincoln:

> The whole State must be so well organized that every Whig can be brought to the polls. So divide the county into small districts and appoint in each a committee. Make a perfect list of the voters and ascertain with certainty for whom they will vote. . . . Keep a constant watch on the doubtful voters and have them talked to by those in whom they have the most confidence. . . . On election days see that every Whig is brought to the polls.

So it can hardly be said that the mobilization plan represented a novel approach to politics. It is of interest, though, for at least two reasons. One is

[12] It should be noted that this basic organizational work—structuring the organization, making key appointments, setting the budget, and communicating campaign plans—required nearly two months. The time required in the out-party to transform a nomination coalition into an electoral coalition should be borne in mind when evaluating periodic suggestions to shorten campaigns. The situation is not unlike that faced by a newly elected president who must pick key personnel, review the outgoing president's budget, and prepare a State of the Union message between election day and January 20 to transform an electoral coalition into a presidential coalition.

that the specific plans employed were adapted in ways appropriate to the technology available and the conditions of American life in the 1960's. The other is the great emphasis placed on the mobilization plan, an emphasis growing out of experience in the California primary where Goldwater won by virtue of superior organization.[13]

The mobilization plans were built around four separate programs: a precinct quota program, a voter canvass, election day activity, and a ballot security program. These four programs were the responsibility of the political education and training division—and since these programs were at the heart of the mobilization campaign, they represented a real augmentation of the importance of that division—and each program was discussed by a staff member of that division.

The vote quota program was explained by Ray Humphreys himself. It had been used by Humphreys in a number of congressional campaigns. The version employed in 1964 was worked out in a 1962 race in the Eighth District of North Carolina. Charles Jonas had held this district for a decade, but faced trouble in 1962 because the legislature had drawn new boundaries for the district to make it more Democratic. Basic political data for each precinct in the new district had been assembled—registration figures, the size of the potential electorate, the number of non-voters who were already registered and the number who could not vote because they were not registered, and the presidential, gubernatorial, and congressional votes cast in 1956, 1958, and 1960. On the basis of examination of these data, a vote quota was assigned for each precinct. The data were presented to the Eighth District county chairmen as "direct, specific information so your vote hunt this fall can be with a rifle and not a shotgun." The quotas, they were told, were realistic goals, but goals which had to be met if Jonas was to be re-elected. The quotas were met: the Pearsonian correlation between the precinct quotas assigned in Anson County (the example used in the 1964 presentation) and the votes cast was .91. If one excludes two of the thirteen precincts, the correlation rises to .99. This had been done, Humphreys explained, "by finding people to accept the individual responsibility to go out and buttonhole their neighbors." In 1964 the hope was to do in each of the 185,000 precincts across the country what had been done in the thirteen precincts of Anson County, North Carolina, two years before.

[13] Here again the importance of the institutional attitudes of coalition leaders should be noted.

In 1964, vote quotas were assigned for every state, county, and congressional district in the country. This called for concentrated work because the entire job had to be completed in time for the state chairmen's meeting on August 15. Under the direction of Ray Humphreys and Mrs. Babette Ransohoff, Republican national committeewoman from Connecticut, 102 volunteers worked for twelve days to compile and reproduce the registration and voting data for 3,700 separate electoral units. When the state chairmen came to Washington, each was handed a booklet containing quotas and supporting electoral data for every county and congressional district in his state.

The vote quotas were assigned by Mr. Humphreys together with Charles S. Burns and Richard N. Rigby, aides to Congressman Jonas who had worked on the vote quota program in the 1962 race. Professor Franklin L. Burdette of the Political Science Department at the University of Maryland acted as a consultant. In assigning the vote quotas, four factors were taken into consideration: an estimate of Republican strength in the state concerned; a knowledge that the total electorate had expanded at a rate of roughly 10 per cent from election to election over a fifty-year period; an examination of the presidential, senatorial, gubernatorial, and congressional votes cast in 1956, 1958, 1960, and 1962; and an examination of the number of non-voters among the potential electorate.

The assessment of Republican strength in each state was quite thorough. The states were evaluated on the basis of the history of the majority vote for Republican presidential candidates since 1948, Goldwater's personal strength with the voters, Miller's personal strength with the voters, present voter acceptance of Republican positions on major national issues, vote-pulling aid expected from 1964 state or congressional tickets, effectiveness of the Republican state committee, productivity of precinct working personnel, harmony within the state organization, vote-pulling aid of local issues, expected honesty of the vote count, friendliness of the press and other communications media, ability to counteract Democratic campaign techniques, grass-roots opposition to Johnson or his administration, adequacy of the state party finances, effectiveness of the Republican Women's Federation, effectiveness of the Young Republicans, the national ticket's appeal to women, support from younger voters, support from the business community, support from labor, support from Negroes, support from other minorities, organized or unorganized farm group support, support from senior citizens, and vote-pulling aid from religious influences. Each of these items was rated on a scale running from zero to four, and this information was used in determining how much departure should be expected from the normal voting pattern in the state because of conditions specific to 1964.

In practice, relatively little use was made of this detailed information about Republican strength in assigning the vote quotas. This, of course, is not surprising, in view of what is known about the limits to human ability to assimilate information,[14] the use of non-comprehensive analysis in decision-making because of these limits on human intellectual capacities,[15] and the tendency to make decisions on the basis of limited information when the decision is urgent and the decision time is short.[16] An additional consideration in this case was the objective nature of the registration and voting data entered on the worksheets (see Figure 3 as an example) compared with the subjective nature of the estimates of party strength in each state. Consequently, the short-term factors were used only to make slight modifications in the national pattern in its application to particular states.

The national quota was 40,155,000 votes. This figure was 117.7 per cent of the 1960 Republican presidential vote. But since those making the plans were assuming a 10 per cent increase in the electorate since 1960, it is better to view the 40,155,000 as a proportion of a total electorate of 75,722,040. This is the number of voters arrived at by taking the total number of votes cast in 1960, 68,838,218, and projecting a 10 per cent growth rate. On this basis, the national quota called for a Republican percentage of 53.0 per cent.

Each state was assigned a vote quota high enough to permit the Republicans to carry the state. The mean of all the state quotas, again assuming 10 per cent more voters than in 1960 and looking at each quota as a percentage of this projected 1964 electorate, was 54.1 per cent.[17] One can see

[14] George A. Miller, "The Magical Number Seven, Plus or Minus Two," *Psychological Review*, March, 1956, pp. 81–97.

[15] Charles E. Lindbloom, "The Science of Muddling Through," *Public Administration Review*, Spring, 1959, pp. 79–88.

[16] Richard C. Snyder and Glenn D. Paige, "The United States Decision to Resist Aggression in Korea," *Administrative Science Quarterly*, December, 1958, pp. 341–78.

[17] The standard deviation from the mean of 54.1 per cent for the fifty state quotas was 4.6 per cent. There were only six states whose quotas did not fall within a range bounded by ± 1 standard deviation: Mississippi (76.2%), Arizona (63.9%), South Carolina (63.0%), Nebraska (59.3%), Kentucky (49.3%), and West Virginia (47.7%). The first four were states where there was a good deal of Goldwater support; the last two were states where the assumption of a 10 per cent increase in the electorate since 1960 was unrealistic.

WHY NOT VICTORY
IN ARIZONA?

CONGRESSIONAL DISTRICT 3	COUNTY all 14	CITY, TOWN, TOWNSHIP various
PRECINCT & ELECTION DISTRICT all 701	POLLING PLACE various	

VOTE HISTORY

YR.	CAND	REPUBLICAN	DEMOCRAT	OTHER	TOTAL	PLURALITY
56	Pres	176,990	112,880	303	290,173	69,110-R
58	Cong					
58	Sen	164,593	129,030	0	293,623	35,563-R
60	Pres	221,241	176,781	469	398,491	44,460-R
62	Sen	163,388	199,217	0	362,605	35,809-R
62	Cong					
62	Gov	200,578	165,263	0	365,841	35,315-R
64	Pres					

VOTES NEEDED FOR VICTORY IN 1964	280,000

1960

680,000	Persons of voting age
398,491	Persons actually voted
281,509	Persons who DIDN'T vote

1964

874,000	Persons of voting age
	Persons registered
	NOT registered

TIME TO REGISTER	BY MONDAY, 21 SEPTEMBER

REGISTRATION

REP.	DEM.	OTHER	TOTAL

Figure 3 *Sample Work Sheet for the Vote Quota Program*

Source: 1964 Campaign, Republican National Committee, Dean Burch, Chairman, Division of Education, Training and Political Organization the influence of the estimates of local Republican strength in modifying the national pattern by looking at two groups of states: those whose quotas called for victories by margins of 56 per cent or higher and those states who were not expected to do better than 52 per cent. The states where Goldwater was expected to do better than 56 per cent were his home state of Arizona; four states in the Deep South—South Carolina, Georgia, Mississippi, and Louisiana; and three Plains states where there was thought to be a good deal of conservative sentiment—Oklahoma, Kansas, and Nebraska. The states where the analysis of Republican strength evidently indicated that the Goldwater candidacy was in trouble were the home states of the Democratic nominees—Texas and Minnesota; three far Western states—Nevada, Oregon, and Washington; three Border states which had gone Democratic in most recent presidential elections—Missouri, Kentucky, and West Virginia; and several industrialized states in the Northeast—Ohio, New Jersey, Connecticut, Rhode Island, Massachusetts, and New Hampshire. If Pennsylvania and New York had been included in this last group of states with relatively low quotas,[18] these vote quotas would have been perfectly consistent with August soundings about probable Republican strength in the various states. But even with these two exceptions, and the still more questionable assumption that the Republicans would carry all fifty states,[19] these quotas represented a serious effort to concentrate campaign effort where it would result in the greatest pay-off in votes.

When this vote quota program was presented to the state and local leaders at the nine regional workshops, the state leaders were encouraged to implement it by selecting target counties and target precincts where they

[18] It *may* be that the assignment of "normal" quotas to Pennsylvania and New York reflected continuing animosity between the Goldwater leaders and the Rockefeller-Scranton leaders who contested the Arizonan's nomination, but I have no evidence that this was the case. More germane to the way these decisions actually were made is the fact that West Virginia, Connecticut, North Carolina, and Alabama all had lower quotas than did contiguous states. In each of these cases, someone with personal familiarity was involved in the assignment of quotas. This would suggest that superior information tended to lead to the assignment of more modest quotas.

[19] The assumption that the Republicans would carry all fifty states is questionable if viewed as a realistic estimate of what was likely to happen in November. It is, however, functional from the standpoint of the requirements of coalition leadership. A national leader with any tact would never *tell* a state chairman his state had been written off.

would focus their effort. Generally they were to be guided by the assumption that the greatest potential for increasing the Republican vote would come from increasing the turnout in areas already casting a heavy Republican vote.[20] The state leaders were advised not to advertise the counties they had chosen as target counties (this was less for reasons of secrecy than to avoid offending the county leaders whose areas were not selected for intensive work), but to select the target counties by mid-September so the target precincts could be selected by late September.

The next person to speak at the regional workshops was Mrs. Rita Bass, who had supervised a very successful canvassing program in Dallas. She began by pointing to electoral successes which could be attributed to canvassing. In Lawrence, Kansas, in 1958, there were two normally Republican precincts. The first had no canvass; the turnout was 60 per cent and there was a Republican majority of five votes. The second was canvassed; the turnout was 80 per cent and there was a Republican majority of 166 votes. She also noted that canvass work in target precincts in Nueces County (Corpus Christi), Texas, had increased the Republican majority in these precincts from a range of 50 per cent to 55 per cent in 1962 to a range of 75 per cent to 80 per cent in 1963. Large turnouts in areas of Goldwater strength could (as in California) contribute to statewide victories.

We need hardly dwell on the basic purpose of the canvassing program, but some of the adaptations in the 1964 program are of interest. First of all, the program fit conditions of life in the suburbs. The canvassing was to be done by couples. Householders, it was argued, would open their doors more readily to a couple in the evening than to a single male, and two proponents were more likely to be able to present an effective case than would one worker. The best recruiters of couples to take part in the canvassing were said to be "busy active people who take part in civic organizations and can contact their friends in these groups such as the PTA, church circles, doctors' wives, engineers' wives, lawyers' wives, bowling league, etc." These

[20] The idea of increasing a party's vote by intensive efforts among natural adherents seems to be prevalent in American politics. E. E. Schattschneider writes: "The American major party is a low-grade organization which has exploited its opportunities by bonanza methods and has worked only the most accessible fields in a very fertile wilderness, i.e., *new* voters, immigrants, newly enfranchised voters, indifferent voters without strong opinions, and others in the great reservoir of nonvoters" (*Party Government* [New York: Rinehart, 1942], p. 50).

instructions echo William H. Whyte, Jr. on the suburban life of the organization man.[21]

The second point of some interest is the extent to which this couples canvass was subject to centralized control. This was not the routine operation in which state parties are exhorted to conduct registration and get-out-the-vote drives. Detailed instructions were prepared in Washington and passed down through state and county levels to the precinct workers. Centralized control, it was said, would "insure uniformity and correctness. No material is left out and no undesirable material is added." The instructions were quite detailed. The county canvass committee was to have a chairman, a volunteer recruiting chairman, a kits and materials chairman, an advance men chairman, and a records chairman. The precinct chairmen were given such instructions as: "The day of the canvass, CALL YOUR CANVASSERS and remind them to come and TO BRING A FLASHLIGHT. Emphasize the importance of not 'letting you down' at the last moment. It makes for a more pleasant occasion if you plan to serve refreshments of some sort when the canvassers return." The canvassers themselves were given some ten specific injunctions such as: "Never argue! A pleasant smile is the most powerful weapon you have," and "Don't go inside the house—you won't have time to complete your calls if you do." The conversation was prescribed: "Good evening, Mr. or Mrs. __________. I'm __________, and this is __________. We are volunteers calling tonight to ask you to vote for Barry Goldwater for President. May we count on your vote? (Pause and wait for response.) We also want to ask you to vote for the other Republican candidates. May we count on your vote for them? (Pause and wait for response.)" From that point on, the conversation branched, depending on whether the householders were for or against Goldwater. If for Goldwater, they were encouraged to undertake some activities which would aid Republican chances. If undecided or opposed, the canvassers were enjoined to close the conversation by saying: "We want you to know that we think enough of your vote and our candidates to come by and ask you to vote for them."

21 "With sixty-six adult organizations and a population turnover that makes them insatiable for new members, Park Forest probably swallows up more civic energy per hundred people than any other community in the country. For the wife who gets fully involved, the blackboard in the kitchen is indispensable, for scheduling oneself to keep from being expected at two different meetings at the same time is not always easy. Every minute from 7:00 a.m. to 10:00 p.m. some organization is meeting somewhere" (Whyte, *The Organization Man* [New York: Simon & Schuster, 1956], p. 287).

A final point about the 1964 canvass was that the canvassers were as interested in laying the groundwork for a successful election day operation as they were in soliciting votes. After the canvass, they were to return to a central headquarters to record the names of all known Republican voters on tally lists. Just as instructions came down the "chain of command," reports were to flow back up on the number of voters contacted, the proportion of Republican voters, and so forth, at regular intervals. And the entire canvass was to be stopped a week before the election in order to permit collation of the results on high-speed data processing equipment to produce accurate lists of Republican voters in time for election day work. At the regional workshops, John Grenier told the story of an Alabama county where they canvassed until the last minute, located 4,750 "canvass votes," but then had no election day list and had to be content with 2,100 actual votes cast.

The canvassing program was inaugurated in all but four states (Iowa, Michigan, Ohio, and New York), which had programs of their own. There were 1,052 target counties designated, and canvassing operations were actually begun in 912 of these counties. Reports reached the political education and training division in Washington on completed canvasses in 437 counties in 39 states. These reports indicated that a total of 3,388,632 voters had actually been contacted by the canvassing program. Given the probable inefficiency of reporting procedures, we may assume that these last figures underestimate the number of counties in which the program was carried through and the number of voters reached by the couples canvass.

The reports also gave reasonably accurate estimates of the progress of the campaign. Of course, some assumptions have to be made in interpreting these figures. If one assumes that Goldwater would receive half the undecided vote, then the canvass reports showed the Republican ticket carrying 33 of the 39 states reporting. A more realistic assumption would be that those intending to vote for Goldwater would tell this to Republican workers, while those intending to vote for Johnson would either report a Democratic preference *or* say they were undecided. This suggests the use of the reported Goldwater vote as the basis of prediction. On this assumption, the Pearsonian correlation between the percentages reported by each state and the percentages of the vote actually cast was .74, a prediction which accounts for slightly more than half the variance. (See Figure 4 for a scatter diagram of these data.) If one further restricts the comparison to those 17 states from which reports from more than 10 counties were received, the correlation rises to .85, a figure that accounts for 72 per cent of the variance. By way of

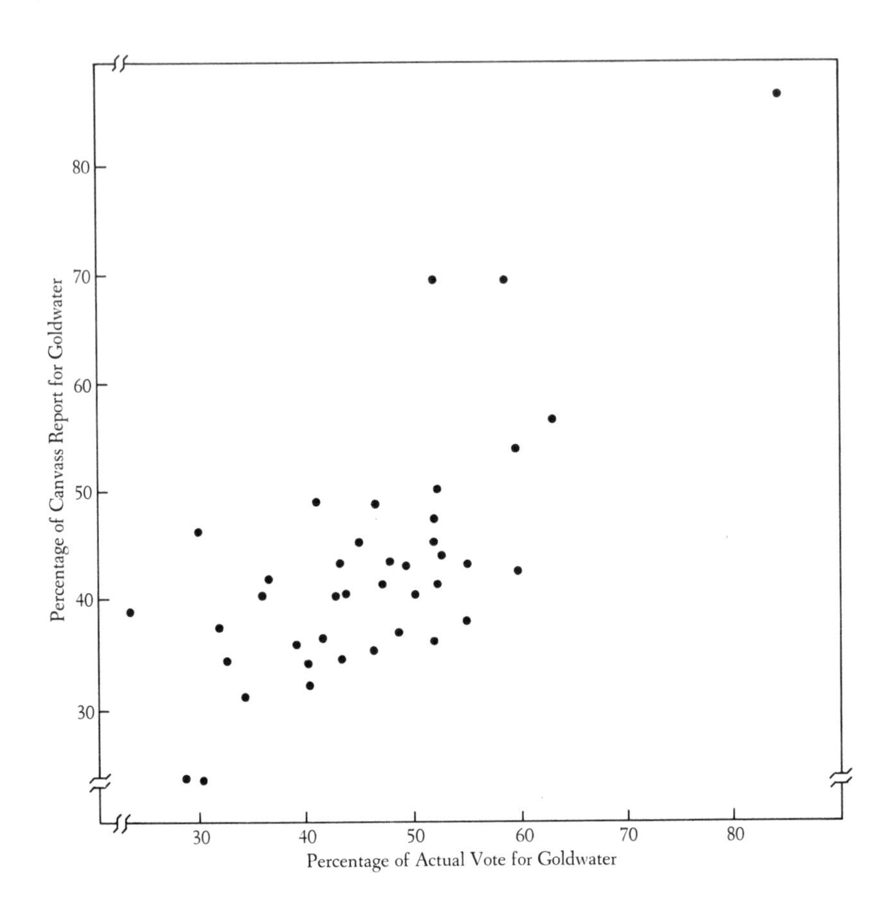

Figure 4 *Canvass Reports and Actual Vote*

comparison, the correlation between vote intention and reported vote in the 1964 election study conducted by the University of Michigan Survey Research Center was .81.[22] So the couples canvass produced a great deal of effort to reach voters, and yielded some not unreliable estimates of what these voters intended to do.

The third phase of the mobilization program, election day activity, was

[22] This correlation figure is Kendall's Tau-b, a rank-order measure of association which produces a figure lower than the Pearsonian r. Of course, the professional standards in the Survey Research Center study should produce a more accurate estimate.

discussed at the regional workshops by Charles S. Burns, Congressman Jonas' administrative assistant who had worked on the successful North Carolina race two years earlier. Burns related the mobilization program to the sales program of a business firm. "The precinct quota is what you can reasonably expect to get in your sales territory. The more calls you make in the canvassing program, the more sales you make. The pay-off is in sales, though. And in politics, the point of sales is the ballot box."

The election day procedures Burns outlined were routine. Volunteers should work on the basis of the list of Republican voters identified through the canvass program. The names of those who voted should be checked off by poll watchers. Republicans who had not voted by mid-afternoon should be phoned. "Good afternoon, Mr. Jones. I'm George Matthews, calling as a Republican volunteer. Have you voted yet? (To 'no' answers) Please go vote now. Our reports indicate a close election. May I help you get to the polls?" The only way this might vary from the procedure followed by the Democratic party is that Republican suburbanites, who must vote before leaving for work in the central city or after returning home, face a little more of a problem because of the volume of early and late voting.

The fourth phase of the mobilization campaign, the ballot security program, was a direct result of Republican experience in 1960. The election had been lost by 118,574 votes out of 68,838,219 cast. There had been a number of charges of irregularity, particularly in Illinois and Texas. If these two states had been in the Republican column, Vice President Nixon would have had the 270 electoral votes necessary to elect him. And just as the Jacobites believed the Stuarts were entitled to the throne of England after 1688, many Republican loyalists believed Richard Nixon was entitled to the White House in his own right. Mr. Nixon took the position that he did not want to raise the constitutional question involved in challenging the vote count in the courts, and that, even if there was a question about the propriety of the election, it was the Republicans' fault for not having enough poll watchers to insure an honest count. Consequently, the 1964 instructions contained such words as: "Planning, organization, and training in Ballot Security must begin at once and be advanced rapidly as part of the existing political organization and program. Frantic efforts on election night to round up the lost, strayed, or stolen votes needed to win another close election will again be too late. Unless Ballot Security is made a part of the campaign it may be nothing more than a 'morning after' headline."

The ballot security program was explained at the regional workshops by

Harlington Wood. Much of his presentation was devoted to known methods of vote fraud. He wanted to make sure local leaders were aware of such techniques as having the ballot box partly filled at the beginning of voting, chain voting when the voter receives a marked paper ballot before entering the polling place and then brings his blank ballot back out so it can be marked for the next person, using false addresses which appear to lie within the precinct boundaries, recording the wrong vote after the vote is counted, ballot boxes having a broken seal or no seal at all, advancing the count on a voting machine so the count is not zero when voting begins, using the real voting machine as the "practice" machine, switching the names on a voting machine so the votes cast for one candidate will be counted for another, giving instructions to voters in a foreign language or telling voters to be sure to pull the "red" or "blue" or "green" lever to make sure their vote counts, and hanging the curtain on the machine so it does not close all the way.

Mr. Wood also urged that attorneys be appointed to head the ballot security program wherever possible. Lawyers could easily familiarize themselves with the provisions of the applicable election code. They could make advance arrangements with the local officials whose responsibilities included the judicial supervision of elections. In case any irregularities occurred, particularly those leading to an arrest or other legal action, attorneys would know exactly what steps should be taken in order to preserve Republican rights. Since it would be difficult to recruit enough legal help to assign one attorney per precinct, small teams of lawyers should be assembled which could be dispatched on election day whenever a report of difficulty was received.

Finally, the ballot security program involved publicity. There are always some areas where a party organization lacks the personnel to do an adequate job. Publicity about a comprehensive ballot security program presumably exerts some deterrent effect in these uncovered areas, and advance publicity can strengthen the hand of volunteers in handling difficult situations where the party can provide poll watchers. So the local leaders were encouraged to secure as much press coverage as possible—and a good deal of national publicity was later released on what came to be called "Operation Eagle Eye."[23]

Of course, all these organizational efforts—assigning vote quotas, distributing detailed instructions for the couples canvass, emphasizing election day activity, setting up a separate ballot security program—were never in-

[23] The appropriateness of this name for the ballot security program is somewhat dependent on one's point of view. Hubert Humphrey responded to the publicity about "Operation Eagle Eye" by calling it "Operation Evil Eye."

tended to be more than a part of the total campaign. The campaign plan discussed at the regional seminars explicitly distinguished between mobilization and motivation. The task of motivating the voters was the responsibility of the candidates, the policy group, and the public relations division. The official view was that the mobilization campaign was half of a smoothly coordinated total effort.

Some political veterans were less certain that a balance was being maintained. One who played a central role in the campaign was asked in mid-August what he thought of the Goldwaterites' campaign strategy. His reply was simple: "I don't think they have one." Another organizational loyalist was more explicit. "They're trying to win this," he observed, "with precinct politics. You can't do that on the national level. On the national level, you have to create an atmosphere of enthusiasm. This permits the organizational work to go forward on the state and local level."

As one proceeded outward from the center of the Goldwater coalition, one encountered more and more criticism of the way the campaign was being conducted. In part, this was because only those at the peak of the organization were aware of all phases of the campaign. Another reason was that the campaign strategy reflected the attitudes of at least four different groups in the Goldwater coalition. Since the strategy was determined by the intersection of the attitudes of the member groups, it was not completely satisfactory to any one group, and it was least satisfactory to those groups on the periphery of the coalition. To understand this more fully, we must turn from questions of coalition leadership and deal directly with coalition strategy.

THREE

☆☆☆☆☆☆☆☆☆☆☆☆☆☆☆☆☆☆☆☆☆☆☆☆☆☆☆☆

Coalition Strategy

7

The Goldwater Strategy

A campaign organization is brought into being for a purpose: It is assembled to help the candidate communicate with the voters. This over-all goal subsumes the many more specific tasks—writing speeches, buying television time, raising money, and the like—which, as we saw, require so much effort. But a campaign organization is not a neutral instrument which can generate any set of ideas thought to be persuasive to the public. The strategy employed will be a product of the attitudes of the groups making up the electoral coalition. Hopefully, the ideas stressed will advance the candidate's cause with the electorate, but they are ideas urged upon him by those already committed to his cause. This places the candidate in a position where he must maintain a delicate balance: He must be responsive to the wishes of his followers if he is to retain their loyalty, and, at the same time, appeal outwardly to uncommitted members of the electorate.

This dual task of coalition leadership usually is easier for a front-runner. He is an attractive candidate who can lend his strength to groups associated with him and, if elected to office, one who will be in a position to do many more favors. Moreover, if the coalition he leads has been in existence for a period of time, the relationship between group goals and coalition goals is likely to be well understood by all the participants. In these circumstances, the group leaders are likely to approach the candidate with a certain amount of deference. They are more likely to listen to his thoughts than to insist that he advocate policies more acceptable to them. Now consider the plight of a candidate who is thought to be running behind. The reasons for his difficulty are usually sufficiently ambiguous that any group leader can claim the candidate's standing will improve if only the candidate will adhere more closely to the goals of that particular group. Moreover, whenever a coalition leader needs help, the group leader is in a stronger bargaining position. A candidate in difficulty therefore is likely to be assaulted with advice from all sides as his campaign develops.

A candidate may do several things with this problem. He may, for example, try to accommodate himself to advice coming from different quarters. A nominee following this course often seems to be saying one thing one day, and something else the following day. He may be stiff-backed and tell his advisers a particular strategy has been decided upon, and that, for better or worse, this is the strategy which will be followed. Or, if he has a sufficiently powerful mind, he may find underlying themes which knit together the varying attitudes of his supporters.

Barry Goldwater tended to resist suggestions that he alter any of his own tactics or ideas. His self-perception was that he was a man of high principle. Any suggestion implying a sacrifice of integrity was likely to be rejected. He also felt there had occurred dips in his political fortunes when, as in New Hampshire, he had adopted unfamiliar campaign techniques at the urging of others. So, many a suggestion was felled by the Goldwater comment, "They're trying to change me."

The question of his mental prowess is more difficult. A common view is that of a foreign observer: "Barry Goldwater's ideas are all right for a Senator from Arizona, but since he has become a presidential nominee his thoughts have been scrutinized by some of the best minds in the Western World—and they just don't add up!" A very different impression was conveyed by one of the top Republican strategists who said: "Senator Goldwater has a very quick mind. Often before you even get into the pros and cons of a certain decision, he's already there. He'll tell you right away what he wants to do and why." A political reporter who had traveled with the Senator expressed his private judgment this way: "For my money, Barry Goldwater's thinking stops when the problem gets difficult. I'm convinced that he's perfectly sincere in saying that he is for civil rights and that he is for states' rights. But he doesn't go ahead to think about possible conflicts between these two positions."

What manner of man inspires comments as divergent as these? Certainly not a simple man, one who can be defined quickly with such words as "good," "bad," "smart," or "dumb." Perhaps a man who had been an activist most of his life. Aside from business and politics, after all, he had been a prize-winning photographer, a man who had shot the Colorado River rapids, and who had spent a good deal of time with his ham radio set. These are the pursuits of one who enjoys doing things rather than one who reflects on the meaning of ideas. In any case, it is not necessary to solve this puzzle about Barry Goldwater completely. For our purposes, it is enough to know that whatever his mental alacrity, he rarely concerned himself with the *implications* of ideas. Each of his principles could be regarded as a separate impetus for action, rather than as a component of a coherent ideology. Barry Goldwater did not have that quality of mind which would rebel if the ideas he espoused on Friday were not fully consistent with the speech he had given on Tuesday. For this reason, as well as because of the dynamics of a losing campaign, the membership of the Goldwater coalition is an important key to understanding the Goldwater strategy.

As we have already noted, each of the major groups in the Goldwater coalition had some representation at campaign headquarters. These groups were not, however, equally well placed to affect campaign strategy. Nor were they equally interested in the content of campaign strategy. The core group of Arizonans, for example, had spokesmen in key posts. It is difficult to overstate Denison Kitchel's influence with Senator Goldwater. Dean Burch was in charge of all day-to-day operations at the national committee. But both Kitchel and Burch were far more interested in serving the interests of their friend, Barry Goldwater, than they were in urging any particular strategy on him. Kitchel and Burch participated in most key decisions, but more as decision-makers than as advocates of a particular point of view. Other groups acted as advocates. Their representatives were located at points within the campaign organization where strategy decisions were being made, and they had certain reasonably precise ideas about strategy to which they were committed. These groups were the organizational loyalists, the Southerners, the foreign policy hard-liners, and the conservative ideologues.[1]

The organizational loyalists were those who had not been active in Goldwater's nomination drive and who thus were never completely embraced by the Arizonans. From the Goldwaterites' point of view, they were acceptable to a degree because of their long records of Republican activity. From their own point of view, they accepted the Arizona Senator as the party leader, once he received the Republican nomination. One organizational loyalist

[1] These names are intended to suggest attitudes important in determining campaign strategy.

expressed himself this way: "Of course I'm working for Barry Goldwater! As far as I'm concerned, if the Republicans were to nominate Joe Klutz—whoever he is—I'd be working just as hard for him." Although this group was more concerned with increasing the candidate's standing with the electorate than with any ideology, these organizational loyalists tended to be happier when they heard themes familiar from the Eisenhower-Nixon years than they were when someone spoke of the need to give the voters "a real choice." The most prominent members of this group were Leonard Hall and Ray C. Bliss. The organizational loyalist who had most to do with day-to-day decisions about campaign strategy was the veteran publicist Lou Guylay.

The Southerners had decided ideas about how the campaign ought to be run, but they were not in a very good position to implement their beliefs. These ambitious young men were interested in building Republican parties they could control in their home states at the same time as they worked for the election of Senator Goldwater. They believed "the Democratic party went off and left us when it became socialistic." A typical view of Goldwater's nomination was that it constituted "the finest thing that has happened in America since I have been old enough to be aware of what happens politically. People will have a choice and I think they will return government to the people." And, of course, the Southerners felt strongly about "states' rights," a phrase which implied, but was by no means limited to, a status quo position in the area of civil rights.[2] Their principal spokesman in the coalition leadership was John Grenier. Grenier had considerable authority, but as executive director was as much occupied with organizational questions and tactical matters as with general questions of strategy.

The foreign policy experts attracted to Goldwater saw a politically divided planet: the free world led from Washington, the communist world from Moscow. These hard-liners did not agree that the bipolar postwar world had dissolved into a polynucleated system. They saw our most important duties to be strengthening ourselves and taking a firm stand against our enemy. Parallel to this concern with diametrically contending forces was a fascination with weaponry, an interest often found among men like Barry Goldwater whose military experience influences their foreign policy attitudes. The Senator's Air Force associates were represented in the policy group by Dale Smith, a retired general who worked with the speechwriters on mili-

[2] Bernard Cosman, "The Case of the Goldwater Delegates: Deep South Republican Leadership" (University of Alabama: Bureau of Public Administration, 1965), pp. 4–5, 19–20.

tary matters. Most of Goldwater's foreign policy statements came from Karl Hess, a writer who has consistently taken militant anti-communist positions, and from G. Warren Nutter, a University of Virginia economist who is a student of Soviet growth rates. W. Glenn Campbell, director of the Hoover Institution on War, Revolution and Peace, contributed a number of ideas, but was less inclined than the others to reduce complex international situations to questions of "us" and "them."

Quite a few members of the Goldwater coalition could be said to be "conservatives." Many of the businessmen there were attracted to the Goldwater cause because it appeared to offer a chance to strike a blow for free enterprise and the "American way of life." "This is the year we've been waiting for!" was a statement heard time and again at Republican headquarters during the early weeks of the campaign. Many of these businessmen were highly placed within the Goldwater organization. Retired General Electric President Ralph Cordiner was finance chairman and Wisconsin industrialist Wayne J. Hood was director of the campaign division. Cordiner was concerned with keeping the campaign on a pay-as-you-go basis and Hood was occupied with questions of campaign scheduling. As we have seen, both these activities had an obvious bearing on the execution of campaign strategy. But neither had much to do with shaping campaign speeches. Another consideration was that while many businessmen were dedicated to conservative principles, their ideas about what these principles implied were relatively vague. The campaign required speeches discussing conservatism in some detail. No matter how dedicated to "the American way of life," a candidate cannot spend half an hour on nationwide television reciting the Pledge of Allegiance. The real need was for conservative ideologists who could spell out programs which a Goldwater administration might follow.

A Washington, D. C., organization which had been devoting a good deal of attention to conservative policies was the American Enterprise Institute for Public Policy Research. Because the AEI had precisely the scarce talents required by the Goldwater campaign, many who had been connected with it in one way or another came to play important roles in shaping the Goldwater strategy. William J. Baroody took a leave of absence from the presidency of AEI during the campaign. Karl Hess,[3] already mentioned in

[3] Remember we are using group to mean a set of individuals characterized by a set of shared attitudes and a set of interacting behaviors. There were some persons (Karl Hess and Warren Nutter, for example) who were members of more than one such group.

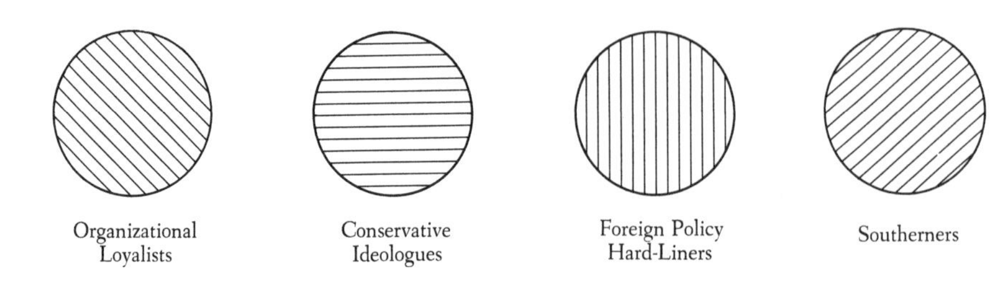

Figure 5 *Groups in the Goldwater Coalition*

connection with foreign policy, had been employed by AEI before he became the principal Goldwater speechwriter. Conservative intellectuals known to the AEI also played key roles. Charles Lichenstein, who had obtained a Master's Degree in political science at Yale and taught at Notre Dame before becoming a speechwriter for Vice President Nixon, was in charge of the day-to-day activities of the speechwriters in the research division. Scholars known to these principals, such as economist Warren Nutter, foundation official Richard Ware, and Claremont political theorist Harry Jaffa, came to Washington during the campaign. Others, such as University of Chicago economist Milton Friedman, contributed ideas from their home institutions. While these persons might quibble over the details of conservatism, they were in agreement in one important respect. This was that ideology was more important than winning. "The American people may decide to reject the conservative alternative," one conservative ideologue declared shortly before the Goldwater nomination, "but when this campaign is over, at least they're going to know what conservatism means!"

When one looks at the interplay among the attitudes of these four groups, the intersection was largest between the foreign policy hard-liners and the conservative ideologists. There was a smaller intersection between

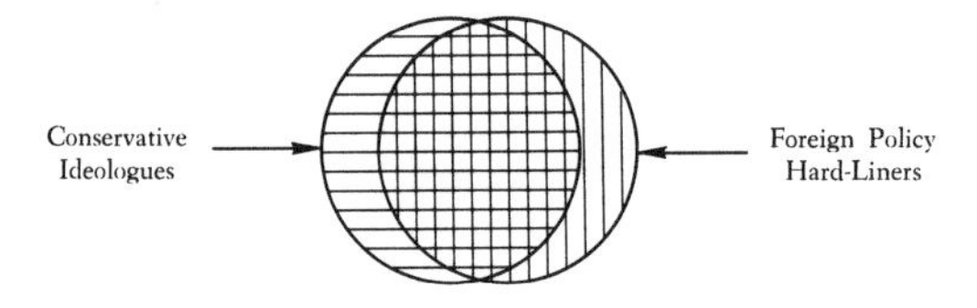

Figure 6 *A Union of Two Attitudes*

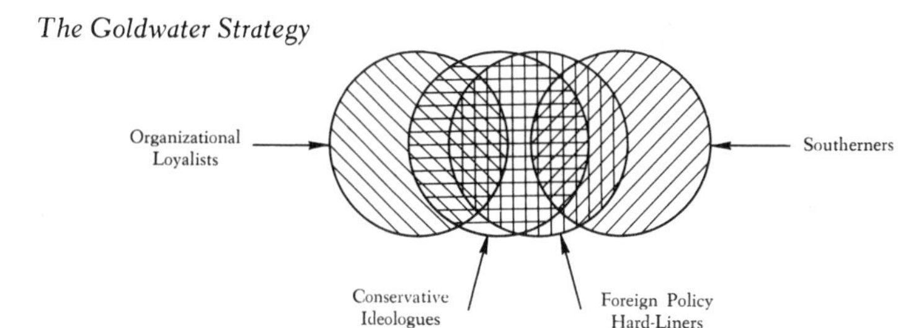

Figure 7 *The Goldwater Coalition*

these attitudes and those of the Southerners, who would have preferred a more conservative thrust, and between these central attitudes and those of the organizational loyalists, who would have preferred a more moderate strategy. Venn diagrams are helpful in visualizing a relationship such as this. In Figure 5, each circle represents a set of attitudes. There was substantial agreement between conservative ideologues and foreign policy hard-liners. Their attitudes were not identical. A tax cut advocated by conservative ideologues, for example, would have prevented acquisition of new weapons systems desired by the foreign policy hard-liners. A Venn diagram of their attitudes would look something like Figure 6.

The organizational loyalists and the Southerners both held certain attitudes in common with the conservative ideologues and the foreign policy hard-liners. For all practical purposes, though, the organizational loyalists and the Southerners did not have any interests in common with each other. So when one adds these sets of attitudes to the figure, it resembles Figure 7. This "picture" of the attitudes of the Goldwater coalition implies the strategy Goldwater would follow as the campaign developed. For reasons already discussed, the attitudes of groups within the Goldwater coalition were more important in determining strategy than was any perception of the voters' attitudes. Therefore, the core of the Goldwater strategy lay within the intersection of the attitudes of the Goldwater coalition shown in Figure 8. Occasionally, there occurred a departure from these central attitudes in order to

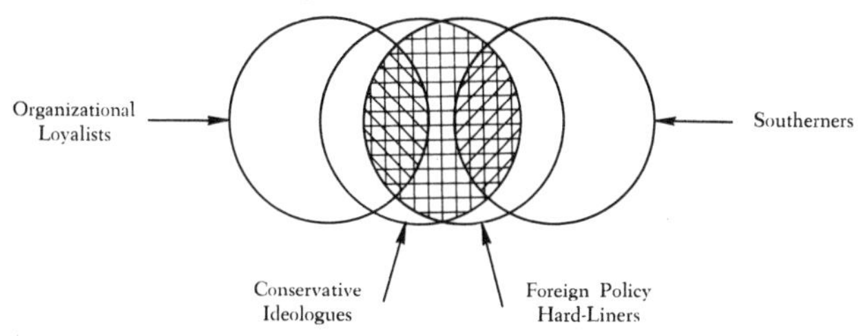

Figure 8 *Central Attitudes of the Goldwater Coalition*

respond to needs of one of the peripheral groups or the practical exigencies of the campaign.[4]

The first phase of the Goldwater strategy was impelled by the need to unite the party behind the nominee. The problem of party division, as has already been noted, was acute in 1964. The disputed sentences in Goldwater's acceptance speech, "Extremism in the defense of liberty is no vice. Moderation in the pursuit of justice is no virtue," even caused some delegates to leave the convention floor. They moved a political veteran to say: "It'll take a month to put this thing back together." The political veteran was right in his estimate of time. The first month of the campaign was devoted to healing wounds opened by these two sentences. It can be argued, however, that the outcry caused by these words was only symptomatic. The Goldwater leaders and the moderate Republicans never did learn to communicate with each other. To understand the events in this phase of the campaign, it is necessary to know something about the two groups' perceptions.[5]

For one thing, the moderate Republicans had expected the Goldwater leaders to proceed in a customary manner to restore party unity once the nomination had been settled. "We were ready," said one the morning after the acceptance speech. "Bill (Scranton) made his speech (Wednesday night in support of Goldwater), but they forgot to move Barry back to the center. I saw some delegates in tears!" Even more important, many of the

[4] Since each group in the coalition has a set of attitudes (both ideological and non-ideological), this analysis interprets coalition strategy as an n-dimensional problem rather than as a function of the distribution of groups along a single ideological dimension. The simpler model is used by Anthony Downs. See Downs' *Economic Theory of Democracy*, Chs. 8 and 9; Donald E. Stokes, "Spatial Models of Party Competition," in Campbell *et al*, *Elections and the Political Order*, Ch. 9; Philip E. Converse, "The Problem of Party Distances in Models of Voting Change," in Kent Jennings and Harmon Zeigler, eds., *The Electoral Process* (Englewood Cliffs, N.J.: Prentice-Hall, 1966), Ch. 9; John H. Kessel, "Some Non-Programmatic Dimensions of Parties" in *American Behavioral Scientist*, March, 1961, pp. 22–23.

[5] A good deal of analysis of international conflict is devoted to the actors' perception of the situation. See, for example, Dean G. Pruitt, "Definition of the Situation as a Determinant of International Action," and James A. Robinson and Richard C. Snyder, "Decision-Making in International Politics," in Herbert C. Kelman, ed., *International Behavior* (New York: Holt, Rinehart & Winston, 1965). Intra-party conflict, of course, has characteristics different from those of international conflict, but the actors' perceptions are central phenomena in both.

moderate Republicans knew they were in serious political trouble. A poll in one major eastern state, for example, projected a Goldwater vote of only 22 per cent. It indicated that a Republican senator facing a tough battle for re-election would lose 10 per cent of his support if he endorsed Barry Goldwater. These leaders were quite apprehensive about the possibility of a Goldwater campaign which would create greater difficulties for them. They could not fathom Goldwater's reasons for doing things that would cause them trouble.

For their part, the Goldwater leaders could not understand why moderate Republicans were reluctant to endorse the Arizona Senator. They had taken Goldwater's convention margin and the unanimous election of Dean Burch as national chairman to be indices of support for Goldwater within the Republican party. They were also mindful of Senator Goldwater's past campaign exertions for moderate Republicans. If Senator Goldwater had given speeches in their behalf, why were moderate Republicans now unwilling to return the courtesy? By and large unaware of the threat posed by the Goldwater candidacy to other Republicans, the Goldwater leaders saw the question as one of simple party loyalty. They failed to see any good reason why moderate Republicans should not be working hard for Goldwater. Given these perspectives, it was hard for the moderate Republicans to understand why Senator Goldwater had made his statement about extremism and moderation in the first place, and hard for the Goldwater leaders to understand the furor caused by the statement.

The organizational loyalists were in a key position to establish a link between the Arizonans around Goldwater and the moderate Republicans. They shared the attitudes most salient in the thinking of the other two groups. They knew the Goldwater nomination was going to cause political difficulty, but they also had a deeply ingrained sense of party loyalty. Therefore, they wanted to settle the dispute in a way which would mitigate the threat to other Republican candidates *and* reunite the party. This implied a strategy of running Goldwater along "normal Republican" lines.

Two ranking Republicans who were working to overcome the problems of party division were Dwight D. Eisenhower and Richard M. Nixon. For months, Eisenhower had been pursuing a course of neutrality among the rival aspirants in order to serve as a symbol of unity after the battle was over. One of Nixon's real skills had long been in stating an issue so as to maximize the number of groups to which it will be acceptable. So, on August 6, a meeting took place at Gettysburg between Eisenhower, Nixon, Goldwater, and vice-presidential candidate William Miller. Bryce Harlow, a former presidential assistant who still wrote many of Eisenhower's speeches, and Edward McCabe, Goldwater's research director who had also been on the Eisenhower White House staff, took notes.

The first product of this meeting was a reply to a Nixon letter giving Goldwater an opportunity to clarify the controversial passage in his acceptance speech. On August 4, Nixon had written:

Dear Barry:

Since our convention in San Francisco, I have received several inquiries as to the intended meaning of two sentences in your acceptance speech: "Extremism in the defense of liberty is no vice. Moderation in the pursuit of justice is no virtue."

The charge has been made that in using these phrases you were, in effect, approving political recklessness and unlawful activity in achieving the goals of freedom and justice.

When the two statements in question are read in the full context of your speech I feel certain this interpretation of your remarks is unwarranted. . . .

I have assured all of those who raised this question with me that you would be the first to reject the use of any illegal or improper methods to achieve the great goals of liberty and justice we all seek.

I believe, however, that it would be most helpful to clear the air once and for all in this regard, and I would appreciate it if you would send me any further comments you may wish to make with regard to the intended meaning of these two sentences. . . .

Sincerely,
Richard M. Nixon

On August 7, Goldwater replied.

Dear Dick:

Your letter concerning the two sentences in my acceptance speech which have occasioned so much comment is most welcome. Misunderstandings must not be permitted to stand in the way of the unity of principle and purpose that is essential to a Republican victory in November.

During these past weeks much has been said about the "context" in which these two sentences were used. It is, therefore, essential that the context of my remarks be correctly identified. . . .

One portion of that correct context . . . was the paragraph immediately preceding the two sentences in question. In it I urged that we resist becoming captives of "unthinkable labels." . . . I was urging, in effect, that we understand and view the great problems of the day in their essence and not be diverted by glib political catch words. In that context the sentences that followed were but examples. . . .

They were examples, chosen consciously and deliberately, because of another portion of the correct context, namely, that of the whole body of my acceptance speech. This was a speech of affirmation of certain great principles: the principle of constitutionalism, the principle of ordered freedom, the principle of equal justice under and within the encompassing framework of law. We may implement these principles, in the practicalities of day to day affairs, either well or badly—but we must affirm them unreservedly. . . .

If I were to paraphrase the two sentences in question in the context in which I uttered them I would do it by saying that whole-hearted devotion to liberty is unassailable and that half-hearted devotion to justice is indefensible. . . .

Sincerely,

Barry Goldwater

While this balm was being applied to the immediate cause of difficulty between the moderate Republicans and the "Arizona Mafia," McCabe was working out an even more important statement for Goldwater. A unity conference had been summoned to meet at Hershey, Pa. on August 12. The invitation list included Eisenhower, Nixon, Goldwater and his ranking advisers, and the most important group of moderate Republicans in the country, the Republican governors and gubernatorial candidates. The Republican governors had been trying to obtain an acceptable statement of Goldwater policy ever since the Senator's victory in the California primary. Now, thanks to the efforts of Dwight Eisenhower, they were about to get it.

The Goldwater "remarks" dealt specifically with three subjects which had been quite controversial in San Francisco: foreign policy, civil rights, and extremism. Goldwater-Miller foreign policy was pictured as a continuation of Eisenhower's.

The Republican party is . . . the Party of Peace. We don't claim the Democrats are a war party. But America might well question the caliber of leadership which has blundered into three wars in my lifetime. . . . That same leadership demonstrates today, in the wake of Laos, Viet Nam and the Bay of Pigs that . . . it understands far too little now about leading the Free World in the cause of peace. . . .

> We will hear over and over again until November such words as "impulsive," "trigger-happy," "imprudent," "hip-shooting," and the like. . . . Was there anything "impulsive" or "imprudent" about Dwight Eisenhower when he moved with firmness and clear purpose in Lebanon and the Formosa Straits? Compare the Eisenhower-Dulles policies in those situations with the appalling actions of this administration in such places as Laos and the Bay of Pigs. I have said, and will continue to say, that a Goldwater-Miller Administration will mean an immediate return to the proven Eisenhower-Dulles policy of Peace through Strength.

The comments on civil rights were calculated to place Republican platform pledges in a positive light. They had been regarded by those who drafted them as fairly strong pledges in the first place. Goldwater's comments brought this out.

> A Goldwater-Miller Administration pledges, in the literal wording of the President's Oath of Office "faithful execution" of the 1964 Civil Rights law, and all other civil rights laws. This solemn pledge for full implementation is included in our 1964 Platform. For myself, I reject any suggestion that I would do otherwise based on my individual vote as a Senator when the 1964 Act was approved by the Senate. Further I say to you—as I have also said in every corner of the land throughout this campaign—that I will use the great moral influence of the Presidency to promote prompt and peaceful observance of civil rights laws.

And there was a rejection of extremist groups by name—a step the Republican platform committee had been unwilling to take. The John Birch Society was not mentioned because it was not on the Attorney General's subversive list, but Goldwater did attack two of the three extremist organizations condemned by Governor Mark Hatfield in his keynote speech at San Francisco.

> Let me reiterate what I have said over and over in this campaign: I seek the support of no extremist—of the left or of the right. I have far too much faith in the good sense and stability of my fellow Republicans to be impressed by talk of a so-called "extremist takeover" of the Party. Such a thing cannot happen under Bill Miller and me. We repudiate character assassins, vigilantes, communists, and any group such as the Ku Klux Klan that seeks to impose its views through terror or violence.

Elsewhere in the speech Goldwater made comments in favor of social security and the United Nations, two other topics on which he had taken stands disturbing to moderate Republicans.

When the unity conference assembled, former President Eisenhower made it clear that Senator Goldwater had given satisfactory answers to the questions Eisenhower had put to him. He invited others to bring up the matters troubling them.[6]

> I think I have had more experience than most people in organizing groups that were made up of disparate types and sometimes of different nationalities. And I just know this: It's got to be done on the basis of honest conciliation of views. We do have different views on details sometimes, and sometimes on something a little deeper. But let's bring them out and see whether there isn't an honest answer that all of us can support, and do it with all the might and energy which the Good Lord gave us.

Problems were brought up for discussion. How were the militant conservatives who had worked for Goldwater's nomination going to be integrated into the campaign so they wouldn't be a threat to existing county chairmen? How were Republicans who disapproved of Goldwater going to be persuaded not to bolt the party? How was the farm issue going to be handled? Nelson Rockefeller, William Scranton, Charles Percy, and George Romney all spoke about the issues causing trouble in industrial states. Some of the exchanges dealt with central questions with unvarnished candor. Governor Romney, for example, was concerned about civil rights: "All I am trying to indicate is that as far as I can determine, people are concerned about whether this is a racist campaign, and that this point has to be dealt with and dealt with effectively." In reply Senator Goldwater said: ". . . I will promise you with every degree of seriousness and strength that I have that I will never talk about racism. . . . I am scared to death of it. I know your big cities in the Northeast and the Middle West—not only on the West Coast—are just tinderboxes, and I'll be darned if I will have my grandchildren accuse their grandfather of setting fire to them."

Such answers satisfied most of the participants. "I had some reservations about Senator Goldwater when I came in here," declared one conferee, "but I don't now." "It was just like we had the Tuesday night balloting (on the platform amendments at San Francisco) all over again," recalled another. "The only difference was that this time we won." Governor Scranton told the Goldwater leaders he would devote ten to twelve days to campaigning for Goldwater. Richard Nixon said he would spend five weeks on the hustings. And Dwight Eisenhower indicated a willingness to address several meetings.

[6] A transcript of the unity conference has been published in the appendix of Karl Hess, *In A Cause That Will Triumph* (Garden City, New York: Doubleday, 1967).

This Goldwater strategy of emphasizing aspects of his policies pleasing to moderate Republicans ended as soon as a reporter asked Goldwater his first question at a press conference that afternoon. Did he regard his speech as conciliatory? "No," the Senator replied to the astonishment of those who regarded the central purpose of the unity conference as conciliation. "I merely consider it as an expression of my positions that I've had, some of them for years, some of them not for years, but this is no conciliatory speech at all." Part of the reason for this answer was Goldwater's resistance to anyone who suggests he is not steadfast to his principles, but there was more to it than that. The political weakness of the Goldwater candidacy was so important in the thinking of the moderate Republicans that they believed Goldwater finally understood the danger of a "truly conservative" campaign. Goldwater and his advisers, however, saw the event only as a necessary exercise to unify the party, not a fundamental modification of strategy. Discussing the meeting at a Congressional campaign school a few days earlier, National Chairman Dean Burch had said: "It will be short and—we hope—sweet. (Afterward) we will have established unity in the party." In other words, the Goldwater core group did not see the Hershey conference as the beginning of the campaign, but rather as a prelude to the campaign. And the strategy of the campaign to come was to be dominated by the central attitudes of the Goldwater coalition, not by the views of the organizational loyalists.

Other Goldwater speeches were heard during the month of August. On August 10, he told the National Association of Counties that "at the very heart of the domestic difference between the two great American parties is their performance in regard to local governments." Nine days later, he told those attending the Illinois State Fair that "there is a mood of easy morals and uneasy ethics that is an aching truth in our land. And no one in a position to set the examples that might set this right can avoid the responsibility for what is wrong." Attacking the public announcement that American planes would retaliate for the attack on the destroyer *Maddox*, Senator Goldwater denounced "the administration and its civilian generals, such as Field Marshal McNamara (who) take full credit for this remarkable strategy of warning our enemy that our planes were on their way." Remarks on the Senate floor on August 21 were released calling attention to Senator Goldwater's vote for expansion of social security benefits. And, on August 25, he suggested to the Veterans of Foreign Wars meeting in Cleveland "that a way be developed to provide NATO with its own stock of small, tactical, nuclear battlefield weapons—what may truly be called *conventional* nuclear weapons." These were all typical Goldwater statements. In many respects, they presaged themes to be developed later. But they were "occasional speeches"—not part of an integrated strategy.

The general planning of campaign strategy had been attended to immediately after the Republican convention. Denison Kitchel had met with Dean Burch, Edward McCabe, Tony Smith, Lou Guylay, Peter O'Donnell, John Grenier, and Miller advisers William Warner and Robert Smalley to chart campaign strategy. As they saw things, little campaigning would be necessary to win votes in the South because of the natural conservatism of the area. No amount of campaigning, on the other hand, could win electoral votes in New England and on the East Coast. Therefore, the campaign should be directed to the Midwest and the West. In terms of electoral college arithmetic, this meant the large votes of New York and Pennsylvania were being written off as hopeless. Emphasis was to be placed on building support in Ohio, Indiana, Illinois, Texas, and California.

The strategists also decided it was to be a campaign of ideas. Several major speeches were to be given. Each one would outline Goldwater's thinking in detail on some topic. Beyond this, Kitchel and his associates planned to get general guidelines from surveys being undertaken by the Opinion Research Corporation.[7] When their data first became available in mid-August, there was one bit of information of particular interest to the Goldwater strategists. This was that 41 per cent of the American public regard themselves as conservative, 31 per cent as liberal, and 28 per cent as somewhere in between. Furthermore, 65 per cent of the Republican respondents classified themselves as conservative and 41 per cent of the Independents did so. This Goldwater and his advisers regarded as confirming their idea that a conservative campaign could be successful.[8] So the general strategy called for a conservative appeal to the Midwest and West.

The speech which inaugurated this strategy was made on September 3 in Prescott, Arizona, in the same Court House Square where Goldwater had begun two earlier campaigns. After some opening words about the im-

[7] This is a Princeton, New Jersey firm founded by the late Claude Robinson. It has worked closely with Republicans for many years.

[8] An estimate implicit in these same data is that if one takes *all* the Republicans and Independents who consider themselves to be conservatives or "in between," one arrives at a total of 41 per cent of the electorate. This was *not* called to the attention of the Goldwater strategists.

portance of the occasion and the consequences of the choice to be made in November, the Senator stated his theme:

The campaign we launch today is dedicated to peace, to progress, and to purpose. . . .

When we speak of these things we mean something far different from the opposition party. *We* mean:

—Peace *through preparedness*

—Progress *through freedom*

—Purpose through *Constitutional* order

These are the themes that we shall make resound across this great land of ours, and across an anxious, troubled, and listening world.

Here, stated as the central themes of the campaign, were the central attitudes of the Goldwater coalition: a resolute foreign policy with an emphasis on military preparedness and a domestic conservatism stressing free enterprise and law and order.

As the speech progressed, each of the three themes was discussed. Foreign policy came first.

We are preoccupied with peace! And we are fearful that this administration is letting the peace slip away, as it has slipped three times since 1914, by pretending that there are no threats to it. I am trying to carry to the American people this plain message: this entire nation and the entire world risk war in our time *unless* free men remain strong enough to keep the peace.

Republicans, the Senator said, understood the nature of the communist enemy, and understood that the military needed flexible, balanced weapon systems manned by trained volunteers. For this reason, Republicans would end the draft (a promise which generated more headlines than anything else in the address).

Turning to his second theme, progress through freedom, Senator Goldwater balanced a pledge of ending governmental regulation of economic affairs with a promise that the transition would not be too precipitous.

This country has grown great and strong and prosperous by placing major reliance on a free economy. What we have we owe to the ceaseless strivings of tens of millions of free men to better their own condition and to provide a better future for their children and their children's children.

Increasingly . . . government has been absorbing or controlling more and more of our resources, our energy, and our ambition. . . . This cancerous growth . . . must and shall be stopped. . . . (But) prudence requires that we proceed slowly and steadily in withdrawing the central government from its many unwarranted interventions in our private economic lives. Only so can the private economy adjust smoothly to its properly broadened tasks. . . .

Among things which could be given immediate attention by the government were a cut in government spending, fostering an economy that would provide millions of new jobs, and due attention to the problems of the needy and the aged.

Near the conclusion of his speech, Senator Goldwater dealt with his third theme, the concentration of power in the federal government as a threat to purpose and order in our society.

The leadership of this present administration . . . becomes the natural ally of the result reached by the use of power. . . . To a constitutionalist, it is at late power, and grow rich from power. . . . Facing the power seekers is the lone man, the citizen, the forgotten man whose rights our government was designed to make secure.

Because those who held high office had not exhibited high moral purpose, he argued, there was crime in the streets.

When men use political advantage for personal gain, we can understand the decline of moral strength generally. It is a responsibility of the national leadership, regardless of political gain, political faction, or political popularity to encourage every community in this nation to enforce the law, not let it be abused or ignored.

Having launched his campaign in his native state, Senator Goldwater began his first full week of campaigning on September 8 in California. After a luncheon speech in San Diego, he headed for Los Angeles. Here was the city which had played a crucial role in his June primary triumph, and here, before 53,000 of the faithful assembled in Dodger Stadium, Barry Goldwater delivered the first of the projected speeches spelling out his views on particular subjects. His topic of the evening was tax revenue. He presented a plan developed for him by conservative economists Milton Friedman and Warren Nutter. It was based on an assumption that growth in the gross national product would produce a disposable tax surplus in the foreseeable future.

I will, as one of my first actions in the White House, ask the Congress to enact a regular and considered program of tax reduction. . . . . That reduction would represent part of the increase in revenues that our growing economy is producing. The balance of that increase would be used to eliminate our present deficit, to cut nuisance taxes imposed on so many things you buy, and to reduce the debt. The legislation for which I will ask would provide an across-the-board reduction of five per cent per year in all income taxes—both individual and corporate. . . . [This] is not the impulsive, massive, politically motivated tax cut gimmickry we have seen employed by the present administration.

The proposed 5 per cent cut was to be a cut in the amount of tax due each year, it was explained, not a 5 per cent cut in the tax rate. Shortly afterward, Milton Friedman publicly stated his belief that, win or lose, the Goldwater candidacy was bound to advance the conservative cause.

In mid-week, the campaign headed north to Seattle, where Goldwater attacked the administration's handling of the Bay of Pigs, the Cuban missile crisis, the Berlin Wall, Laos and Vietnam, then east to Minneapolis for a speech on the increase in crime which charged that Washington, D. C., had become "a city embattled, plagued by lawlessness, haunted by fears." On Friday, the campaign jet turned south once more. Goldwater headed for Illinois, another of the big states he had to carry.

The American Political Science Association was meeting in Chicago at the time, and, because this group was professionally concerned with the problems of government, the Goldwater strategists had decided that this audience would hear a major speech. The topic was constitutional philosophy. The Senator sought to explain why he opposed the trend toward strong legislatures, strong executives, and strong courts.

Some of the current worship of powerful executives may come from those who admire strength and accomplishment of any sort. Others hail the display of Presidential strength, or judicial strength . . . simply because they approve of the result reached by the use of power. . . . To a constitutionalist, it is at least as important that the use of power be legitimate as that it be beneficial. . . . To me, the political heroes of this nation . . . are those who refrained from power when they doubted the legitimacy of its exercise.

Goldwater dealt at greatest length with what he regarded as arrogations of power by the Supreme Court.

I weigh my words carefully when I say that . . . today's Supreme Court is the least faithful to the constitutional tradition of limited government, and to the principle of legitimacy in the exercise of government.

He went on to say that there had been only the most limited effort to defend the Court decisions about school prayers and reapportionment on grounds that they were within the intent of the framers of the Fourteenth

Amendment. Instead they were said to be desirable. This, said Goldwater, was "raw and naked power." Lawyer Denison Kitchel regarded this discussion of constitutional principles as "the most exciting thing we've done in the campaign so far."

The following weeks the Senator headed for eight Southern states[9] in his longest foray south of the Mason-Dixon line during the campaign. This region presented a problem. The Southern electoral votes were absolutely essential to Goldwater's chances, and the possibility of his getting them would be enhanced if the Democratic state organizations did not work too hard. Therefore Goldwater preferred to have Southern Republicans concentrate on the presidential election. The ambitious young Southerners, however, were determined to build local Republican parties. This meant running local candidates to take advantage of the conservative thrust of the 1964 campaign—and this activity was precisely what might stir dormant Democratic organizations to life. This provides a good illustration of the general situation in which the attitudes of one member group do not fully coincide with the central attitudes of the coalition. There was tension because of conflicting attitudes, in this case the higher Southern priority on local races and the greater coalition interest in getting electoral votes for the presidential candidate. At the same time, there were enough attitudes shared by group leaders and coalition leaders, such as the desirability of a vigorous presentation of the conservative case, to ensure that the Southerners would provide a warm welcome for Senator Goldwater when he came to their states.

The most important political event of the week was the party switch of Senator Strom Thurmond. Speaking to a statewide television audience, Senator Thurmond said:

> The Democratic Party has turned its back on the spiritual values and political principles which have brought us the blessings of freedom under God and a bountiful prosperity. . . . It is leading the evolution of our nation to a socialistic dictatorship. . . . I cannot foretell what success will reward Senator Barry Goldwater's efforts to return the National Government to its Constitutional role and our nation to its rightful place of strength and respect in the world. . . . But I do know that we have a fighting chance under Barry Goldwater's leadership and that we are welcomed to his banner.

[9] He did not campaign in Virginia or Mississippi. Goldwater felt that Senator Byrd's silence about supporting either presidential candidate might speak more eloquently to the voters if he stayed out of the Old Dominion and he did not wish to become involved in the turmoil of Mississippi.

Hopes were expressed that Senator Thurmond's switch would be the first of many, and his speech was given wide distribution throughout the South. But a speech given by Senator Goldwater the same day, September 16, was more important to the strategy of having the Arizonan spell out what he meant by conservatism. In Montgomery, Alabama, he turned again to the possibility that growth in the economy would produce a disposable surplus. This time, he linked it to a possibility of reform in the federal system.

> Over the years, state and local government have become increasingly dominated by the ever-growing system of so-called Federal grants-in-aid. There are now over a hundred such programs totalling over $10 billion in annual Federal spending. They cover every major activity of state and local governments. In this way, these governments have been made subservient to a huge Federal bureaucracy with its center in the White House. . . . We must bring government back closer to the people. And a Republican Administration will do just that. . . . Because of existing commitments, we cannot do this overnight. But we can gradually replace this undesirable and complex system with a much simpler and more sensible one. The Federal government . . . should return to the states a share of the income taxes collected from them, and permit a greater credit on estate taxes. . . . Such a system of unconditional grants—*in place of the present programmatic grants*—would give each state needed resources for use within the state, free of control by the Federal bureaucracy.

Goldwater's speeches elsewhere in the South that week illustrate some important characteristics of his campaign as it was developing. One was redundancy. In almost every speech, he was repeating large portions of previous speeches. The Montgomery speech, for instance, used material from the Prescott address on ending the draft and repeated most of what had been said in Los Angeles about a disposable surplus and income tax reduction before it took up the new point about block grants to the states. Material from the Minneapolis speech about rising crime rates was repeated in St. Petersburg, Florida, and almost the entire Chicago speech attacking the Supreme Court was given again in Charlotte, North Carolina. There are two reasons for this redundancy. One is that speechwriters have only so many fresh ideas and can produce only so many stirring phrases amidst the hubbub of a campaign. Therefore a campaign must imitate a television network and rely on a certain number of "summer re-runs." The other cause of redundancy is that a candidate must repeat himself if he is going to be heard at all. A political campaign is a classic example of a "noisy channel." A presidential candidate is competing with his rival, with the World Series, with dramatic foreign events, and a host of other things in an attempt to capture the attention of preoccupied and often apathetic citizens. It is a very boring thing for a presidential candidate (not to mention those traveling with him) to say the same thing over and over and over. But this is often the only way communication can be achieved.[10]

Another characteristic of the Goldwater strategy that became obvious while the candidate was in the South was the deliberate choice of "unsympathetic" audiences. He criticized the Supreme Court on reapportionment in Atlanta, a city long hostage to rural Georgia because of the county-unit system of voting. Speaking in Knoxville, Tennessee, he alluded to his suggestion that the government sell the TVA by saying this was up to Congress, but "what I said with respect to TVA is within the general framework of (a private enterprise) philosophy, and I stand by it." And he went to Charleston, West Virginia, near the heart of Appalachia, to tell the voters that the war on poverty was "as phony as a three dollar bill." These statements left some veteran political observers in a state of bewilderment, but they were not accidental. To paraphrase Marshall McLuhan, the place was the message. These were statements which reflected the central attitudes of the Goldwater coalition. But uttering them where they would be sure to cause comment, the Senator hoped to emphasize his own courage and candor. But, beyond that, he was saying that his ideology was more important to him than winning the election. Here were his thoughts. If the voters agreed with these thoughts, they could vote for him. If not, they were still his thoughts.

A speech which underscored this supremacy of ideology first, regardless of the political consequences, was given to the National Plowing Contest at Fargo, North Dakota. On the border between the Midwest and the West, his major political targets, he did not pledge his administration to support farm income. Instead, he called for a gradual reduction of farm supports, something which would be good for the farmers.

> Farm income certainly should be improved. But the question is—how should it be improved? By arbitrary handouts subject to the whim and caprice of an arbitrary farm boss in direct contact with the dealer in the White House? Or by the healthy and fair forces of flourishing and expanding mar-

[10] Redundancy complicates the problems of the analyst. The selective method being used here does not indicate how often a particular message has been transmitted. On the other hand, a formal content analysis of everything said in the campaign does not discriminate between the more important items and those which are necessary "filler."

kets? There is no doubt what your answer will be. It will be the same as mine and Bill Miller's. . . . Bill Miller and I will stop this bureaucratic meddling in your private affairs.

And with that, he concluded his discussion of agricultural policy and switched over to a discussion of foreign affairs.

As the Senator's plane headed away from North Dakota, however, this second phase of his campaign was already almost over. It did not formally end at a given hour on a given day, but there were difficulties which were causing the strategists to recast their thinking. One was the tone of the Johnson campaign. In its eagerness to present the electorate with a real choice, the Goldwater core group has assumed that if Senator Goldwater presented his views in detail, President Johnson would indicate his opinions on the same subjects and thus the issues would be joined between them. Lyndon Johnson, however did not respond in the manner they had anticipated. His statements were very general and on topics of *his* choosing. Rejoinders to Goldwater came from lower-ranking aides. Goldwater's public comments on this reflected his strategists' private frustration.

You have heard me discuss many things in this campaign, all important. You have not heard my opponent discuss anything at all. We are both running for the Presidency of the United States. We are both running for the first time. Yet he will not face the issues, he will not face me—he will not face *you*. . . . We keep hearing that the White House announces something or that the Pentagon says such-and-such. The Pentagon talks so much that I've suggested that it be given a name—like Peter Pentagon. It is an interesting thing, a building with five sides and a hole in the middle. Apparently, it can talk. Can my opponent talk? What does my opponent have to say? . . . I demand of him—debate!

The other difficulty was that Goldwater was not catching up with his rival. His private polls said much the same thing as did the public polls.[11] Two issues in particular struck his advisers as troublesome: nuclear responsibility and social security. Mid-September polls showed that 57 per cent of the respondents thought Johnson would do better in handling nuclear weapons, 13 per cent thought Goldwater would do better, and 30 per cent saw no dif-

[11] This does *not* mean that Goldwater and his advisers regarded polls as vital information. Survey information was taken into account, but was regarded simply as one more source of intelligence about the campaign. "I didn't need a poll to tell me social security was causing trouble," was a typical statement. Polling was cancelled by Dean Burch in mid-October.

ference or had no opinion. On the question of improving social security, 63 per cent thought Johnson would do a better job, while only 10 per cent thought Goldwater would do a better job. As Table III shows, even Republicans lacked confidence in Goldwater's ability to handle these matters.[12] No set of political strategists could come up with an easy answer about how the candidate of a minority party ought to handle issues on which he does not have even the support of his own partisans. One alternative favored by Lou Guylay was for Goldwater to remain silent on these matters while concentrating on issues more favorable to him. Strategists closer to the center of the Goldwater coalition, however, felt that these issues were hurting so badly that some answer had to be given to them. So, after a brief first phase emphasizing reconciliation with the moderate Republicans and a longer second phase attempting to spell out the meaning of conservatism, the Goldwater campaign entered a third, essentially defensive, phase. The major concern during this phase was clarifying the Senator's stand on nuclear responsibility.

If a time can be assigned to the beginning of this defensive phase of the campaign, it was at 9:30 p.m. on Friday, September 18. This was the hour that Barry Goldwater's first half-hour address was shown on nation-

Table III *September Survey Data*

	Type of Respondent		
Answer	Democrat	Independent	Republican
Who would do a better job of keeping the peace?			
Johnson	71%	54%	35%
Goldwater	4	14	32
No difference, no opinion	25	32	33
Who would do a better job of handling social security?			
Johnson	76%	61%	41%
Goldwater	4	9	23
No difference, no opinion	20	30	36

Source: Opinion Research Corporation Poll, September 15, 1964.

[12] A more general foreign policy question is used in Table III, but the point is the same.

wide television.[13] He had barely said good evening before he got to the business at hand.

> Before this half-hour is over, you will know exactly where I stand regarding the most important problem in the world today. And that problem is *peace*, peace for you and your children, and peace in a world in which free people and free nations can live the kind of lives they choose for themselves.

If he talked about arms, the Senator said, it was because in a world threatened by communism, the only realistic policy was peace through preparedness.

> The Republican Party is the party of peace—because we understand the requirements of peace, *and because we understand the enemy*. We know he'll run risks, take advantage, push and prod for openings, the minute he spots a weakness. . . . He's the schoolyard bully. . . . Let him push you around and eventually you'll have to fight. Just stand up to him, though, . . . and he'll back down and there will be no fight. . . .
>
> If our role is to be the guardian of the peace and the leader of the free world—then to fulfill that great role, we must be strong. And we must remain strong. And this is the whole point of all that I have been saying, and all that I have been writing, in all my campaigning through the years.

The speech closed with words to the same effect by Winston Churchill—spoken in 1938.

The following Tuesday, another nationwide television show was presented. This time it was "Conversation at Gettysburg," a dialogue between Barry Goldwater and Dwight Eisenhower filmed on the General's farm.[14] At the end of the half-hour, the Senator mentioned that "our opponents are referring to us as warmongers," and asked the General's opinion.

> Well, Barry, in my mind this is actual tommyrot. Now, you've known about war, you've been through one. I'm older than you, I've been in more. But, I tell you, no man who knows anything about war is going to be reckless about it. Now, certainly the country recognizes in you a man of integrity, good will, honesty and dedication to his country. You're not going to be doing these things—what do they call it—push the button? I can't imagine anything you

[13] The decision to use half-hours of television rather than a much greater number of short spots reflected Kitchel's belief that the Goldwater personality needed the longer time period to come through to the viewer.

[14] The Trendex ratings, incidentally, were 25.1 for "Peyton Place," 19.6 for "Petticoat Junction," and 6.5 for "Conversation at Gettysburg." This led an all too short-lived television program, "This Was the Week That Was," to "quote" Senator Goldwater as saying, "Gettysburg is a nice place to visit, but I wouldn't want to live there."

would give more careful thought to than the President's responsibility as the Commander-in-Chief of all our armed forces, and as the man conducting our foreign relations. I am sure that with this kind of an approach you will be successful in keeping us on the road to peace.

On Thursday, September 24, National Chairman Dean Burch delivered a carefully drafted speech before the National Press Club in Washington. He said that the "nuclear thing" seemed to have become the basis for the entire Democratic campaign, and that responsible handling of this issue was a challenge to the Fourth Estate. Burch's speech handled the problem of Senator Goldwater's varying statements on the matter by referring to an "official statement" and a "definitive article" which said that the Supreme Commander of NATO ought to have authority over tactical nuclear forces. Burch then turned to the Democratic use of the issue.

> On July 25th . . . President Johnson was asked about Senator Goldwater's proposal to give the NATO commander greater latitude in nuclear control. Johnson responded that "I believe that the final responsibility for all decisions on nuclear weapons must rest with the civilian head of this Government, the President of the United States." There is a difference between "responsibility" and delegation of authority. Senator Goldwater has never suggested relinquishing responsibility. Anyone familiar with organizational precepts recognizes the difference between these two terms.

The address then went ahead to call the journalists' attention to the difference between what Democrats were saying and articles in *U. S. News and World Report* and *Time.*

The two-page piece in *U. S. News,* based on interviews with "military men," tended to support the Arizona Senator.

> Some military men say that . . . it will be found that the Administration and Senator Goldwater were actually not far apart at the time the issue was first brought up in the campaign. . . . Military men say they are dismayed by (the) kind of "fact(s)" produced by political appointees in the Pentagon. . . . What the Administration has done—military men assert— . . . not only confuses, but frightens people.[15]

The cover story in *Time* faulted both candidates for their handling of the issue, but did say:

> Johnson lets on that he can't and won't (delegate such authority). The fact is that he already has and does, as did Presidents Eisenhower and Kennedy before him.[16]

[15] *U. S. News and World Report,* September 28, 1964, pp. 49–50.
[16] *Time,* September 25, 1964, pp. 15–19.

Other Republican voices joined the swelling chorus. On Capitol Hill, the joint Senate-House Republican leadership issued a call to President Johnson to tell the American people the truth about the allegations in the two magazine articles. Ten days after that, a "Task Force on Peace and Preparedness" headed by former Defense Secretary Neil McElroy said that recent actions by the Administration had undermined the confidence of our NATO allies. Richard Nixon announced his agreement with the Task Force report. He said that Presidents Eisenhower and Kennedy had both given the NATO commander the right to use tactical nuclear weapons under clearly specified conditions, and "if President Johnson has changed this policy he should inform the American people."

While all this attention was being lavished on "the nuclear thing," relatively little concern was being devoted to social security. One pamphlet containing the remarks made on the Senate floor in August was prepared, but otherwise this issue was not featured any more prominently in campaign material than a good many other topics. The Goldwater position was outlined in a radio spot announcement, but the same tape also contained Goldwater statements on freedom, disarmament, foreign aid, fiscal policy, peace, and the administration. A voter who happened to lay hands on a campaign pamphlet such as "Meet Barry Goldwater" or "Where He Stands" could thumb through and find the Goldwater position.

> I favor a sound Social Security system and I want to see it strengthened. I have always voted for improvement in the system. I want to see every participant receive all the benefits the system provides. And I want to see these benefits paid in dollars with real purchasing power.

With social security mentioned in the small type of campaign pamphlets and nuclear responsibility splashed across the cover of *Time*, it seems unlikely that the domestic issue came to the attention of as many people as did the foreign topic.[17]

It was not until early October that Barry Goldwater made any major statement on social security. He was handed an opportunity when a bill expanding social security benefits died in conference committee.[18] The Senator

[17] More material devoted to Goldwater's social security position was ultimately prepared, but not until very late in the campaign. Full-page advertisements were placed in newspapers on Sunday, November 1.

[18] The House conferees voted 3–2 against accepting any social security bill with medicare; the Senate conferees voted 4–2 against accepting any social security bill without some kind of health care provision.

had spent the week on a campaign train chuffing across the key states of Ohio, Indiana, and Illinois. Daytime whistle-stops alternated with nighttime rallies in such cities as Cincinnati and Toledo. When the campaign train reached Moline, Illinois, on October 3, Senator Goldwater assailed the President for

> . . . denying retired and disabled breadwinners a cost-of-living increase in their benefits that is only fair and just. He is denying widows and surviving children the same cost-of-living increase.

Pointing out that he had voted for expanding social security benefits—as he had voted for broadening coverage in 1954, 1956, 1958, and 1961—the Senator charged that the Administration was putting politics ahead of the needs of social security recipients.

> Now you know who the friends of Social Security are—and you know why. Now you know who the enemies of social security are—and you know why.

During this defensive phase of the campaign, members of the Goldwater coalition were becoming increasingly critical of campaign strategy. The common element in the criticism was that Goldwater was not coming across, but the exact complaint depended on the point of view of the particular group. The organizational loyalists were deeply disturbed by reports from trusted sources about the lack of progress in the campaign, and were apprehensive about how much this ideological binge would eventually cost the party. The Southerners were disturbed that civil rights had not been given greater prominence in the campaign. Conservative ideologues were unhappy that Senator Goldwater did not have the quality of mind to mount a sustained, coherent critique of liberal practices, while others saw the conservative ideologues as a tight clique who had cut the Senator off from better sources of advice. With this restiveness, some kind of change in strategy was highly probable. Actually, it had already been decided that Senator Goldwater should switch back to the offensive in his speech Tuesday, September 29 at the Cincinnati Gardens. The audience was right, but national television time could not be booked. Consequently, the shift back to the offense was delayed. As one strategist recalled:

> This was why we were getting all the criticism about no content to the Senator's speeches. The timing of the criticism was right—it came when we were ready to make the switch. But we were hung up for about a week.

One formal statement of the strategy of this new phase of the campaign is to be found in "Operation Home Stretch: A Public Relations Strategy," drafted by Lou Guylay. This seven-page campaign plan was not formally approved by the strategy committee until October 11, but it represented Guylay's thinking during this period. In his opinion, the way to respond to the Democratic advantage on nuclear responsibility and social security was not to answer directly. A direct answer would only focus attention on disadvantageous issues. Instead, an "override issue"—one which would divert the voters' attention—was needed. "Operation Home Stretch" was the attempt of an organizational loyalist to formulate an override strategy acceptable to the Goldwater coalition.

> Brief—concise—the summation of our case. We charge the Administration has let the people down. We had great promises in '60 but they have not been kept.
>
> 1. Instead, we have seen a shocking decline in political morality—moral decay—a national disgrace.
>
> 2. This has led to crime and violence on the street—a breakdown of law and order—terrorizing our people.
>
> 3. Meanwhile in the world arena we have weakened ourselves and permitted our enemy to make gains all over. Our alliances are failing—the war in Vietnam persists. Cuba is a cancer spreading its poison throughout the Americas—and the Johnson administration plays politics with our defenses. Communism is on the march and the Johnson Administration flounders.
>
> 4. And finally, our national leadership has failed to inspire us or the world. Is Johnson a true national or world leader? Or is he a selfish politician more interested in buying votes than in the welfare of our people and the future of the country. He is a wheeler-dealer not a leader. And his running mate is a creature of the ADA which has goals dangerous to our best interests.
>
> Let's get rid of the wheeler-dealers and put conscience back in government.

Next came the positive side. The key here was to tie the Senator's statements to the theme of "Our Hope for a New America."

> America is aware of the failures of the past four years.
>
> We are all *concerned* about it. We *promise* to do something about this and we hold out *hope* for a new America.
>
> The formula is there:
>
> 1. Awareness
> 2. Concern

3. Promise
4. Hope

All four are important. All four should be part of every speech—long or short.

But the last is especially important. The voters are looking for inspiration. Nothing is better than the Senator's own words: "I see a new America. . . ."

The remainder of the brief document dealt with means of transmitting these messages. Repetition and contagion were the techniques advocated.

We need to bring the power of our entire campaign organization and all its communication facilities to bear in a concentrated selling effort. We need to use the powerful device of *repetition*. We must not be diverted by side issues or fall into the trap of defending our positions. And we must not get cluttered up with too many issues or too much detail.

We need the *sound* of contagion. . . . We need the *sight* of contagion. Crowds of happy people fighting to shake Goldwater's hand—to wish him well—this is why we recommend that some of the television half-hours feature huge rallies.

The polls have turned upward. The gap will narrow. We need to publicize this coming on of the underdog. . . .

We are positioned right—on the move upward while Johnson is slipping.

Senator Goldwater inaugurated this second offensive phase of the campaign with an address before the Annual Conference of United Press-International Editors and Publishers in Washington on the afternoon of October 6. His speech was that which would have been given in Cincinnati a week earlier had it been possible to obtain television time. Taking exception to the view that there were no issues in the campaign, Senator Goldwater gave his audience a *tour d'horizon* scanning all the issues he regarded as important. Social security, the power of the federal government, the make-up of the coalitions supporting the two candidates, the increasing power of the executive branch, the need for a strong defense, whether communism was mellowing, how to deal with communism, the development of new weapon systems, nuclear responsibility, civil rights, and law and order were all cited as instances of real issues on which he was taking one position and President Johnson was taking another. At the conclusion of the prepared remarks, the Arizona Senator added some words of his own:

. . . This is the type of a campaign that I . . . have been looking forward to for years. . . . I don't have the desire, nor do I have the particular interest of getting down into what I think will make this particular district of the country respond to me, or that particular district respond to me. I think these are problems that are recognized by Americans east, north, south and west, and there is no trying to separate them. There is no way you can speak for the Constitution in New York and not speak for it in Ohio, or go before a farm group and try to promise them more on the basis that the only responsibility the Republican party has is to try to out-promise the Democratic party. We have been doing this for too long. My contention is that people are now concerned with basic issues. . . .

The same evening another half-hour program was shown on nationwide television. This, too, was designed to put the Senator on the offensive regarding the issues. The format employed was that developed in the California primary in which films of persons asking the Senator questions were shown on a back screen, and Goldwater was photographed as he answered the questions. This introduced a degree of spontaneity at the same time it guaranteed that precious television time would not be wasted answering a frivolous question. During this half-hour, a teamster asked about Goldwater's tax-cut proposal, an executive secretary inquired about the conflict between China and Russia, a dairyman asked if Cuba could be freed from communism without war, a California housewife gave the Senator a chance to restate his view that preparedness was the best guarantee of peace, a 76-year-old retired supervisor asked about social security, a narcotics specialist said he was concerned about foreign aid, and an electrician asked if Senator Goldwater felt the war on poverty was genuine. After answering the specific questions, the candidate concluded with pledges about the nature of a Goldwater-Miller administration. He began by stating that America would be strong against the communists, then turned to the theme of hope.

I pledge an Administration that knows the sources of America's greatness, the ideals, the convictions, the hopes and dreams of a free people and will cherish this priceless heritage. I pledge an Administration that knows the secret of this nation's economic miracle, that will encourage individual initiative and reward individual enterprise. I pledge an Administration that knows the inner meaning of the American dream. . . .

I pledge an Administration with public servants who hold sacred their public trust. . . . During our Administration, the White House must and shall be once more a symbol of the ideals that all Americans share so that, with God's blessing, we shall achieve the American dream. And all these . . . are not just political promises in the heat of a political campaign; they are pledges of the heart. . . .

The Senator spent the next day—"National Bobby Baker Day," he called it—in New Jersey, then headed for the Southwest and West once more. In the President's home state, Goldwater charged that Johnson's statements on television were

> deceptions and distortions which, in a political campaign being waged by a man known as a master politician, probably are nothing more than we should have expected and should continue to expect.

On Friday, while the Senator himself was campaigning in California, another telecast was shown. This time Richard Nixon and Barry Goldwater both spoke on "The Real Job of the Presidency." The former Vice President spoke first about the dedication which was increasing the prospects of a Goldwater victory.

> Everywhere I've been, beginning about October first, there's been an up-turn, an up-turn particularly significant among workers, people that are thinking about these issues, people that are going to produce the greatest army of volunteer workers in America's political history on November the third.

Then he introduced Senator Goldwater, ". . . a reasonable man, . . . a calm man, . . . a patriotic man." The Senator's address first dealt with his approach to the campaign itself.

> You have probably been reading and hearing about some of the unorthodox things I have been doing. . . . I have done all these things deliberately. . . . *I will not attempt to buy the votes of the American people. . . . I will not treat any of you as just so many special interests. . . . I will not appeal to you as if you were simply pocketbooks . . . surrounded on all sides by self-serving concerns.*

After contrasting his approach to the campaign with that of the "interim President," the Arizonan turned to foreign policy.

> *The great power of your President . . . indeed his chief responsibility . . . is direction of foreign policy and leadership of this nation among all the nations of the world.* You *must* hold him responsible for the state of our affairs throughout the world.
>
> And, I say to you tonight . . . *they are in shambles* . . . from Egypt to Cambodia . . . from India to Viet Nam . . . from the Congo to Algeria, to Cuba, to Laos. *And you know it.*

Mr. Nixon concluded with an attack on President Johnson:

> With all the power that a President has, the most important thing to bear in mind is this: you must not give that power to a man unless, above everything else, he has character. Character is the most important qualification the President of the United States can have.

And on that score, a cloud hangs over the White House tonight . . . because the present President . . . has refused to disassociate himself from political hanky-panky, from corruption, in his official family, in the Bobby Baker case. . . .

Senator Goldwater concluded his week of hard campaigning with Saturday speeches in three western states: Washington, Oregon, and Utah. The most important address was in the evening in Salt Lake City. Speaking in the Mormon Tabernacle, Senator Goldwater asked why we saw riot and disorder, a rise in juvenile delinquency, and corruption around our highest offices. This he linked to the Supreme Court's decision banning required prayers in the schoolroom. The Senator pointed to the many eminent persons who had criticized this action.

. . . there is clearly a deep and widespread public interest—nonpartisan and nonsectarian in nature—in rectifying the Supreme Court's decision through the Amendment process. . . . This is why the Republican Party gave strong endorsement in its 1964 Platform to a "Constitutional Amendment permitting those individuals and groups who choose to do so to exercise their religion freely in public places."

The Democratic platform, Senator Goldwater pointed out, was silent on this issue. Perhaps, he said, this is because Hubert Humphrey and the Americans for Democratic Action were totally opposed to any form of prayer amendment. "I pledge," the Senator concluded, "my every effort to a reconstruction of reverence and moral strength, those great pillars of human happiness in our land."

The other major speech of this fourth phase of the Goldwater campaign was delivered in Chicago after another week of campaigning in the Midwest and Plains States.[19] It was here on October 16 that Senator Goldwater finally addressed himself to civil rights. In addition to its intrinsic importance, this speech was significant for what it told about relationships within the Goldwater coalition. Many Southerners had been urging that Senator Goldwater make "just one speech" in the South implying that he favored segregation. All such proposals were instantly rejected. The Senator spoke about many things during his September swing through the South, but civil rights was not one of them. So if organizational loyalists were unhappy about Gold-

[19] Both the Salt Lake City speech on morality and prayer and the Chicago speech on civil rights were shown on nationwide television. The Salt Lake City speech was televised on October 20; the Chicago speech on October 22.

water's refusal to repeat themes from the Eisenhower and Nixon campaigns, they could at least take some comfort from the fact that the Senator had not embraced a Southern strategy either.[20]

There was another reason for delay in discussion of civil rights. No one had been able to write a civil rights speech the Senator was willing to deliver. The requirements were clear: a statesmanlike approach which no one would interpret as an appeal to a white backlash. But this was easier said than done, and it was not until mid-October that a speech was ready that met with Senator Goldwater's approval. The principal contributors were political theorist Harry Jaffa and William Rehnquist, an Arizona lawyer. The audience was also carefully selected. Those attending a $100-a-plate fund-raising dinner could be expected to listen to the address with appropriate restraint. No one could charge that the candidate was trying to incite a racist mob.

The speech began with the theme that *e pluribus unum* referred not only to the formation of one nation from many states, but also to the formation of one people from many races, colors, and creeds. It went on to condemn both compulsory segregation and compulsory integration.

> It is wrong to compel children to attend schools restricted to members of their own race. . . . It is also wrong to forbid children to attend schools restricted to members of another race. I condemn that sort of segregation because it is *compulsory*.
>
> There is another way that people may separate and distinguish themselves from each other. Far from being compulsory, it is the necessary result of freedom—the freedom of association. Throughout this land of ours, we find people forming churches, clubs and neighborhoods with other families of similar beliefs, similar tastes, and similar ethnic backgrounds. No one would think of insisting that neighborhoods be "integrated" with fixed proportions of

[20] There have been a number of statements by political scientists that Senator Goldwater followed a Southern strategy and/or that he was appealing to segregationist sentiment. These analyses are plausible, but they are also incorrect. Part of the error is due to a failure to distinguish carefully enough between statements made by Senator Goldwater's supporters (some of whom did advocate a Southern strategy or a racial appeal) and statements coming from the Senator or those he had placed in charge of his campaign. So far as Goldwater himself was concerned, there was very good evidence he consciously avoided an appeal to segregationist sentiment. He sought a meeting with President Johnson (on July 24) where he agreed to eliminate appeals to racial passion from the campaign; he promised Republican leaders at the Hershey unity conference "with every degree of seriousness and strength that I have that I will never talk about racism"; he did not even mention civil rights in the South until the closing hours of the campaign.

Anglo-Americans, German-Americans, Swedish-Americans—or of Catholics, Protestants, and Jews.

To me, it is just as wrong to take some children out of the schools they would normally attend and bus them to others. . . . It is wrong . . . because it reintroduces through the back door the very principle of allocation by race that makes compulsory segregation morally wrong and offensive to freedom.

. . . what can those in national office do about this problem? Some laws will help, but they cannot be relied upon to provide the full solution—indeed, even a major part of it. This is a moral problem, and local leadership is needed to make headway in solving it. The best thing the President can do is to use his office to persuade and encourage localities to take up the task of leadership.

Our aim, as I understand it, is neither to establish a segregated society nor to establish an integrated society. It is to preserve a *free* society.

Goldwater himself was pleased with the reaction to the speech, and Theodore H. White was later to term it "the best effort of his campaign."[21]

A campaign, however, is not all speeches. There are some events which do not form part of the strategy plans of either candidate. Often they cannot be anticipated at all. But dramatic events—whether domestic or foreign—can cause headlines, and these can appreciably alter a candidate's ability to communicate with the voters. Just as freak atmospheric conditions can bring in a radio signal from a great distance, and just as static can make it difficult at times to hear a local radio station, the "channel capacity" of a political campaign can be altered by events unplanned by any strategy committee. And while Barry Goldwater was occupying himself on the plains and prairies this mid-October week, events were occurring elsewhere which were to have an important effect on his campaign.

One event had taken place a few days earlier. On October 7, Walter Jenkins, a presidential assistant and long-time confidant, was arrested on a morals charge. It took a few days for this intelligence to reach the top levels of both parties, but when it did a behind-the-scenes struggle took place over whether the story would be made public. Clark Clifford, one of the ranking Johnson strategists, and Abe Fortas, later to be named to the Supreme Court, visited Washington papers. Pointing out that Jenkins had suffered a nervous collapse, they asked the editors to consider carefully before taking steps which would cause additional injury to a married man with children. The Republicans' position was that the arrest of an assistant to the President

[21] *The Making of the President 1964* (New York: Atheneum, 1965), p. 331.

ought to be made known to the public. Republican public relations specialists exerted pressure to bring about publication by having out-of-town papers ask their wire services to supply them with the story. The story was finally put on the wires on the evening of Wednesday, October 14. Once available, it was page-one news everywhere. The *Baltimore Sun*, for example, made it the lead story with an eight-column headline; there was a two-column headline in the *Washington Post;* there was a five-column headline in the *New York Herald Tribune.*

The political impact on the Goldwater campaign, of course, was the coincidence between the nature of the story and the political offensive which had been launched a week earlier. The central thrust of this was an effort to establish a contrast between moral decay around President Johnson and Senator Goldwater's hope for a new America. The Jenkins story, distressing though it was, tended to substantiate statements Republicans had been making. At least, Republicans hoped, voters might listen a little more closely to what the Senator was saying.

The hopes of the Goldwater strategists were short-lived. Washington is not the only source of news, and, in mid-afternoon, October 15, the teletype chattered out: "FLASH MOSCOW—OFFICIALLY KHRUSHCHEV OUT AS PREMIER." The replacement of Khrushchev with Leonid Brezhnev and Alexei Kosygin was more dramatic news than the arrest of a presidential assistant. And if that wasn't enough to blanket the Jenkins story, the same day brought the news of a hairbreadth Labour victory carrying Harold Wilson to power in Great Britain, and the next day the Chinese exploded an atomic device in Sinkiang Province. Just as one story had briefly illuminated the issue of moral corruption, now others swung the focus back to foreign policy. On Saturday, October 17, vice presidential candidate William Miller told Californians that the Russian and Chinese developments showed that Goldwater had been right all along in demanding a firm foreign policy backed up by military strength. In Lansing, Michigan, Richard Nixon said that our State Department had been caught flat-footed by the Kremlin shakeup and that we should expect the new Russian leaders to take a harder line. And as Yia Bi Kin was moving through western skies, speechwriter Karl Hess was making use of the plane's advanced communications equipment to contact friends in universities to check on the meaning of these latest developments in order to prepare a Goldwater position.

On Sunday evening, President Johnson addressed the nation from the White House. Republicans took the position that this was a partisan speech and demanded equal free time so candidate Goldwater could present his views. NBC and CBS turned down the request, but ABC offered fifteen minutes to national chairman Dean Burch.[22] At first Burch was not inclined to accept the ABC offer, but Lou Guylay urged him to do so and drafted a speech for him.

> . . . This Administration has repeatedly tried to manipulate the news; unfavorable news is suppressed and favorable news is broadcast far and wide.
>
> ITEM: President Johnson, through his acknowledged ability to control the Democratic Congress, killed the Senate investigation in the Bobby Baker case. . . . Issue suppressed: morality and national security.
>
> ITEM: President Johnson . . . killed the Amendment to section 315 of the Communications Act dealing with equal time. If he had not done that, we might not have been in the position we are in today. Issue suppressed: all issues.
>
> ITEM: President Johnson has consistently and absolutely refused to accept Senator Goldwater's challenge to debate the real issues, either on a shared expense basis or entirely at Senator Goldwater's expense. Issue suppressed: all issues.
>
> . . . On October 17, 1964, some 48 hours after the occurrence of these events the Democratic National Committee attempted to purchase from N.B.C. a 15 minute time slot. Candidate Johnson then put on his Presidential hat and demanded that the networks give him free time to address the nation on a matter of "national significance."

Chairman Burch went on to label the President's address "the most uninformative half-hour I've ever seen," and said that Senator Goldwater would present his views on Wednesday evening *if* those watching sent in enough money to buy the television time. This speech elicited 140,000 contributions and brought in more than a million dollars.[23]

[22] There was a precedent for the request. In 1956, all three networks had given Adlai Stevenson free time to respond to President Eisenhower's analysis of events in Suez and Hungary. The Federal Communications Commission later ruled this had been unnecessary. The networks based their 1964 action on this FCC ruling.

[23] A number of Senator Goldwater's speeches had been followed by a trailer in which Raymond Massey asked for contributions. This money, however, was sent to a Los Angeles post office box, and the California committee had ideas of their own about how the money ought to be spent. The Burch speech for the first time gave the Goldwater strategists in Washington, D. C., the financial capability to transmit messages when they desired.

Senator Goldwater's speech, taped Tuesday and presented Wednesday evening, interpreted the Russian and Chinese developments as underscoring the need for the kind of foreign policy he had been urging. He said that the Administration had been distinguishing between "good" and "bad" communists, and this was a serious mistake. He quoted the exchange of fraternal greetings in which the Chinese congratulated the new masters of the Kremlin as evidence that the Sino-Soviet rift was now being patched up. He pointed out that Russians had continued to support "wars of national liberation," and that the communist definition of "peaceful coexistence" was

> a form of the class struggle between capitalism and socialism (which) provides, as the events of recent years have shown, a favorable climate for the revolutionary struggle of all peoples.

The incumbent Administration, the Arizonan continued, had confused "peaceful coexistence" with "peace," and the Secretary of State had admitted on television that the State Department had been surprised by the Russian developments. Senator Goldwater concluded his speech with his own prescription for foreign policy.

> Here are three things we can do immediately in establishing a sensible policy toward Communism. First . . . we must rebuild our once grand alliances. And we must start with the North Atlantic Treaty Organization. . . . I have already pledged that one of my first acts as President will be to initiate a call for a North Atlantic conclave. . . . The second thing we must do is to recognize that Communism is our enemy . . . the whole of Communism . . . not just some faction of the movement. . . . The third thing we must do is to confront Communism with a firm policy of resistance.

Senator Goldwater was on nationwide television four times that week. On Tuesday evening, his speech at the Mormon Tabernacle was shown; on Wednesday, his analysis of the shifts in the Kremlin was on; on Thursday, his Chicago speech on civil rights was televised; and on Friday, a "Brunch with Barry" on which he chatted with leading distaff Republicans coincided with Republican brunches across the country. This was not, however, Barry Goldwater's best week. His traveling schedule had to be hastily revised because of the need to tape the Wednesday night speech and to attend Herbert Hoover's funeral in New York on Thursday. He had to take time to settle a dispute over a film called "Choice." This film, purporting to be a documentation of moral decay, was to be shown on television sponsored by "Mothers for a Moral America." After a private viewing, the Senator demanded it be withdrawn and threatened to publicly disavow it if it was shown. But these troubles were minor compared to difficulty caused by the events in Russia and China. These developments had made it most difficult to communicate about domestic political issues. On the front page of the *New York Times* News of the Week in Review section the following Sunday, for example, the lead article (39 column-inches) concerned the shift in power in Russia and the second piece (25 column-inches) was a view of China as a nuclear power. Only in the lower right-hand corner could the reader find 10 column-inches devoted to the campaign. The political meaning of this was that the dramatic events in Moscow and Sinkiang had broken the momentum of Barry Goldwater's October offensive, and time was running out.

Senator Goldwater did not hold press conferences during the campaign. His off-the-cuff comments in New Hampshire had caused too much trouble. He did, however, hold a weekly "backgrounder"[24] whenever possible. Stories generated by a backgrounder in Texas on October 24 gave Senator Goldwater's estimate of the situation as the campaign entered its final week. The articles all but said the Arizonan did not expect to win. He regarded Illinois and Texas as even bets because of the strength of the Percy-for-Governor and Bush-for-Senator candidacies, but thought he was in trouble in California. (All three were "must" states in the Goldwater strategy.) He admitted that he had never been as bullish as some of his backers about carrying the South, citing Tennessee, Florida, and Georgia as "toss-ups," and said Kentucky and Arkansas looked as if they would be tougher propositions. He asserted that he had a "chance" to defeat President Johnson in the election, but anyone with the least skill in adding up electoral votes could look at the estimates in particular states and know that by now the likelihood of success was almost nil.

The final week of the campaign represented a fifth phase of the Goldwater strategy. The change which could be noted was not a conscious decision on the part of Goldwater strategists that their political offensive was finished. It was the political fact that it was over. Signs of discouragement and fatigue were evident. Major appearances were scheduled in New York, Cleveland, Pittsburgh, and Los Angeles. But the candidate was also spending

[24] In this form of "press conference," correspondents normally may use the comments proffered to write stories on their own authority but cannot attribute them to the person giving the interview.

time in Salisbury, Maryland; Dover, Delaware; Bristol, Tennessee; London, Kentucky; Belleville, Illinois; Cedar Rapids, Iowa; Oshkosh, Wisconsin; Altoona, Pennsylvania; Cheyenne, Wyoming; and Las Vegas, Nevada. These are not communities where voters are to be found in large numbers. It was as if the managers had lost control over the campaign in its closing days.

His speeches during this final week revealed an increasingly defiant Goldwater. As hope for electoral victory receded, the man who had not been terribly interested in running for the presidency in the first place began to place more and more emphasis on beliefs which were important to him. The most important speech of the week was delivered to an overflow crowd in Madison Square Garden in New York on Monday evening and later televised for a national audience. It began with a question:

> I can't help wondering, sometimes, if you've asked yourselves why my campaign is what it is. I wonder, my fellow Americans, if you think I don't *know* what views would be most popular. Do you think I don't know what Labor wants to hear, what Management wants to hear, what housewives and diplomats and white collar workers want to hear? Do you honestly think, after all these years in politics, that I don't *know* the easy way to get votes? The promises to make? The subjects to talk about—and the ones to avoid? . . .
>
> One thing we all know, and I assure you I do, that (there is) a much easier way to get votes than in my way. (There) always has been. It's political daddyism and it's as old as demagoguery and despotism.

He went on to say that he did not expect to get the votes of Nazi and fascist types, of communists, of lazy dole-happy people, or of the Socialist, ADA-type followers of Hubert Horatio Humphrey. He charged that the Administration was pursuing a "Closed Till After Election Day" policy, and concluded with a plea to return America to sound conservative principles.

In Kentucky, the next day, Goldwater asked his audience: "Do we want raw and naked power and ambition in the White House, power stripped of humanity, stripped of common honesty, devoid of any morality except the morality of get, the morality of grab and the morality of gifts to the favorite few?" In Iowa, on Wednesday, the candidate charged that the president had "kidnapped the Democratic party, tied it up in a neat bundle for eventual delivery to the Americans for Democratic Action, the most effective radical socialist organization in the land." In Pittsburgh, he chose to deal at some length with the case of Otto Otepka, a State Department employee whose dismissal had been ordered for allegedly passing classified documents to a Senate subcommittee. "Dean Rusk," the Senator asserted, "has coddled the liars, the wiretappers, the brutal abusers of government power who tried to railroad Otepka. But, the final responsibility . . . is with Lyndon Johnson who has been informed about this case for many months but has done nothing but delay decisions until after the election." Such were the messages being transmitted in the last week.

If most of these speeches suggested fatigue on the part of candidate and speechwriters, there was one which illustrated a final shift in strategy. This was delivered on Saturday night, at the end of the final week of campaigning. There were no new messages in the speech. The words had been uttered before—in New York, in Chicago, or elsewhere. But this speech was given in Columbia, South Carolina, and it was televised on eighty-seven stations throughout the South. Appearing with Senator Goldwater on this hour-long program were former Secretary of State James F. Byrnes, Senator Strom Thurmond and Representative Albert W. Watson of South Carolina, former Democratic state chairman James Grey and one-time Representative Iris Blitch of Georgia, and Congressman John Bell Williams of Mississippi. The longest section of the speech, moreover, concerned civil rights. The words were identical with those used in the Chicago address, but spoken over a Southern television network from a South Carolina rostrum in the company of the 1948 Dixiecrat candidate for president, the connotation was inevitably different. Senator Goldwater never did yield to Southern pleas that he take a segregationist stand, but he did move this close to a Southern strategy. In this closing phase of the campaign, he was now fighting hard for what had once been regarded as certain Goldwater territory.

These, then, were the five phases through which the Goldwater strategy passed. The Goldwater coalition was made up of five groups: the core group of Arizonans, the organizational loyalists, the conservative ideologues, the foreign policy hard-liners, and the Southerners. The story of the campaign can be interpreted in the light of the relationships within the Goldwater coalition, and of the Goldwater coalition's reaction to certain external events. In the first phase, the organizational loyalists played a key role in the one attempt to assuage the feelings of the moderate Republicans. For most of the campaign, the attitudes of the conservative ideologues and the foreign policy hard-liners were dominant within the coalition. This was true during the second, third, and fourth phases of the campaign, phases characterized by offense, defense, and offense once again. And during the fifth phase the campaign lurched on to a conclusion with an increasingly strident Goldwater coming as close as he ever did to adopting a Southern strategy.[25]

The Columbia rally did not officially close the campaign. Further efforts took place, in particular a last major speech in San Francisco on Monday, November 1. This was a return to the beginning. Senator Goldwater was returning to the city in which he had obtained the Republican nomination, and he chose to repeat, word for word, the address with which he had launched his campaign. This was a point of pride with Senator Goldwater. By ending his campaign with the same words he had used in beginning it, he could illustrate his unswerving loyalty to his principles. But repeating the same words had another meaning as well. The campaign was over—and candidate Goldwater had no further communication to make.

[25] The attitude of the organizational loyalists by this last phase of the campaign is told in two "Peanuts" strips which were posted in a headquarters office. In the first, Linus, nominated for school office, is addressing his fellow students. "Hallowe'en will soon be with us," Linus begins. "On Hallowe'en night the Great Pumpkin rises out of the pumpkin patch, and brings toys to all the good little children." He is interrupted by an explosion of laughter. In the next day's strip, Linus is confiding in Snoopy. "So I told them about the Great Pumpkin and they all laughed! Am I the first person ever to sacrifice political office because of belief? Of course not! I simply spoke what I felt was the truth. . . ." In the last two panels, Snoopy walks off talking to himself. "I've never pretended to understand politics," the dog muses, "but I do know one thing. If you're going to hope to get elected, don't mention the Great Pumpkin."

8

The Johnson Strategy

The role of the candidate is always important, but Lyndon Johnson was able to dominate the strategy of the Johnson coalition to an unusual degree. Several things enabled him to do this. He was President of the United States —with all that implies about power and prestige. He appeared to be ahead in the polls, and politicians are as unlikely to question the tactics of a front-runner as they are overanxious to give advice to a lagging candidate.[1] The Johnson strategy was reasonably familiar to the groups in the Johnson coalition. Certain aspects of the 1964 campaign were unique, but the President was taking positions not dissimilar to those advocated by every Democratic nominee for a generation. And beyond all these considerations, there was the compelling personality of Lyndon Baines Johnson. He had the will to lead.

Neither President Johnson nor Senator Goldwater has ever been accused of being a bookish man. Both are regarded as activists, as doers. But their interests are quite different. Barry Goldwater is interested in gadgets and nature. It is easy to think of him photographing the Colorado River rapids.

[1] This does not mean, of course, that the President was free from all criticism. Particularly in the months before the campaign, there were many critical comments about Mr. Johnson's unwillingness to take over the Democratic National Committee, to reorganize the party, and so on. This statement means only that he was the target of less intra-party criticism than was Senator Goldwater, a condition which usually is true when one candidate is perceived to be winning and the other is thought to be losing.

With Lyndon Johnson, the key words are "men" and "power." He has an instinctive feel for the strengths and weaknesses of human beings, and brings all his tremendous energy to the task of leading diverse individuals toward some common goal. There is a statement of Johnson's political beliefs which has often been quoted:

> I am a free man, an American, a United States Senator, and a Democrat, in that order.
>
> I am also a liberal, a conservative, a Texan, a taxpayer, a rancher, a businessman, a consumer, a parent, a voter, and not as young as I used to be nor as old as I expect to be—and I am all these things in no fixed order.

The second sentence in this declaration provides a valuable clue to Lyndon Johnson's style of thinking. A student of political philosophy might not have been so willing to proclaim himself simultaneously a liberal and a conservative. He would have been sensitive to inconsistencies between these positions. But Lyndon Johnson is not a man to whom ideas are all-important. With him, the key is empathy for the concerns of others. And since he could understand the beliefs of both the liberal and the conservative, he could work with both.

There was much in Lyndon Johnson's experience in Texas and in the Senate to prepare him for a role as a mediator between contending political forces.[2] He came from a large, diverse, and rapidly changing state, one "concerned about money and how to make it, about oil and sulfur and gas, about cattle and dust storms and irrigation, about cotton and banking and Mexicans."[3] Texas was a state which could produce both agrarian populists and business-oriented conservatives. Lyndon Johnson, with memories of rural poverty and with new-found affluence, could communicate with both.

When he was first elected to the Senate, he was almost at once found to be in the middle of the Democratic party in that body.[4] Elected to the Floor

[2] There are three sources which I have found most valuable in understanding the pre-presidential Johnson. A sympathetic account appears in Michael Janeway's honors thesis, "Lyndon Johnson and the Rise of Conservatism in Texas" (Unpublished, Harvard College History Department, 1962). A somewhat more critical evaluation is Selig S. Harrison, "Lyndon Johnson's World," *New Republic*, June 13, 1960, pp. 15–23. The third source is Ralph K. Huitt, "Democratic Party Leadership in the Senate," *American Political Science Review*, June, 1961, pp. 333–44.

[3] V. O. Key, Jr., *Southern Politics*, p. 254.

[4] David B. Truman, *The Congressional Party* (New York: Wiley, 1959), p. 113.

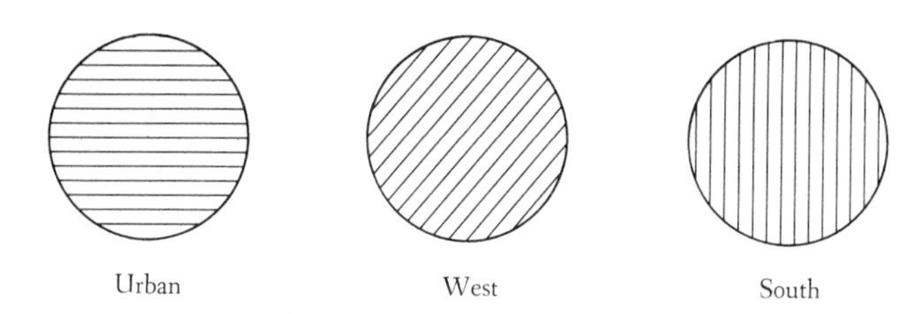

Figure 9 *1932 Democratic Coalition*

leadership, he had to look in both directions to hold together a party which extended from such Southerners as Byrd, Eastland, and Stennis to such metropolitan spokesmen as Lehman, Douglas, and Clark. By 1960, Johnson could contentedly run for re-election to the Senate from Texas on a rather conservative platform and for Vice President of the United States on a very liberal platform.

Lyndon Johnson did not simply find himself in the center; he used the center. Whether by conscious preference or by subconscious improvisation, he worked out a strategy which he employed time and again. It was not just balancing, though this could be found. (The Texas Senator voted for bread-and-butter liberal measures such as dams, rural electrification, etc., while he also cast budget-cutting votes and votes for defense appropriations pleasing to the business community.) Repeatedly, Johnson would locate the political center, then expand the boundaries of that center while he kept its content more or less undefined. By so doing, he could enlarge the area of consensus and persuade doubters to support that developing consensus. Michael Janeway gives us this description of the policy of "moderation" employed by Majority Leader Johnson:

> "Moderation" was a strategy designed to rebuild the center of the Democratic Party at a time when left and right were tearing it apart. . . . It was also a strategy of legislative technique, whereby Johnson created for himself an invaluable area of maneuverability wherein he could ambiguously appear to be at once helping liberals and protecting Southern conservatives. Without such maneuverability he would have been unable to persuade conservatives to give liberals anything, or liberals to give conservatives any reason for giving up anything.[5]

[5] Janeway, "Lyndon Johnson and the Rise of Conservatism in Texas," p. 83.

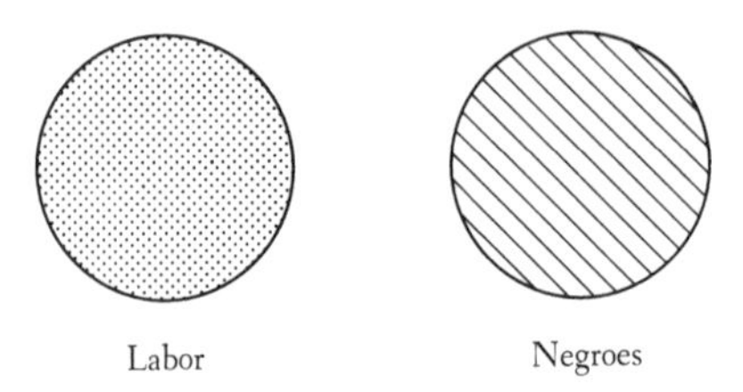

Figure 10 *Groups Joining the Democrats During New Deal Era*

Johnson's most characteristic response thus leads to political solutions emphasizing the desires of the largest number of people who can be assembled the center of the political spectrum. It is likely to cause anguished protests from dedicated men of the left and of the right, but it is one of the classical forms of coalition leadership.

The application of this form of leadership to 1964 campaign strategy can be understood by reflecting for a moment on the nature of the Democratic coalition. When Franklin Roosevelt took over the leadership of the Democratic party in the 1930's, the three major groups were conservatives from the South, agrarians from the West, and urban politicians from the Northeast. Again using Venn diagrams, one could say that the groups in the 1932 Democratic coalition may be represented by Figure 9. During the New Deal era, the strength of the urban wing of the Democratic party was augmented by the growth of the political influence of labor and the switch of Negroes from the party of Lincoln. With the addition of the new groups in Figure 10, the Democratic coalition came to look something like Figure 11.

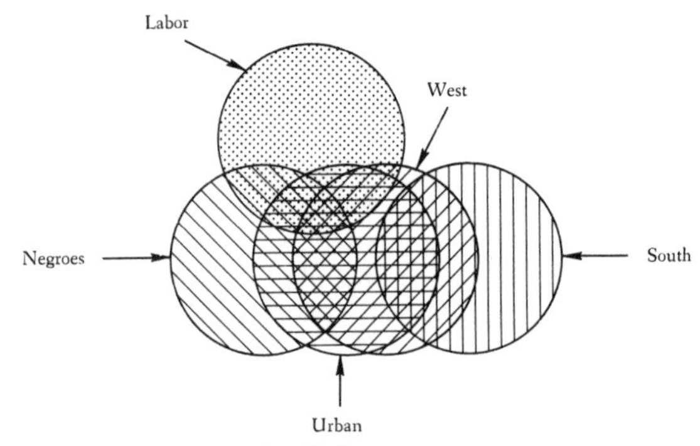

Figure 11 *Normal Democratic Coalition*

The Negro, urban, and labor groups in the Democratic coalition had more votes to contribute in presidential nominating conventions and elections while the Western and Southern groups had more influence in Congress.[6] In a very real sense, the Kennedy-Johnson ticket in 1960 symbolized this coalition. The Senator from Massachusetts was more acceptable to the Negro, urban, and labor groups; the Senator from Texas had more support among Westerners and Southerners; and neither man had taken extreme positions. When John F. Kennedy was assassinated, Lyndon B. Johnson inherited the task of holding this coalition together. The story of the Johnson strategy in 1964 is the application of Johnson's tactics to this task of coalition leadership.

The theme of the campaign began to emerge in addresses at two universities in the late spring. Speaking to University of Michigan graduates on May 22, the President introduced the idea of a "Great Society."

> In your time we have the opportunity to move not only toward the rich society and the powerful society, but upward to the Great Society. The Great Society rests on abundance and liberty for all. It demands an end to poverty and racial injustice, to which we are totally committed in our time. But that is just the beginning.
>
> The Great Society is a place where every child can find knowledge to enrich his mind and to enlarge his talents. It is a place where leisure is a welcome chance to build and reflect, not a feared cause of boredom and restlessness. It is a place where the city of man serves not only the needs of the body and the demands of commerce, but the desire for beauty and the hunger for community.
>
> It is a place where man can renew contact with nature. It is a place which honors creation for its own sake and for what it adds to the understanding of the race. It is a place where men are more concerned with the quality of their goals than the quantity of their goods. But most of all, the Great Society is not a safe harbor, a resting place, a final objective, a finished work. It is a challenge constantly renewed, beckoning us toward a destiny where the meaning of our lives matches the marvelous products of our labor.

President Johnson spoke to another university audience, this time at the University of Texas, on May 30. In his Ann Arbor address, he had defined

[6] The membership, attitudes, and behavior within each of these groups had, of course, changed over time. The Westerners, for example, had become much more urbanized, even though they continued to have some distinctive interests—land, water, minerals, timber—which were unlikely to excite a congressman from Brooklyn.

his goal in vague and glowing terms. In Austin, he spoke more directly about the task of political leadership.

> It is one of the great tests of political leadership to make our people aware of (the real voice of America), aware that they share a fundamental unity of interest, purpose and belief.
>
> I'm going to try to do this. And on the basis of this unity, I intend to try and achieve a broad national consensus which can end obstruction and paralysis, and can liberate the energies of the Nation for the work of the future.

These emphases on a brighter tomorrow and unity were perfectly consistent with Lyndon Johnson's penchant for working from a broad, vaguely defined center. The strategy also offered a number of political advantages. He could not only hold the Democratic coalition together, but he also could emphasize the common interests of the component groups. By enlarging the set of attitudes common to all of the member groups, he could ameliorate the intergroup rivalries which had done so much to stall Democratic-sponsored legislation.[7] His goal was defined so nebulously and so attractively that it would be politically difficult to challenge it effectively. And by urging all of the country to work together, he could reunite the South with the rest of the country and thus heal the wounds still remaining from sectional conflict a century earlier.

All these purposes were being served as President Johnson went about his business that summer. As many Kennedy appointees as could be persuaded to stay were kept at work while Texans learned the arts of managing the Johnson coalition. The President employed his superior legislative skills to obtain passage of much of the legislation which John Kennedy had advocated. Leaders of many important sectors of American society were invited to the White House. Business leaders, labor leaders, public school superintendents, state university presidents, women's groups, foreign language publishers, newspaper bureau chiefs, civil rights leaders, community relations committee members, students, congressmen, governors, and mayors were all invited to the White House where assurances were given that there was an important place for each in the Great Society.

[7] As one bit of evidence on the difficulties of leading the Democratic coalition, there is a public statement by President Kennedy: "... there isn't any doubt that there is in a party as large as the Democratic Party those who do not support a good many of the programs. The alliances may change but, of course, we lose a third or a fourth (of the Democratic votes in Congress), and we have since 1938" (Press Conference, July 23, 1962).

Now what did the nomination of Barry Goldwater imply for this centrist strategy? It meant that the major thrust of the Johnson strategy would go unchecked. For the first time in at least a generation, the two major parties would not try to occupy the same political ground, and President Johnson was free to develop his unity theme as he wished. It meant that the Republican nominee could be portrayed as an extremist by selective use of the quotable statements Barry Goldwater had made so freely during his years of public life. By simply saying he was in favor of social security or that he was not going to sell TVA, the President could easily suggest that Barry Goldwater stood well outside the area of consensus on public policies, while he was in the center. The general outlines of the Johnson strategy did not need any alteration.

The Goldwater nomination, however, did suggest special attention to two groups. The nomination of a conservative opponent was a threat to the South. Lyndon Johnson, the first Southerner to occupy the White House since the Civil War, was not about to cede the South to any opponent. He wanted to bring it closer to the center of his coalition. At the same time, the Goldwater nomination presented the possibility of adding another group, moderate Republicans, to the Johnson coalition. The President quickly sensed this opportunity and acted to take advantage of it. Consequently, the 1964 Johnson coalition included six groups whose attitudinal relationships are indicated in the Venn diagram in Figure 12. There were three points to

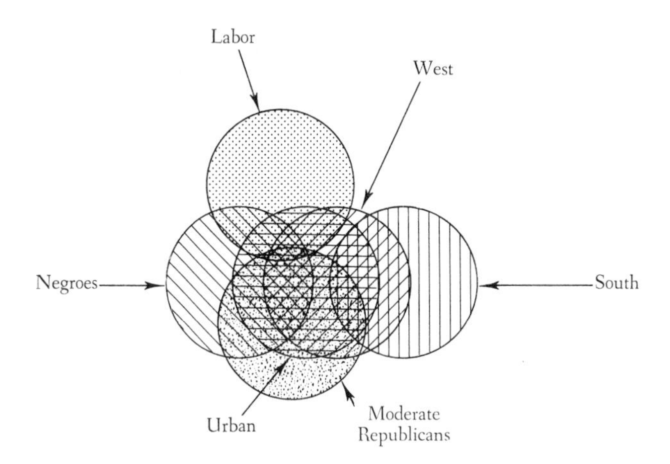

Figure 12 *The Johnson Coalition*

the 1964 Johnson strategy: to maintain support from four groups in the normal Demcratic coalition, labor, Negroes, urbanites, and Westerners; to defend the South by reducing antagonism between Southerners and other Democratic groups; and to convince moderate Republicans that their attitudes were closer to those of the Johnson coalition than those of the Goldwater coalition.

The convention which met in Atlantic City was a Johnson convention. His unity theme—One Nation, One Party—was prominently displayed and featured in the platform. Anything which might shift the spotlight from him was altered. A memorial to John F. Kennedy that had been scheduled for the opening night of the convention was shifted to the closing session lest an uncontrollable demonstration of Kennedy sentiment should develop as it had for Alben Barkley in 1948. Cliff Carter, Johnson's untitled liaison man with the Democratic National Committee, manned the Atlantic City end of a telephone line to the White House. Major decisions had to be cleared through him. And there was not a single roll call vote taken during the convention.

The convention presented the President with two important challenges. One, long anticipated, was the selection of a vice presidential nominee. The other, upsetting plans and time tables, was the problem presented by the Mississippi Freedom Democratic Party. The Freedom Democratic delegation, a largely Negro group, challenged the seating of the regular Mississippi delegation on the ground that Mississippi Negroes had been systematically excluded from participation in the process of delegate selection. Technically, this was a question of whether the regular delegation or the Freedom Party had valid credentials, one which should have been settled by the credentials committee after it examined the evidence. But the matter was far too important for routine handling. Not only were the television cameras focusing on the Freedom delegates instead of the intended theme of "One Nation, One Party," but this fight involved most of the important groups within the Democratic coalition. The lawyer for the Mississippi Freedom Democratic Party was Joseph L. Rauh, Jr. Rauh was a key figure on the liberal side of the Democratic coalition. He was chairman of the District of Columbia Democratic Central Committee, a close friend and adviser of Walter Reuther of the United Automobile Workers, and a national vice chairman of the Americans for Democratic Action. As this implies, the resolution of the issue had to be satisfactory not only to Negroes, but also to labor and to urban politicians. At the same time, the Southerners could not be alienated because this part of the Democratic coalition was already threatened by the conservative appeal of Goldwater. So a special credentials subcommittee was set up. It consisted of Walter Mondale, later appointed to the United States Senate from Minnesota; Charles Diggs, a Negro congressman from Michigan; Sherwin Markham of Iowa; Irving Kahler of Georgia; and former Governor Price Daniel of Texas. The subcommittee, including both liberals and Southerners, stayed in touch with Hubert Humphrey in Atlantic City and Lyndon Johnson in Washington while it groped for a solution. The ultimate resolution of the issue was that two Freedom delegates were to be seated as delegates-at-large, no regular Mississippi delegate was to be seated unless he signed a party loyalty pledge required of all delegates, and in 1968 and thereafter, no delegation would be seated from a state which deprived citizens of the right to vote for reason of race or color. This was not acceptable to all. Negro demonstrations continued. Mississippi (and Alabama) delegates who refused to sign the loyalty pledge departed from the convention. But the resolution was agreeable to the important groups within the Democratic coalition. Most Negro, urban, and labor leaders recognized it as a real victory, and the resolution was achieved in a way which did not offend most Southerners.

The treatment of the Mississippi Freedom Party presaged the manner in which the South would be handled in the fall. Essentially, this was a trade of the old for the new. Some delegates from Alabama and Mississippi walked out, but they were spokesmen for vanishing attitudes. Their loss could be accepted as long as moderate Southerners—especially those who would be influential in coming years—could be persuaded that their best interests could be served within the Democratic party. The Tennessee, North Carolina, and Georgia delegations—who already had Negro members—were unlikely to be troubled by a requirement of Negro participation in the delegate selection process in 1968. Several senior Southern senators did not attend the Democratic convention because of "pressing business" in Europe, but a number of younger Southern leaders were very active. Atlanta's Charles Weltner, a congressman who had voted for the 1964 civil rights bill, gave a speech which declared:

> And to that new generation, who soon must choose where it will go, I say: Come with us! Our party is dynamic, and bold, and exciting as youth itself.

Oklahoma's Carl Albert, a former Rhodes Scholar now in line to become Speaker of the House one day, was chairman of the platform committee. Georgia's 39-year-old Governor Carl Sanders was chairman of the rules committee. And John Connally of Texas, another capable Southern governor, was one of those placing Lyndon Johnson's name in nomination. The pattern was fairly clear. By fighting for the South along these lines, the Southern group in the Johnson coalition would be reconstituted with new leaders holding more moderate views. If this strategy worked, the task of coalition leadership would become easier.

No one besides President Johnson, of course, knows exactly why Hubert Humphrey was selected as the vice presidential nominee. His public statement was simple.

> I picked Humphrey because, in my judgment, and after checking all over the country, I was convinced that he would be the best man to be President if anything ever happened to me.

This is consistent with thinking that in view of America's global responsibilities in the nuclear age, Roosevelt's death, Eisenhower's heart attacks, and Kennedy's assassination, old-fashioned ticket balancing is somewhat out of date. However, the selection also fit in with Johnson's view of coalition leadership. Senator Humphrey had relationships of much longer standing than the President with labor, urban, and Negro leaders, but he also had been active in efforts to hold the national Democratic coalition together. He had served with Virginia's Governor Battle on a committee to settle the loyalty oath dispute that was splitting the Democratic party along North-South lines in the early 1950's. He had worked with Majority Leader Johnson in the Senate, and had ultimately become an activist Majority Whip himself. By 1964, Senator Humphrey had worked with Southerners and Westerners long enough to be able to claim some support from all of the important Democratic groups. So Hubert Humphrey was tapped to stand by the President's side in the center of the Johnson coalition.[8]

Hubert Humphrey's acceptance speech emphasized the contrast between Johnson and Goldwater which would be the theme of Democratic strategy throughout the campaign. Senator Humphrey began with a tribute to President Johnson:

> . . . the President of the United States must be a man of clear mind and sound judgment and a man who can lead, a man who can decide, a man of purpose and conviction, and Lyndon Johnson is that man. He is a man with

[8] For another interpretation of Humphrey's selection, see Gerald Pomper, "The Nomination of Hubert Humphrey for Vice-President" in *Journal of Politics*, August, 1966, pp. 639–59.

> the instinct of a teacher who would rather persuade than compel, who would rather unite than divide. President Johnson is respectful of the traditions of the Presidency and he understands the compelling need for restraint in the use of the greatest power ever assembled by man. In President Johnson's hands our people know that our power is for justice. In his hands our people know that our power is for peace; and in his hands our people know that our power is for freedom.

In contrast to this portrait of Lyndon Johnson as a gentle and understanding leader, Barry Goldwater was said to be a man who was impetuous one moment and indecisive the next. Most Democrats and most Republicans in the Senate, Humphrey told the delegates, had voted for the nuclear test ban treaty, the tax cut, the civil rights bill, the establishment of an arms control and disarmament agency, an expansion of medical education, the National Defense Education Act, and emergency funding for the United Nations, "but not Senator Goldwater!" Senator Goldwater was not even a typical Republican, and therefore Republicans were invited to join the Johnson coalition.

> Yes, yes my fellow Americans, it is a fact that the temporary Republican spokesman is not in the mainstream of his party, in fact he has not even touched the shore. . . . I say to those responsible and forward-looking Republicans—and there are thousands of them—we welcome you to the banner of Lyndon B. Johnson; we welcome your support. Yes we extend the hand of fellowship. We ask you to join us tonight for . . . (Lyndon Johnson) is the President in the great American tradition—for labor and for business; no class conflicts; for the farm family that will receive the unending attention and care of this President and for the city worker; for North and for the South; for East and for the West.

Lyndon Johnson began his acceptance speech by restating the unity theme.

> Tonight we offer ourselves on our records and by our platform as a party for all Americans, an all-American party for all Americans! This prosperous people, this land of reasonable men, has no place for petty partisanship or peevish prejudice. The needs of all can never be met by parties of the few. The needs of all cannot be met by a business party, or a labor party; not by a war party or a peace party; not by a Southern party or a Northern party.

The President continued by speaking of prosperity and peace, of strength and restraint, of equality and order. Lyndon Johnson's penchant for balance was even maintained to the point of promising great new achievements without disturbing existing social, economic, or political values. Attractive goals could be reached if only the status quo were not upset:

> We do offer the people a choice. A choice of continuing on the courageous and the compassionate course that has made this nation the strongest and the freest and the most prosperous and the most peaceful nation in the history of mankind.

To make sure that doctors, lawyers, and Indian chiefs all knew they were welcome in the Johnson coalition, a fairly extensive citizens operation was set up. In contrast to the Goldwater leaders, who regarded the Citizens for Goldwater-Miller as auxiliary, the Democratic strategists used this as a central part of their campaign. The general director of the effort was James H. Rowe, Jr. who had directed Hubert Humphrey's 1960 campaign until Humphrey was defeated in the West Virginia primary and had thereafter supervised Lyndon Johnson's quest for the nomination. He was, in other words, an experienced political tactician who was a confidant of both men at the top of the Democratic ticket. The twenty-six units functioning under his general supervision included Lawyers for Johnson and Humphrey, Scientists and Engineers for Johnson-Humphrey, Rural Americans for Johnson-Humphrey, Veterans for Johnson and Humphrey, Young Citizens for Johnson-Humphrey, National Independent (Business) Committee for President Johnson and Senator Humphrey, Educators for Johnson and Humphrey Committee, District Attorneys Committee for Johnson and Humphrey, Senior Citizens for Johnson and Humphrey, Artists and Entertainers for Johnson and Humphrey, and Professors for Johnson and Humphrey.

The typical organization of these groups was a prestigious letterhead committee (i.e., a number of well-known people who would permit the use of their names, but would not be expected to do much work) and an executive director who had interest-group experience or some other background which would give him access to mailing lists and knowledge about making contacts within his profession. The "initial organizing group" of the Scientists and Engineers, for example, included Detlev W. Bronk, Harrison Brown, Michael De Bakey, George Kistiakowsky, Polykarp Kusch, Clark Millikan, Albert Szent-Gyorgyi, Harold Urey, Paul Dudley White, and Warren Weaver. The letterhead committee for the lawyers included five former presidents of the American Bar Association and eight law school deans. The veterans' committee chairman was John W. Mahan, former National Commander of the Veterans of Foreign Wars, while Daniel F. Foley, immediate past National Commander of the American Legion, was listed as special adviser. The business group, the National Independent Committee for President Johnson and Senator Humphrey, included two Eisenhower cabinet members, Robert B. Anderson and Marion Folsom, in its letterhead committee, and Maxwell Rabb, secretary to the Eisenhower Cabinet was designated as counsel. Typical executive directors were Mrs. Mary Condon Gereau of the Educators Committee, one-time Montana Superintendent of Public Instruction, and Charles E. Odell of the Senior Citizens, on leave from the United Automobile Workers' Department of Older and Retired Workers. Other executive directors included Donald A. MacArthur of the Scientists and Engineers, a cousin of Mrs. Johnson's, and James F. Fitzpatrick of the Young Citizens, on leave from the law firm of the President's long-time friend, Abe Fortas.

The Democratic platform opened with the words "America is *One Nation, One People,*" and spoke in the following paragraph about "the sharing of responsibilities as well as benefits by all our people." The tone of the pamphlets prepared by these committees, however, came closer to following the instructions in Lawrence O'Brien's campaign manual: "The Veteran's Chairman should emphasize the various liberal programs to benefit veterans that have been advanced by the Democratic party, and stress President Johnson's close cooperation with veterans." Accordingly, the Veterans' Committee pamphlet was entitled "60 Key Laws: Four Years of Democratic Accomplishment in Veterans Affairs," and concentrated on medical care for the disabled, an increase in compensation and pension adjustments, education for orphans and children of the 100 per cent disabled, G.I. housing, and so forth. The Rural Americans for Johnson-Humphrey pointed out that the Democratic candidates had supported a feed grain program, agricultural conservation, merger of farm cooperatives, the food stamp program, food for peace, REA loans, and a price freeze, whereas Senator Goldwater had not. A women's pamphlet illustrated a Johnson quote, "I am unabashedly in favor of women," by pointing to fourteen specific programs benefiting female Americans. The lawyers' pamphlet pointed out that "beyond our general concern as citizens, a number of issues have emerged in this campaign on which we can speak with special competence as lawyers." The issues cited were the rule of law in world affairs, violence in the streets, civil rights, the right to a fair trial, and integrity of the judiciary. The scientists and engineers published a booklet whose cover proclaimed (in blue) "Johnson-Humphrey Must Be Elected" and (in red) "The Alternative is Frightening."

The inside pages contrasted "The Black and White World of Mr. Goldwater" with "The Case for Johnson-Humphrey"; ". . . even if by temperament they are not attracted to politics," the booklet began, "scientists, engineers, and physicians have been forced to acknowledge a duty to contribute their competence and understanding to the resolution of many basic questions facing the nation."

While scores of people were marshaling support through occupational channels, others were concerned with the defensive strategy being developed for the South. Four separate activities were involved in defending this exposed flank of the Johnson coalition from Republican incursions: mobilization of the newly registered Negro voters, an appeal to traditional Southern loyalties by Mrs. Johnson, support from elements friendly to the President in key spots in the Democratic party throughout the South, and an economic appeal. A Southern Regional Council study issued on August 2 indicated that in the Peripheral South[9] the proportion of Negroes registered varied from 27.7 per cent in Virginia to 67.2 per cent in Tennessee. In the Deep South, the proportions varied between 6.7 per cent in Mississippi and 39.1 per cent in Georgia. Checked against census figures, this meant that Negroes could be a decisive voting bloc in closely contested elections, particularly in the Peripheral South. Negroes constituted 5.7 per cent of the potential electorate in Virginia, 7.1 per cent in Texas, 9.1 per cent in Florida, 9.3 per cent in Arkansas, 11.0 per cent in North Carolina, and 11.1 per cent in Tennessee. In many areas, to be sure, the Negro turn-out rate would not be very high, but in some other areas Negroes were politically active and had been accepted by local Democratic politicians. The Durham (North Carolina) Committee on Negro Affairs, for example, had organized down to the block level.[10] And southern Negroes, as Negroes throughout the country, could be expected to vote almost unanimously against Barry Goldwater because he "chill(ed) them more than any other presidential candidate in memory." Negro leaders were convinced "that Goldwater had the support of known anti-Negro elements in local communities across the nation . . .

[9] This is a classification adopted by Donald Matthews and James Prothro in *Negroes and the New Southern Politics* (New York: Harcourt, Brace & World, 1966). The Peripheral South consists of Virginia, North Carolina, Arkansas, Tennessee, Texas, and Florida; the Deep South is made up of South Carolina, Georgia, Alabama, Mississippi, and Louisiana.

[10] Lewis Bowman and G. R. Boynton, "Coalition as Party in a One-Party Southern Area," *Mid-West Journal of Political Science*, August, 1964.

(and) it was this, the nature of the local elements supporting Goldwater, that turned the Negro anti-Goldwater tide into a raging flood."[11]

A second element in the Southern strategy was the invocation of traditional Southern support for the Democratic party. Lyndon Johnson himself had sought Southern support for the Kennedy-Johnson ticket in 1960 by speaking from the rear of a train which wended its way through the South. In 1964, this role was played by the President's Alabama-born wife. In early October, the "Lady Bird Special" departed from Alexandria, Virginia. The President came to see his wife off, and some government employees were given time off to swell the crowd. The message of a "New South" was not muted on this trip, but it was dressed for the occasion in crinoline and cotton. "I want to make this trip," said Mrs. Johnson on her departure, "because I am proud of the South and I am proud that I am part of the South." In North Carolina, she allowed that her main reason for coming "was to say to you that to this Democratic candidate and his wife, the South is a respected, valued, and beloved part of this country." And in a less sympathetic Alabama, Mrs. Johnson remarked: "You might not like all I am saying, but at least you understand the way I'm saying it."

It was also significant that as the "Lady Bird Special" crossed eight Southern states, every governor (or his wife) save Alabama's George Wallace climbed aboard. Southern Democrats had been accustomed to presidential Republicanism, voting for a Republican presidential candidate on an otherwise straight Democratic ballot, since the 1920's. The challenge presented in 1964 was something else. Now Southern officeholders, heretofore unconcerned with what the "national Democrats" did in Washington, D. C., could be reminded that the Republican threat was a threat to congressmen, district attorneys, and sheriffs. At the Southern Governors Conference, Governor John Connally announced that Goldwater's campaign had "just not caught fire," and that Johnson should carry all but four Southern states. Florida's Governor Farris Bryant predicted that the President would carry Florida by a narrow margin. Governor Carl Sanders declared that "the strong sentiment for Goldwater seems to have subsided," and Kentucky's Governor Breathitt told reporters that civil rights was a dead issue. The word was being passed. Men who had never had to think past a primary election were now very concerned with November.

[11] Louis Lomax, "The Basic Issue in the Presidential Campaign," *Washington Star*, October 4, 1964, p. C–3.

The final, most important, element in Johnson's strategy for the South was an economic appeal. The crucial change in the South in recent decades has been economic growth. Per capita income in the South remains below the national average, but it has grown more rapidly there. By 1960, per capita income was more than 400 per cent of what it had been at the beginning of the depression.[12] This economic development, as Hugh Douglas Price has reminded us, has had real political consequences:

The postwar South has been torn between two basic, and largely contradictory urges: the Whiggish enthusiasm for industry, and the old issue of race. One might boil it down a bit crudely, to a contest between business greed and racial prejudice, in which the former has steadily triumphed in most Southern cities, and in every Southern state except for Mississippi and Alabama.[13]

In 1964, Lyndon Johnson clearly chose to emphasize economic development. His views had been spelled out in an address on May 8 to an Atlanta breakfast audience which included Georgia's governor and many Georgia legislators. The President pointed to the equal employment opportunity plan "born here in the great state of Georgia at the Lockheed plant" and urged his listeners to move forward on the racial question.

In your own search for justice the Constitution of the United States must be your guide. Georgians helped write that Constitution. Georgians have died to protect that Constitution. . . . I believe Georgia will join with the entire nation to ensure that every man enjoys all the rights secured to him by the Constitution. Because the Constitution requires it, because justice demands it, we must protect the Constitutional right of all citizens regardless of race, religion or the color of their skin.

These progressive words on civil rights were preceded, however, by a review of the economic progress made by the South under Democratic auspices.

Franklin D. Roosevelt sent me to the South in 19 and 36 to survey conditions in our Southern states. He sought to turn the conscience of the nation to the cares of its neighbors. The South was then a forgotten and a forbidding land. Its mills were idle and its banks were shut. Misery was on the faces of its farmers and hunger scarred the faces of its children.

[12] Arthur Goldschmidt, "The Development of the U. S. South," *Scientific American*, September, 1963, p. 229.

[13] Hugh Douglas Price, "Southern Politics in the Sixties: Notes on Economic Development and Political Modernization," a paper prepared for delivery at the 1964 Annual Meeting of the American Political Science Association.

What little there was trickled north, leaving the South barren of its own bounty. Many thought the South had suffered its final defeat. These were the faint of heart and I was not among them. And, thank God, the people of Georgia were not among them.

The results are here in the new South. The average income in the South has increased six times since 19 and 30, rising much faster than the national average. Malaria and pellagra are going and hunger is going. The acreage yield of our farms has doubled and the gross income per farm in your state has risen eight times. Nearly every home in Georgia has water and electricity and every child can go to school.

This theme of economic progress was brought home to rural and urban voters in a drumbeat of messages throughout the campaign. The chairman of Rural Americans for Johnson and Humphrey was Robert W. Scott, the 1964 Democratic nominee for lieutenant governor of North Carolina. When President Johnson came to Raleigh, North Carolina, he argued that the termination of the farm subsidy program, called for in Goldwater's *Conscience of a Conservative*, would take money out of farmers' pockets.

For the nation, (termination of farm subsidies) would mean that our $12 billion net farm income would be cut in half. . . . North Carolina would lose at least a third of a billion dollars a year.

Virginian Henry Fowler, an active member of the National Independent Committee who was to become Secretary of the Treasury, was busy reminding Southern businessmen of their interest in economic development . And when President Johnson, in another intersection with the "Lady Bird Special," spoke in New Orleans, he quoted a nameless old Southern senator as saying:

I would like to go back there and make them one more Democratic speech. I just feel like I've got one more in me. Poor old state, they haven't heard a Democratic speech in thirty years. All they ever hear at election time is Negro, Negro, Negro! The kind of speech they should have been hearing is about the economy and what a great future we could have in the South if we just meet our economic problems, if we just take a look at the resources of the South and develop them.

That a Southern politician would have the courage to tell a Southern audience they had been hearing too much "Negro, Negro, Negro" generated more headlines, but the economic emphasis was more important.

President Johnson began his campaign in the North with the traditional

Labor Day address in Detroit's Cadillac Square. The opening words reminded his listeners of the precedents.

> Sixteen years ago, an American President came here and promised that America would "enter a new period of hope." That President was Harry S Truman. You gave him support and he gave you that hope.
>
> Four years ago, another great American stood where I stand today, and he said, "Give me your hand . . . and this country can move again." That man was John Fitzgerald Kennedy. You reached out your hand, and America began to move.
>
> I have come here today to pledge that, if all Americans stand united, we will keep moving. . . .

Several hundred words later, he turned to a dream he had first when he was young and "looked up at the scattered Texas sky."

> . . . my dream . . . is not the grand vision of a powerful and feared nation. It concerns the simple wants of a people. But that is what America is really about. All the rest—the power and the wealth, the life of freedom and the hopes for peace, the treasured past and the uncertain future—all of this will stand or fall on this. Reality rarely matches dream, but only dreams give nobility to purpose.

The speech began as standard Democratic text and ended with authentic Johnson references to a better tomorrow for the common people. There were, however, unusual aspects to the setting of the speech. There were relatively few references to "the Democratic party" in the speech and Governor and Mrs. George Romney were on the platform along with Walter Reuther and assorted Democratic politicians. Officially the Governor was present to greet the visiting President. But his presence also served his need to overcome Barry Goldwater's considerable unpopularity in the state of Michigan, and Lyndon Johnson's desire to add moderate Republicans to the Johnson coalition.

Johnson's appeal to Republicans was made more explicit in a speech three days later in Harrisburg, Pennsylvania. Speaking before an audience composed exclusively of Democrats, the President stated that he had not come to Pennsylvania as a partisan. He uttered kind words about the last Republican president, Dwight Eisenhower, and about the Pennsylvania governor who had fought the last fight to prevent Goldwater's nomination, William Scranton. His opponents were not Republicans, but extremists

> contemptuous toward the will of majorities, callous toward the plight of minorities, arrogant toward allies, belligerent toward adversaries, careless about peace.

In contrast, voters of all persuasions could rally around the Johnson banner. And so it went. Another "nonpartisan" address was given at Johns Hopkins University in early October. The President went out of his way to praise Milton Eisenhower (who had nominated Governor Scranton in San Francisco), pointed to Arthur Vandenberg and Henry Cabot Lodge as fine men who had supported a bipartisan foreign policy, and argued that the Democrats had done their part by supporting Dwight Eisenhower's foreign policy. In the postwar era, Mr. Johnson recalled,

> We have formed together—across the sea—an alliance of purpose between the two largest associations of free men in the world. America's part in this achievement has been possible because (nothing) was ever permitted to override the noble spirit of united (American) purpose.

And, campaigning in Indiana, Lyndon Johnson acknowledged that Hoosiers had often supported Republican presidential candidates, but declared, "I'm not sure whether there is a real Republican candidate this time."

Nor was an appeal to Republicans neglected in the Johnson television campaign. One widely used spot showed a man presumably walking away from the San Francisco convention stepping on posters bearing pictures of Rockefeller, Romney, and Scranton. Meanwhile, the announcer's voice recalled pre-San Francisco statements by Senator Goldwater's Republican rivals. Governor Rockefeller, for example, was quoted as saying that Goldwater's policies could "spell disaster for the (Republican) party and the country." At the end, the announcer tied this message directly to voters' attitudes by saying that if they had doubts about Goldwater, they were in pretty good company. A longer (4½ minute) television appeal was called "Confessions of a Republican." This accented several themes, a fear about "that crowd" which had taken over the Republican party, a belief that Goldwater was reckless and vacillating, and a latent preference on the part of some Republicans that Goldwater lose the November election. This, too, was designed to assure wavering Republicans that they were not the only ones skeptical about Barry Goldwater.[14]

The advertising agency which created these spots, Doyle Dane Bernbach, had been selected at the insistence of Bill Don Moyers and Lloyd Wright, who were in charge of the media campaign. They had been favor-

[14] Description of the Democratic television campaign is based largely on two sources: Pete Hamill, "When the Client is a Candidate," *New York Times Magazine,* October 25, 1964, pp. 30–31, 128–130, and Walter Pincus, "Democrats Split on Ad Agency Value," *Washington Star,* November 18, 1964, p. A–7.

ably impressed by the agency because of its work with the Peace Corps. The best known component in the campaign created by Doyle Dane Bernbach was the so-called "daisy spot." This was an announcement that began with a little girl pictured in a field of daisies. She picked one and began plucking off the petals one at a time. As she removed the petals, the voice on the sound track began a countdown. When it finished, the girl disappeared in a mushroom cloud. "These are the stakes," the voice continued, "to make a world in which all of God's children can live or go into the dark. . . . The stakes are too high for you to stay home." As the announcer concluded, a message on the screen admonished the audience to vote for President Johnson on November 3. This spot, touching raw nerves in the viewing audience,[15] was put on in the best available time period. Many who did not see it had their attention called to it by the ensuing protests from Republicans and neutral observers. It was shown once only, but this was all that had been intended. The media strategists had been certain that once would be enough to stimulate substantial comment about one of Goldwater's weakest areas: nuclear responsibility.

Several less controversial television spots dramatized other themes central to the Johnson strategy. One of these showed a social security card being torn up while a voice on the sound track said: "Goldwater has said he would change the system. Even his running mate admits that the voluntary plan would ruin the system." Another gave the viewers a chance to see a wooden East Coast falling into a swimming pool "ocean" and being moved away by a hidden swimmer while the announcer recalled the Goldwater quote: "Sometimes I think our country would better off if we could just saw off the Eastern seaboard and let it float out to sea." A backdrop of the Grand Canyon was used while the sound track implied Senator Goldwater opposed federal benefits everywhere except in his home state of Arizona, and Appalachian faces were shown on the screen while a voice over a folk music background stated: "Millions of families are caught in circumstances of poverty beyond their control. Their children will live lives of poverty unless the cycle is broken." A pretty little blonde girl was shown licking an ice cream cone as a female voice read: "Know what people used to do? They used to explode bombs in the air. You know children should have lots of vitamin A

[15] This spot caused trouble for a good many parents when young children, just becoming aware of their own mortality, began asking anxiously if they were going to be blown up.

and calcium. But they shouldn't have strontium-90 or cesium-137. . . . Now there's a man who wants to be President. . . . (who) wants to go on testing more bombs. His name is Barry Goldwater. If he's elected, they might start testing all over again." And there was a spot featuring a reflective President Johnson in the White House while the announcer talked about the qualities a President ought to have. "The way an agency functions with a political party is not much different from the way it functions with any other account," recalled James Graham, the account executive who supervised the Democratic efforts. "They know what they want to say, and we know how to say it."[16] What the Johnson strategists wished to emphasize was nuclear responsibility, social security, and anti-Goldwater Republicanism. Doyle Dane Bernbach transmitted these messages for them.[17]

As we have seen, the Goldwater strategy was characterized by an oscillation as it shifted back and forth between offense and defense. There was also an oscillation to the Democratic strategy, but in this case the dynamic was between a front-porch campaign with Lyndon Johnson remaining in the White House and making news by just being the President and the alternative of actively taking to the hustings. At first, the President leaned toward spending much of the time in Washington. He told a September 5 White House press conference:

> We are not going to plan our activities for the next few weeks based on any traditions or any practices of Presidents who have preceded us. Our first obligation is to do this job that we are doing here, today, and I will be doing it all day today, and I will be doing it all day tomorrow, right in this house. But if I can get off a few hours Monday, I am going out there and speak to the folks there at their Labor Day meeting like I would go to the Fourth of July, if I do, and then I am coming right back here to burn some midnight oil.

Senator Humphrey would fly around the country to make political speeches while President Johnson remained in Washington most of the time. If the President left the nation's capital, it would be for quick in-and-out trips, as his September 7 journey to Detroit and his September 10 evening speech

[16] Hamill, "When the Client Is a Candidate," p. 128.

[17] An early October survey by Opinion Research Corporation showed respondents recalled these things from the Johnson television commercials: convention posters of Rockefeller, Scranton, and Romney; Republicans are not supporting Goldwater; the little girl and the atomic explosion; the social security card being torn up; that Johnson is the better man for the country; that they should vote for Johnson.

in Harrisburg. There were some union speeches scheduled—the machinists on September 15 in Miami Beach, the steelworkers on September 22 in Atlantic City, and the electricians on September 23 in Washington—and he was going to take part in some ceremonies with our North American neighbors. On September 16, he would fly to the Northwest to join Canadian Prime Minister Pearson at the International Peace Arch on the Washington-British Columbia border, and on September 25 he would fly Southwest to join Mexican President Lopez Mateos in ceremonies marking the return of some 437 acres to Mexico.

The President was among friends as he spoke to the union audiences. He was repeatedly interrupted by applause. In Miami Beach, Mr. Johnson cited some specific gains for the machinists.

> Our success, the success of all the American people, is running at the flood. In all our years, never have any other Americans known the prosperity that you know today. . . . Average weekly earnings set a new record for August of $103—$4.50 more than August, 1963, and $10 a week more than August, 1961. This is what our late, beloved President, John Fitzgerald Kennedy, talked about when he said, "We are going to get America moving again." . . . In the 42 months before January 1961, the workers' average weekly earnings, after taxes, rose only $1.25. But in the next 42 months they rose $8.43—let me repeat, seven times as much.

Speaking to the steelworkers in Atlantic City, the President declared he was opposed to the philosophy of the soup line, and said the nation would help the poor, the helpless, and the oppressed. Departing from his prepared text, he added:

> We will do these things because we love people instead of hate them; because we have faith in America, not fear of the future; because you are strong men of vision instead of frightened cry babies; because you know it takes a man who loves his country to build a house instead of a raving, ranting demagogue who wants to tear down one. . . .

The following evening Lyndon Johnson told the International Union of Electrical Workers in Washington (and five other unions who were watching on remote television in other major cities) about the political choice as he saw it.

> Americans are faced today with a concerted bid for power by factions which oppose all that both parties have supported. It is a choice between the center and the fringe—between the responsible mainstream of American experience and the reckless and rejected extreme.

In short, American labor was part of the Johnson centrist coalition; labor was sharing in substantial benefits under the existing order of things; and the status quo was under attack from the fringes. Or, as George Meany told the steelworkers, "It is not a sure thing that Barry Goldwater will not win. We must get out the vote for Lyndon Johnson."

President Johnson managed to make a number of political stops on his trips to the borders. At a "Salute to United States and Canadian Partnership in Progress" in Seattle, Mr. Johnson told "my fellow Westerners" that he wanted to talk about one of the most solemn responsibilities of the president, the duty to direct and control the nuclear power of the United States:

> Our experts tell us as of today that a full-scale nuclear exchange between the East and the West would kill almost 300 million people around the world, and in the midst of that terror and tragedy we could expect that weapon after weapon would engulf a portion of mankind. . . .
>
> Now in the face of these facts, every American President has drawn these same conclusions:
>
> President Harry Truman said: "Such a war is not a possible policy for a rational man."
>
> President Eisenhower said: "In a nuclear war, there can be no victory—only losers."
>
> President Kennedy said: "Total war makes no sense. . . ."
>
> And I say we must learn to live with each other or we will destroy each other. . . .
>
> I believe the American people should know the steps that we have taken to eliminate the danger of accidental attack by our strategic forces. . . . (First,) the release of nuclear weapons would come by Presidential decision alone. Complex codes and electronic devices prevent any unauthorized action. . . . (Second,) by protecting our power against surprise attack, we have given ourselves more time to confirm that war has actually begun. . . . I do not want to fight a war that no one meant to begin. . . .
>
> Third, we have developed ways to meet force with appropriate force by expanding and modernizing our conventional forces. . . .
>
> Fourth, we have worked to damp down disputes and to contain conflict. . . .
>
> Fifth, we consistently work toward arms control. . . .

In Portland, Oregon, the next day, Lyndon Johnson declared that conservation is a bipartisan affair, and outlined a five-point program for a "new conservation" which would embrace cities and suburbs as well as river basins. And speaking from the steps of California's capitol, Commander in Chief Johnson disclosed the existence of two hitherto secret weapons: a radar which "will literally look around the curve of the earth" and a system which could intercept and destroy armed satellites.

On his trip to the Mexican border the following week, the President promised to "go to any remote corner of the earth, any place, any time, to promote freedom and peace." Speaking en route at the dedication of the Eufaula Dam in Oklahoma, Lyndon Johnson spoke again in favor of conservation:

> The government has a responsibility not to waste the taxpayers' money. But the government also has a responsibility not to waste the nation's resources. The real wasters, the real spendthrifts, are those who, by neglecting the needs of today, destroy the hopes of tomorrow.

And on his way back, he stopped off at Texarkana to speak in favor of civil rights—"Today, we ask for equality and justice for all citizens under our Constitution"—and sounded his make-the-South-part-of-the-nation theme by quoting Robert E. Lee: "Abandon all these local animosities and make your sons Americans."

Large crowds greeted the President everywhere and, as a man sensitive to people and one who enjoys contact with them, he was drawn farther and farther away from the strategy of posing as a working president who was too busy to campaign. On Monday, September 28, he finally left Washington for what he conceded to be a political tour. It lasted but a single day, but it was a day organized by Connecticut's John Bailey so the Democratic president could visit all six New England states. His themes that day were familiar. In Providence, he cried, "We're in favor of a lot of things, and we're against mighty few"; in normally Republican Vermont, he warned, "One of the great parties has been captured by a faction of men who stand outside the whole range of common agreement and common principles which have brought us to the summit of success"; and in Manchester, New Hampshire, he declared the four pillars of American foreign policy were "the effort to persuade adversaries that attack would bring their destruction, a strengthening of the independence of others, working for peaceful settlements in world affairs, and lessening the danger that nuclear weapons will destroy mankind." There was, in other words, room in the large center of the Johnson coalition for almost everyone, and he wished to extend a particular invitation to moderate Republicans and men interested in peace.

This was a day, however, when people were more important than words. One reason for making the trip was to dispel the notion that a Texan president would not be popular in New England. At his first stop of the day, the

President noticed crowds at the edge of the airport. Telling journalists, "If you want to see crowd reaction, follow me!" he started off on a day of pressing the flesh which did not end until well after midnight. Lyndon Johnson obviously loved the reception he was getting, and New England was responsive to the President. No Democratic candidate had ever swept all of New England's electoral votes, but the crowds in Providence, Hartford, Burlington, Portland, and Manchester were larger than they had been for Franklin D. Roosevelt, Dwight D. Eisenhower, or John F. Kennedy.

The candidate had hit his stride now. He was relaxed, confident but not over-confident, hoping for a landslide, and willing to work for it. The front-porch strategy was forgotten, and additional political trips were added to the President's schedule. On the day after the "Lady Bird Special" departed for the South, Lyndon Johnson himself left Washington for a week-long fifteen-state tour. He began with the Midwest. Although this had been traditional Republican territory, both polls and political reports indicated Johnson's chances of success were bright. The normally reliable Iowa poll projected a Johnson vote of 64 per cent, and private polls gave the President a 55–45 margin in Indiana. Campaign director Lawrence O'Brien had just completed a series of conferences with state leaders in the Midwest and West and his reports were equally good.

The plan for this trip was to mix serious speeches before set audiences with hoopla along the way. As Johnson and his party reached Chicago on the evening of October 7, his first national speech was being telecast. In this address, the President argued in favor of the status quo.

> Few presidential elections in our entire history have presented, as this one does, a basic choice that involves the fundamental principles of American life. We must decide whether we will move ahead by building on the solid structure created by forward-looking men of both parties. Or whether we will begin to tear down this structure and move in a radically different and—I believe—deeply dangerous direction.

In Gary, Indiana, the next morning, he advocated reform of immigration laws.

> . . . two-thirds of the total immigration quota goes under (the McCarran-Walter) law to people who never use their quota. . . . We want to abolish those discriminatory quotas gradually over a five-year period and raise the overall limit by 9,000—or 1/80 of 1 per cent of our work force.

Four days later in Montana, the President spoke of a "Bill of Responsibilities," goals which should be pursued to give greater meaning to the rights of citizens. These goals included prudence in spending, full development of the economy and natural resources, social security, education for all, equal opportunity, domestic tranquility and protection against violence, world peace, proper discharge of world leadership, and a government of service rather than of mastery. At the Denver Coliseum that evening, the President pledged himself to make educational opportunities freely available.

> I intend to put education at the top of America's agenda. And if you do not quite understand the details of what I mean by the top of America's agenda, I will say this: That regardless of family financial status education should be open to every boy and girl born in America up to the highest level which he or she is able to master.

On many other stops during this swing, Lyndon Johnson used more earthy language. In Springfield, Illinois, he urged his listeners to "vote for peace in the United States between labor and business and government . . . vote for peace among all people." Then, reaching a peak, he told his audience they should "vote for Molly and the babies." In Peoria, in an off-the-cuff speech to an AFL-CIO meeting, the President asked: "Are we going to do it up brown?" Then he reminded his listeners that work was necessary, and that on election night he was going to be "at my little ranch home on the banks of the Pedernales . . . waiting until we hear from the great state of Illinois." On Sunday, he flew eight hundred miles to attend church services in Phoenix. This was to show that he could outdraw his opponent in his home state—and on a Sunday. And the presidential car was stopped by crowds seven times on the way to church, and ten times on the return trip. In Reno, he told his audience: "Sometimes I think (my opponent) is running against the office of President instead of for it. Somebody better tell him most Americans are not ready to trade the American Eagle in for a plucked banty rooster." And when he reached Denver Monday evening, he used a bull horn to invite residents to come to his rally.

> Come on down to the Coliseum. . . . Get in your cars and come. You don't have to dress. Just bring your children and dogs, anything you have, with you. It won't take long. You'll be back in time to put the kids to bed. Come on down to the speakin'. We're gonna have a hot time in the old town tonight.

The crowd reaction to Johnson on this trip led such a careful observer as David S. Broder to write:

> To describe this week's work on this first frankly political junket as "effective campaigning" is like calling Hurricane Hilda "a bit of a blow."

Hoarse-voiced but happy, he returned . . . with even the skeptics convinced that he has built a vast and enthusiastic personal following of his own. He is no longer just John Kennedy's successor. He is a towering political figure, with a constituency that is his, and his alone.[18]

This political style had many advantages. By relying on personal empathy and by pledging himself *in principle* to work for popular goals, he could avoid discussion of thorny political problems. In his Denver education speech, for example, he did not take up the question of federal aid for classroom construction, and he did not discuss Vietnam or our relations with NATO at any time on his trip. By leaving many details of the Great Society rather vague, it was easier for him to entice additional recruits into his political coalition. This, as has already been noted, was consistent with the centrist political tactics employed by Johnson for many years. And there was another political advantage to the combination of pledging actions in certain areas and leaving the rest in vague outline. Lyndon Johnson did not give his political opponents any target. Arthur Hoppe wrote a delightful dialogue about an alleged spy episode which illustrates an opponent's difficulty in debating with the President.

> Oh, I can just see the jubilant scene in Republican headquarters as their master spy slips stealthily in and triumphantly draws forth from under his cloak the advance text of Johnson's address to the Muncie, Indiana, Hog Improvement Association.
>
> *Head strategist:* You've got it!
>
> *Master spy* (wearily): Yes. It's bloodstained here and there. But let us not think of the cost in human lives.
>
> *Head strategist:* . . . Oh, we'll undercut him on every issue before he can raise them.
>
> *Chief speech writer:* Wonderful! What an opportunity to change the course of history. What's he say?
>
> *Head strategist* (reading): "Howdy, folks. How y'all? It sure is good to get down here and press the flesh of so many fine, friendly . . ."
>
> *Chief speech writer:* Try the next paragraph.
>
> *Head strategist:* Well, let's see. That seems to be a story about a Baptist minister down Texas way who . . .
>
> *Chief speech writer:* Try the next page.

[18] "Johnson Creates a Campaign Style," *Washington Star,* October 13, 1964, p. 1. I have relied heavily on three Broder articles published in the *Washington Star* on October 8, October 11, and October 13 in describing this particular campaign swing.

Head strategist: ". . . and the minister says to this here fellow running for Congress . . ."

Chief speech writer: Better skip a couple of pages.

Head strategist: . . . Here we are! Listen, "Well, now, that's enough funning, folks. I know you came down here tonight to hear me talk about the issues. And I'm going to tell you all tonight right smack dab where I stand on the issues. I'm against poverty, shooting from the hip, wasteful spending, war, sin, the Ku Klux Klan and infectious dandruff."

Chief speech writer (rubbing his hands): Great. We've got him cold. All we have to do is come up with a brilliant speech assailing his stand on the issues. Tell me, which do you think we ought to come out for more strongly, poverty or the Ku Klux Klan?[19]

Lyndon Johnson was no sooner back in the nation's capital than he was off again. This time he headed for the Empire State to campaign with Robert Kennedy. And it was here that word reached the President of the collapse of Walter Jenkins. Though this was doubtless a personal blow to Lyndon Johnson, it did not involve a large commitment of presidential time. The affair already had been handled in Washington by Johnson's old and close friends, Clark Clifford and Abe Fortas. When word reached him, Johnson simply confirmed their action recommendations. And the next day—before any shift in strategy could have been implemented—word came of the change in leadership in the Soviet Union.[20]

Now the working President took the spotlight back from candidate Johnson. He made a brief reference to Khrushchev's ouster in a speech in Madison Square Garden. It "may or may not be a sign of deeper turmoil or may be a sign of changes in policies to come. . . . But we must keep our eyes and our vision on the stars, and our feet—both of them—on the ground." On Friday, October 16, he met with Secretaries Rusk and McNamara, CIA Director McCone, Under Secretary of State George Ball, Presidential Assistant McGeorge Bundy, and Russian expert Llewellyn Thompson. Later

[19] *San Francisco Chronicle*, October 15, 1964, p. 43.

[20] Theodore H. White reports that Oliver Quayle was commissioned to do a quick telephone survey on the impact of the Jenkins affair. On the basis of preliminary results—and prior to news of the foreign events—Quayle had recommended continuing the campaign as planned (*Making of the President 1964*, pp. 369–70).

in the morning he received Soviet Ambassador Dobrynin who brought word from the new Soviet leaders that there would be no radical departure from established Russian foreign policy. The next day he canceled a weekend campaign trip to Texas, convening instead a meeting of the National Security Council for a review of the meaning of the events in Russia and China. And, on Sunday evening, he requested time from all three television networks for a report to the American people.

Just as Barry Goldwater examined the events and found that they confirmed the wisdom of his call for a tougher foreign policy, Lyndon Johnson listened to his experts and concluded that the events showed that the United States had been following the correct course in foreign policy. The President began his address with a discussion of the transfer of power in the Kremlin.

> It means at least four things:
> *First:* . . . A time of trouble among the Communists requires steady vigilance among free men and most of all among Americans. For it is the strength of the United States that holds the balance firm against danger.
> *Second:* There will be turmoil in the Communist world. . . . [This] is not all bad because men who are busy with internal problems may not be tempted to reckless external acts.
> *Third:* This great change will not stop the forces in Eastern Europe that are working for greater independence. . . .
> *Fourth:* Our own course must continue to prove that we on our side are ready to get on with the work of peace.

Next he turned to the Chinese nuclear device exploded "near a lake called Lop Nor in the Takla Makan desert of the remote Central Asian province of Sinkiang."

> I discussed . . . this event in a statement on Friday. The world already knows:
> —That we were not surprised,
> —That our defense plans take full account of this development,
> —That we reaffirm our defense commitments in Asia,
> —That it is a long, hard road from a first nuclear device to an effective weapons system,
> —And that our strength is overwhelming now and will be kept that way.
> But what I have in mind tonight is a different part of the meaning of this explosion at Lop Nor. . . . The lesson of Lop Nor is that we are right to recognize the danger of nuclear spread. We must continue to work against it—and we will.

Then he devoted a few words to the victory of the Labour Party in Great Britain.

> The British Labour Party is the same party that held power when the Atlantic Alliance was founded, when British and American pilots flew the Berlin airlift together, and when Englishmen joined us in Korea. . . . They are our friends—as the Conservatives before them are our friends—and as governments of both parties have been friends for generations. We congratulate the winners. We send warm regards to the losers. The friendship of our two nations goes on. This is our way with all our trusted allies.

The President closed on the note that "what happens in other countries is important, but the key to peace is to be found in the strength and good sense of the United States of America."

The next morning, Mr. Johnson held a meeting with the congressional leadership of both parties to relate his observations arising from conversations with Prime Minister Wilson, Ambassador Dobrynin, and others. He was joined in this highly classified briefing session by the Secretaries of State and Defense, CIA Director McCone, and Glenn Seaborg, chairman of the Atomic Energy Commission. On Tuesday, he held a two-hour cabinet meeting devoted to an examination of the meaning of these foreign events. Afterward he issued a statement which said:

> Changes in the Communist world and the free world do not at this time indicate any sharp or serious changes in our policy. We shall pursue a course of reasonable and responsible watchfulness. . . .

He also revealed that he had ordered the cabinet officers to enter and leave the White House by way of the West Wing (where newsmen congregate) so they could be more accessible to correspondents and presumably originate more news. And, on Wednesday, he had another meeting to discuss the same foreign developments, this time with a group of elder statesmen most of whom were Republicans. Then he left for St. Louis for a campaign speech. Here he discussed the series of meetings with governmental leaders so as to contrast his policies with what were presumably the Goldwater alternatives.

> All those men that I met with, men from both the Democratic and Republican parties, were in agreement about the broad course of American foreign policy. No one advised me to break the Nuclear Test Ban Treaty. Instead, we discussed ways of making it apply to other nations. No one advised me to break off relations with the Soviet Union. Instead, we discussed ways to make our relations with the new Soviet leaders more productive. No one advised me to withdraw from the United Nations. Instead, we talked

about the need to strengthen it. No one advised me to make threats or issue ultimatums, or to talk about lobbing one into the men's room at the Kremlin. Instead, we talked about how we could avoid expanding conflicts, instead we sought the means of trying to reason together and resolve any differences that exist between the nations.

As the campaign entered its closing days, candidate Johnson again replaced the working President on the front pages of the nation's newspapers. The President had generated about as many stories as he could in connection with the events in Russia and China—and there were cities influencing large blocs of electoral votes that Lyndon Johnson wished to visit prior to election day. Monday was devoted to the South, but Tuesday found the President campaigning in Pittsburgh and Houston; Wednesday he was in San Diego, Los Angeles, and other points in Southern California; Thursday he was in Philadelphia, Friday in Chicago, and Saturday he went to New York City for a final rally in Madison Square Garden.

The themes during the final week remained as they had been throughout the campaign—special strategies directed at the South and moderate Republicans and a general strategy aimed at gathering as many groups as possible into the ambiguously defined center of the Johnson coalition. Mr. Johnson made his Southern appearances in three states thought to be close, Florida, Georgia, and South Carolina. Polls indicated that the Democratic candidate had pulled ahead in Florida, but was in trouble in Georgia and South Carolina. Trouble or no, the President did not modify his "new South" appeal. Speaking in Augusta, Mr. Johnson told his audience:

> The only place in the world where nothing has to be explained to me is the South. I know the burdens the South has borne. I know the troubles the South has seen. I know the ordeals that have tried the South through all these years. With all that is in me, with all the feeling in my heart, I say to you this afternoon that I want to see those burdens lifted off the South.

It was important to Lyndon Johnson to win Southern support, and he was willing to fight for it. But if he was going to win that fight, he was going to win it on his terms.

Mr. Johnson found more sympathetic audiences outside the South, and in these settings he sounded a bit more like the victorious candidate. "We will win this election," he told a capacity crowd in Chicago Stadium. This had all the marks of a triumphant party rally—and it was. The President was escorted to the stadium by a torchlight parade and spoke before heroic-size portraits of the most important party leaders in the country—which in Chicago meant Mayor Richard J. Daley, President Lyndon B. Johnson, and Senator Hubert H. Humphrey. But the President had made some more important, and more newsworthy, comments at Rockford, Illinois. Here he once again invited moderate Republicans to join the Johnson coalition. He promised them

> . . . that so long as Lyndon Johnson may serve as your President, I will share with them the opportunity as well as the obligation of saving America and saving our system of free enterprise.
>
> . . . every good Republican in this nation and every good independent who yearns for peace, who believes in prosperity . . . every businessman who believes in profits and prudence, every labor man who wants adequate wages and reasonable working conditions . . . (ought) to do some heavy thinking now.

Mr. Johnson did not apologize for being a Democrat, but he pointed out:

> I have always been the kind of Democrat who could and would work together with my fellow Americans of the party of Lincoln and McKinley, Herbert Hoover and Dwight Eisenhower, Robert Taft, Arthur Vandenberg, and Everett Dirksen.

In a non-campaign setting, there would be nothing unusual in a President speaking in Illinois bracketing the name of an old congressional colleague with other distinguished leaders of Everett Dirksen's party. But here was candidate Johnson four days before the election lavishing praise on the man who had nominated Barry Goldwater for president of the United States. Such words could leave little doubt about Lyndon Johnson's interest in obtaining Republican support.

Perhaps the most interesting speech of Johnson's final week of campaigning, though, was delivered in San Diego on the second anniversary of the settlement of the Cuban missile crisis. Mrs. Johnson had commented in a television interview that when the President spoke extemporaneously "he is infinitely better, and much more himself." The San Diego speech proved to be such a revealing off-the-cuff effort.[21] In the course of his reminiscences about foreign policy, he linked himself with the Kennedy administration, with the development of postwar bipartisanship, mentioned his own experi-

[21] Long excerpts from this speech were printed in the *Washington Star*, November 1, 1964, p. B–2.

ence, and defended his handling of the crises which had confronted him. He began with the 1962 Cuban missile episode.

In all the history of man, there has perhaps never been a moment of greater peril than the Cuban confrontation. I attended thirty-eight meetings with the President and his Security Council, the generals and their stars, the admirals and their braid, the Secretary of State, a Rhodes scholar with his great diplomatic experience, the Secretary of Defense, the former President of the Ford Motor Company at $550,000 a year, and the President went around the table and got the suggestions from all those present, including the Vice President.

There were moments when I guess some men were a little more hot headed than others. There were moments of distress and indecision while we were looking at the facts, because no man's judgment on any question is any better than his information on that question, and yet, when all is said and done, it gave me a great deal of satisfaction that you lay people of the United States had selected the Commander-in-Chief by your votes, and the coolest man in that room during all those thirty-eight meetings was John Fitzgerald Kennedy.

During that time, that was the moment when human understanding caught up with nuclear knowledge, and reason regained its rule over force.

Later in his remarks, he took up the theme of bipartisanship in foreign policy.

Harry Truman had a problem with the Communists taking over Greece and Turkey and he drew the line, the Truman doctrine, because he felt if they took Greece and Turkey they would sweep all Western Europe right after World War II. And the man that stood up by his side and did the most to help him was a Republican, Senator Arthur Vandenberg, of Michigan. He put his country ahead of his party.

When General Eisenhower was elected President, I was elected Democratic leader of the Senate, and the first thing I told my colleagues was "when he is right I am going to support him. When he is wrong, I am going to oppose him, but I am going to do it with decency, and with dignity, and without character assassination." . . . And when he had the crisis in Suez, and when he had the crisis in the Formosa Straits, the Democratic leader Lyndon Johnson stood up on the Senate floor and held his arm high. . . .

And when President John Kennedy decided your children were drinking milk that they shouldn't be drinking, and you faced problems that we shouldn't face, and we were breathing air that was polluted, it was Everett Dirksen, the Republican Senator from the state of Illinois, that came to the White House and sat there with us and agreed that we would pick up that

Kennedy treaty proposal and he would carry it on his broad shoulders right through the Senate.

That is the bipartisan foreign policy that is an issue in this campaign. Are we going to junk it? We have had it for twenty years. Are we going to flush it down the drain and let us go to evils we know not of? Well, we are not, if you elect me. . . .

Finally, the President discussed the foreign crises he had faced in his months in the White House and defended the decisions he had made in each case.

I am proud to be a Democrat, and I want to make that clear. But I am humble in the belief that on the issue of war and peace I share the view of the presidents of both parties who have preceded me and I share the view of what I think is the overwhelming majority of Americans today. We believe . . . you demonstrate courage by handling carefully and never carelessly any test which may arise. And there are many of them, and there is no way to prevent them. We must be ready to handle them when they come. We must do it with care, and coolness and courage. This we have done.

We were tested at Guantánamo, right after I went into office, and in Panama. They took a thermometer and put it in my mouth and took my temperature. They knew we had lost our President. They wanted to see what kind of transition we could have. And Castro went out and turned off the water at our Guantánamo base. . . . We finally decided after we talked to the best advisors we could get that it was a lot wiser to send one little admiral down there to cut the water off than to send in all these Marines to turn it on. . . . When we were tested in the Gulf of Tonkin, when they shot at our destroyers, we answered appropriately and promptly. . . . What we wanted was where those PT boats were nesting. . . . We looked at the targets and picked this one, and then your heart kind of comes up in your throat, but you say, "go on in, men" . . . and those boys got their planes off the deck and they went in and they destroyed their nests, and nearly all of them came back.

So the world knows, all the world knows, what you know tonight, that America says what it means and means what it says about keeping the peace against aggressors. And . . . all Americans know in this world of danger that we must be calm and we must be clear.

Thus did Lyndon Johnson defend his stewardship and the status quo.

By the time the President returned to his home state on the day before election, he had given attention to every group in the Johnson coalition. The special strategies for the South and the moderate Republicans were unusually important in 1964, but the President had also spoken to unions about gains for the laboring man, to Westerners about conservation, to Negroes about civil rights, and to urbanites about a better life in cities of the Great Society. And through citizens' organizations, television spots, and the

President's own speeches the word had gone out: there must not be any marked departure from established practices in domestic and foreign policy. To be sure, there were some who were concerned that Mr. Johnson's all-things-to-all-men approach left the precise contours of the future a little vague. A *Dallas Morning News* editorial, for example, complained that Johnson was supported by a confused bandwagon of "business tycoons, left-wing laborites, corporation lawyers, New Dealers, anti-New Dealers, etc."[22] But in case there is any doubt that the 1964 Democratic coalition bore the brand of Lyndon B. Johnson, it should be noted that this editorial was written in 1948.

[22] Quoted in Janeway, "Lyndon Johnson and the Rise of Conservatism in Texas," p. 64.

9

The Impact of Strategy

The strategies of the Goldwater and Johnson coalitions were quite different. The Goldwater strategy, though it passed through some five different phases, was essentially an explication of conservative doctrine. It emphasized issues rather than appeals to groups, and aimed for victory by adding the Midwest and West to a presumably already sympathetic South. The Johnson strategy, on the other hand, emphasized group appeals in an effort to build a consensus with as large a coalition as possible. Because of the nature of the Goldwater challenge, the Johnson strategy included special efforts to keep Southerners in the Democratic column and to woo discontented Republicans. What impact did these strategies have? Did the candidates succeed in communicating to the voters? Or were the voters effectively insulated from the messages the candidates were trying to transmit?

To answer these questions, we must concern ourselves with the relationship between the behavior of the electoral coalitions and the attitudes of the electorate. Specifically, we must look for evidence of *impact,* observable changes in the attitudes of the electorate that correspond to the strategies of the candidates. For this purpose, we shall treat strategies as independent variables and the attitudes of the electorate as dependent variables. Our measure of impact thus becomes an observable change in a dependent variable. There may arise problems in defining impact so narrowly, but unless some attitudinal modification can be shown we are forced to conclude either that the exertions of the candidates exactly offset each other or that the attitudes of the voters were so stable that the candidates could not sway them.

High quality data on the electorate's attitudes are available from the 1964 election study of the University of Michigan Survey Research Center.[1] The basic data have been drawn from responses to the now familiar sequence of questions: "I'd like to ask you what you think are the good and bad points about the two parties. Is there anything in particular that you like about the Democratic party?" "Is there anything in particular that you don't like about the Democratic party?" "Is there anything in particular that you like about the Republican party?" "Is there anything in particular that you don't like about the Republican party?" "Now I'd like to ask you about the good and bad points of the two candidates for president. Is there anything in particular about Johnson that might make you want to vote *for* him?" "Is there anything in particular about Johnson that might make you want to vote *against* him?" "Is there anything in particular about Goldwater that might make you want to vote *for* him?" "Is there anything in particular about Goldwater that might make you want to vote *against* him?"

The analysis of these data has been conducted in a somewhat different manner than those published by the Survey Research Center.[2] One of the latter's principal research foci has been the development of a parsimonious explanation of voting. Therefore techniques of data reduction were used to produce a six-factor model. Our interest is in the impact of strategies on attitudes. In order to observe as much of this as possible, we want to retain as many different attitudes as we can rather than reduce them to a few summary forces. Consequently, we shall present these data in twenty-nine attitudinal categories.

The data for the sample of the total electorate are presented in Figure 13. The figure itself is a little complex, as it reflects two different aspects of each attitude, salience and favorability. Each bar in the histogram represents

[1] These data were made available through the facilities of the Inter-University Consortium for Political Research. Needless to say, neither the Survey Research Center nor the Consortium bears any responsibility for the secondary analysis of these data reported here.

[2] Here I am referring to Donald E. Stokes, *et. al.*, "Components of Electoral Decision," *American Political Science Review*, June, 1958, pp. 367–87 (which also appears in *The American Voter*, pp. 523–31), and Donald E. Stokes, "Some Dynamic Elements of Contests for the Presidency," *American Political Science Review*, March, 1966, pp. 19–28.

Democratic Party

	N	% +
People in the Party	215	65
Management of Govt.	283	28
Philosophy of Govt.	374	38
Domestic Policies	645	70
Foreign Policies	226	38
Relation to Groups	598	90
Genl Party Loyalty	536	56

Republican Party

	N	% +
People in the Party	294	39
Management of Govt.	178	63
Philosophy of Govt.	399	71
Domestic Policies	268	35
Foreign Policies	146	64
Relation to Groups	424	17
Genl Party Loyalty	591	39

Johnson

	N	% +
Exper'ce, Ability	972	84
Character & Background	910	50
Personal Attraction	261	54
Domestic Policies	741	69
Foreign Policies	206	62
Relation to Groups	260	93
Pty Representative	558	61
Successor to JFK	219	93

Goldwater

	N	% +
Experience & Ability	252	48
Character & Background	1095	39
Personal Attraction	232	54
Domestic Policies	969	36
Foreign Policies	391	31
Relation to Groups	154	16
Pty Representative	624	19

800 400 0 400 800

Positive Comments *Negative Comments*

In this figure, the total length of each bar corresponds to N (the number of comments in each category) while the proportion to the left of the center line corresponds to % + (the proportion of positive comments).

Figure 13 *Attitudes of the Electorate*

one category of response. The over-all length of each bar represents the total number of responses falling into that category. The proportion of the bar lying to the left of the center line represents the proportion of positive comments; the proportion to the right signifies the proportion of negative comments. Hence, the total length of each bar indicates the salience of an attitude and the proportion to the left or right the favorability or unfavorability of the attitude to a party or candidate.

The attitudes about the parties are quite familiar. The Democratic party enjoys slightly greater visibility than the Republican; five comments were made about the Democrats to every four about the Republicans. The great Democratic advantages lie in the voters' perceptions of Democratic domestic policies, and in being regarded as the party more helpful to population groupings such as farmers, labor, minorities, and so forth. A lesser, but still significant, Democratic advantage is found in general party loyalty. Republican advantages continue to be found in the electorate's perception of their philosophy and conduct of government, and in foreign policy. Both parties tend to be weak in the areas where their opponents are strong.

The attitudes about the candidates, however, were far more salient than the attitudes about parties, and President Johnson enjoyed a little more visibility than Senator Goldwater. The questions about candidates engendered half again as many comments as the questions about parties, and eleven comments were made about Johnson for every ten about Goldwater. Mr. Johnson benefited particularly from a positive perception of his experience and ability,[3] the attractiveness of his domestic policies, and his being the Democratic nominee. Senator Goldwater was especially handicapped by negative references to his character and background (most frequently uncertainty as to the positions he was taking or negative references to his intelligence or impulsiveness), an unpopular domestic program, and his being the nominee of the minority party.

The queries about the candidates also differed from those about parties in that they seemed to tap short-term attitudes specifically related to 1964. The most striking example of this is found in the relatively undeveloped (and hence unstable) attitudes about foreign policy. Here negative attitudes

[3] As usual with first-year presidents, public approval of Johnson was very high, but the attitudes were diffuse. The respondents expressed themselves in such general phrases as "He's a good man," and "He seems to be doing all right." On the general record of presidential popularity, see Robert A. Dahl, *Pluralist Democracy in the United States* (Chicago: Rand McNally, 1967), pp. 106–7.

about the Democrats' foreign policy were cancelled by the attractiveness of Johnson's foreign policy. The usual Republican advantage on foreign policy, on the other hand, was more than offset by negative views about Goldwater's foreign policy. Another topic specific to 1964 was what might be called the "assassination effect." Whereas the comments about Goldwater aside from those reported in Figure 13 were sufficiently limited and random that they could be abandoned with little analytic loss, there were a large number of miscellaneous comments about President Johnson which took the form of "He's just begun" or "He'll carry out Kennedy's policies." This favorable attitude toward Lyndon Johnson as John Kennedy's successor was of the same order of salience as the President's relation to groups, and it was helpful to him.

When one looks at the estimates of attitudes of particular populations, this general pattern is repeated with variations caused by other relevant attitudes of the population in question. Table IV presents the attitudes of those who regard themselves as Democrats, Independents, and Republicans. (For the sake of simplicity, the number of comments in each category is not shown. The salience of attitudes did not vary much when party identification was controlled.) Significant[4]—and usually predictable—differences are found between the three party identification types. Perhaps the most interesting data in this table are those few which depart from normal expectation. There is a little partisan gradient in the comments about President Johnson's experience and ability, but this attitude was quite favorable to the President with all three types of party identifiers. The (less salient) attitudes concerning Mr. Johnson's helpfulness to various population groupings, and his "right" to the White House as John F. Kennedy's heir also went across party lines. On comments relating to the Republicans, the large number of negative comments about people (principally Senator Goldwater) in the Republican party, and the relatively weak appeal of party loyalty as a reason for a favorable perception of either the party or the candidate are notable. But,

[4] The significance of these data was tested by arraying them in a slightly different form than that in which they are presented here. A 7 by 3 frequency matrix was prepared for the pro-Democratic comments with type of comment as the column entry and party identification as the row entry. Chi-square and a contingency coefficient were calculated. Similar frequency matrices were prepared for the anti-Democratic, pro-Republican, anti-Republican, pro-Johnson, anti-Johnson, pro-Goldwater, and anti-Goldwater comments. The data are presented in a more condensed fashion in Table IV, however, because their meaning can be more readily apprehended in this form.

Table IV *Positive Comments by Party Identification*

	Democrats	Independents	Republicans
	Democratic Party		
People in the party	74%	74%	41%
Management of govt.	49	27	10
Philosophy of govt.	61	33	14
Domestic policies	79	64	46
Foreign policies	62	32	7
Relation to groups	96	85	57
General party loyalty	84	44	18
	Republican Party		
People in the party	36	46	41
Management of govt.	32	63	82
Philosophy of govt.	39	71	97
Domestic policies	21	49	82
Foreign Policies	36	84	92
Relation to groups	6	23	66
General party loyalty	16	31	62
	Johnson		
Experience and ability	90	84	67
Character and background	70	41	27
Personal attraction	68	45	35
Domestic policies	79	65	37
Foreign policies	82	52	33
Relation to groups	96	96	73
Party representative	85	47	17
Successor to JFK	95	92	82
	Goldwater		
Experience and ability	28	42	71
Character and background	21	37	64
Personal attraction	49	52	64
Domestic policies	20	39	61
Foreign policies	16	39	52
Relation to groups	5	16	67
Party representative	6	14	46

in the main, the attitudinal patterns of the party identification types are what one would expect given the general pattern and the usual effects of party identification.

A regional analysis[5] also reveals significant differences,[6] but a pattern that is far less regular than that caused by party identification. Table V presents the favorable comments by region. There is a general ordering to these data which is best shown in the comments about domestic policies of the Democratic party. Here one finds a drop in approval from 82 per cent to 43 per cent as one moves from East to Midwest to West to Peripheral South to Deep South. But there occur certain exceptions to this ordering which seem to reflect special regional characteristics. For example, there was almost no variation in the comments about Goldwater's experience and ability except in the Deep South, where 78 per cent of the comments were favorable. The approval rate for Democratic foreign policy and Johnson's foreign policy was highest in the Peripheral South, while the proportion of favorable comments about Republican foreign policy was somewhat higher in the East and strikingly so in the Midwest. And the appeal of President Johnson's experience and ability, his relationship to groups, and the assassination effect seemed to flow across regional boundaries just as clearly as it went across party lines. In short, an inspection of the attitudes of the electorate reveals a pattern decidedly favorable to the Democrats with quite predictable party variations and less predictable regional variations.

Now, bearing in mind both the strategies of the electoral coalitions and the attitudes of the electorate, we are in a position to ask what impact the strategies had. Can we find populations whose attitudes vary from the general population in ways which correspond to the strategies which were being followed? The answer is that at least three such populations can be

[5] Normal Survey Research Center regions are used in this analysis except for the South. Here I have followed the Matthews-Prothro distinction (in *Negroes and the New Southern Politics*, pp. 169–172) between a Deep South and a Peripheral South. The Deep South consists of South Carolina, Georgia, Alabama, Mississippi, and Louisiana; the Peripheral South includes all other southern states. I have also included the Border States with the Peripheral South because I found fewer attitudinal differences between the Border States and the Peripheral South than between the Peripheral South and the Deep South. Making this distinction caused a methodological problem. Because the Survey Research Center controls its sample between its eight subregions, but not within a subregion, there happened to be many more respondents in the Peripheral South than in the Deep South. Consequently, the data for the Deep South are much less reliable than those for other regions. The decision to use the Deep South as a separate region was one I made more as a political scientist who thought the data were interesting than as a properly cautious amateur statistician.

[6] The pro-Republican comments ($p = .5$) are the major exception to this. The relationship between region and anti-Johnson comments ($p = .1$) is also weaker than statistical significance implies.

Table V *Positive Comments by Region*

	East	Midwest	West	Peripheral South	Deep South
		Democratic Party			
People in the party	76%	69%	56%	59%	50%
Management of govt.	33	22	33	31	9
Philosophy of govt.	36	31	34	38	33
Domestic policies	82	72	69	57	43
Foreign policies	42	39	24	45	x
Relation to groups	90	90	91	90	96
General party loyalty	59	58	63	88	88
		Republican Party			
People in the party	31%	41%	40%	46%	57%
Management of govt.	59	69	59	60	x
Philosophy of govt.	71	75	73	66	73
Domestic policies	38	44	27	33	21
Foreign policies	67	80	55	58	50
Relation to groups	17	20	14	19	9
General party loyalty	41	41	39	37	24
		Johnson			
Experience and ability	86%	83%	81%	83%	86%
Character and background	57	47	48	51	38
Personal attraction	63	57	54	40	29
Domestic policies	83	67	73	63	55
Foreign policies	65	61	62	71	63
Relation to groups	93	97	91	94	92
Party representative	66	59	52	61	67
Successor to JFK	91	96	89	94	x
		Goldwater			
Experience and ability	49%	48%	44%	47%	78%
Character and background	31	41	42	38	72
Personal attraction	49	54	65	47	75
Domestic policies	34	30	31	43	59
Foreign policies	21	32	33	37	11
Relation to groups	3	18	13	23	19
Party representative	16	19	17	20	30

x = number of comments too small to report.

found. One reflects the success of the Republican mobilization effort; the other two show the success of the special strategies of the Johnson coalition with respect to discontented Republicans and the Peripheral South.

In Chapter 6, we reviewed the detailed Republican effort to mobilize potential Goldwater voters through vote quota, canvassing, election day, and ballot security programs. Survey Research Center data show that this portion of the Republican campaign was successful. Twenty per cent of the respondents said they had been contacted by a Republican party worker, while only 15.5 per cent said they had been contacted by the Democrats. This means that the minority party was able to reach four potential voters to every three reached by the majority party. Moreover, there occur significant differences in the attitudes of those contacted by the Republicans while no significant differences were found when the attitudes of respondents contacted by the Democrats were compared with those who had not been contacted. Table VI shows the contrast between those contacted by the Republican party and those uncontacted by either party. The most important effect of a Republican contact was to communicate a positive case for Barry Goldwater. Every one of the attitudes about the Senator was apparently improved by contact, and the contacted voters' perception of Barry Goldwater's experience, ability, and relation to groups was much more favorable. The Republican party, however, was not so well served. Explanation of Goldwater's foreign policy seems to have brought the voters' attitudes about this into closer relation with their views about Republican foreign policy, but this helped the Senator at the expense of the party.

It is also possible to find respondents whose views were probably shifted as a result of the Democratic campaign. As we have seen, nearly half the Republican voters were particularly unhappy about Goldwater's nomination.[7] And while the Arizona Senator disdained the support of any who did not agree with him, Lyndon Johnson went to very considerable effort to add these dissident Republicans to his coalition. The results of this can be seen when one compares interviews with these two types of Republican. The first is with a sixty-year-old retired school teacher in Mt. Pulaski, Illinois. He had wanted to see Goldwater nominated.

(*Is there anything in particular that you like about the Democratic party?*) They do have some conscientious members, I'm sure, and they are trying to

[7] See pp. 127–129 and Table I for a discussion of the frequency of these attitudes among Republicans, and for the questions which were used to discern respondents holding these views.

Table VI *Republican Success: Organizational Contact*

Positive Comments by Category	Contacted by Republicans	Uncontacted*
	Democratic Party	
People in the party	63%	65%
Management of govt.	18	29
Philosophy of govt.	28	39
Domestic policies	60	71
Foreign policies	22	37
Relation to groups	76	91
General party loyalty	60	56
	Republican Party	
People in the party	43%	39%
Management of govt.	55	65
Philosophy of govt.	88	69
Domestic policies	35	35
Foreign policies	56	65
Relation to groups	19	16
General party loyalty	43	38
	Johnson	
Experience and ability	75%	84%
Character and background	36	51
Personal attraction	74	53
Domestic policies	67	70
Foreign policies	61	62
Relation to groups	87	93
Party representative	37	61
Successor to JFK	69	93
	Goldwater	
Experience and ability	70%	47%
Character and background	42	39
Personal attraction	53	54
Domestic policies	51	34
Foreign policies	44	30
Relation to groups	56	10
Party representative	31	18

* The figures on which these percentages are based were arrived at by an estimating procedure because 9.5% of the respondents were contacted by both parties.

save the country as far as that goes. (*Anything else?*) I can't think of anything more. I don't think the country will go to pot if they stay in.

(*Is there anything in particular that you don't like about the Democratic party?*) Political machines—too much. Too much big government. Too much "papa knows best." Too much government interference in local affairs. And too much federal government handout.

(*Is there anything in particular that you like about the Republican party?*) I like their attempt to stay away from local contests and attempt to speak with authority on world affairs and cut down on federal spending. At least that's their promises. And I feel they are honest and forthright in their ideas.

(*Is there anything in particular that you don't like about the Republican party?*) In the past, they have failed to live up to some of their ideals. (*Anything else?*) No, that's the principal thing I dislike.

(*Is there anything in particular about Johnson that might make you want to vote for him?*) Very little. I think he's *trying* to do a good job.

(*Is there anything in particular about Johnson that might make you want to vote against him?*) He's wishy-washy. He plays up to different organizations and changes ideas depending on who he's talking to and gives something to everybody. A typical "politician." Undesirable. (*Anything else?*) That's enough!

(*Is there anything in particular about Goldwater that might make you want to vote for him?*) He's honest—says what he thinks. Believes in action and won't take any backtalk from foreign countries or any pressure groups.

(*Is there anything in particular about Goldwater that might make you want to vote against him?*) A trifle impulsive.

Another Goldwater supporter, a thirty-seven-year-old mechanical engineer who lived in southern California, was more succinct.

(*Like about Democrats?*) They are progressive. (*Anything else?*) No.

(*Dislike about Democrats?*) They are socialistic. (*Anything else?*) They are too free-spending.

(*Like about Republicans?*) Their objectives are more in keeping with respecting individual rights. (*Anything else?*) They are more conservative. They are more apt to retain existing policies.

(*Dislike about Republicans?*) No, not as a party.

(*Like about Johnson?*) Outside of his being a God-fearing man, no.

(*Dislike about Johnson?*) Yes, he does things for political expediency rather than to uphold the rights of individuals. (*Anything else?*) He is socialistically inclined.

(*Like about Goldwater?*) Yes, he upholds the Constitution and Bill of Rights in preference to political expediency. (*Anything else?*) His objectives are realistic.

(*Dislike about Goldwater?*) No.

These persons' attitudes were quite clear. They knew who they were for and who they were against.

Republicans upset by Goldwater's nomination, on the other hand, were subject to very real cross-pressures. A young Japanese-American medical technologist, a resident of Gardena, California, was about to cast her first vote. She was quite explicit about the mental anguish she felt. Almost as soon as the interview began, she burst out:

> Since this is the first time I voted, I don't see why things must be so hard for me. I stay awake nights trying to decide what way to vote. Why did it have to be a moral issue my first time?

Her comments about the parties and candidates revealed she saw good and bad points about both.

> (*Like about Democrats?*) The Democratic party is more for human rights, I believe. (*Anything else?*) No.
>
> (*Dislike about Democrats?*) Yes, their foreign policy. The Vietnam situation for one thing. They take more rights away from the individual person, but give more rights to all people. One morality. I guess that is right.
>
> (*Like about Republicans?*) I believe in less central government. Things like medicare. All this welfare. I think people should help themselves more. The Republicans believe that also. They believe in more states' rights.
>
> (*Dislike about Republicans?*) As far as the Republican platform itself, there was nothing I did like. (*Anything at all?*) No.
>
> (*Like about Johnson?*) I think his role in civil rights in general, especially since he is a Southern man. The feeling he gives you. He has a warm feeling for people, and you feel he is a fair man.
>
> (*Dislike about Johnson?*) I don't know anything about his personal life. If some things could be hidden like the Bobby Baker case. (*Anything else?*) Not against him personally, but since I am a registered Republican I wanted to vote that way. Now I really don't know.
>
> (*Like about Goldwater?*) Yes, he would do a better job in handling foreign policy. His concern for communism in this country. (*Anything else?*) No.
>
> (*Dislike about Goldwater?*) He is too impulsive. His stand on civil rights. He would not do a good job in enforcing the civil rights bill and that would lead to more trouble. He seems to be a cold hard man.

A fifty-six-year-old housewife in upstate New York was not suffering as much torment from cognitive imbalance, but still told the interviewer:

> Actually I'm voting against my own views—I'm a Republican.

Her comments also included positive and negative comments about both parties.

> (*Like about Democrats?*) I like what they're doing about social security.
> (*Dislike about Democrats?*) I think they spend too much money.
> (*Like about Republicans?*) I like their conservatism.
> (*Dislike about Republicans?*) I don't like Goldwater. I think sometimes they're a little slower about arriving at important decisions.
> (*Like about Johnson?*) I like his whole attitude. I think he is definitely and sincerely trying to do better things in Washington, and he is a sincere type of person who really wants to do things for the people.
> (*Dislike about Johnson?*) No, I wouldn't say so.
> (*Like about Goldwater?*) No.
> (*Dislike about Goldwater?*) Yes, everything. It's a personal reaction. I don't like his approach and I think he's been doing more mud-slinging than the rest. This has been the dirtiest campaign I've seen.

As can be seen, Republicans unhappy with Goldwater tended to handle the cognitive dissonance between their positive attitude toward the Republican party and their negative attitude about the Republican candidate by adding positive attitudes about the Democratic candidate. The data in the first two columns of Table VII compare the attitudes of the two groups. The comments of the two groups about the Republican party are not too dissimilar, but other attitudes show the combined effect of Democratic wooing and Republican neglect. The sharpest differences are to be found on Democratic domestic policies, and Johnson's and Goldwater's domestic policies, foreign policies, and relations to groups—all salient aspects of Johnson's compaign to attract liberal Republican support.

Table VII also compares the attitudes of Independents from the Peripheral South with those of other Independents. The Peripheral South was an area for which the Democrats devised a defensive strategy and to which the Republicans did not devote as much effort as they did to the Midwest and West. Some impact of Democratic efforts on the Independents from the Peripheral South can be seen in the comments on Republican and Democratic domestic policy.

The reason why the attitudes of Independents from the Peripheral South were not more favorable to Johnson when compared with other Independents is that Northern Independents were leaning in such a decidedly Democratic direction. Again, sample interviews help to give the flavor of the

Table VII *Democratic Success: Target Populations*

Positive Comments by Category	Republicans unhappy with Goldwater	Other Republicans	Independents from Peripheral South	Other Independents
		Democratic Party		
People in the party	63%	19%	x	76%
Management of govt.	6	12	14	30
Philosophy of govt.	20	12	18	38
Domestic policies	68	34	71	61
Foreign policies	19	2	33	32
Relation to groups	60	56	79	86
General party loyalty	32	15	43	45
		Republican Party		
People in the party	29%	57%	x	44%
Management of govt.	72	87	60	64
Philosophy of govt.	93	98	77	69
Domestic policies	75	87	44	50
Foreign policies	82	97	x	86
Relation to groups	55	73	x	21
General party loyalty	57	64	53	27
		Johnson		
Experience and ability	74%	63%	79%	85%
Character and background	43	18	18	45
Personal attraction	36	34	27	45
Domestic policies	55	29	50	69
Foreign policies	63	31	x	50
Relation to groups	100	59	88	97
Party representative	33	8	50	47
Successor to JFK	83	81	86	93
		Goldwater		
Experience and ability	52%	79%	33%	43%
Character and background	40	75	59	34
Personal attraction	35	80	86	47
Domestic policies	37	71	50	37
Foreign policies	29	63	x	32
Relation to groups	20	81	33	14
Party representative	28	58	26	12

x = Number of comments too small to report.

attitudes. First is an interview with a thirty-year-old German-born chemist living in Orlando, Florida.

(*Like about Democrats?*) No.

(*Dislike about Democrats?*) Well, it seems to me the Democratic party is getting too much power. I don't like this.

(*Like about Republicans?*) It seems to me the Republicans are more fair to the public on general issues.

(*Dislike about Republicans?*) No.

(*Like about Johnson?*) No.

(*Dislike about Johnson?*) Yes. The main issue is the civil rights bill. I don't like what's been done on that.

(*Like about Goldwater?*) Yes, he seems to be more fair and open-minded in seeing things the way things really are. He seems to be closer to the truth, I think.

(*Dislike about Goldwater?*) No.

Balanced against this clearly pro-Goldwater interview is one with a fifty-seven-year-old patent examiner. He had grown up in Batavia, New York, but now lived in Arlington, Virginia.

(*Like about Democrats?*) Moderate socialism and a sound foreign program.

(*Dislike about Democrats?*) Nothing specific.

(*Like about Republicans?*) It's changed so much. It used to represent big business and level-headed conservatism. It doesn't appear to stand for anything now. No positive approach.

(*Dislike about Republicans?*) My attitude is mainly negation I guess. I can't see that they're doing anything constructive. Just needling the Democrats.

(*Like about Johnson?*) He seems like a practical politician. He won't upset the applecart. He won't make any ignorant errors. He has a strong hand. I hope he'll outlive his money-grabbing days.

(*Dislike about Johnson?*) Well, he's certainly an opportunist. He's been closely associated with some pretty questionable characters.

(*Like about Goldwater?*) Yes, I think he's frank and honest and good-hearted. He likes people.

(*Dislike about Goldwater?*) He's made some wildly ill-advised comments. Mostly campaign talk, and to be discounted some.

And there was a thirty-four-year-old housewife who lived in rural North Carolina. She mentioned that her children took up all her time, and her limited comments (positive about Johnson, negative about Goldwater) were put in simple, personal terms.

(*Like about Johnson?*) I like him. He's a good husband. I don't know too much about him.

(*Dislike about Goldwater?*) I don't like him. He talks too much.

These statements, indicating a split in sentiment between the President and his Republican opponent, were not nearly so pro-Johnson as those offered in interviews with Independents from the North. Take, for example, the views of a Teaneck, New Jersey, Jewish housewife.

(*Like about Democrats?*) Well, talking about the Democratic party I like the liberal policies—civil rights program, medicare, anti-poverty—

(*Dislike about Democrats?*) The same as politics in general. (*You mean?*) All parties have to play politics.

(*Like about Republicans?*) At the present time, nothing at all.

(*Dislike about Republicans?*) They allied themselves with Goldwater.

(*Like about Johnson?*) No—except he has done a job he has taken over and he has done it well.

(*Dislike about Johnson?*) No.

(*Like about Goldwater?*) No, nothing at all.

(*Dislike about Goldwater?*) Yes—everything he stands for.

But if the interviews with the Independents from the Peripheral South were less favorable to the President than this, they were far more favorable than the responses from Independents in the Deep South. Here is a sample from a retired woodwork and machinery dealer in Montgomery, Alabama.

(*Like about Democrats?*) I can't think of a thing that would make me like the party. I vote Democratic in local elections, but I vote for the Republican party nationally. I don't like Johnson.

(*Dislike about Democrats?*) Nationally I don't know of anything I like about them. They have misled this country. I don't like Kennedy, and I despise Rusk and Mennen Williams.

(*Like about Republicans?*) I like the conservatism.

(*Dislike about Republicans?*) I don't like the new gangsters running the party. Goldwater is not a gangster. I'll clarify that. By gangster I meant Rockefeller and his bunch. Goldwater is a good man.

(*Like about Johnson?*) I don't know of anything. He is a Texas boy, but I don't believe he will spare any whips on anybody. A man can't change his mind every morning and still expect you to believe him.

(*Dislike about Johnson?*) Just listen to him talk. Sometimes I don't think Johnson is a real American. Johnson didn't get his feet wet in the last war. I think he served about three months.

(*Like about Goldwater?*) I think he is an upright American citizen.

(*Dislike about Goldwater?*) I don't know of anything. I don't approve of all he says, but I don't believe a thing Johnson says.

The comments from Independents in the peripheral South may not have been full of praise for Johnson and the Democrats, but they were certainly more favorable to them than this.

If the Democratic strategy produced these attitudes on the part of moderate Republicans and Independents from the Peripheral South, then it can be counted a success. Given the distribution of party identification types, the Democrats can almost win by getting all the Democratic votes whereas the Republicans need both Republican and Independent votes to do so. The implication of the data we have just reviewed is that the strategy of the Johnson coalition resulted in favorable attitudes among Democrats, Independents, and some Republicans in the East, Midwest, and West, and maintained favorable attitudes among Democrats and some Independents in the Peripheral South. Hence, the Democratic strategy had created (or at least permitted) the attitudinal basis for a massive victory at the polls. The Republican achievement lay in a very good organizational campaign which, as we have also seen, helped create attitudes favorable to the Goldwater cause. In the political environment of 1964, this, too, must be counted as a real success. So both parties achieved some measure of victories. The over-all attitudinal configuration bode well for the Democrats; hard organizational work by the Republicans created a counterforce of pro-Goldwater attitudes.

Thus far we have singled out particular populations who were the targets of campaign strategy, and have sought evidence of impact in differences between the attitudes of these groups and comparison groups. Now what about the temporal impact of the strategies? Were any attitudes changed as the campaign progressed? In order to assess this, the survey has been treated as a quasi-panel. The interviews have been separated into those which took place before October 4, those from October 4 through October 17, and those from October 18 through November 2.[8] Although this is less

[8] 432 interviews were conducted before October 4, 643 interviews from October 4 through October 17, and 496 interviews from October 18 through November 2. To compensate for the unequal number of interviews, the results for the period before October 4 were multiplied by a factor of 1.51, and the data for the October 18–November 2 period were weighted by multiplying by a factor of 1.29. The subsamples created for this quasi-panel were compared with respect to

satisfactory than a panel with re-interviews with individual respondents, it does give us blocks of interviews which represent three two-week intervals before the election. We can inspect these to see if any temporal changes in attitudes were taking place.

The choice of these time periods was dictated primarily by the analytic need to have comparable time periods containing a sufficient number of interviews. However, these two-week periods also coincide with shifts in campaign strategy and with outside events likely to capture the attention of the electorate. During the first period, Senator Goldwater was following a defensive strategy. The speech which signaled his return to the offense came on October 6, just two days after the second "wave" of interviews began. A week later the Goldwater offensive got some unexpected help with the news of the arrest of Walter Jenkins, an external event tending to give credence to Senator Goldwater's charges of "a shocking decline in political morality." But within twenty-four hours there were other headlines. Khrushchev was ousted in Russia, a Labour Government was elected in Britain, and the Chinese exploded their nuclear device. On the evening of October 18, the first day of our third time period, President Johnson took cognizance of these foreign events in a television address to the country. Analyses of the meaning of the Russian power shift and the Chinese nuclear capability continued to dominate the news for the next several days. So our three time periods do have some relation to shifts in strategy and important external events.

The data on the temporal impact of strategy are presented in Figure 14 and Table VIII. The immediate impression created by inspecting these is that the attitudes are rather stable. And so they are. The impact of strategies is to be found in the modification of specific attitudes rather than in the creation of a wholly new attitudinal pattern. We must understand that the histograms in Figure 14 are variations on an established general pattern, and seek the impact of strategies in perceptible modifications of attitudes on specific topics.

---

education, region, party identification, and vote to guard against the possibility that those who were interviewed at one time might differ from respondents who were interviewed at a different time. The results of this comparison suggest that the statistics from these subsamples can be used although they should be treated with appropriate caution. The sample estimate of the Johnson vote for the total sample was 67.5%; the estimates of the Johnson vote from the three subsamples were 68%, 67%, and 67%, respectively.

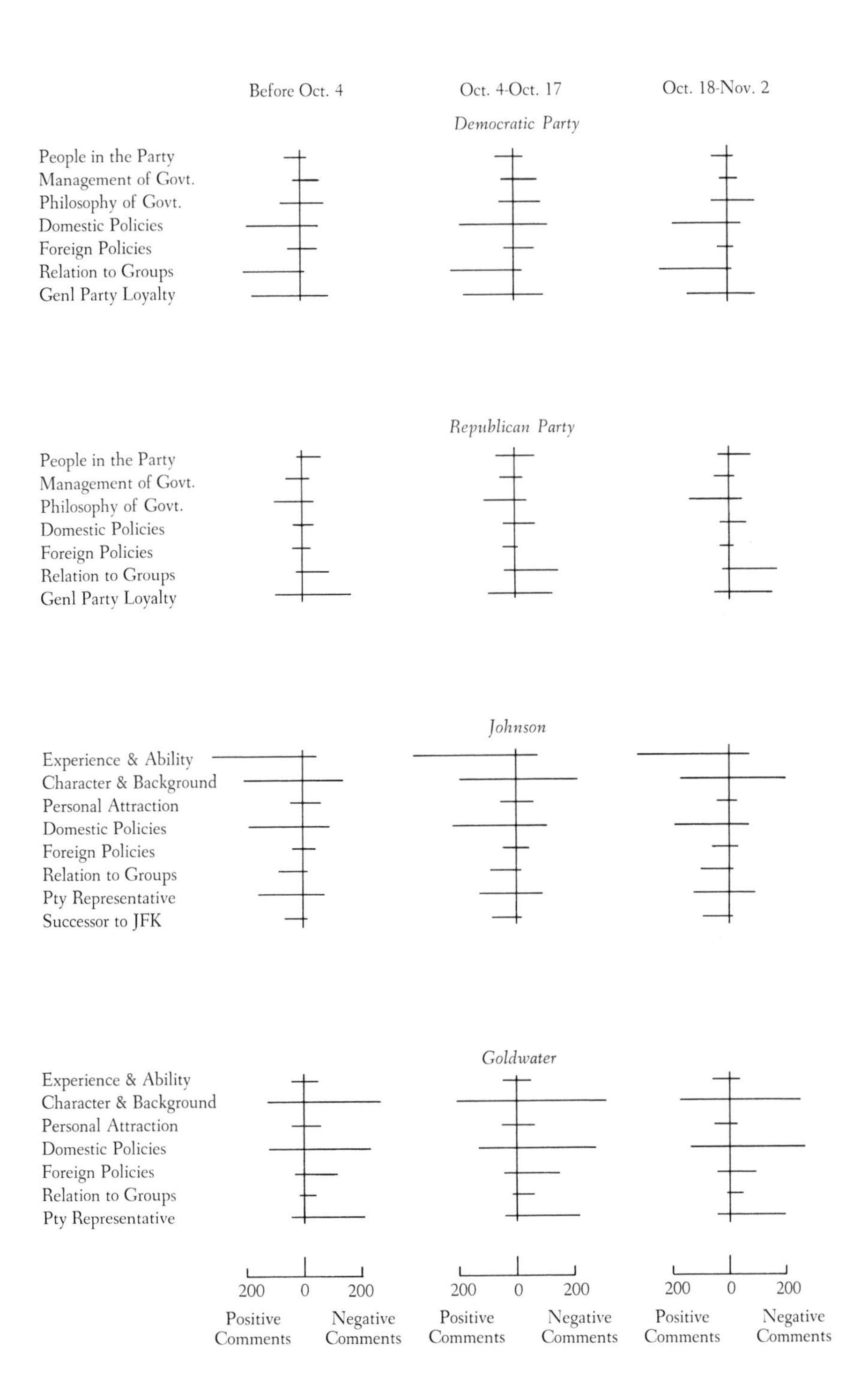

Figure 14 *Attitudes of the Electorate by Interview Date*

Table VIII *Attitudes of the Electorate by Interview Date*

	Before Oct. 4		Oct. 4–Oct. 17		Oct. 18–Nov. 2	
	N*	%+	N	%+	N*	%+
	Democratic Party					
People in the party	87	66	105	65	69	64
Management of govt.	97	27	128	32	116	22
Philosophy of govt.	159	47	149	34	155	35
Domestic policies	258	72	298	64	242	75
Foreign policies	102	40	101	36	72	39
Relation to groups	218	91	253	89	261	89
General party loyalty	268	66	272	64	243	59
	Republican Party					
People in the party	95	35	130	42	117	32
Management of govt.	89	64	78	64	70	70
Philosophy of govt.	146	75	150	69	182	74
Domestic policies	94	44	119	34	112	31
Foreign policies	77	58	62	65	43	70
Relation to groups	119	15	189	21	187	12
General party loyalty	276	40	223	39	199	26
	Johnson					
Experience and ability	365	87	427	83	394	82
Character and background	339	60	408	47	356	46
Personal attraction	113	48	108	53	83	52
Domestic policies	287	68	323	66	276	73
Foreign policies	81	48	91	57	90	70
Relation to groups	106	90	95	94	105	94
Party representative	242	66	228	59	219	58
Successor to JFK	76	89	95	93	95	95
	Goldwater					
Experience and ability	103	51	104	52	99	41
Character and background	383	34	507	41	422	41
Personal attraction	100	43	121	50	75	64
Domestic policies	353	39	416	35	412	34
Foreign policies	149	26	189	28	141	39
Relation to groups	61	23	72	15	55	11
Party representative	258	21	265	18	242	18

* N's have been weighted to compensate for the number of interviews which took place in each time period.

The impact of Goldwater's questions about the wisdom of federal dominance of all political affairs can be seen in the increasing salience of the Republican party's philosophy of government. His advocacy of different domestic policies (and Democratic criticisms of these policies) had an impact, too, albeit a less helpful one. By comparing responses elicited during a given two-week period with those made during the preceding periods, one can see that the comments about Republican domestic policies and Goldwater domestic policies became less favorable. The Republican defense of Senator Goldwater's foreign policies eventually was beneficial, however. Negative comments about Republican foreign policies and Goldwater foreign policies occurred less frequently; hence, the balance on this topic became more favorable.

The emphasis of the Johnson campaign on benefits for various groups (and Goldwater's disdain of such an approach) likewise had an impact. One can see this in the increasing salience of this subject in comments about the Democratic and Republican parties. And although it might seem unlikely that Johnson, who began his campaign with a 90-10 favorable balance on the subject of groups, would be able to increase the favorability of this attitude, or that Goldwater, who started off with a 23–77 negative balance about groups, would be able to lose more support, this is exactly what happened. In addition to this impact of his group appeal, President Johnson was able to maintain support for Democratic domestic policies and his own domestic policies at levels which varied between 2-to-1 and 3-to-1, and to increase support for his foreign policies.[9]

We can also see the impact of the personalities of the candidates. The public reputations of both men's experience and ability declined somewhat, Johnson's from 87% favorable to 82% favorable, and Goldwater's from 51% favorable to 41% favorable. Lyndon Johnson came to be seen as less trustworthy; positive references to his character and background dropped 14%. The electorate also came to perceive Barry Goldwater as a more likeable human being; positive references to his personal attractiveness rose some

[9] That both Johnson and Goldwater were able to increase support for their respective foreign policies does not seem so paradoxical if one remembers that: (a) attitudes on this topic were less well developed and so probably less stable; (b) Johnson's support rose to 70% while Goldwater's rose to only 39%; and (c) if one listened to the candidates' own foreign policy statements rather than the opponents' caricatures of their positions, one could note that Johnson and Goldwater often made very similar statements.

21%. And the perception of Lyndon Johnson as John Kennedy's successor who ought to be given a chance became even more favorable to the President. The margin of positive comments among those who mentioned this topic rose from 8-to-1 to 19-to-1.

There is something else in these data in Figure 14 and Table VIII which tells us of changes in the attitudes of the electorate during the course of the campaign. Look at the figures on the salience of a topic which relates to the respondents' interest in the campaign itself—the number of comments about people in the party or about the character and background of the candidates. Here is evidence that the campaign was most visible to the voters in mid-October. Either the voters were tiring of the whole business in the last two weeks, or something had happened to distract their attention.

There is reason to believe that this decrease in interest in the campaign was at least in part a reflection of "channel noise,"[10] specifically the leadership change in the Kremlin and the Chinese atomic explosion. In order to see this—as well as get a better idea of what was happening with respect to issues—we must look at responses to a question which focused directly on issues. The general queries about parties and candidates elicit so much in the way of traditional political views that issue references are a relatively minor theme. A more specific question is needed to tap the voters' thinking on issues. We shall look at the responses to: "What do you personally feel are the most important problems the government should try to take care of when the new President and Congress take office in January?"[11]

[10] In communication theory, "noise" refers to any signal (whether a vital message or simple static) which is not originated by the transmitter, and which reduces the "channel capacity" linking the transmitter to his intended destination. Using this term for important events simply calls attention to the communications problem faced by a candidate who must compete with many other sources of information (sporting events, stock market slumps, Latin-American revolutions, and so forth) for the voters' attention. It does not involve any judgment about the relative importance of the events. Some of the clearest explanations of this theory are to be found in Wilbur Schramm, "Information Theory and Mass Communication," *Journalism Quarterly*, Spring, 1955, pp. 131–46; R. Duncan Luce, "The Theory of Selective Information and Some of its Behavioral Applications," in R. Duncan Luce, ed., *Developments in Mathematical Psychology* (New York: The Free Press of Glencoe, 1960), and Colin Cherry, *On Human Communication* (New York: Wiley Science Editions, 1961).

[11] This was one of a series of questions about problems the government ought or ought not to handle. 1,241 people mentioned one problem requiring positive action, 907 mentioned two problems, and 436 three problems. 724 respondents mentioned one area the government ought to get out of, 306 two areas, and 111 three problems the government should not try to handle. Table IX is based on

Table IX *Salience of Issues by Interview Date*

	Number of Comments about Topics*		
	Before Oct. 4	Oct. 4– Oct. 17	Oct. 18– Nov. 2
Topics of Relatively Constant Salience			
Schools, aid to education	21	21	25
Medicare	47	49	46
Poverty, depressed areas	50	42	45
Labor relations**	11	12	8
Taxes	32	25	31
Farm problems**	20	20	19
Pro-civil rights responses	68	68	62
Anti-civil rights responses	21	30	27
Cuba	32	28	32
Topics of Declining Salience			
Neutral civil rights responses	79	64	62
Foreign aid	50	40	35
Topics of Highest Salience in Mid-Campaign			
Public disorder	23	31	21
Graft, corruption, Baker, Jenkins	8	18	14
Threat of communism	14	28	22
Fiscal and monetary policy	15	21	14
Aged and social security	30	39	26
Employment, unemployment	42	49	43
Vietnam	82	94	67
Topics of Highest Salience at End of Campaign			
Russia, cold war, etc.	27	12	37
War and peace	36	24	39
Must maintain position of strength	11	22	27

* N's have been weighted to compensate for number of interviews in each time period.
** These categories are not comparable to others. See footnote 11.

the first two positive responses. The N's in Table IX are comparable over time, but the number of references about farm problems and labor relations cannot be compared with the others. When a general topic (welfare, economics, civil rights, other domestic problems, foreign problems) included a great many comments, Table IX includes only those comments that could be put under reasonably identifiable subheads. Comments about labor relations and farm problems, on the other hand, were so scattered that all references are included under a single general heading.

Table IX shows the frequency of reference to specific issues. Here we see that there were four distinct patterns of salience during the campaign.[12] The number of persons mentioning education, medicare, labor relations, farm problems, and certain other topics remained almost constant. For whatever reason, whether the references reflected personal concerns that were independent of the campaign, or whether the candidates simply lacked the ability to communicate on these issues, the salience of these topics did not vary appreciably. There were a couple of topics of declining salience. The drop in neutral comments about civil rights suggests that those who did not feel involved in this controversy were beginning to shift their attention elsewhere. But the most suggestive evidence about the nature of the messages being communicated to the electorate comes from the third and fourth categories. The third category is made up largely of "political" subjects. Here we see four issues stressed during the Goldwater offensive: public disorder, corruption in high office,[13] the threat of communism, and government spending. We also find two Democratic issues: social security and jobs.[14] The fourth category, on the other hand, consists of cold war issues. The content of these categories seems to be related to the differing patterns of public attention which characterized them. The domestic political issues were marked by a noticeable increase in salience during the second period and an equally noticeable decrease in the third time period. The foreign issues were declining in interest in the second period, but something happened to refocus attention on these topics in the third time period. Since the dramatic events in Russia and China roughly coincided with the division between the two time periods, it seems plausible to infer that they generated channel noise which made it more difficult for the domestic political messages to be apprehended.

More evidence on the impact of these external events comes from the respondents' comments on the likelihood of war. The question put to

[12] Classification of topics within these patterns was done on the basis of inspection alone. A few issues did not clearly fit any pattern. Their classification had to be rather arbitrary.

[13] Note that an increase in the number of references to "graft, corruption, Baker and Jenkins" coincided with an increase in the number of negative references to Lyndon Johnson's character and background.

[14] It would be fascinating to speculate why the salience of these two topics could be increased, while the level of interest in schools, medicare, poverty, etc., remained relatively constant.

them was: "Looking ahead, do you think the problem of keeping out of war would be better handled in the next four years by the Republicans, or by the Democrats, or about the same by both?" As has already been reported, 1964 was the first time during the Survey Research Center election studies when the responses to this query showed a Democratic advantage.[15] Our concern here is with the reasons given by those who thought one party or the other would do a better job. As Table X shows, these responses fell into four categories. One set of respondents based their judgments on the abilities of the candidates. Here Johnson held a sizeable, and rather constant edge. A second grouping based their answers on the abilities of the parties. The Democrats had a better than 3-to-1 edge with these respondents at the beginning of the campaign, but by election time the Republicans had nearly caught up. A very few referred to specific trouble spots. But nearly half the respondents gave such simple answers as "The Democrats will keep us out of war" or "Goldwater will get us into war." The generality of this reaction suggests these respondents had the weakest informational base for their attitude. Whether or no, the shift is remarkable. The Democrats began with a 5-to-1 advantage with these voters; the Republicans cut the Democratic lead to 2½-to-1; then, suddenly the Democratic lead jumped back to its original size. Again, given the coincidence of timing, it would seem probable that this shift in the nature of the general responses is more evidence of impact.

More fragmentary evidence on the effect of the Kremlin power struggle and the mushroom cloud over Sinkiang Province may be found by reading interviews which took place shortly after these events. The basic queries about the candidates elicited a number of adverse comments about Goldwater's belligerence and declarations that the country ought to stay with an experienced man such as Johnson. Concern with these events also emerged when the respondents were asked about problems the new administration ought to handle. An insurance agent in Orlando, Florida, said on October 19 that the government should "just keep peace with Russia and Red China." They should "approach these matters with care or just wait and see what's going on now that Khrushchev is out." The same day, a housewife in Wyandotte, Michigan, was saying, "They shouldn't jump to conclusions now that Khrushchev is out. They should go along with the new leaders and find out what they are like first." And the next day, a Salt Lake City waitress

[15] Philip E. Converse, Aage R. Clausen, and Warren E. Miller, "Electoral Myth and Reality: The 1964 Election," p. 332.

Table X *Relation Between Parties and War by Interview Date*

Reason Given	Before Oct. 4	Oct. 4–Oct. 17	Oct. 18–Nov. 2
Handled better by Democrats because of Johnson's capacity	14%	14%	12%
Handled better by Republicans because of Goldwater's capacity	4	2	3
Handled better by Democrats because of Democrats' capacity	23	19	18
Handled better by Republicans because of Republicans' capacity	7	10	14
Trouble spots (Berlin, Vietnam, Cuba) better handled by Democrats	1	1	0
Trouble spots better handled by Republicans	1	1	0
Handled better by Democrats, general response*	41	38	44
Handled better by Republicans, general response	9	15	8
N**	295	247	273

* The Democrats (Johnson) will keep us out of war; the Republicans (Goldwater) are the war party, will get us into war.

** N's have been weighted to compensate for the number of interviews in each time period. These N's are low because reasons were given only by those who had asserted that one party or the other could do a better job of keeping the country out of war.

told an interviewer the most important problem for the new administration was "Red China and that—just came up the other day. I'd like to see them control Red China about that—that ban on bombs." She mentioned Russia as a second problem because, as she phrased it, "I was a little shook up when Khrushchev got put out." So there is a good deal of evidence that these dramatic foreign events increased the salience of foreign policy, and caused enough concern to modify the impact of the campaign.[16]

Now what can be said about *influence,* the relationship of campaign strategies to the voting behavior of the electorate? Thus far we have been concerned with *impact,* the modification of attitudes. Our theoretical position is that the relationship of the behavior of the electoral coalitions to the behavior of the voters is indirect. The campaign strategies exert influence by modifying attitudes which in turn motivate the voters to cast their ballots in one way or another. In our consideration of influence, the campaign strategies are still conceived as independent variables, the attitudes of the electorate become intervening variables, and voting behavior now becomes the dependent variable upon which we shall focus. Sometimes we shall look at a simple relationship between campaign events and voting behavior, leaving the effects of the intervening attitudes unstated. Sometimes, having already shown a relationship between strategies and attitudes, we shall just trace out the last half of the linkage. It is a little simpler to present the data this way, but to understand all the implications, the complete path from coalition behavior to voters' attitudes to voters' behavior should be kept in mind.

Something of the temporal influence of the campaign may be seen in Table XI. Here is evidence from the pre-election interview and the post-election interview. In the first, respondents were asked about their voting intention. Their answers have been organized according to the time periods used in our quasi-panel. The data suggest that President Johnson's strength was holding fairly steady while Goldwater's support was increasing. After the election, respondents were asked whom they had voted for and when

[16] The short-lived Walter Jenkins affair did not have nearly as much impact. Perception of its importance probably ran more along party lines. An Inglewood, California, horse owner, a strong Republican, said he disliked Johnson's advisers. "One has been arrested on morals charges and there's the Bobby Baker and Billy Sol Estes scandals." But a Worcester, Massachusetts, bricklayer, a strong Democrat, said, "I'm broad-minded. I know all about the Bobby Baker case and the others, but I don't blame Johnson. He trusted them and it wasn't his fault they were dishonest and connivers." Both interviews took place October 15, the day the news about Jenkins was made public.

Table XI *Vote Intent by Interview Date and Vote by Time of Decision*

Vote Intent	Before Oct. 4	Oct. 4–Oct. 17	Oct. 18–Nov. 2
Johnson	63%	64%	63%
Johnson with qualifications	5	3	1
Undecided	7	9	6
Goldwater with qualifications	3	1	2
Goldwater	22	23	28
N *	530	510	495

* N's have been weighted to compensate for the number of interviews in each time period.

Time of Decision	Vote: Johnson	Vote: Goldwater	N
"Knew all along"	74.3%	25.7%	191
Pre-convention	79.8	20.2	253
At time of convention	67.7	32.3	269
During campaign	60.3	39.7	224
Last two weeks	45.7	54.3	94
Election day	51.3	48.7	39

Gamma = .292*

* Gamma is the Goodman-Kruskal measure of association for ordered data. It should be +1.0 for perfect positive association, 0 when no association exists, and −1.0 in the case of perfect negative association. With the data arrayed as they are, a positive gamma indicates those who made later decisions had a greater tendency to vote for Goldwater. For a description of the measure, see Morris Zelditch, *An Introduction to Sociological Statistics* (New York: Holt, Rinehart & Winston), pp. 180–83, or L. A. Goodman and W. H. Kruskal, "Measures of Association for Cross-Classification," *Journal of the American Statistical Association*, December, 1954, pp. 748–54.

they had decided to vote as they did.[17] Analysis of the responses to these retrospective questions leads to the same conclusion as inspection of the pre-election questions: Goldwater did relatively well during the campaign.

[17] Why one makes up his mind at a particular time is, of course, a complex question that depends on the number of conflicting attitudes and many other considerations. However, analysis of responses to "time of decision" questions

The longer a person waited to make up his mind, the greater the likelihood he would vote for the Arizona Senator.

Why did Goldwater do relatively well as time went on? There are at least two possible explanations for this relationship. One is that Goldwater's campaign was exerting more influence. The other is that those who were making late decisions possessed characteristics which predisposed them to vote for Goldwater. The latter hypothesis might imply, for example, that Democrats found the choice easy, and decided quite early to vote for Johnson, while Republicans waited until the last moment before making up their minds to vote for Goldwater. It is possible, but it didn't happen this way. Table XII gives the data for vote by decision time with party identification controlled. Late Republican decisions did not cause the apparent Goldwater success. In fact, the sign of the rank order correlation is negative because Republicans were more likely to make early decisions to vote for Goldwater. Independents and Democrats who postponed their decisions until the fall were more likely to vote for Goldwater. The relationship between a late decision and an increased tendency to vote for Goldwater also holds for every section of the country. The gamma rank order correlations for the regional subsamples are: East .355, Midwest .187, West .340, Peripheral South .363, and Deep South .546.

It is necessary to apply two controls simultaneously to come close to eliminating the positive relationship between time of decision and a tendency to vote for Goldwater. It turns out that the populations thus identified—Re-

---

suggests the proportion of persons who make up their minds at particular stages is relatively constant from one campaign to the next, and certain types of persons tend to be overrepresented among those deciding at each stage. The first persons to decide are traditionalists, persons whose attitudes strongly predispose them to cast Democratic or Republican votes and who do so almost as a matter of course. Next come the activists, persons who are themselves involved in politics and who tend to acquire information about the candidates and issues rather early. During the campaign proper, "policy-oriented" citizens pay close attention to what the candidates and parties are saying, and tend to make issue-based decisions. Finally, just before the election, weakly motivated voters finally have their attention caught by the mounting hoopla of the campaign. The inclinations of these "peripheral citizens" are hard to predict because of their lack of real involvement, and they are rather easily moved from one camp to another. For a discussion of the relation between attitudes and time of decision, see Campbell *et al.*, *The American Voter*, pp. 78–83. On policy-motivated voters, see Carl C. Hetrick, "Issues and Politics: An Exploration in Policy-Motivated Political Behavior" (Unpublished Ph.D. dissertation, University of Washington, 1966).

Table XII *Vote by Decision Time by Party Identification*

Time of Decision	Vote: Johnson	Vote: Goldwater	N
Democrats			
"Knew all along"	96.7%	3.3%	121
Pre-convention	97.5	2.5	159
At time of convention	90.7	9.3	140
During campaign	82.0	18.0	100
Last two weeks	50.0	50.0	36
Election day	62.5	37.5	8
Gamma = .662			
Independents			
"Knew all along"	90.0%	10.0%	20
Pre-convention	66.7	33.3	45
At time of convention	69.4	30.6	49
During campaign	57.6	42.4	59
Last two weeks	59.1	40.9	22
Election day	66.7	33.3	15
Gamma = .204			
Republicans			
"Knew all along"	12.5%	87.5%	48
Pre-convention	33.3	66.7	48
At time of convention	26.6	73.4	79
During campaign	29.2	70.8	65
Last two weeks	33.3	66.7	36
Election day	31.2	68.7	16
Gamma = −.156			

publicans unhappy about Goldwater's nominations and Independents from the Peripheral South—were the target groups for the special Democratic strategies already discussed. And it *happens* that their votes were split rather equally between the two candidates.[18] The gamma between vote and decision

[18] There is no reason why this should have been so. If a population gave the same proportion of its vote to both candidates (whether 90–10, 70–30 or 50–50) during each period of the campaign, the rank order correlation between vote and decision time would be zero.

Table XIII *Distribution of Party Identification by Region, 1964*

	Strong Democrats	Weak Democrats	Independents	Weak Republicans	Strong Republicans
East	5.3%	4.7%	5.6%	4.3%	2.7%
Midwest	6.5	7.3	8.8	4.7	4.5
West	4.6	3.8	3.5	2.4	1.7
Peripheral South*	8.2	6.4	3.3	1.6	1.8
Deep South*	2.1	2.8	2.2	.9	.3

* The proportions in the Peripheral South and Deep South have been weighted to compensate for having too many interviews in the Peripheral South and too few interviews in the Deep South.

time for Republicans unhappy with Goldwater was .039; 49.5% of them voted for Johnson.[19] The President received slightly more than half the votes of those Republicans who made up their minds before the fall campaign, and slightly less than half of those who made their decisions during the fall. The gamma between vote and decision time for Independents from the Peripheral South was .092; 45.1% of them voted for the President.

We now have two sets of data, attitudinal data and voting data, which together enable us to say that the Johnson campaign influenced these particular groups of voters. The implications of Johnson's ability to reach these voters are fairly clear if we consider the distribution of party identification types throughout the country. These data are given in Table XIII with each cell entry giving the percentage of the total electorate made up by that particular type. (The upper left-hand cell entry, for example, tells us that strong Democrats from the East constitute 5.3% of the total electorate.) Two minimal Democratic majorities are suggested by the lines on the chart. The vertical line indicates a straight party-line vote. If all Democrats voted

[19] Another population with very similar behavior was the Eastern Republicans. Gamma for vote and decision time =.037; Johnson received 42.3% of the vote. As Table I shows, the Eastern Republicans and Republicans unhappy with Goldwater were not identical populations. Sixty per cent of the Eastern Republicans were unhappy with Goldwater's nomination, but only 37.8% of the Republicans unhappy about Goldwater's nomination lived in the East.

for Johnson, and all Republicans and Independents voted for Goldwater, Johnson would win with 51.7% of the vote. If, as suggested by the broken line, Goldwater got the votes of the weak Democrats in the Deep South, Johnson could more than make up for it by getting the votes of Independents in the East, and win with 54.5% of the vote. In other words, when the President was getting roughly half the votes of Republicans unhappy with Goldwater[20] and half the votes of Independents from the Peripheral South, he was receiving support from groups whose votes weren't necessary. The front lines of this political engagement were well within Republican territory.

If President Johnson was reaching target groups whose identity portended a Democratic landslide, then how can we conclude, as we did after examining the relationship between vote and time of decision, that Senator Goldwater was doing relatively well during the campaign? Part of the answer to this, of course, lies in the words *relatively well*. If Senator Goldwater received, as our sample estimate indicates, 42.3 per cent of the votes of those who made up their minds during the campaign,[21] this is a substantial improvement over the 26.2 per cent of the votes he received from those who made up their minds before the campaign began. But even the better of the two figures does not imply that Senator Goldwater was winning the campaign.

The other reason for Senator Goldwater's relative success in the face of President Johnson's ability to reach key groups in the population lies in the efforts of Republican workers. We have already seen that the attitudes of persons contacted as part of the mobilization campaign were likely to be significantly different from the attitudes of those who were not. Table XIV presents the voting data for those who were contacted. We see that those who were contacted by a Democrat were slightly less likely to vote for President Johnson than those who weren't contacted by a Democrat. Republican

[20] Thirty-six per cent of the weak Republicans and 26 per cent of the strong Republicans fell into this category.

[21] The alert reader will have noticed by this time that the sample estimates for the Johnson vote are high. The estimate for the Johnson vote for the total sample is 67.5% as compared with an actual Johnson vote of 61.5%. In a detailed study of this discrepancy, Aage Clausen concludes: "The pre-election interview stimulates voting participation among the least interested voters who are most susceptible to short-term influences." In 1964, the short-term influences were in a pro-Democratic direction. Hence, these least interested voters (whose counterparts in the general population were not taking the trouble to vote) were

Table XIV *Vote by Party Contact*

Entire Sample

	Democratic Contact?		Republican Contact?	
Vote	No	Yes	No	Yes
Johnson	68.4%	65.6%	72.4%	55.6%
Goldwater	31.6	34.4	27.6	46.4
N	901	195	833	263
	Gamma = .051		Gamma = .375	

Vote by Republican Contact by Party Identification

	Republican Contact?	
Vote	No	Yes
Democrats		
Johnson	91.0%	84.6%
Goldwater	9.0	15.4
N	458	117
Gamma = .286		
Independents		
Johnson	71.1%	50.0%
Goldwater	28.9	50.0
N	166	50
Gamma = .398		
Republicans		
Johnson	32.2%	17.2%
Goldwater	67.8	82.8
N	208	93
Gamma = .361		

likely to cast Johnson ballots. See "Response Validity: Vote Report" (University of Michigan Survey Research Center, January, 1967, mimeographed).

contacts, on the other hand, significantly increased the likelihood of a Goldwater vote.

Even with the attitudinal data, this relationship between a Republican contact and a Republican vote requires further analysis before we can be sure it is not spurious. Precinct workers are notorious for contacting the already committed. How can we be sure that Republican contact of Republican voters has not produced an accidental relationship? The answer is to use a party identification control.[22] These data are also included in Table XIV. This tells us that Republican workers did reach more Republicans than Independents or Democrats. Thirty-one per cent of the Republican respondents reported that someone from the party "called them up or came around to talk to them during the campaign," whereas 23 per cent of the Independents and 20 per cent of the Democrats did so. But the relationship between a Republican contact and a vote for Goldwater does not disappear with any group of party identifiers. The same is true when regional controls are applied. The gamma rank order correlations for the regional subsamples are: East .419, Midwest .322, West .264, Peripheral South .427, Deep South .746. Hence, we can be reasonably confident that this phenomenon was general, that the national figures are not a spurious reflection of organizational effort concentrated in certain regions or of Republican workers contacting only voters who would be likely to vote for Goldwater whether contacted or not.[23]

[22] This form of analysis begins with an original relationship $X \rightarrow Y$. With any such two variable relationships, there is a possibility that the two are not in fact related to each other, but only appear to be related because both are related to some third variable as $X \leftarrow Z \rightarrow Y$. In this case, the original $X \rightarrow Y$ relationship is said to be spurious. The check is to hold constant any third variable which might cause such an accidental relationship. If the original relationship was spurious, the correlation should disappear. See Herbert Hyman, *Survey Design and Analysis* (Glencoe, Ill.: The Free Press, 1955), Chs. 6–7.

[23] The 1964 Republican success in voter contact may well be unique in recent presidential elections. Using a probability model to analyze 1952, 1956, and 1960 Survey Research Center data, Gerald Kramer has found party contacts did not significantly alter turnout or the likelihood of voting for one party or the other. See Gerald Kramer, "Decision Theoretic Analysis of Canvassing and Other Precinct-Level Activities in Political Campaigning," (Unpublished Ph.D dissertation, Massachusetts Institute of Technology, 1965). In more recent work with 1964 data, Kramer has found significant turnout and conversion effects in the case of Republican voters contacted by Republican precinct workers. These data were presented in a lecture at a Conference on Mathematical Applications in Political Science, Blacksburg, Virginia, June, 1966.

With this information and the attitudinal data in Table VI, we can conclude that this organizational work did influence votes, and that it represented genuine Republican success.[24]

Now what about the linkage between particular attitudes and voting choice? The subjects mentioned as problems facing the incoming administration (Table IX) give some idea about the issue uppermost in the voters' minds. Welfare, civil rights, and foreign policy were the most salient topics. Specific questions asked about each of these subjects make it possible to relate these attitudes to voting behavior. As Table XV indicates, attitudes about welfare were most closely related to the voting decision. The data presented are those on medicare, but other welfare issues showed the same general pattern. The gamma rank order correlations between vote and the other welfare questions scaled with an intensity component (Is your mind made up or do you have some doubts?) were: public power .596, jobs and living standards .531, and aid to education .514. On all these issues, Goldwater did reasonably well with opponents of welfare while Johnson received lopsided majorities from supporters of welfare activity.

Civil rights, a major question of national policy in 1964, does not appear to have been as influential as welfare issues with respect to voting. There is some possibility that the data on the relationship between one's general attitude on segregation and vote, given in Table XV, understate the effect of civil rights on the election. Three other specific civil rights questions were scaled with an intensity component (as the general question was not), and two of them have much stronger relationships to voting choice. The gamma rank order correlations were: job integration .453, school integration .372, and residential integration .173. However, none of these relationships were as strong as those between welfare attitudes and vote, and President Johnson received a majority of both integrationist *and* segregationist support on all of these issues.

Vietnam was the foreign problem most frequently mentioned as one the new administration would have to act on. (Indeed, it seems to have been

[24] Not a few post-election analyses said one reason for Senator Goldwater's defeat was division within the Republican party. If this means that Senator Goldwater himself was unpopular with many Republican voters, it is accurate. But if "division in the Republican party" is meant to imply that Republicans did not work for Goldwater, it is in error. These data on organizational effectiveness show clearly that Republicans were working very hard in the service of an untenable candidacy.

Table XV *Relation Between Specific Issues and Vote*

Position of Respondent	Percentage Voting for Johnson	Percentage Voting for Goldwater	N
"Some people say the government in Washington ought to help people get doctors and hospital care at low cost, others say the government should not get into this. What is your position?"			
Favors medicare, mind made up	85.9%	14.1%	461
Favors medicare, has doubts	76.2	23.8	63
It all depends	59.7	40.3	77
Opposes medicare, has doubts	50.0	50.0	36
Opposes medicare, mind made up	36.3	63.7	306
Gamma = .693			
"Are you in favor of desegregation, strict segregation, or something in between?"			
Desegregation	75.3%	24.7%	360
Something in between	64.6	35.4	497
Strict segregation	62.8	37.2	223
Gamma = .192			
"Which of the following do you think we should do now in Vietnam?"			
Pull out of Vietnam entirely	63.4%	36.6%	93
Keep our soldiers in Vietnam, but try to end the fighting	81.9	18.1	276
Take a stronger stand even if it means invading North Vietnam	51.8	48.2	382
Gamma = .390			

more salient to the voters than to the candidates.) President Johnson drew most of his support from those who wanted to continue what was then our policy in Vietnam. He received a reduced majority from those who wanted to pull out entirely, and much less support from those who preferred a more aggressive posture. Since the relationship was curvilinear, the gamma actually underestimates the very strong association between attitude and vote. The gammas between vote and other specific foreign policy questions were: admit China to U.N. .367, intervene in Cuba .346, trade with communist nations

.338, and foreign aid .231,[25] So a relationship can be shown between a host of attitudes on foreign and domestic policy and voting behavior.

Still stronger relationships can be found by looking at more general issues, specifically the power of the federal government and the success of American foreign policy. These issues were broad enough to subsume most of the specific issues already discussed. And quite aside from their generality, they are attitudes one would expect to be influential. As long as one deals with specific issues, there are going to be many speeches in which they go unmentioned by candidates and many voters who are so unconcerned with these particular topics that they do not "hear" anything when the candidates do mention them. Hence, no impact. The opposite set of conditions is present with general issues. When these are woven into the fabric of almost every speech, a voter with even a minimum interest in the campaign is likely to receive some cues as to where the candidates stand. In 1964, President Johnson and Senator Goldwater did take opposite sides regarding the power of the federal government and the success of American foreign policy. As Table XVI shows, these were the dominant issues of the campaign. The voters were divided in their judgments, and their judgments were closely related to their voting decisions. And, as in the case of medicare, Goldwater received fair margins from those who agreed with him, while Johnson was getting lopsided majorities from those who favored the status quo.

Tables XVII and XVIII give further evidence that the power of the federal government was the most influential issue of the campaign. Table XVII shows an analysis of the relationship between that attitude and vote by region. Here it can be seen that everywhere but in the Deep South, Senator Goldwater was receiving majorities *only* from those whose minds were made up that the federal government was too powerful. And Table XVIII shows that this attitude was the one most closely associated with vote in every region of the country. President Johnson and Senator Goldwater would doubtless have agreed that if a single attitude had to decide the election, this should be it, but Senator Goldwater might have been surprised that this attitude would be so strongly related to votes for the President.

On more specific domestic questions, medicare was more important in every section of the country than segregation. In fact, outside the East and the South, civil rights was a most unimportant question. In the area of

[25] The questions on China and foreign aid were scaled with intensity components. Those on Cuba and trade with communist nations were not.

Table XVI *Relation Between General Issues and Vote*

Position of Respondent	Percentage Voting for Johnson	Percentage Voting for Goldwater	N
"Some people are afraid the government in Washington is getting too powerful for the good of the country and the individual person. Others feel that the government in Washington has not gotten too strong for the good of the country. What is your feeling?"			
Government not too strong, mind made up	90.2%	9.8%	315
Government not too strong, has doubts	77.9	22.1	86
It all depends	74.2	25.8	31
Government too powerful, has doubts	60.7	39.3	56
Government too powerful, mind made up	30.1	69.9	299
Gamma = .783			
"Would you say that in the past year or so the United States has done pretty well in dealing with foreign countries, or would you say that we haven't been doing as well as we should?"			
Pretty well	84.1	15.9	496
Well in some ways, not well in others	62.7	37.3	102
Not too well	43.2	56.8	361
Gamma = .662			

foreign policy, there is another interesting regional distinction. The voters' general impressions of foreign policy had a closer relation to their voting decisions than the specific question of Vietnam in every section of the country *except* the East. And, as one compares the five regions, it is impossible to avoid noticing the extreme polarization of attitude in the Deep South. So divided is opinion in the Deep South that civil rights, with a correlation of "only" .695, turns out to have the least influence[26] of any of the five issues.

The analysis of the influence of issues by region leads to a still more general question. When all the attitudinal forces we have been discussing are summed up, how did they influence the voting behavior in each region?

[26] The rank order correlation between issue and vote provides a fair estimate of the influence of a particular issue. A better measure could be obtained by multiplying the rank order correlation for a particular population by the departure from normal vote for that population.

Table XVII *Power of Federal Government and Vote, by Region*

Vote	Government Not Too Strong		It All Depends	Government Too Powerful	
	Mind Made Up	Has Doubts		Has Doubts	Mind Made Up
East					
Johnson	89.6%	73.9%	85.7%	50.0%	40.0%
Goldwater	10.4	26.1	14.3	50.0	60.0
N = 177, Gamma = .703					
Mid-West					
Johnson	89.3%	76.3%	61.5%	57.9%	28.6%
Goldwater	10.7	23.7	38.5	42.1	71.4
N = 257, Gamma = .751					
West					
Johnson	89.5%	90.9%	100.0%	50.0%	23.2%
Goldwater	10.5	9.1	—	50.0	76.8
N = 141, Gamma = .841					
Peripheral South					
Johnson	93.1%	78.6%	66.7%	85.7%	33.0%
Goldwater	6.9	21.4	33.3	14.3	67.0
N = 194, Gamma = .832					
Deep South					
Johnson	83.3%	—	—	—	—
Goldwater	16.7	—	—	100.0%	100.0%
N = 18, Gamma = 1.0					

One way of answering this question is to ask how each group of party identifiers voted in each region. Ordinarily, a party ought to receive the votes of approximately 19/20 of their strong party identifiers, about 5/6 of their weak party identifiers, and roughly half the independents. The voting patterns for each section, shown in Table XIX, reveal that the campaign had a varying

Table XVIII *Relation Between Issues and Vote by Region*

	Gamma Rank Order Correlation Coefficients				
	Power of Federal Govt.	Medicare	Segregation	Foreign Affairs	Vietnam
Entire Sample	.783	.693	.192	.662	.390
East	.703	.677	.406	.362	.467
Midwest	.751	.615	.000	.612	.244
West	.841	.846	−.107	.776	.552
Peripheral South	.832	.641	.274	.815	.293
Deep South	1.000	1.000	.695	.947	.962

influence in different parts of the country. President Johnson did very well outside the South, receiving 3/5 of the weak Republican vote in the East and 2/3 of the Independent vote in the Midwest and the West. In the Peripheral South, there was a little more voting for the candidate of the rival party than one might expect, but the proportion of each group voting for Johnson bears a resemblance to normal expectations. The figures for the Deep South provide still more evidence of the strong appeal of the Goldwater candidacy in this region.

A more elegant way of estimating the net influence of the strategies in each region is the use of Philip Converse's concept of the normal vote.[27] The

Table XIX *Voting Patterns by Region*

	Percentage Voting for Johnson				
	Strong Democrats	Weak Democrats	Independents	Weak Republicans	Strong Republicans
East	98%	88%	80%	60%	17%
Midwest	100	90	69	36	9
West	98	74	67	40	4
Peripheral South	90	77	47	23	7
Deep South	90	20	0	20	0

[27] Philip E. Converse, "The Concept of a Normal Vote," in Angus Campbell, Philip E. Converse, Warren E. Miller, and Donald E. Stokes, *Elections and the Political Order* (New York: Wiley, 1966).

normal vote is based on the distribution of party identification types in any population grouping. The calculations reflect estimates of turnout probability and the probability of voting for a given party in an election when pro-Democratic and pro-Republican attitudes are equally balanced. The normal vote thus provides a base-line against which we can compare the actual vote in any particular election. The departure from the normal vote for any population grouping can be regarded as a fair estimate of the net effect of the short-term attitudinal forces in that election.

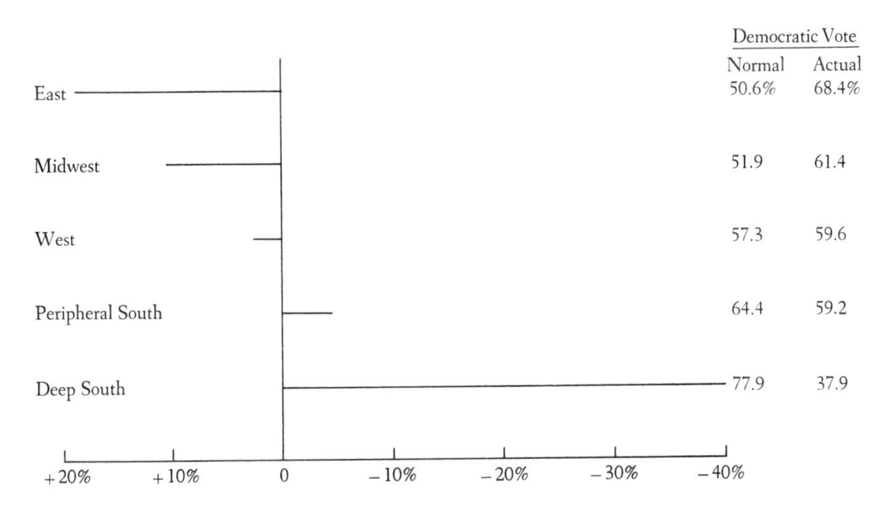

Figure 15 *Departure from Normal Vote by Region*

A normal vote for each region has been calculated using party identification data collected during the 1960's.[28] The normal votes for the East, Midwest, and West are based on data from the Survey Research Center election studies for 1960, 1962, and 1964. The normal votes for the Peripheral South and Deep South are based on data gathered in these national studies for 1960

[28] Calculation of a normal vote presents an important methodological problem because it depends on the accuracy with which party identification has been measured. There are two sources of inaccuracy in the measure, responses from almost apolitical persons who do not comprehend the meaning of the party identification question and responses of some more active voters who interpret the "generally speaking" question in terms of their *current* feelings. (An extreme case was the woman from upstate New York, a portion of whose interview was quoted earlier, who began by saying she was voting against her own views because she was a Republican, but insisted she was an Independent by the time the

and 1964 and on party identification data from the Matthews-Prothro study of political participation in the South.[29] Figure 15 shows the departure from the normal vote for each region. Here we can see quite clearly the different influence exerted from region to region. The most important indicators of the success of the candidates' strategies are in the Midwest, the West, and the Peripheral South. These, after all, were the regions which both hoped to carry. The deviations from the normal vote show that Goldwater did very badly in the Midwest and not quite so badly in the West. The Arizona Senator did make some inroads in the Peripheral South, but Lyndon Johnson's defensive strategy held Democratic defections within tolerable limits. The more dramatic data, of course, are the departures from the normal vote in the East and the Deep South. These were essentially uncontested areas. Goldwater made no serious effort to carry the East and Johnson's strategy conceded at least part of the Deep South to his opponent. Given the existing attitudes in these regions, it may be that no Goldwater strategy could have been very influential in the East and that no Johnson strategy could have been very influential in the Deep South. But the combination of effort by one candidate, little opposition by his rival, and a set of regional attitudes

---

party identification question was reached.) The first group of errors are sufficiently random to cancel out over time, but the second cause the party identification measure to sway in the direction of current influences. "Any reasonable inspection of the data points makes clear that one is dealing with some more systematic term than sheer sampling error. That is, the lowest (most Republican) point in the series occurs in connection with the 1956 Eisenhower landslide; the highest point in connection with the Johnson landslide in 1964. Hence it seems clear that in addition to an inevitable sampling error term, the distribution of party identification sways slightly in response to national tides surrounding a given election" (Letter from Philip E. Converse dated March 4, 1966). Because of this measurement problem the person who would calculate a normal vote faces a dilemma. If the party identification data are from a single year, he picks up some of the effects of a single election. On the other hand, if he aggregates data from past elections in order to cancel out the effects of the single election, he biases the measure in a "backward" direction by including data from voters now dead and excluding data from current voters who were too young to be interviewed at the time of an earlier survey. The decision to calculate a normal vote based on data gathered in the 1960's is a compromise between these two dangers.

[29] I should like to thank the Louis Harris Political Data Center at the University of North Carolina for making these data available.

The addition of the Matthews-Prothro data means that we have enough cases to make a reliable calculation of the normal vote. As pointed out in footnote 5, the other sample estimates for the Deep South are based on too few cases.

already receptive to the policies urged by the first candidate seems to have been enough to produce the most dramatic departure from traditional voting habits seen in a good many years.

In summary, then, we can say the Johnson strategy met with greater success. The President was able to win the votes of those who agreed with the policy positions he took. His group emphasis was an unqualified success. His bid for the support of moderate Republicans netted him half their votes, and his defense of Democratic strength in the Peripheral South was sufficient to hold all the electoral votes in this region. And if he did not increase his support throughout the campaign, he still kept enough of it to make for a landslide victory.

The successes of the Goldwater coalition were less consequential, but still noticeable. Goldwater increased his support as the weeks wore on. The number of voters contacted and persuaded to vote for Goldwater showed the Republican organization to be stronger than that of their rivals. The Goldwater offensive of early to mid-October was having some impact until dramatic foreign events diverted the attention of the electorate. All things considered, these were some very real accomplishments. If they were not apparent, it was because they were particular successes set in a context of general disaster.

FOUR

☆☆☆☆☆☆☆☆☆☆☆☆☆☆☆☆☆☆☆☆☆☆☆☆☆☆☆

Coalition Theory

10

☆☆☆☆☆☆☆☆☆☆☆☆☆☆☆☆☆☆☆☆☆☆☆☆☆☆☆☆☆☆

Some Results of the Election

The most important effect of the 1964 election was the most obvious. Since Lyndon Johnson won the election, the Johnson presidential coalition continued in office. (The Johnson presidential coalition was not identical with the Johnson electoral coalition, even though the membership was similar. The institutional setting was different, and there were persons, particularly subject-matter experts such as McGeorge Bundy, who were much more important in the presidential coalition than in the electoral coalition.) The central attitudes of the Johnson coalition were therefore important in shaping the massive legislative program submitted to the 89th Congress, and in the other important business of the Administration.

Beyond saying that one of the candidates was the victor, and this had certain consequences for public policy, one's estimate of the effects of the election depends very much on one's theoretical perspective. We are considering American political parties in terms of sets of attitudes and behavior. The voting behavior which determines the outcome of any particular election is a reflection of the attitudes of the electorate at a single point in time. But these attitudes continue to exist after the election is over, and continue to be susceptible to modification as new information is received. Since these attitudes (as later modified) will control the political activity of the electorate in the future, it is important to ask how they may have been changed during the campaign. If it can be shown that the basic attitudes have been shifted in a pro-Democratic or a pro-Republican direction, then the campaign may have an effect which lasts long after the election is over.

Many attitudes motivate citizen activity, but the central attitude around which the others are organized is party identification. It is subject to change, but this usually requires a number of other dissonant elements in the same attitudinal cluster. Moreover, there is no other political attitude nearly as stable. Because of its importance, either within the system of political attitudes of a single individual or within the system of attitudes and behaviors in terms of which we are regarding political parties, this sense of belongingness is vital to any political party. If one thinks about the prospects of a party over a series of elections, party identification can be seen as the long-term asset which a party should attempt to guard most closely.[1]

The Survey Research Center has been asking its party identification question since it began its series of national political surveys in 1952. The basic data gathered are presented in Table XX. Until 1964, the distribution of party identification had been remarkably stable. In the surveys taken

Table XX *Distribution of Party Identification, 1952–1964**

	Oct. 1952	Oct. 1956	Oct. 1960	Oct. 1962	Jan. 1964	May 1964	Oct. 1964
Strong Democrat	22%	21%	21%	23%	23%	24%	26%
Weak Democrat	25	23	25	23	27	22	25
Ind. Democrat	10	7	8	8	9	7	9
Independent	5	9	8	8	10	10	8
Ind. Republican	7	8	7	6	6	5	6
Weak Republican	14	14	13	16	14	17	13
Strong Republican	13	15	14	12	9	11	11
Apolitical	4	3	4	4	2	4	2

* The May, 1964, data are reported by Angus Campbell in "Interpreting the Presidential Victory," in Milton C. Cummings, Jr., ed., *The National Election of 1964*, p. 278. The others are from various Survey Research Center publications.

[1] This point has been so well established that it is being stressed by party leaders. In a report presented to the Republican National Committee on January 31, 1966, Ray C. Bliss noted: "The strong party identifiers . . . will vote for their party's candidates 82 per cent of the time regardless of the candidates or the issues. Obviously, it is imperative that we expand the number of these firmly committed Republicans" (*Elements of Victory* [Washington: Republican National Committee, 1966], p. 23).

during the Eisenhower years, and in those of October, 1962, and May, 1964 (as well as in many surveys unreported in Table XX), the proportion of Democrats in the electorate had varied from 44 per cent to 47 per cent, and the proportion of Republicans was bounded by limits of 27 per cent and 29 per cent. This much variation can be accounted for by sampling error alone. In the studies of January, 1964, and October, 1964, however, we find a majority of respondents now reporting themselves to be Democrats and a little less than a quarter saying they consider themselves Republicans. The Democratic advantage of 3-to-2 had changed to 2-to-1.

This is the most substantial change noted since the Survey Research Center began charting party identification. Why should such a change emerge in January and October, 1964, but not in May? As noted in Chapter 9, the measurement of party identification is in some degree responsive to short-term forces. Therefore, it seems logical to infer that certain strong short-term forces were applied to the voters' attitudes at those particular times. In view of the timing of the surveys, a plausible explanation is that the system of attitudes reacted to the shock of the Kennedy assassination by bending in a Democratic direction,[2] had begun to recover its normal contours in late spring, and then was hit with the second shock of the Goldwater campaign.

There are some data which permit us to pursue this question a bit further. Some retrospective questions were asked about changes in party identification[3] at the time present party identification was ascertained. These data leave much to be desired. Responses to such questions, especially those which ask about events remote in time, "may be distorted and colored by subsequent experiences and characteristics of the respondents."[4] The data

[2] See Bradley S. Greenberg and Edwin B. Parker, eds., *The Kennedy Assassination and the American Public* (Stanford: Stanford University Press, 1965), especially the article by David O. Sears, "Effects of the Assassination on Political Partisanship."

[3] The questions were: Was there ever a time when you thought of yourself as a (member of the other party) rather than a (member of your present party)? When did you change from (the other party) to (your present party)? What was the main thing that made you change from (the other party) to (your present party)?

[4] Herbert Hyman, *Survey Design and Analysis*, pp. 207–8. A fairly extreme example of the trouble with retrospective questions is provided by the 1964 Survey Research Center question about the 1960 presidential vote. Of those who said they voted for Nixon or Kennedy, 64 per cent said they voted for Kennedy. Obviously, some replies were affected by memories of the late President's popularity and Mr. Nixon's post-1960 slump in public esteem.

Table XXI *Time of Party Switch by Former Party*

Time of Change in Party Identification	Former Party		N
	Democrats	Republicans	
Prior to 1919	50.0%	50.0%	4
1920's	30.0	70.0	10
1930's	41.7	58.3	48
World War II	75.0	25.0	12
Truman Era, 1946–51	69.2	30.8	26
Eisenhower Era, 1952–59	30.0	70.0	60
Kennedy Era, 1960–63	40.3	59.7	77
1964	56.5	43.5	46
Don't know time of switch	49.2	50.8	59

in Table XXI, the *former* party of those reporting a change in party identification arrayed against the time of the reported change, illustrate some of the difficulties. Analysis of aggregate voting data shows that the largest shift in the loyalties of the electorate in modern times occurred during the depression of the 1930's. Yet only 14 per cent of those who changed parties recall having done so during the depression. Given the lapse of time, some of this decrease can be attributed to death, but there are doubtless others who cannot recall their state of mind of thirty years before with much accuracy. Still, the time pattern bears some resemblance to known electoral history. The Republicans lost ground during the depression, regained strength reaching a high point during the early '50's, and suffered another attrition thereafter. And while panel data on changes in party identification would be preferable, we do not have them. So our best course is to use the available retrospective data with due caution.

Table XXI does make two important points about changes in party identification. One is that stability in the over-all distribution does not mean that individual party identification has been equally stable. Roughly one respondent in five said there was a time when his party identification had been different. The normal stability in the over-all distribution results from compensating individual changes in opposite directions. It takes a substantial departure from the 50–50 mark among those who are changing to produce a *net* change in the over-all distribution. Of those reporting a switch in 1964 pre-election interviews, 55 per cent had changed from being Republicans and 45 per cent had switched from regarding themselves as Democrats. Hence the over-all distribution shows a small net change in the Democratic direction.

The other important point in Table XXI is the date of the reported change in party identification. The largest reported changes were said to have taken place during the Eisenhower and Kennedy administrations. Yet we know from earlier surveys that such changes were not occurring at that time.[5] The Democrats were making some small gains at the expense of the Republicans, but certainly not at the rate suggested by these retrospective data. So the important question is why persons interviewed in 1964 *said* they had changed their party identifications some years earlier. One plausible explanation is to consider party identification as the central organizing attitude in a cluster of political attitudes. Since it is a central value, it can survive in the face of *a few* dissonant attitudes, but if there is too much dissonant information, then it is necessary to change the central attitude to permit cognitive reorganization to handle the new information. Now what had happened in the late '50's and early '60's? First, there was dissatisfaction with the Eisenhower administration's handling of the 1958 recession (leading to heavy Republican losses that year). Then, there was a popular Democratic president whose public image was enhanced after his assassination. Finally, there was the Goldwater campaign. We know that the distribution of party identification did not change much until 1964. What this implies is that a person's system of political attitudes can survive random shocks from different directions without changing party identification, but that successive shocks from the same direction cumulatively can bring about such a change. If true, this would explain the finding that changes occurred in 1964, but were then "back-dated" to some prior event or figure such as the

[5] This refers not only to the stability of the over-all distribution or party identification, but also to what is known from the Survey Research Center panel study of 1956–58–60. Of 1956 respondents who were reinterviewed in 1958, 81.6 per cent reported the same party identification, 5.0 per cent reported a shift within the same party, and 13.4 per cent reported a shift in categories. Of those changing from one party to another, 44.2 per cent shifted from Republican to Democrat, 6.9 per cent from Republican to Independent, 15.0 per cent from Democrat to Independent, and 33.9 per cent from Democrat to Republican. The percentages for comparison with Table XXI are that 51.1 per cent of the changers were former Republicans, and 48.9 per cent were former Democrats. This is strikingly different from the 70%–30% gradient for that time period in Table XXI.

Table XXII *Reason for Party Switch by Former Party*

Reason	Former Party		N
	Democrats	Republicans	
Depression or recession	10.5%	89.5%	19
Other economic reasons	57.9	42.1	19
FDR, Truman, Eisenhower	48.1	51.9	54
Kennedy	43.8	56.3	32
Johnson	50.0	50.0	12
Goldwater	50.0	50.0	24
Other national political (A change is good, should vote for men or issues, etc.)	63.6	36.4	44
Foreign policy	57.1	42.9	7
State and local politics	66.7	33.3	18
Temporary change, 1964 only	30.8	69.2	13

very popular late President. The Goldwater campaign may have caused changes in party identification by confirming feelings the voters had after the Kennedy assassination.

Some additional data which tend to support this argument are presented in Table XXII. Here we see the reasons given by those who had shifted their party loyalties. The most important causes of Republican losses were the depression and John F. Kennedy. The more modest Democratic losses have been associated with general economic or political philosophy, with foreign policy, and by voters' reactions to state and local politics.[6] So, important changes in party identification did occur in 1964, and this seems to have been caused by the combination of the Kennedy administration and the character of the presidential campaign which followed.

[6] Another fragment of evidence on this matter is that Republican gains tended to be obtained in the East where moderates set the tone of the party, and in the West where there are some visible moderates (for example, Governors Anderson, Love, Smylie, Hatfield, and Evans). Republican losses tended to occur in the Midwest and the South, bastions of G.O.P. conservatism.

The importance of these attitudinal changes as an effect of the election depends, of course, on how lasting they are. "If the shift turns out to be a temporary reaction to the circumstances of the moment," wrote Angus Campbell, "the future of party competition in this country will probably not differ greatly from what has been seen in the recent past. If it is the first sign of a true realignment of party attachments, the implications for the future may be far reaching."[7] There was some hope for a revival of Republican strength in the proportion of persons who reported a temporary change relating only to 1964. More than two-thirds of them were Republicans, but since less than 1 per cent of the sample said they had made such a temporary shift, this can hardly be cited as a substantial omen.

The latest data available at the time this is being written are those gathered by the Survey Research Center in its 1966 election study. These are shown in Table XXIII with 1962 and 1964 data added for comparison. It can be seen that the Republican party is still in a slightly weaker posture than prior to 1964, but that the events of 1964–66 seem to have weakened the Democratic party as well. During the 1960's, both parties have lost strong identifiers, and there has been a notable increase in the number of independent voters who do not think of themselves as close to either party. It would be fascinating to speculate on the causes of these further shifts, but this lies quite beyond the scope of our present inquiry. All that can be said

Table XXIII *Recent Shifts in the Distribution of Party Identification*

Party Identification	Oct. 1962	Oct. 1964	Oct. 1966
Strong Democrat	23%	26%	18%
Weak Democrat	23	25	28
Independent Democrat	8	9	9
Independent	8	8	12
Independent Republican	6	6	7
Weak Republican	16	13	15
Strong Republican	12	11	10
Apolitical	4	2	1

[7] "Interpreting the Presidential Victory," in the *National Election of 1964*, p. 280.

now is that the competitive posture of the two parties is moving back toward its pre-1964 status (the normal vote for a Democratic candidate would now be 56 per cent), but the behavior of the electorate is likely to be more volatile. Whether either party will succeed in anchoring the loyalties of the voters once again remains to be seen.

When we turn our attention from the electorate to group behavior, we also find some interesting aftereffects of the 1964 election. Returns were still being announced in Boise, Idaho, when Robert Smylie, chairman of the Republican Governors' Association, placed a call to George Romney, who had just been re-elected Governor of Michigan. After extending congratulations on his triumph, Smylie turned to another topic very much on his mind. "Dean Burch has to resign and I think we should call for that resignation at the next Governors' meeting. When the Yankees lost the series, they went out and hired a new manager the very next day. We've got to do the same thing." As election night wore on, Governor Smylie also placed calls to Daniel J. Evans, the newly elected governor of Washington, to Nelson Rockefeller in New York, to John Chafee who had run far ahead of Goldwater in winning re-election in Rhode Island, and to Tim Babcock, the victor in neighboring Montana. The next morning another call went to William Scranton in Harrisburg.[8]

That weekend Governor Smylie appeared on CBS's *Face the Nation.* He called attention to the electoral successes of moderate gubernatorial candidates (Avery 5 per cent ahead of the presidential ticket in Kansas, Boe 8 per cent ahead in South Dakota, Babcock 10 per cent ahead in Montana, Knowles 13 per cent ahead in Wisconsin, Evans 19 per cent ahead in Washington, Romney 23 per cent ahead in Michigan, Volpe 26 per cent ahead in Massachusetts, and Chafee 39 per cent in Rhode Island), and noted that the Republican governors controlled states casting 209 electoral votes, a fair base on which to rebuild the party. Smylie said that the Republicans needed to "get back into the broad middle of the road that established the last consensus satisfactory to the American people," and that in order to do so it was necessary to have a new national chairman. Asked about his own willingness to serve, the Governor said he would be willing to accept the position because he felt so strongly about "the need to make our party better able to serve as an instrument of the wishes of the American people." He was not particularly anxious for the position, but mentioned his availability

[8] *Newsweek,* November 16, 1964, p. 27.

to provide leaders of Republican groups with an alternative for consideration.

Actually, the attitudes expressed by many Republican leaders in the wake of the election were remarkably unaffected by the election results. Leaders of committed groups took positions quite similar to those they had been taking all along, and alluded to the election results as "proof" they had been right. Moderate leaders said the election showed how unwise it had been to stress conservative doctrine. New York state chairman Fred Young declared the party had "paid a shattering price for the erratic deviation from our soundly moderate, 20th-century course." Maryland state chairman Newton Steers said: "The election was a sharp and stunning rejection of the Goldwater brand of conservatism." Iowa state chairman Robert Ray stated that "bold, drastic steps will have to be taken to keep the two-party system in Iowa." Michigan national committeeman John B. Martin called for Burch's resignation. Governor Rockefeller told an ABC *Issues and Answers* audience that pleas for Burch's resignation were "reasonable." Pennsylvania Senator Hugh Scott told a news conference: "The present party leadership must be replaced—all of it. I don't even know where the leadership lies in that morass down there."

Leaders of conservative groups in the Republican party saw a very different verdict in the returns. The first question asked of Senator Goldwater at his post-election press conference was whether he had hurt the conservative cause. "No," he replied, "I don't feel that the conservative cause has been hurt; 25 million votes is a lot of votes and a lot of people dedicated to the concept of conservatism. I don't think it has been hurt." Denison Kitchel declared: "We may have to wait four years, but we're going to get this government back where it belongs." Texas Senator John Tower suggested that a liberal Republican nominee might have lost all 50 states instead of just 44, and argued the election could not be considered a defeat for conservatism because it was a battle of personalities rather than issues. Georgia state chairman Joe Tribble said that the calls for new leadership were "wishful thinking on the part of the leftists."

The attitudes of a third group, which might be called "centrists," did show some effects of the election. They admitted there were lessons to be learned from the election, but still deplored intra-party fighting and sounded unity themes. Michigan's Governor Romney disagreed with his state's national committeeman, saying a call for Burch's ouster was "to say the least, premature." Speaking to a post-election news conference, Romney said:

"Obviously there is great need in this situation to broaden and unify the party, [but] you don't broaden the party by kicking a lot of people out." Governor Mark Hatfield said that calls for Burch's resignation smacked "of trying to put the finger on a goat for the defeat. Every Republican shares in this defeat. . . . We have to draw together all the remnants of the party and get back to the middle of the road." Ohio's Ray Bliss said this was not the time for recrimination. "All responsible Republicans," argued Bliss, "should join together in planning sensibly for the future by developing a program to broaden our party base." 1964 platform chairman Mel Laird picked up this theme, saying: "This is no time to hunt for scapegoats, no time to indulge in intra-party bickering, no time to pursue personal ambition. Above all this is no time for anybody to read anybody else out of the Republican party." Laird acknowledged, however, that it would be "suicidal to ignore the election results and try to resist any change in the party." Former national chairman Thruston Morton told interviewers he was opposed to the removal of Dean Burch for failure to conduct a better campaign just as he was opposed to the removal of Thomas Kuchel as Republican Senate whip for failure to support Barry Goldwater. Richard Nixon declared the "strong conservative wing of the Republican party . . . deserves a major voice in party councils, and the liberal wing deserves a party voice, but neither can dominate or dictate—the center must lead."

So, after the election, as before, it was still possible to distinguish at least three Republican groups: moderates, conservatives, and centrists. The attitudes of the moderates and the conservatives had not been altered. The question was whether the attitudes of the centrists had been sufficiently affected to persuade them to join the moderates. This would determine whether a new coalition could be formed to take charge of the electoral machinery of the party, or whether the Goldwater coalition would retain control of this institutional base. This was discussed by Goldwater leaders during their post-campaign vacation at Montego Bay, Jamaica. At a press conference which followed, Barry Goldwater made a number of points. He reiterated his support for Dean Burch. "The National Chairman is contracted for four years and I expect the Republican party to live up to that contract." But he also said that he thought it would be a happy thing for the voters to choose up sides again with conservatives on one side, and liberals on the other. He equated the Republican party with conservatism in this proposed realignment, and referred to Governors Rockefeller and Romney and Senators Kuchel and Scott as "so-called Republicans." Three days later,

Governor Smylie announced that a meeting of the Republican Governors' Association was scheduled to take place in Denver on December 4 to discuss and plan the party's future.

In the two-and-a-half weeks between the Goldwater press conference and the Smylie announcement, there was much visiting and telephoning by emissaries of both sides. The results of this are unclear, but an Associated Press poll of members of the Republican National Committee probably was not too far off. Ninety-seven of the 132 committee members replied. Thirteen said they had no confidence in Chairman Burch; fourteen said they would support him; seventy had no opinion. A few leaders of one of the two groups of protagonists had made a decision. The rest were waiting to see what happened.

When the governors and governors-elect gathered in Denver, Governor Smylie delivered a strong keynote address.

> For the Republican party this is a time for a calm, cautious, dispassionate, rational and productive consideration of the age old question that reads where do we go from here.
>
> It is not a time for dictatorial pronouncement . . . [b]ut neither is it a time for squeamishness or irresolution. . . .
>
> As Governor Reed has pointed out, there was much good in the content of the recent campaign. He included the emphasis that was placed on restraining the growth of big government, on the importance of moral standards, on strength in the face of the obvious Communist menace, and on the importance of strong states working within the framework of a Federal union to accomplish satisfaction of the needs and aspirations of their people.
>
> To say that we did some things right, however, is not to say that we did nothing wrong. We did convey the impression that we had an equivocal position with respect to the civil rights of all Americans. Many thought we were opposed to the Social Security System, when in fact we were not. Many thought, rightly or wrongly, that we were sabre rattlers and thus not to be trusted with the Nation's security.
>
> It would be futile indeed to argue why or how this happened. This is what the people obviously believed when they voted. This is why we need now to set about repairing the image of the party in the Nation's consciousness, to restore it to a posture that will bring us all together again in a great consensus of America that can be useful to the people in the preservation of their freedom. . . .
>
> In the interest of repairing this historic house which is our political home, we might properly recommend to the National Committee that in our considered judgment the Committee itself might consider making appropriate changes in its leadership.

There was no mincing of words here, but, as we have seen, there was no doubt in Smylie's mind about the need for immediate action. The question on the gubernatorial agenda was whether his fellow chief executives would heed Smylie's call to action. It was not at all certain that this would happen. Robert Smylie had presented the moderate position, but there were also a few conservatives among the governors, as well as centrists who wished to avoid any precipitate action that might exacerbate intra-party rivalries. If the governors were to act as a group (and given the state of affairs in the party, any action they took would not be very effective unless they were united), they had to discover shared attitudes.

The most important session of the governors' meeting came Friday evening. Paul Fannin had interrupted a Mexican vacation to fly to Denver to present the Goldwater point of view. Fannin was popular with his fellow chief executives—he had been chairman of the Western Governor's Conference—and had been able to block action in Cleveland which he thought would be inimical to Goldwater. But in June he had been speaking for his party's probable presidential nominee. In December, he was speaking for those responsible for an electoral disaster, and the result of his determined presentation of the Goldwater case was to remind centrist governors of the many attitudes they shared with the moderates. The crucial moment came when Fannin proposed that the Republican Governors' Association *endorse* the national committee leadership. Amidst the dismay which followed, William Scranton leaned forward: "Mr. Chairman, I move you appoint a committee to draft a statement expressing the consensus of this meeting." Govenor Smylie promptly appointed a committee consisting of Governors Scranton, Rockefeller, Romney, and Babcock.

The "Denver Declaration" drafted by this committee was truly a group product. The four governors worked into the small hours of the morning; then aides worked throughout the night to have a draft ready for consideration at breakfast Saturday morning. The draft they prepared stated in part:

> Our experience as Governors and the Republican records of achievement in the various States clearly indicate that certain policies firmly anchored in the great Republican tradition and truly responsive to the modern needs of our nation, must be emphasized once again to make the Republican Party once again a national majority. Here are but some of the priorities:
>
> —Republican governors support all necessary action, public or private, to root out discrimination and the effects of discrimination throughout the United States. . . .

> —The Republican governors vigorously oppose all forms of narrow political radicalism, whether of the right or left, which seek to disrupt the orderly development of the great experiment in self-government that is the United States.
> —Government today is necessarily active in many areas of human need. Republican governors believe that some of these are: Old age security, hospital and medical care, decent living standards, public education, mental health and the needs of youth. . . .
> —Republican governors believe that the development of modern, responsive state and local government techniques is fundamental to the preservation and extension of individual liberty. . . .
> —Republican governors believe in private competitive enterprise as the best vehicle to serve the interests and rights of consumers, owners, management and labor. . . .

The statement also called for a Republican leadership conference including spokesmen for the House, Senate, governors, national committee and other party elements, and announced plans for the Governors' Association to put itself on a permanent basis by opening a Washington office. But the most important paragraph read:

> We need to appeal to *all* Americans. *We need to become inclusive rather than exclusive. We need to win elections and serve America as a great broadbased political party, far greater and far more effective than any narrow, exclusive political clique can ever hope to become.*

And the statement recommended that the national committee "adopt leadership which clearly represents a broad view of Republicanism and practices a policy of inclusion, not exclusion."

Seventeen of the governors and governors-elect were willing to sign this statement; Paul Fannin was not. Shortly before the press conference for release of the statement was scheduled to begin, Washington's Dan Evans, a young man with more than the normal quota of steel in his backbone, asked Fannin if he couldn't examine his purposes and find it within himself to join them in signing. Fannin did so, and unanimity was achieved.

Stating the issue in terms of the desirability of an inclusive, broad-based political party made unanimity possible. Not all governors were agreed on the meaning of this statement. Nelson Rockefeller said flatly that it was a call for Burch's departure: "If it isn't, you can shoot me." The New York Governor spoke for the majority. Montana's Tim Babcock, on the other hand, argued that Chairman Burch ought to "have the opportunity to end, if he can, the factionalism that is disrupting us. He has earned and is entitled to this chance. I choose not to see him forced out of office as a scapegoat."

The selection of this issue for emphasis also placed the governors in a relatively strong position vis-à-vis the Goldwater leaders. The governors did not quibble over whether Dean Burch had a "contract" because of his election by the national committee, nor did they raise any questions about what had been accomplished during his stewardship. The point on which the contest was focused was Senator Goldwater's preference for an ideologically oriented party supporting conservative causes versus the governors' preference for an inclusive, broad-based party that aimed at becoming a national majority.

The moderates who wanted to see the national committee under new leadership needed to be on strong ground. It was one thing for the Republican Governors' Association to call for a more inclusive party; it was quite another to replace the national chairman. The moderates were a majority among the governors; they were anything but a majority on the national committee. Here some institutional considerations are important. First, the structure of the national committee, equal representation from each state, acts to maximize small-state, conservative influence. Second, unless state law makes some other provision, the members of the national committee are elected by the state delegations to the national convention. This also skewed national committee attitudes in a pro-Goldwater direction. And Republican state chairmen are national committee members if their states cast Republican majorities in the presidential, congressional, or gubernatorial elections. As a result of the 1964 election, twelve state chairmen had lost their seats on the national committee while the state chairmen of South Carolina, Georgia, Alabama, Mississippi, and Louisiana had gained seats. These institutional rules meant that the Goldwaterites were in a very strong position on the national committee.

The names of several persons had been suggested as possible national chairmen. Richard Nixon, Robert A. Taft, Jr., Charles Percy, Walter Judd, John Anderson (the retiring Governor of Kansas), Robert Smylie, Leonard Hall, and Thruston Morton were all proposed by one person or another to succeed Dean Burch. But there was one name mentioned more frequently than any other: Ray C. Bliss. Ohio's Ray Bliss had a towering reputation within the party because of the job he had done as state chairman. At one point, he had been the choice of all of the potential nominees to head the national committee during the 1964 campaign. That had come to naught, but his reputation remained. And, because of his reputation, he was the man most likely to be able to command the votes to be elected as the next national chairman. So the question came to be whether Bliss or Burch could command more support within the party.

A private meeting which had been scheduled between Senator Goldwater and General Eisenhower was called to the attention of the press and broadened (apparently by Goldwater) to include Richard Nixon and Dean Burch. Governor Smylie wired General Eisenhower, saying he hoped the General would not lend his influence to any move to oppose the position taken by the governors in Denver. Eisenhower's reply was: "I now hear that the meeting scheduled originally to be merely bilateral has been broadened to include a number of individuals, but I shall be a party to no action or statement that denies the need for re-examination and assurance of early restructuring." The day before the Goldwater-Eisenhower meeting in New York, Governor Scranton flew to Gettysburg for an unpublicized meeting with the General. He brought along a copy of the Denver Declaration which he left for Dwight Eisenhower to study at his leisure. This resulted in an Eisenhower note to Scranton: "I've read the Governors' proposals with great care and have nothing but admiration for them." When the Goldwater-Eisenhower meeting finally took place, it was unproductive from Goldwater's point of view. Dean Burch was excluded from the meeting, and there was no joint statement to be given to the press indicating a Goldwater-Eisenhower agreement.[9]

The next indication of the direction of the political wind was a nationwide survey of Republican voters. Goldwater leaders had been arguing that replacing Dean Burch would be offensive to the 27 million persons who had voted for Goldwater. The poll revealed that only a fifth of the Goldwater voters could be thought of as strong Goldwater supporters. Moreover, among those calling themselves *conservative* Republicans, less than a quarter wished Goldwater to have the dominant voice in party affairs. The Arizonan ranked fourth, after George Romney, William Scranton, and Richard Nixon. This "confidential" poll, sponsored by an unidentified group allegedly including some large contributors to Goldwater's campaign, quickly became public knowledge.

The Senator's next move was to write to Republican leaders asking their advice on the future of the party. The dominant reply was that the governors' recommendations should be implemented. This was followed by an end-

[9] This paragraph is based upon "Goldwater's Little Summit Lesson" by Richard Dougherty, *New York Herald Tribune*, December 13, 1964, p. 7.

of-the-year personal appeal from the Senator to the members of the national committee. "I feel," Goldwater wrote, "the removal of Dean Burch now would be a repudiation of a great segment of our party and a repudiation of me. For the Republican party to turn its back on our cause now would be to destroy the two-party system—and that would be the prelude to the destruction of our nation." But the outcome of the contest between the conservative and moderate groups for the support of the centrists was more accurately foreshadowed in a quotation from the last Federalist President, John Adams: "Once the erosion of power begins it develops a momentum of its own."[10] Shortly after Goldwater appealed for support, he was visited by Nebraska National Committeeman Donald Ross and by Ray Bliss. The votes were available, they told the Arizonan, to elect Bliss national chairman. In these circumstances, wouldn't Goldwater be willing to support Bliss and so permit him to take over the difficult job of rebuilding the party with the support of all important Republican groups? The Senator acceded to their request. At the January meeting of the national committee, Dean Burch submitted his resignation, to take effect April 1. Ray C. Bliss, who had begun his career in Republican politics in Akron, Ohio, thirty-two years before, was unanimously elected to take his place.

The initiative taken by Republican moderates, and their subsequent success in forming a new coalition to place an experienced organizer in charge of the party's electoral machinery, was not the only instance of a group reaction to the 1964 election results. Another took place in the House of Representatives. The election had substantially changed the nature of the Republican membership in the House. The Republicans gained ten seats from the Democrats while losing forty-eight, and the Republican losses were concentrated among the conservatives. Forty Republican Representatives with ADA scores of 20 or less were replaced.[11] In districts carried by President Johnson by substantial majorities, liberal Republicans were much more likely to be re-elected than were conservative Republicans.[12] Sixty-two House Republicans had endorsed Barry Goldwater's candidacy for the Republican

[10] This quotation was used by Arthur Edson in an Associated Press story on the future of the Republican party published November 29, 1964.

[11] A score of 100 would mean that, in the judgment of the Americans for Democratic Action, the representative had a voting record that was as liberal as possible. A score of 0 would mean that his voting was regarded as being as conservative as possible.

[12] Milton C. Cummings, Jr., "House Nominations and Elections," in *The National Election of 1964*, pp. 248–50.

nomination; twenty of these Republicans were defeated in the November election. Another, quite unusual, result of the election was the defeat of many senior Republican House members. Hence, the Republican House membership was not only more liberal, but also younger. Two-thirds of the Republicans returning for the Eighty-Ninth Congress had entered Congress after 1956.[13]

There had been dissatisfaction with Charles Halleck's leadership before the election took place. Members who were anxious for a more constructive image for the party were disturbed by his normal tactic of marshalling a solid Republican vote *against* Administration proposals. Younger Republicans, a majority of the Republican membership, resented his tendency to restrict his consultations to the old boys with whom he was more familiar. Yet, no rebellion took place immediately after the election. Once the shock of the size of the Democratic gains wore off, there was a tendency to wait to see what happened. Unlike the relatively liberal Republican governors, no one seized the initiative. It took a series of unplanned, uncoordinated incidents to set the stage for group action.

This first was a letter from Thomas Curtis of Missouri to his colleagues. Curtis, who long has had an interest in stimulating more of an exchange of ideas among Republicans, wrote in part:

> Let's get our leadership established on one basic premise, if no other, that major decisions on Party organization and policy matters be made on as broad a base as possible. It may take a little more time and patience, but the net result will be, I am certain, a better organization, better policies, and better politics. In order to do this, I suggest that we have a party caucus within the next two or three weeks. . . .

Two of the Republicans who received this letter, Charles Goodell of New York and Robert Griffin of Michigan, saw real possibilities in this suggestion. Goodell and Griffin were two very able young men who had already won their spurs in Republican organizational politics and in substantive policy matters.[14] They saw the suggested meeting as a testing ground for Republi-

[13] Robert L. Peabody, *The Ford-Halleck Minority Leadership Contest, 1965*, Eagleton Institute Cases in Practical Politics (New York: McGraw-Hill, 1966). The remainder of this description of the Ford-Halleck contest is based on Peabody's analysis.

[14] They had organized the campaign to elect Gerald Ford chairman of the Republican Conference in 1963. Griffin (since elected to the Senate) was co-author of the Landrum-Griffin Bill, and Goodell deserved much of the credit for the passage of the Manpower Retraining Bill in 1962.

can leadership, and an opportunity to gain publicity for Republican proposals. In late November, Curtis, Goodell, and Griffin met with Albert H. Quie of Minnesota and Donald Rumsfeld and John Anderson of Illinois (able, younger members from large-state delegations) to discuss the possibilities of a mid-December meeting. This group concluded that a caucus was desirable, that the question of a leadership change should *not* be part of the agenda, and that Conference Chairman Ford should be asked to convene such a session.

Ford, with Halleck's reluctant consent, called such a meeting for Wednesday, December 16. One hundred and nineteen Republican House members attended, and from the viewpoint of those who wanted a full discussion of legislative issues, organizational questions, and the like, it was a productive session. But Minority Leader Halleck reacted defensively. He treated suggestions as if they were attacks on the way he had been doing things. The result was that a small group meeting in Goodell's office after the meeting concluded that an attempt should be made to change the House Republican leadership, that Gerald Ford would be the best candidate to support, and that Ford would stand a good chance of winning. Goodell, Griffin, and Quie reported this to Ford the following morning, and—after further consultations with interested parties—Ford agreed to enter the race.

The group who had urged Ford to make the race (those already mentioned, plus Silvio Conte of Massachusetts and Robert Ellsworth of Kansas) now faced the problem of building a coalition to support him. One strategy quickly decided upon was the need to keep the Ford-Halleck contest isolated from other intra-party battles. It must not be linked to the effort to remove Dean Burch in another institutional setting, lest Goldwater supporters be alienated. It should not appear as the project of the Wednesday Club (a group of generally liberal House Republicans), or conservative groups could not be recruited. If Ford should appear to be the candidate of the group of new congressmen just elected from the South, liberal groups would not support him. Similar considerations barred any tie between Ford's candidacy for the minority leadership and Mel Laird's aspirations for the conference chairmanship. Ford and Laird were good friends, and Laird's campaign was being organized by some able young conservatives, many of whom were also supporting Ford. But Laird still had enemies because of the platform fight in San Francisco, and any Ford-Laird "ticket" would make it hard to persuade these people to vote for Ford. So, isolation of the Ford contest was the order of the day.

The next question was what attitudes could unite a coalition including such dissimilar groups as the Wednesday Club and Southern conservatives. It could not be ideological. Not only was there relatively little intersection between the sets of attitudes of the groups whose support was necessary, but Ford and Halleck had quite similar voting records. Both had been part of the Republican leadership in the preceding session, and both were moderate conservatives. Therefore, it was decided to take advantage of the number of younger members by calling for full use of *all* Republican talent to "promote and communicate the image of a fighting, forward-looking party seeking responsible and constructive solutions to national problems." Ford sent each of his Republican colleagues a telegram reading:

> Today I am announcing my candidacy for the minority leadership of the House. During the next two years our performance as Republican congressmen will have a great impact on the future of our party. I am convinced that our House Republican talent, energy and dedication can and must be utilized fully if we as a party are to better represent and promote the best hopes of the American people and if we are to become a majority party. I hope I have your support. I look forward to a personal visit with you in the near future.
>
> My best wishes for a happy holiday season.

Ford's telegram, needless to say, cut short the "happy holiday season" of Charles Halleck who was vacationing in Florida. Halleck's statement, sent to the members and released to the press, stressed the extent of party agreement under his leadership.

> . . . the decision is for the Republican Members of the House to make. In making that decision I would assume that my record over the past six years would be an important consideration. . . .
>
> On vote after vote Republicans from the North, South, East and West—from urban and rural areas—have stood shoulder to shoulder on issues of vital importance to America. On six major issues over the past two years, our roll call votes averaged 162 to 3, an amazing example of teamwork. A study of Republican votes in the House from January 1961 to mid-1964 shows that whenever we had a policy position, the Republicans averaged 150 to 14 on 51 House roll calls.
>
> With our numbers reduced it is more important than ever that we continue this sort of teamwork.
>
> This would be my purpose as Republican leader.

The central attitude of the Halleck coalition, then, was the importance of unity on party issues. This unity could be most easily forged for a minority party by a policy of opposition to Administration proposals.

The core groups in the Halleck coalition would be his own Indiana delegation and other leaders with whom he had worked most closely in his years in the top party post. These other leaders included Leslie Arends of Illinois, who had first come to the House with Halleck in 1935 and was now Republican whip, and the deans (senior members) of large-state delegations. So, in terms of the membership of the core groups, this was a contest between generations. The senior members emphasized party unity behind an experienced legislative tactician while the younger generation stressed broader participation to produce constructive Republican alternatives.

The emphasis of both campaigns to build legislative coalitions was on a group of supporters who were committed to one of the candidates contacting members who were undecided. The Ford coalition had an initial advantage because its core group was in Washington while Halleck and most of his supporters were off vacationing. They decided to press this advantage by getting as many firm commitments as possible before Halleck returned. About thirty members who wanted a change of leaders began phoning colleagues to urge support for the Michigan legislator. They were reasonably confident after making their contacts, but after Halleck's core group got busy on the weekend immediately preceding the vote, they began to have doubts. After the Halleck counterattack, they initiated another round of telephoning which lasted until Sunday midnight.

The uncertainty which attends coalition building in the legislative setting[15] is best illustrated by comparing the final estimates of the coalition leaders with the vote which took place Monday morning. The leaders of the Ford coalition estimated 67 solid for Ford, 22 leaning to Ford, 7 undecided, 8 leaning to Halleck, and 36 solid for Halleck. If the Ford vote was restricted to those "solid or leaning," this should have meant a winning coalition with 89 members. A few days earlier, Halleck leaders had released an estimate of 85 members leaning or solid for Halleck. When the secret vote took place in the Republican Conference, Gerald Ford won by a margin of 73 to 67. The uncertainty was such that Ford coalition leaders, making a deliberate effort to keep their estimates cautious, overestimated the size of their coalition by some 16 votes. The Halleck coalition was 18 votes high in their claims. The contest between the two coalitions had been a very close affair.

[15] There is greater uncertainty when building a coalition in support of a leadership candidate than when doing so for a piece of substantive legislation. An organizational coalition has far-reaching implications, and members are apt to be much more cautious in this situation.

When it was over, Charles Halleck, taking the first step to give his successor the broader support he would need to lead the House Republicans, moved to make the nomination unanimous.

The coalition-building which resulted in the election of Gerald Ford as minority leader was different from that which led to the election of Ray Bliss as Republican national chairman. The institutional settings were different. The contest in the House was largely restricted to groups of legislators, while Republican leaders with several different bases of power were involved in the contest over the national chairmanship. Plans for a leadership contest in the House did not crystallize until after a series of discrete events convinced potential coalition leaders that it was appropriate, in contrast to efforts to build a moderate-centrist coalition to gain control of the electoral institution which had begun immediately after the election. And the contest over the House leadership went to a vote, whereas national committee members never did cast ballots in a contest that pitted Ray Bliss against Dean Burch. Barry Goldwater became convinced that a majority of Republicans wanted Bliss as national chairman, then cooperated in making the change.

Still, both can be characterized as aftereffects of the election. The voting behavior of the electorate increased the salience of change-oriented attitudes among members of the groups involved. The election created conditions which made new coalition-building possible. It resulted in a marked contraction in Barry Goldwater's influence. Without this change, a challenge in a Goldwater-dominated national committee would have been unthinkable. Without the defeat of a number of senior Republicans, it is more than possible that Charles Halleck could have survived a challenge to his leadership in the House of Representatives. And, since it could be argued that more pro-Republican attitudes among the voters were necessary if future electoral debacles were to be avoided, it could also be argued that Republican chances would be better with coalitions led by Ray Bliss and Gerald Ford. For it was certain that the voters' perception of the behavior of these coalitions—as well as those led by Lyndon Johnson and the Democratic legislative leaders, those led by the governors in their own states, and the Republican coalition in the U. S. Senate—would reinforce or modify voters' ideas about who should be entrusted with the political leadership of the nation. And this was the beginning of the politics of 1968.

11

A Summation of the Evidence

Electorate, group, coalition, institution—how useful are these concepts? We have been able to analyze nomination politics as the combination of groups into coalitions; we have seen some of the leadership problems involved in matching the skills of coalition leaders with the requirements of a given pattern of institutional behavior; we have noted the relationship between the attitudes of member groups and the strategies pursued by the coalitions to which they belong; we have interpreted the impact of these strategies in terms of changes in the attitudes of the electorate. So, at the very minimum, these concepts have provided us with a vocabulary to discuss significant political events. Still, if we want to use these concepts as the basis of a theory of American political parties, we need to make more explicit statements about the relationships between them.

Certain linkages were stated in the definitions. The electorate is a set of persons, potential voters. A group is also a set of persons, a relatively small set of persons who are members of the electorate. A coalition is a set of groups, and an institution is a set of coalitions. Thus, whenever we speak of an institution, we are automatically speaking about coalitions, groups, and persons. The relationships between the sets of persons (or collectivities of persons) are simple and straightforward. Each of the four concepts, though, was also defined in terms of characteristic sets of attitudes and behaviors. What general statements can be made about linkages within this system[1] of attitudes and behaviors?

Two factors limit the kinds of conclusions we can reach. The first is that our data are not comparable with each other *between* analytical levels. When we are dealing with the electorate, we have very rich interview data available. The extensive pre-election and post-election interviews yielded scores of attitudinal and behavioral variables which can be compared with each other in a great many ways. The data on group and coalition behavior, on the other hand, are more limited and of quite a different nature. The most crucial of these data are based on semi-structured interviews with coalition leaders. A "typical interview" consisted of two questions put to a Republican national committee division director in late September.[2]

What are the attitudes you're trying to project right now?

Well, on the positive side there is the whole question of morality . . . Johnson the politician, Bobby Baker, Billy Sol Estes, and the like. This begins to get into the question of the maintenance of law and order, in a way.

There isn't a name for this as a single issue, but that's what it is. I'd put that down as number 1. Law and order is number 2. And then there's fiscal responsibility and so on.

On the negative side there's the nuclear question, and irresponsibility.

[1] The word "system" is used here in the limited sense that the attitudes and behaviors are related to each other, and that a change in one implies compensating changes in at least some of the others. I am not using the word "system" to imply a political system or social system as it might be conceived in functional analysis or in the more primitive input-output analysis.

[2] This particular interview lasted about fifteen minutes because of the continual interruptions to which a top decision-maker is subject during a campaign. Due to the intense time pressure on these men, I deliberately limited my questioning to those topics on which their personal views were crucial or to items no one else knew about. A few of these interviews ran two or three single-spaced pages when transcribed; a good many more "interviews" consisted of single questions asked when I happened to find myself in the subjects' company. There were, of course, many other types of data available of which I made considerable use. These included discussions of the campaign at various meetings (including Senator Goldwater's own accounts at three staff meetings during September and October), speeches, press releases, reports, memoranda, and reporters' accounts and analyses which appeared in the press. (Throughout the book I have cited published accounts if I have relied on them for information.) Data on the Johnson campaign came almost entirely from sources available to the public.

Do you have any survey evidence about this?

That's what's coming through in the polls, too.

There's evidence that we're beginning to get through on this. The positive side is beginning to cut into Johnson's strength, and we're beginning to get an answer out on this nuclear question. We might be getting close to the turning point. I sure hope so.

Data of this kind are invaluable. They permit the observer to be confident of the coalition behavior he is describing. They are not of a character, however, which permit much use of formal measurement techniques. Consequently, we can describe campaign strategies and then inspect attitudinal data for variations which seem to correspond to these known strategies. We cannot use statistical techniques to obtain measures of association between strategy content and electoral response.

In order to calculate the correlations and regressions necessary to test alternative relationships in related causal models to determine which pathways best knit the concepts together,[3] it would be necessary to have group members and leaders respond to questionnaires parallel to those administered to a sample of the electorate, and to have a content analysis of messages transmitted during the campaign in terms of statements about the attitudes being measured in the questionnaires. In short, one would need an integrated study consciously designed to generate comparable data on both the elite[4]

[3] On this, see Hubert M. Blalock, Jr., *Causal Inferences in Nonexperimental Research* (Chapel Hill: University of North Carolina Press, 1964); Hayward R. Alker, Jr., "Causal Inference and Political Analysis," in Joseph L. Bernd, ed., *Mathematical Applications in Political Science II* (Dallas: Arnold Foundation Monographs, 1966); Charles F. Cnudde and Donald J. McCrone, "The Linkage Between Constituency Attitudes and Congressional Voting Behavior: A Causal Analysis," in *American Political Science Review*, March, 1966, pp. 66–72; Donald J. McCrone and Charles F. Cnudde, "Toward a Communications Theory of Democratic Political Development: A Causal Model," in *American Political Science Review*, March, 1967, pp. 72–79, Donald R. Matthews and James W. Prothro, *Negroes and the New Southern Politics*, Ch. 11; and Arthur S. Goldberg, "Discerning a Causal Pattern among Data on Voting Behavior," in *American Political Science Review*, December, 1966, pp. 913-22.

[4] I am not at all sure such an elite study would be feasible. One barrier is time. Amid the demanding circumstances of a presidential campaign, filling out questionnaires for behavioral scientists would likely have a low priority. The other consideration is that, like the presidency, the number of coalition leaders whose attitudes are relevant in a presidential campaign is so low that it might not be meaningful to analyze their attitudes on any statistical basis. Consequently, a this-is-what-they-thought-they-were-about and this-is-what-they-did approach may indicate limits of precision we shall have to live with.

and mass levels. Until such data are available, we shall have to content ourselves with describing relationships rather than measuring them.

A second constraint on our ability to state relationships between the sets of attitudes and behaviors is that each of the concepts has been defined broadly enough to include a wide range of phenomena. The set of behaviors of the electorate, for example, includes all behaviors falling "within the range of citizen activity." This embraces simply being exposed to political cues, reading and talking about politics, voting, trying to convince your neighbor he ought to vote for a particular candidate, wearing a campaign button, making a contribution, and a host of other activities. The set of institutional attitudes includes all coalition leaders' attitudes toward functions assigned to the institution by society. The functions of but one institution, the legislature, include passing legislation, interest articulation, administrative oversight, representation, educating the public, and so on, and coalition leaders often have quite different attitudes about the relative importance of these functions. One result of defining concepts this broadly is that there are several different relationships between each set of attitudes and behaviors.

It is possible to make some summary statements about the relationships on a very general level. Elsewhere, I have suggested that the linkage between campaign strategies, attitudes of the electorate, and voting behavior could be conceived as an *election game*.[5] Here one summarizes Candidate A's strategy in a row vector

$$S_A = (a_1, a_2, a_3)$$

and candidate B's strategy emphases as a column vector

$$S_B = \begin{pmatrix} b_1 \\ b_2 \\ b_3 \end{pmatrix}$$

where the first, second, and third entries refer to the emphases on candidate, party, and issues respectively. Since Mr. Goldwater emphasized issues while

[5] "A Game Theory Analysis of Campaign Strategy," in M. Kent Jennings and L. Harmon Zeigler, *The Electoral Process* (Englewood Cliffs, N. J.: Prentice-Hall, 1966), pp. 290–303. For an explanation of the mathematical operations, see John G. Kemeny, J. Laurie Snell, and Gerald L. Thompson, *Introduction to Finite Mathematics* (Englewood Cliffs, N.J.: Prentice-Hall, 1957), Chs. 5–6.

Mr. Johnson's strategy emphases were somewhat more equally distributed, their strategy vectors would be:

$$S_G = (2/10, 2/10, 6/10) \qquad S_J = \begin{pmatrix} 4/10 \\ 3/10 \\ 4/10 \end{pmatrix}$$

The attitudes of the electorate are considered in pairs, with a utility function assigned to each pair indicating which candidate derives a net advantage from the joint effect of these two attitudes. A simple five-point scale is used with a score of 1 indicating a decided Democratic advantage, and a score of 5 standing for a decided Republican advantage. Since every pair of attitudes in 1964 gave a decided advantage to the Democrats, each cell in the election game matrix would have an entry of 1. An outcome is calculated by multiplying the election game matrix by the strategy vectors, thus:

Goldwater's Strategy × Election Matrix × Johnson's Strategy

$$(2/10, 2/10, 6/10) \begin{bmatrix} 1 & 1 & 1 \\ 1 & 1 & 1 \\ 1 & 1 & 1 \end{bmatrix} \begin{pmatrix} 4/10 \\ 3/10 \\ 4/10 \end{pmatrix}$$

The outcome of this multiplication would be 1 since every entry in the election game matrix is 1. This corresponds to a decided Democratic victory.

The relationship between strategies, voters' attitudes, and voting behavior in this model is unambiguous. It is multiplicative. Moreover, the deductions from this model—that (in this limiting case) Johnson would have won by a large margin regardless of the candidates' strategies, and that the outcome of the election was just that—are correct as far as they go. The difficulty with this approach, particularly in this limiting case, is that it doesn't tell us very much. It does not, for example, tell us why the candidates employed the strategies they did. The more detailed approach used in this book does permit some understanding about this, but it also points to *several different relationships* among the strategies, attitudes, and voting behavior. We have seen that the Republican mobilization campaign, the Democratic offensive strategy to woo liberal Republican voters, and the Democratic defensive strategy for the South all were related to the attitudes and the behaviors of the electorate. When one is aware of several relationships between concepts, it is difficult to combine this knowledge into general statements. Sometimes it can be done only awkwardly, sometimes not at all.

What can be said about the apparent relationships between the attitudinal and behavioral variables is summarized in Figure 16. In view of the

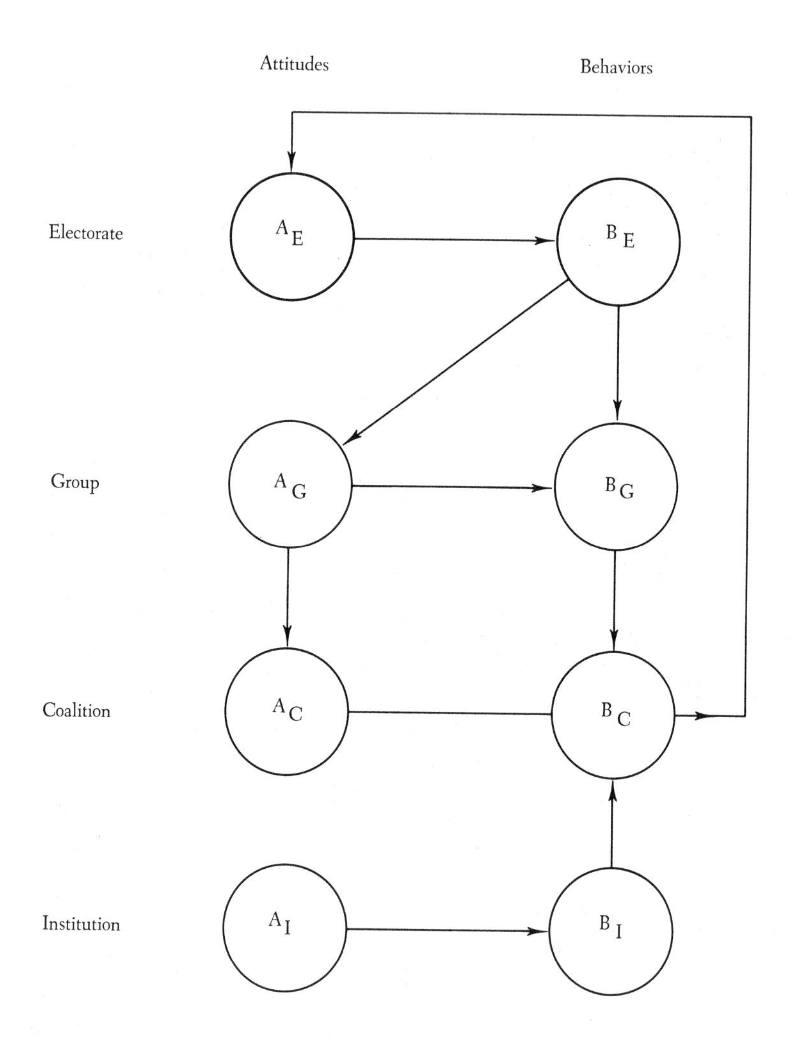

Figure 16 *Relationships in the System*

constraints introduced by the non-comparability of data and the breadth of definitions, one cannot be certain that the pathways diagramed here constitute the best explanatory model. But the evidence we have does point in this direction, so let us examine it one step at a time.

There are many different relationships between the attitudes and behaviors of the electorate, and a choice among them depends on which behavior has been selected as the dependent variable. If one is interested in the entire range of citizen activity, then the dependent variable may be conceived of as a scale of political participation. Lester Milbrath has proposed a hierarchy of political involvement running from apathetics to spectator activities (voting, talking politics) to transitional activities (contacting a politician, attending a political meeting) to gladiatorial activities (working in a campaign, running for office).[6] His summary of the literature indicates that the attitudes affecting participation include political involvement, strength of party identification, political efficacy, personal effectiveness, sophistication of political cognitions, sociability, and an absence of cynicism.[7] Donald Matthews and James Prothro used a five-point scale of political participation, with non-participation as Level I, just talking politics as Level II, talking and voting as Level III, talking, voting and campaigning (giving money, going to a rally, doing campaign work) as Level IV, and the foregoing plus holding office or belonging to a political group as Level V. They found attitudes similar to those noted by Milbrath—party identification, political interest, political information, and sense of civic competence—related to general political participation, and a sense of deprivation, attitude toward change, a sense of racial inferiority, and awareness of local intimidation, damping normal political participation on the part of Southern Negroes.[8]

If one focuses on one aspect of political participation, then certain attitudes become salient. If one wishes to distinguish between voters and nonvoters, then psychological involvement in the campaign (as measured by interest in the campaign, concern over the outcome, a sense of political efficacy, and a sense of civic duty) and intensity of partisan preference are especially important.[9] If the behavioral variable is whether one is likely to

[6] *Political Participation*, p. 18.

[7] *Political Participation*, Ch. 3.

[8] *Negroes and the New Southern Politics*, Ch. 10. Both the Milbrath summary of the literature and the Matthews-Prothro study give much more sophisticated explanations of participation than the relationship with the attitudinal variables discussed here.

[9] Angus Campbell *et al.*, *The American Voter*, Ch. 5

vote Republican or Democrat, then attitudes about parties, candidates, and issues are strongly related. The attitudes about the Republican party, Johnson and Goldwater (introduced in Figure 13 and discussed in the pages following) were all related to voting choice at the .001 level of significance.[10] When these attitudinal data are used in the six-factor Survey Research Center model of voting choice, Donald Stokes tells us "the correlation of estimated and actual majorities over . . . four contests is .98, a figure which increases our confidence that we have faithfully measured many of the immediate attitudinal forces on the electorate's decision."[11]

When one moves to the high end of the scale of citizen activity, participation in some form of active campaigning, persons are apt to have high scores on almost all the attitudes we have been discussing. There have been a fair number of studies of the characteristics and attitudes of political activists,[12] and the point that in "the political stratum, politics is highly salient, . . . individuals tend to be rather calculating in their choice of strategies, . . . an individual's political beliefs tend to fall into patterns that have a relatively high degree of coherence and internal consistency, . . . [and] information about politics and the issues of the day is extensive . . ."[13] has been well substantiated.

One aspect of this more intense form of participation that deserves more emphasis than it has received in the literature is the large number of persons who are involved in campaigns. To be sure, fewer people work for candidates or belong to political organizations than engage in the relatively unde-

[10] Johnson and Goldwater voters' attitudes about the Democratic party, although very different, did not differ at the .05 level because of similar positive views about the Democratic party.

[11] "Some Dynamic Elements of Contests for the Presidency," in *American Political Science Review*, March, 1966, p. 28.

[12] See, for example, Samuel J. Eldersveld, *Political Parties: A Behavioral Analysis*, Part II; Dwaine Marvick and Charles R. Nixon, "Recruitment Contrasts in Rival Campaign Groups," in Dwaine Marvick, ed., *Political Decision-Makers* (New York: Free Press of Glencoe, 1961), pp. 138–92; Lewis Bowman and G. R. Boynton, "Recruitment Patterns among Local Party Officials," in *American Political Science Review*, September, 1966, pp. 667–76; Lewis Bowman and G. R. Boynton, "Activities and Role Definitions of Grassroots Party Officials," *Journal of Politics*, February, 1966, pp. 121–43; and Phillip Althoff and Samuel C. Patterson, "Political Activism in a Rural County," *Mid-West Journal of Political Science*, February, 1966, pp. 39–51.

[13] Robert A. Dahl, *Who Governs?* (New Haven: Yale University Press, 1961), pp. 90–91.

manding sport of talking about politics, but the proportion of those who fall at the high end of the scale of political participation appears to be growing. The Survey Research Center estimate is that, in 1952, 3 per cent of the public worked in a political campaign; in 1964, 5 per cent did so. In 1952, 7 per cent of the S.R.C. sample reported attending a campaign meeting or rally; in 1964, 9 per cent did so. In 1952, 4 per cent said they had given money for one of the parties or candidates; in 1964, 10 per cent responded affirmatively to this question. We seem to be witnessing a "creeping politicization"[14] of the electorate, and we should not let the slow rate of this change blind us to its potential significance.

The total number of persons at the high end of the scale is also greater than is suggested by, say, the five per cent of the respondents who report doing some work for one of the parties or candidates. It happens that scaling efforts are least effective at the high end of the range of citizen activity. If one is a campaign worker, it is a relatively sure thing that he will also vote. It is *not* a sure thing that he will also contribute money or wear a campaign button. Table XXIV presents data (from the 1964 Survey Research Center study) on the extent of overlap between the various types of gladiatorial activities. These data suggest that while a high degree of political involvement is necessary for a person to take part in one of these activities, an individual has enough choice between types of activity to select one which fits his own personality.[15] This has at least two implications. One is that the total number of activists is going to be higher than we might suspect if we look at a single type of campaign behavior. Indeed, one person in every six qualified for our activist category, a proportion which certainly supports description of the American pattern as a *participant* civic culture.[16] The other implication is that as we move to the group level, we are likely to encounter different groups of participants, with intergroup rivalries, for example, between contributors and campaign workers.

The attitudes of party groups are dependent on the behavior of the electorate in two different ways. First, the relationship between the attitudes

[14] Elmo Roper has used the term "creeping suffrage" to call attention to the slow, but significant, increase in voting turnout ("The Politics of Three Decades," *Public Opinion Quarterly*, Fall, 1965, p. 374).

[15] Robert E. Lane, *Political Life* (Glencoe: The Free Press, 1959), pp. 99–100.

[16] Gabriel A. Almond and Sydney Verba, *The Civic Culture* (Princeton: Princeton University Press, 1963), pp. 440–55.

Table XXIV *Overlap Between Forms of Campaign Participation*

First Form of Participation	Proportion of Persons Engaging in First Form of Campaigning Who Also Participate By:				
	Belong to political organization	Work in campaign	Attend meeting or rally	Make contribution	Wear button or display bumper sticker
Belong to political organization	—	48%	64%	59%	52%
Work in campaign	31%	—	64%	44%	56%
Attend meeting or rally	29%	38%	—	52%	44%
Make contribution	22%	19%	42%	—	50%
Wear button or display bumper sticker	13%	18%	23%	32%	—

of the electorate and group attitudes is an indirect linkage through citizen behavior. This is so because the group members do not constitute a random sample of the membership of the electorate. Only those persons who are sufficiently motivated to fall at the high end of the scale of political participation become members of party groups. Hence, there is no necessary correspondence between the attitudes of political groups and the attitudes of the electorate as a whole.

Table XXV shows that attitudes of activists were different from those of the general public on the most salient issues of the 1964 campaign. The activists were more skeptical about the concentration of power in the federal government, less favorably disposed to welfare measures, somewhat more supportive of desegregation, less optimistic about the success of American foreign policy, and more hawkish about Vietnam. Much, but not all, of this difference in attitudes between party groups and the general public is due to the far more conservative attitudes of the Republican activists. As Table XXVI shows, the association between political activism and skepticism about

Table XXV *Attitudes of Political Activists*

	Activists	Non-activists	N
Power of Federal Government			
Govt. not too strong, mind made up	28%	45%	452
Govt. not too strong, has doubts	9	10	110
It all depends	3	5	49
Govt. too powerful, has doubts	6	7	72
Govt. too powerful, mind made up	52	33	401
Gamma = −.316			
Medicare			
Favors medicare, mind made up	36%	56%	695
Favors medicare, has doubts	2	7	83
It all depends	11	7	96
Opposes medicare, has doubts	4	4	49
Opposes medicare, mind made up	47	26	389
Gamma = −.377			
Civil Rights			
Favors desegregation	38%	31%	491
Favors something in between	47	45	686
Favors strict segregation	16	24	352
Gamma = .169			
Foreign Policy			
U.S. has done pretty well	38%	57%	719
Well in some ways, not well in others	6	10	128
U.S. hasn't done too well	56	32	478
Gamma = −.392			
Vietnam			
Pull out entirely	9%	15%	125
Stay, try to end fighting	26	41	352
Take stronger stand	65	44	450
Gamma = −.360			

the power of the federal government is not completely eliminated when one focuses on Democrats and Independents, but it is sharply reduced. Republican party activists are not only more conservative than the general public,

Table XXVI *Activists' Attitude about Federal Government by Party Identification*

	Activists	Non-activists	N
Democrats Only			
Govt. not too strong, mind made up	50%	56%	296
Govt. not too strong, has doubts	15	10	56
It all depends	1	5	25
Govt. too powerful, has doubts	13	6	39
Govt. too powerful, mind made up	21	23	120
Gamma = −.062			
Independents Only			
Govt. not too strong, mind made up	30%	36%	84
Govt. not too strong, has doubts	10	13	30
It all depends	10	6	16
Govt. too powerful, has doubts	7	4	11
Govt. too powerful, mind made up	43	40	95
Gamma = −.103			
Republicans Only			
Govt. not too strong, mind made up	11%	23%	55
Govt. not too strong, has doubts	5	9	23
It all depends	3	3	8
Govt. too powerful, has doubts	2	10	22
Govt. too powerful, mind made up	78	55	181
Gamma = −.428			

but much more conservative than *Republican* voters.[17] But regardless whether the differences between attitudes are general or concentrated among groups of activists of one party, "these gross differentiations between participation strata probably have real significance for public policy."[18] They certainly have significance for this system of attitudes and behavior.

[17] This is consistent with Herbert McClosky's finding that Republican activists (convention delegates and alternates) were "out of touch" with the attitudes of Republican voters ("Issue Conflict and Consensus Among Party Leaders and Followers," *American Political Science Review*, June, 1960, pp. 406–27).

[18] V. O. Key, Jr., *Public Opinion and American Democracy* (New York: Knopf, 1961), p. 186.

The other way in which the set of attitudes of party groups is linked to citizen behavior is that electoral behavior is one of the most important factors in the group's political environment. Hence, most party groups have some kind of attitude about the nature of voting behavior. This attitude may be crude ("Well, no one knows the psyche of the voter, but perhaps . . ."), but it is likely to be a central attitude, and hence important in group behavior. As we saw, this remained one of the major attitudinal differences between groups of Republican moderates and groups of Republican conservatives from the days of the Dewey-Taft contests to the nomination struggle of 1964. Moderates felt that the Republican party must follow more progressive policies to appeal to voters, while conservative groups believed there was a "hidden" conservative vote among the electorate. According to the "hidden vote" hypothesis, conservative voters were alienated by too-liberal policies espoused by both parties, and ready to turn out in large numbers to support a conservative nominee.

Some group attitudes about electoral behavior are susceptible to modification by interpretation of election results. Whether modification occurs depends, of course, on how strongly the attitude is held in the first place. In our canvass of post-election Republican attitudes in the last chapter, we noticed that leading moderates and leading conservatives both continued to talk in late November as they had in mid-June. Moderates felt the conservative course of the party had been disastrous; conservatives believed the party should continue to follow this path. The "centrist" group, however, shifted some of its attitudes. It continued to speak about the importance of party unity. But whereas in the summer "party unity" had meant acceptance of the Goldwater point of view, this was not the case after the votes had been counted. After the election, centrists also referred to the needs "to broaden the base of the party" and "to learn the lesson of the election."

In the flow diagram in Figure 16, group behavior is shown as dependent on group attitudes and the behavior of the electorate. We have just been discussing the indirect relationship in which the behavior of the electorate affects group behavior by (sometimes) modifying group attitudes. The direct relationship comes about by electoral behavior creating conditions in which group action is possible. The post-election behavior of the group of moderate Republican governors who wanted new party policies and new party leadership and of the group of Republican congressmen who wanted younger House leadership was stimulated by the election. The election also made it possible for both groups to succeed by reducing Goldwater influence among members of the national committee, and by defeating many senior conservative Republicans in the House.

Group attitudes are linked to coalition attitudes by definition. The set of attitudes of a coalition consists of those which lie within the intersection of the sets of attitudes of member groups. Coalition behavior, in our conceptualization, is dependent on both group behavior and coalition attitudes. A central question for the validity of this theory is whether coalition behavior, as exhibited in coalition formation and the strategies the coalitions followed, can be shown to be consistent with this hypothetical linkage.

Viewing nomination politics as a stochastic process, the most important transition probability is that governing whether a proto-coalition will become a winning coalition. This depends on the size the proto-coalition has already attained, and on the extent of overlap between the attitudes of the proto-coalition and the attitudes of as yet unrecruited groups. Bearing this in mind, we can assess certain critical stages of the nomination process in the light of what might have happened to cause groups within the party to join one coalition or another.

The first critical stage of the nomination process came after the New Hampshire primary. Conservative groups, though disappointed at Goldwater's lack of success, were still willing to join the Goldwater coalition because of the identity in attitudes. But moderate groups and those non-ideological groups who simply wanted an attractive candidate did not have as clear a choice to make. They were not likely to join the Rockefeller coalition after the New York Governor had run third, but the Lodge coalition lacked the resources to mount a serious campaign and Scranton was inert in Harrisburg. A move which could have altered the eventual outcome would have been a Rockefeller withdrawal in favor of either Lodge or Scranton.[19] Henry Cabot Lodge was unpopular with many groups in the Republican party, but if Rockefeller-like resources had been placed at the disposal of the leaders of the Lodge coalition, it is conceivable Lodge could have won several important primaries. If this had happened, there would have been a proto-coalition of sufficient size (New York, New England, and groups won in primaries) and enough attitudinal overlap with moderate and centrist groups to have had a good chance of winning. Governor Scranton was more

[19] I am not trying to argue that this was something which coalition leaders were likely to do or ought to have done. I only wish to point to behaviors which might have altered the transition probabilities in the nomination process.

acceptable to leaders of Republican groups, but less well-known to the general public. Since he was accepted by the general public when he finally did enter the lists, there is no reason to believe that he would not have been well received if he had done so earlier. At this juncture, a Scranton coalition based on Pennsylvania, New York, New Jersey, Maryland (and Ohio?) also would have stood a good chance of attracting enough groups to have won.

It would have been more difficult to change the outcome later, when the Goldwater coalition had grown in size, but another potential turning point would have been a Lodge victory in Oregon. A slight redistribution of votes between the two front-runners could have made some difference. If Lodge and Rockefeller had split their 61 per cent of the vote with 31 per cent going to Lodge and 30 per cent to Rockefeller, a Lodge victory suggesting that both men were quite popular, it might have made it easier for a successful Lodge-Rockefeller coalition to function in California. If, to continue this might-have-been sequence a bit further, Ambassador Lodge had returned from Vietnam on the eve of the California primary, and had been met at the airport by Governor Rockefeller where they jointly pledged to keep the Republican party within the mainstream of American thought, enough life might have been breathed into a moderate coalition to produce a Rockefeller victory in the California primary. (The actual behavior of the moderate coalition in California, in contrast, points up the dependence of coalition behavior on group behavior. Coalition behavior, in our formulation, is interdependent in the sense that all groups must act in concert for the coalition to succeed. In an institutional setting such as nomination politics where no one is "in charge," one or more groups may fail to act as necessary to achieve the coalition goal. If so, the coalition fails.)

The California primary was, of course, a third opportunity to affect the outcome of the nomination process. If the Rockefeller coalition had won (with or without more help from the Lodge coalition), it is likely more moderate groups would have been selected in the post-California state conventions. In these circumstances, conservative groups would have been in the Goldwater coalition, and moderate groups would have been in several smaller coalitions. The Goldwater coalition would have been in a stronger bargaining position because of its larger size, but the lack of overlap in attitudes between the moderates and the conservatives would have acted to prevent much shifting back and forth. If neither the conservatives nor the moderates had been able to build a coalition to majority size, then a Nixon coalition (or perhaps one organized in support of Governor Scranton or

Senator Morton) would have been in a strong position because of the number of attitudes such a coalition would have shared with both moderates and conservatives.

These might-have-beens, however, are much more useful as illustrations of the implications of the theory than as evidence of its validity. What actually happened is that the Goldwater coalition grew stronger as it grew in size. It did so in a way that suggests the transition probability relating to nomination victory is dependent on size of the proto-coalition and overlap in attitudes with still unrecruited groups as outlined in Chapter 2. Once the Goldwater coalition reached a size such that the prospect of victory neared certainty, all Republican groups joined *except* those moderate groups whose sets of attitudes barely intersected with the set of attitudes of the Goldwater coalition. One instance of coalition formation does not provide much evidence, particularly when no attempt at formal measurement has been made,[20] but it does suggest this theory fits better with the facts of American nomination politics than one which is based on the principle that "in social situations similar to n-person, zero-sum games with side payments, participants create coalitions just as large as they believe will ensure winning and no larger."[21] The Goldwater coalition was much larger than this. It had two-thirds of the votes at the end of the first ballot in San Francisco.

Now are the strategies which the electoral coalitions followed consistent with the assertion that the characteristic attitudes of a coalition lie in the overlap between the sets of attitudes of the member groups? Obviously, they are. But what is less obvious, and hence gives our theory greater explanatory power, is that the strategies employed were by no means the only strategies that would have been plausible in the circumstances. There are at least two other strategies the Goldwater coalition could have followed, and three other strategies which would have made some sense for the Johnson coalition.

[20] For a theory of coalition-formation which has been operationalized, see William A. Gamson, "Coalition Formation at Presidential Nominating Conventions," *American Journal of Sociology*, September, 1962, pp. 157–71. For a theory which accounts for parliamentary coalitions in Sweden, France, and Italy, see Michael A. Leiserson, *Coalitions in Politics: A Theoretical and Empirical Study* (unpublished Ph.D. dissertation, Yale University, 1966).

[21] William H. Riker, *Theory of Political Coalitions*, pp. 32–33. Since nomination situations are not zero-sum (because groups in losing nomination coalitions often receive pay-offs when they join their party's electoral coalition), this would be a social situation *dissimilar* to that envisioned by Riker. Hence, he would not expect his model to apply.

In the case of the Goldwater coalition, once it had won the nomination, it would have been perfectly feasible for it to have followed a strategy not unlike that pursued by candidates Eisenhower and Nixon. It could have continued to take a more conservative posture than President Johnson, but at the same time made policy proposals more consistent with those advanced by previous Republican candidates. It could have done so to appeal to Republican voters who were nervous about Goldwater's nomination, and as a method of uniting party members behind the candidate. This course of action could have been explained to conservative groups on the grounds that it was necessary to elect a conservative president before any conservative ideology could be implemented, and polls had shown such a strategy was necessary to attract the necessary votes.

A second possible strategy would have rested on an assumption that it was impossible for a conservative candidate to win in 1964, and the Goldwater coalition should therefore act to keep control of the Republican party against the day when voters would finally recognize the wisdom of the conservative cause. The implication of this would have been to adopt a "Southern strategy," at least as much of a "Southern strategy" as would be acceptable in conservative areas of the Midwest and West. The campaign would then have focused resources on these most conservative parts of the country. Such a strategy would have put special emphasis on the election of conservative candidates to Congress and other lesser offices in the hope of making groups of elected Republicans still more conservative. The word could have been passed quietly to friendly members of the national committee to stand by for a fight to retain control of the electoral machinery in the wake of defeat. Then Senator Goldwater could have announced after the election that only a single battle had been lost. This strategy would have been quite consistent with a desire to remold the party system along liberal-conservative lines.

Once Senator Goldwater had been nominated, President Johnson had considerable freedom in the selection of his strategy. One response could have been to shift the Democratic policy emphasis in a more conservative direction. By adopting policies more pleasing to Southerners than those of "national Democrats" who had dominated preceding Democratic administrations, the Johnson coalition would have been in a stronger position to defend Democratic strength in the South from the appeals of Barry Goldwater. There were certainly enough precedents for this in the voting record of Senator Johnson (votes against controls on natural gas, votes for defense expenditures, etc.), and a position could have been taken that an age of affluence, presented questions other than the depression-born need for public welfare. Such a strategy would not have been pleasing to liberal groups in the Democratic coalition, but in 1964 there was no other electoral coalition for them to join.

A second possibility would have been a Johnson decision to fight the campaign along liberal-conservative lines, to debate the merits of the questions Senator Goldwater was raising. This would have shifted the Democratic policy emphasis in a direction pleasing to urban Democrats, labor leaders, and Negroes, and would, of course, have cost the Democratic party support in the South. These losses, especially in the Deep South, could have been compensated for by gains in the North. Moreover, if such a strategy had given the Democratic party an image as the party of the future while dismissing the Republicans as the party of the past, Southern losses might have been temporary. In any case, a closer-knit ideological base within the Democratic party could have been prepared to support liberal legislation in coming Congresses.

A third strategy the Johnson coalition might have followed would have been an attack on the Republican party. Rather than referring to Senator Goldwater as the "temporary Republican spokesman," this strategy would have claimed that the Arizona Senator was the "real voice of the Republican party." Democratic spokesmen could have said: "We've been telling you all these years Republicans were genuine reactionaries and you wouldn't believe us. Now you have proof!" Such an attack on the Republican party would have increased the pressure on moderate Republicans, and probably would have led many of them to vote for Senator Goldwater in a defensive reaction. But it might well have increased the number of people who shifted their party identification away from the Republican party,[22] and so would have been of more long-run benefit to the Democrats.

Each of these strategies was plausible, and each could have been predicted with some alternative hypothesis about coalition behavior. It might be argued for example, that the coalition attitudes will be those of the group regarded as most important. If a single group had been considered, then a Goldwater strategy pleasing to organizational loyalists at the expense of the Southerners, or a "Southern strategy" offensive to organizational loyalists would have been valid courses of action. The same argument holds with a

[22] In view of what we saw about the shifts in party identification that took place anyhow, this must be rated a strong possibility.

"Southern strategy" for the Johnson coalition or a shift in the opposite direction to follow a course pleasing to urban Democrats. Or, if one accepts the size principle that minimum winning coalitions tend to form, then one would expect the Goldwater coalition to have adopted a "normal Republican" strategy to recruit Republicans and Independents for a minimal electoral majority. Johnson, to be consistent with this model, should have opted for an attack on Republicans, to restrict the size of what was almost sure to be a winning coalition and to obtain long-run benefits, or should have shifted Democratic emphasis in a more liberal direction. This would also have restricted the size of the winning coalition and, by increasing the ideological homogeneity of the winning coalition, would have increased the number of pay-offs to the members of the winning coalition.[23]

The point is that none of these strategies were employed, and all were excluded by the requirement that coalition behavior be consistent with attitudes falling into the intersection of the sets of attitudes of member groups. A Goldwater campaign along "normal Republican" lines would have been offensive to Southerners, and perhaps to conservative ideologues and foreign policy hard-liners. A "Southern strategy" would have been inconsistent with the attitudes of at least the organizational loyalists. On the Democratic side, a conservative strategy would have offended liberal groups, and a liberal strategy would have fallen outside the set of attitudes of Southerners (and perhaps some Westerners). An attack on Republicans would not have been excluded by this requirement for the normal Democratic coalition, but in 1964 the Johnson coalition included a group of moderate Republicans, and

[23] Professor Riker can defend his size principle by pointing out that it requires a longer time period to operate than a single election campaign. "The American electorate is many-faceted and its government only slowly responsive to the reshuffling of coalitions" (*Theory of Political Coalitions,* p. 90). Further, reduction in coalition size is apt to occur after a landslide victory. "Every coalition has internal conflicts over the division of spoils. When pressure from an opposing coalition is great, so great that the opposition may win and thereby deprive the coalition of any spoils to distribute, these internal conflicts are minimized. But when pressure from the outside diminishes, there is less urgency to settle the internal conflicts amicably . . . . Those who lose in the intramural contests of an oversized winner tend to leave the coalition and the remaining members are on the whole glad to see them go. Thus the excess size of the winning coalition is itself an essential condition of the reduction in size, which is what the size principal asserts" (*Theory of Political Coalitions,* p. 66). Riker has argued that much of the disaffection toward Johnson since the 1964 election was the result of an oversized coalition returning to normal minimum winning size (Lecture, Conference on Mathematical Applications in Political Science, Blacksburg, Virginia, July, 1966).

this strategy would have been offensive to them. Consequently, we can not only say that the strategies were consistent with our theory, but we can also make the stronger statement that of several possible strategies, those followed were the only ones not prohibited by requirements of the theory.[24]

Two further bits of evidence are available from post-election coalition formation. The moderate group of governors who were instrumental in electing Ray Bliss as national chairman chose to emphasize the need for an inclusive party rather than, say, a need to follow more liberal policies. The attitude they stressed was one acceptable to all the groups who would have to join together to elect Bliss to the chairmanship. And the group of Republican congressmen who organized the Ford coalition emphasized a need for a more dynamic party making full use of the talent of all Republican members. Again, these were attitudes which could unite groups ranging from the Wednesday Club to newly-elected Southern conservatives. So, we can say the observed coalition behavior was consistent with the requirement that coalition attitudes fall within the intersection of the attitudes of the member groups. Hence, coalition behavior appears to be dependent on coalition attitudes.

An additional constraint on coalition behavior is that indicated at the bottom of Figure 16. The freedom of the coalition is limited by its institutional setting. In one sense, the relationship is clear. Because we are focusing on political parties, we are simply limiting ourselves to the relevant institutional arenas. We are not interested in institutional behavior unless it concerns nominations, elections, administration, or legislation. But the question of what the pattern of institutional behavior is, and how it therefore restricts the freedom of coalition action is much more complex.[25]

So far as our theory provides a key to this, it lies in the antecedent linkage between institutional attitudes and institutional behavior. The in-

[24] Another alternative hypothesis about campaign strategy is that it should be dependent on attitudes of the electorate in the sense that the strategy should emphasize the attitudes most favorable to the candidate in question. In our model, however, the attitudes of the electorate are linked to strategy indirectly rather than directly. The reason is that until the coalition leaders become aware of the voters' attitudes, coalition strategy is unlikely to be affected. One possible modification in our model would be a direct link between voters' attitudes and attitudes of coalition leaders to signify the information which coalition leaders obtain through sample surveys, and which may not be known to group members.

[25] For a study of the intricate relationship between Congressional procedure and the strategies employed by Congressmen, see Lewis A. Froman, Jr., *The Congressional Process: Strategies, Rules, and Procedures* (Boston: Little, Brown, 1967).

stitutional attitudes are the coalition leader's attitudes toward functions stipulated by the society (or culture, or policy) of which the institution is a part. The functions of the institution, in other words, are given. They furnish the external constraints which limit the coalition leaders' freedom to modify the pattern of institutional behavior. The stipulation of institutional functions is more complete in the executive and legislative arenas than it is in nomination and electoral politics. But, we still have some examples of coalition leaders' attitudes which have modified "normal" institutional behavior, and instances of regularized institutional patterns which have put checks on coalition activity.

One attitude of the Goldwater leaders was a conception of national politics in terms of hierarchy rather than stratarchy. Consequently, doors were locked at the national committee, guards were stationed to insure that unauthorized personnel did not enter forbidden areas, and there was a good deal more downward communication from party leaders than upward flow of information about the state of affairs at the grass-roots. Another unusual organizational arrangement was the separation between a "policy group" and a "political group." A third attitude with organizational consequences was the belief that neither the candidate nor the national committee should make any special appeal to population groupings. This led to the assignment of specialists in agriculture, labor, and other matters to the Citizens' outpost. A fourth example is the difference made by the Goldwater leaders' "learning experience" in the California primary. Mobilization of friendly voters had enabled the Senator to win that election, so great emphasis was put on organization for vote mobilization in the fall.

There are also instances of well-defined institutional patterns which limited coalition leaders' freedom of action. One good example of this was the plight of the leaders of the Scranton coalition in San Francisco. They knew exactly what they had to do. They had to have a contest with the Goldwater coalition on an issue which would split peripheral groups away from the Goldwater coalition and add them to the Scranton coalition. But they were unable to do this because the institutional pattern was already set, and they ended up fighting with the platform committee rather than their real opponents.

Another clear instance of the constraining effect of an institutional matrix was the need of the Goldwater leaders to fill particular jobs at the national committee. When they were reorganizing the nomination coalition into an electoral coalition, they needed persons able to write speeches, translate conservative generalities into specific policy proposals, put out press releases that newspapers would use, raise campaign funds, and do all the other things necessary to fulfill the functional requirements of a campaign organization. The coalition leaders knew of a good many persons who were enthusiastic about the Goldwater cause, but zealous supporters could not help unless they possessed the specific skills necessary to manage a national campaign.

The final bit of linkage is the feedback relationship between coalition behavior and attitudes of the electorate. We have already noted a number of specific instances of impact: the Republican mobilization campaign, the Johnson attempt to woo moderate Republicans, and so on. Now what general conclusions are justified? The first is that modifications of attitudes are unusual. So far as they could be observed through the quasi-panel technique, most attitudes are stable. If one were to conceive of the attitudes of the electorate at a given point in time as being dependent on its prior attitudes and new information received since the earlier measurement, clearly the prior attitudes would be the more important.

When attitudinal modification does occur, the most common type is a change in the salience of certain attitudes. There occurred several examples of this. There was an increase in the salience of Republican philosophy and of the relation of the Republican and Democratic parties to population groupings, the former presumably in response to Goldwater's emphasis on conservative doctrine and the latter probably related to Johnson's group-oriented campaign. There was an increase in the salience of "political" issues midway in the campaign. There were more references to the "Republican" issues of public disorder, corruption, communism, and government spending, and more references to the "Democratic" issues of social security and jobs. And, after the dramatic foreign events, the power shift in the Kremlin and the Chinese nuclear capability, cold war issues gained in salience at the expense of domestic political references.[26]

[26] That a change in salience is the most common type of attitudinal shift during a campaign is consistent with conclusions reached by the Elmira study. "The [1948] campaign was characterized by a resurgence of attention to socioeconomic matters, at the expense of international affairs. The image of Truman did not change, but the image of what was important in the campaign . . . *did* change to a dominance of socioeconomic issues . . . . The increase of Democratic support from June to October came largely in relation to . . . an *increase* in the saliency of economic labor-consumer 'class' issues" (Bernard R. Berelson, Paul F. Lazarsfeld, and William N. McPhee, *Voting* [Chicago: University of Chicago Press, 1954], pp. 264, 267).

Attitudinal change—a significant shift in the favorability of particular attitudes—occurs more rarely. This requires communication between the candidates and the voters in the sense of the transmission of *new* information. The cases where this did occur suggest general conditions which should be present for such communication. Comments about Goldwater's domestic policies and his relation to groups became less favorable while references to Johnson's stance with groups became slightly more favorable. Here we see the effect of messages from both candidates reinforcing one another. When Johnson and Goldwater *both* say Goldwater isn't very interested in doing things for groups, the information is likely to be transmitted and cause some change of attitudes.[27]

The more dramatic examples of attitudinal change concerned foreign policy. The percentage of favorable references concerning President Johnson's foreign policy rose from 48 per cent to 70 per cent; those concerning Republican foreign policy rose from 58 per cent to 70 per cent; those concerning Senator Goldwater's foreign policy rose from 26 per cent to 39 per cent. Why did these changes take place? This leads to a further question about the properties of attitudes. Newcomb, Turner, and Converse point out that certain attitudinal properties tend to co-occur. If an attitude is weak, it is likely to have low centrality, low personal goal relevance, and little stored information. A strong attitude, on the other hand, has high centrality, high personal goal relevance, and a large amount of stored information.[28] Both of these sets of properties lead to attitudinal stability. The weak attitude is subject to change *if* new information is acquired, but since the object is psychologically remote, threshold mechanisms are apt to prevent the acquisition of much new intelligence. A person having a strong attitude, on the other hand, is apt to perceive a great deal of information, but store the information in accord with already well-organized cognitive categories. The attitude which would be most susceptible to change would be one that is high in centrality, has high personal goal relevance, but is based on *little* information. In these circumstances a person would be attentive to new information and the new information might very well cause him to change his attitude. This unusual combination of circumstances does af-

[27] The same argument about reinforcement probably has something to do with the marked departures from a normal vote in the East and the Deep South.

[28] *Social Psychology*, Ch. 5, pp. 118–21. See also Philip E. Converse, "Information Flow and the Stability of Partisan Attitudes," in *Elections and the Political Order*, Ch. 8.

fect foreign policy attitudes. Since foreign policy can lead to peace or war, it is likely to have a high personal goal relevance for many people. At the same time, because of the complexity of foreign policy and unfamiliarity with foreign countries, foreign policy attitudes rest on a relatively weak informational base. In other words, we see here an instance of an unusual combination of attitudinal properties which does lead to a relatively high probability of attitudinal change.

Finally, there are a number of hints scattered throughout our data about the importance of the Kennedy presidential coalition to the attitudes that existed in 1964. The number of statements that Johnson ought to have a chance to carry out Kennedy's policies, the number of changes in party identification said to have taken place during the Kennedy administration, and the inflation of the 1960 Kennedy vote in the respondents' memory all testify to the impact of the late President. This calls our attention to a gap in our data. Most of the extensive studies of voters' attitudes have taken place during election campaigns. Yet, it is entirely possible that citizens' perceptions of the behavior of executive and legislative coalitions between campaigns may be quite as important in shaping their attitudes.[29] If we are to understand the linkage between coalition behavior and the attitudes of the electorate, we need data on how these attitudes are affected by what party coalitions do in office.

With this survey of relationships between the attitudinal and behavioral variables, the author's job comes to an end. The reader's job is now to judge how adequate this attempt at theory-building has been. This involves answering at least four questions. Have the concepts been satisfactorily related to each other? Is this a useful way of organizing knowledge about American political parties? Are the aspects of political life it focuses upon more significant than other aspects it necessarily neglects? Do the real world data correspond to the concepts used to refer to them? The relative importance of each of these considerations is a matter for the reader's taste. But if the thrust of the answers is in the affirmative, then from my point of view this venture will have been worthwhile.

[29] This is the argument advanced by V.O. Key, Jr., in *The Responsible Electorate*. See also Paul F. Lazarsfeld *et al.*, *The People's Choice*, p. 102, and Angus Campbell *et al.*, *The American Voter*, p. 61.

Index